A Short History of the United States

Also by **Robert V. Remini**

The House: The History of the House of Representatives

Joseph Smith

John Quincy Adams

Andrew Jackson and His Indian Wars

The University of Illinois at Chicago: A Pictorial History
  (with Fred W. Beuttler and Melvin G. Holli)

The Battle of New Orleans

Daniel Webster: The Man and His Time

Henry Clay: Statesman for the Union

Andrew Jackson: A Bibliography, Bibliographies of the Presidents
  of the United States (with Robert O. Rupp)

The Jacksonian Era

The Legacy of Andrew Jackson: Essays on Democracy, Indian
  Removal, and Slavery

Andrew Jackson and the Course of American Democracy, 1833–1845

Andrew Jackson and the Course of American Freedom, 1822–1833

The American People: A History (with Arthur S. Link, Stanley
  Coben, Douglas Greenberg, and Robert McMath)

The Era of Good Feelings and the Age of Jackson, 1816–1841 (with
  Edwin A. Miles)

Andrew Jackson and the Course of American Empire, 1767–1821

The Revolutionary Age of Andrew Jackson

We the People: A History of the United States (with James I. Clark)

Freedom's Frontiers: The Story of the American People
  (with James I. Clark)

Andrew Jackson and the Bank War

Andrew Jackson

The Election of Andrew Jackson

Martin Van Buren and the Making of the Democratic Party

A Short History of the United States

of the

United States

Robert V. Remini

HARPER

An Imprint of HarperCollins*Publishers*
www.harpercollins.com

HarperCollins books may be purchased for educational, business, or sales promotional use. For information, please write: Special Markets Department, HarperCollins Publishers, 10 East 53rd Street, New York, NY 10022.

FIRST EDITION

Designed by Level C

Library of Congress Cataloging-in-Publication Data
Remini, Robert V.
A short history of the United States / Robert V. Remini—1st ed.
p.   cm.
ISBN: 978-0-06-083144-8
1.   United States—History.

E178.R38   2008
973—dc22   2007034811

08   09   10   11   12   WBC/RRD   10   9   8   7   6   5   4   3   2   1

For Joan,
Who has brought nothing but joy to my life

Contents

1 Discovery and Settlement of the New World   1

2 Independence and Nation Building   31

3 An Emerging Identity   63

4 The Jacksonian Era   95

5 The Dispute over Slavery, Secession, and the Civil War   127

6 Reconstruction and the Gilded Age   155

7 Manifest Destiny, Progressivism, War,
and the Roaring Twenties   187

8 The Great Depression, the New Deal, and World War II   215

9 The Cold War and Civil Rights   245

10 Violence, Scandal, and the End of the Cold War   277

11 The Conservative Revolution   305

Reading List   337

Index   343

A Short History of the United States

I

Discovery and Settlement of the New World

THERE ARE MANY intriguing mysteries surrounding the peopling and discovery of the western hemisphere. Who were the people to first inhabit the northern and southern continents? Why did they come? How did they get here? How long was their migration? A possible narrative suggests that the movement of ancient people to the New World began when they crossed a land bridge that once existed between what we today call Siberia and Alaska, a bridge that later disappeared because of glacial melting and is now covered by water and known as the Bering Strait. It is also possible that these early people were motivated by wanderlust or the need for a new source of food. Perhaps they were searching for a better climate, and maybe they came for religious reasons, to escape persecution or find a more congenial area to practice their particular beliefs. Who knows?

Of course some scholars have argued that these ancient people came by sea, and several modern adventurers have sought to demonstrate how it was accomplished. But if a land route did provide the gateway to this New World, when did it happen? How long ago? The best guess—and it is a guess—is that it took place 50,000 years ago, if not more. But was it a single long migration stretching over a number of years? Or did it come in fits and starts during an extended period of time? Scholars have suggested that the migration continued until 2,000 years ago and that extended families came in groups. Over time, these people settled into every habitable area they could find, penetrating to the most southernly region and even occupying the many islands off the coast, especially the eastern coast. These ancients established themselves along an 11,000-mile stretch from north to south, and a distance of 3,000 or more miles, in some places, from east to west. They developed a diversity of cultures, depending in the main on the areas where they took up permanent residence; and they spoke at least 300 different languages. Their individual clans formed tribes or nations, and their governments usually consisted of a council of elders and clan chiefs selected by the elders. The highest ruling member of the tribe was the principal chief, chosen from one of the major clans. But many functions of government were normally handled by an individual clan or by a family.

The economy was mostly agricultural, that is, hunting and gathering. But these natives were limited in what they could do by the fact that they had not invented the wheel; nor did they have important domesticated animals, such as the horse and cow. And they had not learned the skills of metallurgy, apart from the hammering of sheet copper to make primitive tools and gold and silver for personal ornaments.

None of the hundreds of tribes who resided in the area north of present-day Mexico had an alphabet or a written language. Instead they resorted to pictographs to record important events, and they substituted a sign language and smoke signals to communicate over long distances. In the south a more culturally advanced society emerged among the Aztec and Inca tribes. The Aztecs had a written language and a command of mathematics and architecture. Their great stone temples commanded the cities and towns in which they were built. It has been suggested that the cultural level of the southern tribes in the eighth century after Christ was more advanced than that of any of the countries in western Europe. If so, the question immediately arises why it came to a full stop and never advanced. That is another mystery that cannot be satisfactorily explained from evidence presently available.

More mysteries. According to Norse sagas, sometime around AD 1000 Vikings were blown off course while sailing west from Iceland to Greenland, and landed in the New World. Just where they found refuge is uncertain. A little later Leif Eriksson and his crew repeated this

Distribution of American Indians

journey and probably reached present-day Newfoundland, or possibly some place along the coast of modern-day New England. They made camp and explored a wide area, no doubt visiting sections that later became part of the United States. Further explorations by other Vikings may have taken them down the St. Lawrence River.

In any event the Vikings never established permanent settlements in the New World, and nothing came of their discoveries. It took several more centuries for western Europe to begin to initiate important changes in its society that would result in the migration of many of its people to the New World.

THE CRUSADES UNDOUBTEDLY triggered a good deal of these changes. In 1095, Pope Urban II called Christians to liberate the Holy Land from the Muslims who controlled it. Thousands of Europeans responded and traveled to the East, where they were exposed to a different and more exotic culture, a way of life that excited their imagination. Later they returned home from their adventure with new tastes, new ideas, new interests, and new demands for foods and goods that they had experienced in the East, such as spices, cotton, and silk cloth. Their desire for the products of the East was further enhanced by Marco Polo's account of his extensive travels and life in China, published in the thirteenth century. The gold and silver as well as the spices and silk clothing that Polo described captured the imagination of Europeans. Trade routes were developed to bring these products to an eager market. Soon the manorial, agricultural, closed economy of the medieval world gave way to a capitalistic economy based on trade, money, and credit. Existing cities flourished and new ones were founded. This urban development attracted artisans of every stripe who perfected their crafts and initiated a technological revolution. The printing press made possible the wide distribution of books and stimulated learning. It also contributed to the formation of universities in a number of cities. The compass and astrolabe were introduced by which navigation of the seas became safer and encouraged seamen to seek new routes and new worlds beyond those already known.

As a result of these and many other less notable changes the Middle Ages, with their authoritarian and rigid system of beliefs and practices, slowly disintegrated. The power of the pope and bishops who controlled the Catholic church was supplanted by that of ruling monarchs and titled noblemen in emerging nation-states. And after Martin Luther posted his list of ninety-five theses on a cathedral door, the Christian religion no longer consisted of a single set of beliefs.

Capitalism, Protestantism, and the nation-states ruled by ambitious sovereigns combined to bring about modern Europe.

ONCE THE ASTROLABE allowed navigators to determine the longitude of their ships at sea by measuring the angle between the sun and the horizon, daring explorers ventured farther down the coast of Africa. Prince Henry of Portugal, known as Henry the Navigator, subsidized expeditions that ultimately crossed the equator and sailed down the length of Africa. In 1498, Vasco da Gama rounded the Cape of Good Hope, crossed the Indian Ocean, and reached India, where he announced to the natives that he had come to trade.

Reaching the East by the shortest possible route and returning home with gold, silver, spices, and other exotic products became an ambitious quest for many seamen. An Italian navigator, Christopher Columbus, believed he could reach the Orient faster by sailing due west, not around the continent of Africa. Despite the objections of her advisers, who felt that the long voyage by small caravels into the unknown posed dangerous risks, Isabella the Catholic, queen of Castile, who married Ferdinand, king of Aragon, to form the nation-state of Spain, agreed to finance the trip. On August 3, 1492, three ships, the *Nina*, *Pinta*, and *Santa Maria*, manned by about ninety sailors, left Palos, Spain, and—after a brief stop at the Canary Islands off the coast of Africa—headed toward the setting sun. It took enormous courage and superb seamanship to undertake this voyage, but on October 12 at around two AM, Columbus and his crew made landfall on what he called San Salvador (it was later named Watlings Island), in the Bahamas. He next sighted a much larger island, Hispaniola, and called the natives who greeted him Indians, in the mistaken belief that he had arrived in India and that China was just a short distance farther west. He returned home to a hero's welcome and made three further trips to this New World, but he never found the treasures and spices he desired, and he died still convinced that he had reached Asia.

The subsequent exploration of a New World by Portuguese and

Spanish adventurers prompted their respective monarchs, in 1494, to reach an agreement known as the Treaty of Tordesillas, by which they drew a line, north and south, 1,100 miles west of the Canary Islands, wherein the land west of the line belonged to Spain, and the land east of it belonged to Portugal.

The search for a route to Asia, and the treasure that adventurers believed they would find, continued into the next century. Another Italian explorer, Amerigo Vespucci, made several trips along the southern coast of the western hemisphere and wrote vivid, if largely untrue, descriptions of what he called this "New World," which caught the attention of mapmakers and geographers. In 1507 a German mapmaker, Martin Waldseemuller, who published Vespucci's accounts, suggested that this New World be called America in his honor. Now the continents of the western hemisphere had a new name.

Soon other Spanish explorers headed west in search of fortune and glory. These conquistadores were tough, ruthless soldiers who spared no life, Indian or Spanish, to find the riches and honor they sought. They roamed the New World in their search, and in the process of their explorations they established an empire for Spain. They were also convinced that they were performing the will of God by bringing Christianity to heathens.

Hernán Cortés, a particularly brutal but capable leader, made his way to the New World in 1504. He participated in the conquest of Cuba and later commanded an expedition to the Yucatán, where he heard stories of great wealth farther west among the Aztecs, who called themselves Mexics. He set out with 500 men to find it. Montezuma, the Aztec emperor, believed that Cortés was the god Quetzalcoatl returning to his country as foretold in Aztec mythology. To greet this returning god, Montezuma sent him as an offering both food and a huge disk the size of a wagon wheel in the shape of a sun and made of solid gold. The Spanish realized that they had come upon unbelievable wealth, and they meant to have it all. Sharp-witted and resourceful, Cortés played the part of Quetzalcoatl and in 1519 captured Montezuma, who paid a handsome ransom for his release. With the help of surrounding tribes who hated the Mexics, Cortés not only conquered the Aztec Nation but also slaughtered the natives with his guns and cannons. His conquest was also aided by the diseases his troops carried with them, such as smallpox, influenza, measles, and typhus, to which the natives had no immunity.

The plunder the intruders seized from the Mexics inspired other conquistadores to range up and down the continents, north, south, east, and west, looking for precious metals. Francisco Pizarro, one such adventurer in search of glory, was told about a civilization farther to the south, in what is now Peru, that could provide the wealth he sought. After several unsuccessful expeditions he gained the confidence of the Emperor, Charles V of Spain, from whom he received support in exchange for one-fifth of all the treasure Pizarro discovered. In 1531 the conquistador set out with several hundred men and discovered the Inca civilization in Peru. He overwhelmed all resistance, murdered the Emperor, Atahuallpa, and made off with a fortune in gold and silver.

These discoveries and the mines that produced such wealth enriched Spain and financed its expansion as the powerhouse of Europe, but the infusion of so much wealth into Spain also brought about inflation that drove the price of goods upward to unprecedented levels.

Spaniards swarmed over the Americas. In 1565 the Spanish monarch sent Pedro Menéndez de Avilés to establish settlements along the North American coast. In September of that year Menéndez founded St. Augustine in what is now Florida. It was the first permanent European settlement in North America. Colonies were also established in the Caribbean, and in Central and South America, with viceroys appointed to represent the monarch and administer these colonies. But absolute authority resided in the king, who ruled through the Council of the Indies in Spain. The council members nominated officials and drafted the laws and rules by which the colonies were to be governed.

Spanish society in the Americas consisted of several ranks. Those in the highest rank had been born in Spain and were called *peninsulares*. Next came those born in America of Spanish parents. They were known as *criollos*, most of whom were landowners. These two groups formed the upper class of society in New Spain. Those of mixed Spanish and Indian blood were known as *mestizos*. Lower on the social and economic scale were the natives who had adopted Spanish life and culture and constituted the broad laboring class. Next were the mulattoes, those of mixed European and African blood. At the bottom of the ladder were black slaves brought from Africa to work in the mines and fields of the Spanish conquerors.

Most important was the position of the Roman Catholic church. Like Spain, the church and state were intricately entwined, each serving the other to the advantage of both.

Spanish expeditions also resulted in the discovery, in 1513, of the Pacific Ocean by Vasco de Balboa, and Florida by Juan Ponce de Leon. Even the globe was circumnavigated by an expedition that started from St. Lucar in 1519 and led by Ferdinand Magellan, who was killed in a battle with natives in what today are known as the Philippine Islands. Of the five ships and 250 original sailors that set out on this remarkable voyage in 1519, only one ship and eighteen men returned home in 1522.

Hernando de Soto fought his way north into present-day Georgia and the Carolinas from 1539 to 1542, and then westward through Tennessee, Alabama, Mississippi, and Arkansas. And Francisco de Coronado led a force from Mexico in 1540 into the interior of North America in search of the legendary Seven Cities of Cibola, that were believed to be paved with gold. California was explored by Juan Cabrillo in 1542; and Catholic priests established missions to convert Indian tribes to Christianity.

THE GREAT SUCCESS Spain enjoyed in establishing a worldwide empire, and raking in a fabulous fortune in the process, encouraged other emerging nations in Europe to follow suit and carve out areas for colonization for themselves. France began its reach for empire in 1534, when the king commissioned Jacques Cartier to search for a Northwest Passage that would lead to the Indies. Cartier failed to find such a passage, but in several voyages he laid claim to the eastern half of Canada and a slice of land between the Appalachian Mountains and the Mississippi River. Later, Samuel de Champlain explored the St. Lawrence River area and founded the cities of Quebec and Montreal. The lucrative fur trade in the Great Lakes area became a source of wealth, but it did not attract many French settlers. The Indians constituted the bulk of the population in New France, and Champlain succeeded in forging an alliance with the Hurons that helped that tribe defeat their ancient enemy, the Iroquois.

The Iroquois were probably more culturally advanced than some other tribes. They occupied the region south of the St. Lawrence River and Lake Ontario. The Five Nations of the Iroquois included the Seneca, Onondaga, Mohawk, Cayuga, and Oneida, and were later joined by the Tuscarora, becoming the Six Nations.

Farther north, above the St. Lawrence, lived the Algonquin tribes, principally the Hurons, who were leagued with the French. This alliance was a natural one, since the French desired furs and the beaver population in the Algonquin country was judged the best. The Iroquois sought to defeat the Hurons to obtain the furs, which they wanted to exchange for guns, resulting in intermittent Indian wars in which the Iroquois came close to driving the French from North America.

The Dutch also tried their hand at enlarging their possessions and obtaining wealth. In 1609 Henry Hudson sailed up the river that now bears his name and established trading posts. The Dutch West India Company controlled several such posts: the most important of these were New Amsterdam on Manhattan Island, which later became New York, and Fort Orange, which was renamed Albany after the English occupied them following the Dutch War. Like the French, the Dutch concentrated on obtaining furs, not on colonization, and they regularly traded guns for furs with the Iroquois.

THEN THERE WERE the English: those Anglo-Saxons perched on islands in the North Sea and protected by water that they soon ruled. With stout ships and even stouter hearts they searched the world to create an empire. As early as 1497, under King Henry VII, an Italian by the name of John Cabot hunted for a westward passage to the Orient, first along Newfoundland and a year later farther south along the North American coastline, thereby giving England a claim to a large segment of what later became the United States. But not until the reign of Queen Elizabeth I, a Protestant, did the English take a serious interest in the New World. For the most part they struck at Spanish power by attacking its merchant and treasure ships plying the high seas. Buccaneers such as John Hawkins and Francis Drake brought home to their queen a hoard of gold and silver. Elizabeth both disclaimed any involvement in the raids and at the same time knighted Drake after he circumnavigated the globe and scooped up a veritable fortune. Philip

II, the Spanish king, struck back in 1588 with a mighty Armada of 130 ships armed with thousands of cannons, hoping to subdue the English and restore them to Catholicism. Between the intrepid British sailors, their highly maneuverable ships, and punishing storms at sea the armada was crippled, and only about half the original number of Spanish ships reached the safety of their ports. England could now make a bid for possession of a healthy chunk of the North American continent.

A few years earlier, in 1585, Sir Walter Raleigh dispatched a small group of settlers, who landed on a tiny island off present-day North Carolina and named it Roanoke. The attempted invasion of England by the Spanish Armada postponed any effort to keep Roanoke supplied. When assistance did arrive in 1591, the would-be rescuers found the island completely deserted. No one, to this day, knows what happened to the settlers.

Despite this disaster, adventurous English merchants still had hopes of sponsoring colonization of the New World in the expectation of imitating the discoveries of the Spanish. A group of them formed a joint-stock company, the London Company, in which shares were sold to stockholders for twelve pounds ten shillings, in order to sponsor colonization by settlers in North America. A charter granted by James I, the first of the Stuart kings, who succeeded Elizabeth upon her death in 1603, allowed the company to develop the land from the coastline westward to the Pacific Ocean. The area was named Virginia after Elizabeth, known as the Virgin Queen because she had never married. Three ships, the *Susan Constant*, the *Goodspeed*, and the *Discovery*, sailed from England in December 1606 and landed in Virginia in April 1607: the settlement was named Jamestown.

These colonists searched for gold, but there was none. Conditions at the triangular fort they built worsened with each month. John Smith took control of the colony during the terrible winter of 1609–1610 known as the "starving time," and those who survived ate roots, acorns, berries, and even their horses. They received help from the Powhatan tribes who taught them how to grow corn and where best to catch fish. But relations between the Indians and the English became strained to the breaking point because of the rapaciousness of the English, and Smith was taken prisoner by a hunting party while on an exploring expedition. He was turned over to Opechancanough, who was probably the half brother of Chief Powhatan, and threatened with death. As a young boy, Opechancanough had been kidnaped by the Spanish in 1559. He was sent to Spain to learn western customs and culture and the Spanish language so that he could be trained and serve as an interpreter and translator between the Indians and the Spanish. He was even given a Spanish name: Don Luis de Velasco. On his return home, sometime in the late 1570s, he renounced his Spanish affiliations and reclaimed his position of authority within the Powhatan tribe. He may also have been instrumental in the slaughter of the missionaries who accompanied him back to Virginia. Most likely he would have killed John Smith, had it not been for Pocahontas, the favorite daughter of the Powhatan chief.

At the time, Pocahontas was only eleven years of age, so it is unlikely that there was a romantic reason for her action. A number of historians have guessed that in successfully pleading for Smith's life she may have been acting out an Algonquin rite in which the power of Chief Powhatan over life and death was demonstrated by accepting Smith and his fellow settlers in Jamestown into his overlordship. By their acknowledgment of his superior position he granted them his protection. Whatever the true reason for Pocahontas's action, she extended her friendship with other English settlers. She converted to Christianity and married John Rolfe, one of the settlers, in 1614, and their marriage strengthened the friendship between the Powhatans sand the settlers. Pocahontas later traveled to England, where she was treated with the deference due her Indian rank and presented to the king and queen. Unfortunately, she contracted smallpox and died at age twenty-two.

Instead of gold, the colonists discovered the value of tobacco, which the Indians had smoked for centuries. Introduced in Europe, this "filthy" habit, as King James labeled it, became very fashionable, and the increasing demand provided the settlers with a cash crop they desperately needed to survive. The value of the trade brought more and more English settlers to America. As a result, large plantations soon evolved to grow the plant, and Virginia became a thriving colony.

The London Company sent Thomas Dale, a military man, to govern Virginia, and he instituted stern measures to ensure the continued life of the community. Then, in 1619, the company instructed the governor to summon two landowning representatives from each of the small settlements in the colony to meet in Jamestown to provide advice. Twenty-two men gathered in the church in town, disregarded the company's instructions, and proceeded to enact a series of laws for the colony against gambling, drunkenness, idleness, and Sabbath-breaking. This House of Burgesses, as it came to be called, then adjourned. But it was clear right from the beginning that English settlers were prepared to go their own way and address problems they felt were important for their safety and livelihood. Their action demonstrated a degree of independence that would be imitated by future legislative bodies in North America in asserting their right to solve their own problems in their own way.

As the settlers in and around Jamestown prospered, their number steadily increased, so that by 1620 there were roughly 2,000 colonists. Opechancanough watched with dismay the steady strengthening of white men's control of the region to the detriment of the Powhatan tribes. He therefore decided to put a stop to it. Early in the morning of March 22, 1622, a number of Indians who were unarmed circulated in several settlements and appeared to be friendly. Then, suddenly, they seized muskets and axes and began a systematic slaughter of the inhabitants. It was a typical Indian ploy: an outward show of friendship to allay the apprehensions of the colonists, followed by a sudden, swift killing spree. They wiped out about a third of the settlers, who retaliated with lethal force and attempted to drive the tribe further west. The slaughter on both sides and the resulting turmoil were so intense that King James revoked the London Company's charter in 1624 and made Virginia a royal colony. But the change in government did not end the killing. Sometime after Powhatan's death, probably in 1628, Opechancanough became the "Paramount Chief" and renewed the fighting, although sporadically. Then, in 1644, he launched what the colonists called the "great assault" of 1644, in which Opechancanough killed over 500 settlers. But the chief was old, possibly about 100 years, and his faculties were sharply diminished. He was captured and after a short time in prison he was assassinated. Thus ended the Powhatan War.

During the interim the House of Burgesses made every effort to meet regularly, and in 1639 the king instructed the governor to summon the Burgesses together each year, a recognition of what had already become regular practice.

NOT ALL THE settlers who came to America searched for gold or other forms of financial gain. A great number came in pursuit of religious freedom. Following the Protestant Reformation and the religious wars between the various sects and creeds, persecution of opposing religious beliefs became standard practice. In England the Anglican church was established by the monarchy in opposition to the Roman Catholic church, although Anglicanism retained many Catholic ceremonies and rituals. As a consequence, any number of Protestants felt that the Church of England needed to be purified of such trappings, and they became known as Puritans. Others, more radical in their thinking, felt compelled to separate themselves from the Anglican church altogether.

A group of English separatists sought even more religious freedom and fled to Holland in 1608, only to find life in this foreign country totally unsuited to their needs and temperament. They decided to relocate. They gained permission from the London Company to settle in Virginia. Thus authorized, they departed Holland and sailed aboard the *Mayflower* to the New World.

They never got to Virginia. They landed at Plymouth on Cape Cod on November 21, 1620, and before they left the ship to establish their colony, forty-one of them signed a compact by which they pledged allegiance to their "dread sovereign, the King" and did "covenant and combine" themselves into "a civil Body Politick." They further promised to obey whatever laws were thought "meet and convenient for the general Good of the Colony." This Mayflower Compact thereby became the authority by which the settlers made their own laws and chose their own officials. They then disembarked.

It is interesting to note that these settlers made an agreement that they committed to paper, stating their position on government and the means by which they had formed their society. The Mayflower Compact became one of many more such documents to follow, by which the people of this New World spoke openly about the ways they would be governed and the principles on which their government would rest. Relying on a written document as an authority became an American custom in enunciating principles and practices by which the inhabitants in the society would be governed.

It was the Pilgrims' good fortune that they were met by two English-speaking Indians—Squanto, a Pawtuxet tribesman, and Samoset, a Pemaquid—who helped them arrange a peaceful agreement with the surrounding Indian tribes. The Indians also taught them how to raise corn and showed them the best places to fish and hunt. The colony survived and prospered, and the colonists gave thanks for their good fortune.

Back in England, King Charles I, who succeeded the "dread sovereign" James I, gave a group of Puritans permission to form a joint-stock company in 1629 called the Massachusetts Bay Company, by which they could establish a colony in an area north of Virginia that John Smith had described in one publication as New England. John Winthrop, like many other Puritans, had become deeply troubled about the moral life in England and the future of religion. He decided to leave and take his immediate family with him. As an influential administrator of the Company, he was chosen to lead a "Great Migration" of Puritans to America. Numbering more than 1,000 men, women, and children aboard a fleet of 17 ships, these Puritans left England on May 22, 1630, with John Winthrop as their governor, and arrived in America on June 12, 1630, eventually settling in Boston. Upon their arrival, Winthrop assured his followers that if they bound themselves together "as one man," God would protect them and ensure their prosperity. "We shall be as a City upon a Hill; the eyes of all people are upon us. . . . We shall be made a story and a byword throughout the World." They believed that they had formed a covenant with God to build a society based on the teachings of the Bible. Church, state, family, and individuals were bound together as a unit to create a government and community in accordance with demands of the Almighty. Many of the settlers were well educated and had enough money to set themselves up in trade, commerce, or farming. Within a few years the population of the colony numbered 20,000, dispersed among several surrounding towns.

The Massachusetts Bay Company had decided to relocate its entire operation to America, taking the charter along as well. That meant there was no need to consult with or take directions from any group in England in making governmental decisions. To a very large extent, the Company was totally on its own. The colony was administered by the governor and eighteen assistants elected by the freemen, called the General Court. In 1634 the General Court, responding to criticism, allowed each town to elect deputies to sit with the assistants. Then, ten years later, the court divided into two houses, thus creating a bi-cameral legislature to fashion the laws for the entire Massachusetts Bay Colony.

But there were dissenters among them who objected to particular rulings or actions, or the system of government. One of these was Roger Williams, a young Puritan who led a congregation in Salem and who preached unacceptable heresy—at least it was heresy to the ruling clergy in Boston. Williams truly respected the Indian tribes and their culture. He made no attempt to convert them to Christianity. He felt that individuals could differ in the way they worshipped God. He even tolerated different interpretations of the Bible. God's gift of faith in the formulation of one's conscience was the only road to salvation in practicing one's religion, he preached. He was banished from the colony because he questioned the right of a civil government to enforce religious beliefs. But he foiled an attempt to ship him back to England by escaping into the wilderness and fleeing south. With a group of his followers he founded the town of Providence, the first Rhode Island community where religious freedom and separation of church and state were made possible. In 1644 he received a charter for his colony.

Anne Hutchinson, another dissenter, held meetings in her home to discuss religious matters and the worth of individual clergymen. She preached a "covenant of grace" that emphasized an individual's direct communication with God through divine grace. She attracted a considerable following. Condemned as an "antinomian," she was expelled from the colony in 1637. She and her disciples fled to Rhode Island and joined the followers of Roger Williams. She and her family were later murdered by Indians.

One of the most popular preachers in the Massachusetts Colony was Thomas Hooker, and his very popularity generated jealousy among other preachers, most notably John Cotton, the senior minister in the colony. Rather than face expulsion, Hooker decided to lead his congregation across the wooded wilderness to the Connecticut River valley, where his followers established themselves in Hartford, Windsor, and Wethersfield. Hooker himself was instrumental in writing the bylaws for the colony's government, called "The Fundamental Orders of Connecticut." Like Rhode Island, but unlike in Massachusetts, church membership was not a condition for voting; nor were clergymen permitted to participate in politics. A charter was granted in 1662.

In an effort to establish a colony that would be loyal to the Anglican church and would act as a rival to Massachusetts, Sir Ferdinando Gorges obtained a charter to establish a settlement in Maine; but he died before he could attract immigrants, and his heirs sold the charter to Massachusetts. Thus Massachusetts and Maine were joined as a single colony. Moreover, another attempt at colonizing a northern portion of New England in what is now New Hampshire also failed. The area was subsequently settled in 1638 by another preacher who had been banished from Massachusetts, John Wheelwright, the brother-in-law of Anne Hutchinson. The original grant was subsequently revoked, and in 1679 New Hampshire became a royal colony.

Catholics also sought refuge in the New World. George Calvert, the first Lord Baltimore, obtained a charter in which he hoped to establish a colony for Catholics, he himself having converted to that faith. Under his plan, he would be the proprietor, and the land, involving millions of acres, his private estate. Those who settled on this property would pay him a land tax, called a quitrent; he, in turn, was required to pay the king two Indian arrows each Easter. Calvert was empowered to appoint the governor, judges, and councilors; organize the court system; and authorize a legislature to enact the laws. However, George Calvert died before the king had given his final approval to this proprietorship, and it was inherited in 1632 by Calvert's son, Cecil, the second Lord Baltimore, who immediately sent out an expedition to establish the colony of Maryland. Unfortunately, the area impinged on the charter granted to the Virginia Company, provoking repeated conflicts between the two authorities. And although Calvert expected to dictate his wishes to the settlers as commands, the settlers had other ideas. When the first Maryland legislature met in 1635, it insisted on the right to enact its own laws, and Calvert wisely agreed to this. But Catholics did not swarm into Maryland as the proprietor had hoped. Instead many more Protestants took advantage of his liberal land grants, and by the end of the century they outnumbered Catholics ten to one. In 1649 the Maryland assembly accepted Lord Baltimore's proposal and passed a Toleration Act, stating that no person who believed in Christ would be persecuted for practicing his or her religion. But since non-Christians were excluded from the colony, this legislation had only limited claim to toleration.

Thus, over a relatively short period of time, there developed in the English colonies in America three forms of government: royal, corporate, and proprietary.

Another proprietary colony was formed when Charles II paid off a series of debts to a group of eight men who had helped him regain the throne in 1660 after the Puritan Revolution that executed his father, Charles I, in 1649, and established a dictatorship under Oliver Cromwell. This colony lay between Virginia and Spanish Florida, and the charter was granted in 1663. The proprietors expected to attract settlers from Barbados, Virginia, and New England and profit from a trade in rice, ginger, and silk. The area was named Carolina after Charles's wife, Queen Caroline. One distinctive feature of this proprietary colony was the plan of government drawn up by one of the proprietors, Anthony Ashley Cooper, the earl of Shaftesbury, and his secretary, John Locke. It was called the Fundamental Constitutions of Carolina, and it attempted to engraft in America a feudal system with a sharply defined social structure, including titles, and a similar hierarchical judicial system. Although it recognized and legalized slavery—Carolina was the first colony to do so openly—it did provide for religious freedom and a representative assembly. Settlers were drawn to this inviting area, but they disregarded the feudal aspects— which could never take root in America, because of the vastness of the land—and enjoyed the more liberal attractions of the Fundamental Constitutions. By the end of the century some 50,000 colonists populated the region. But they tended to concentrate in two areas: one to the north around Albemarle Sound, in what is presently North Carolina; and one 300 miles to the south around a community named after the king, Charles Town, today's Charleston. Both areas prospered and enjoyed increased migration from other parts of the English colonies.

In North Carolina the inhabitants grew tobacco and provided naval stores to shipbuilders. In South Carolina, because of the moisture, temperature, and soil conditions, the colonists cultivated rice and indigo, which is used as a dye.

Many of the Carolina colonists were Scots-Irish who were predominantly Presbyterian in their religious beliefs and had initially moved from lowland Scotland to northern Ireland, where they remained for many years before crossing the ocean and settling in the Carolinas. They engaged the various Indian tribes in defending themselves against the Spanish in Florida. These tribes included the Wateree, Congaree, Santee, Waxhaw, and Catawba, all of whom belonged to the Siouan group. The most dominant tribe, however, was the powerful and fierce Cherokee Nation, who were concentrated in the mountains to the west and related to the Iroquois farther north.

The Carolina settlers frequently aided one group of Indians against another in combat and regularly sold captured natives into slavery. Before long these settlers had exterminated or enslaved the Indians in the Carolinas, or reduced them to a state of total dependence.

CHARLES II AND his brother James, the Duke of York, who later succeeded Charles as James II, cast covetous eyes on the Dutch colony of New Netherland, especially the attractive port at the foot of Manhattan Island where the Hudson River ran into the ocean. The Dutch had not been as successful as the English in establishing colonies since its citizens lacked the impetus of English settlers in migrating to America. The people in New Amsterdam, for example, had little regard for the Dutch West India Company and its autocratic governors. The most recent dictator, Peter Stuyvesant. arrived as governor in the colony on May 11, 1647, looking "like a peacock." He was all pomp and majesty. He wore a decorated peg leg, having lost his own in a pitched battle several years earlier. Determined to bring order and one-man control to the colony, he ruled for seventeen years by stern decrees that won him few friends and many enemies.

Since England and Holland were commercial rivals, it did not take long for Charles to initiate a war by granting to his brother James all the land between the Connecticut and Delaware rivers. Then a British fleet appeared in the harbor of New Amsterdam and demanded the surrender of Manhattan Island. The governor, Peter Stuyvesant, swore he would never surrender, but the leading citizens overruled him. They knew they could not fight off the well-armed and determined British, so they persuaded Stuyvesant to surrender the colony. And not a shot was fired. James, now the proprietor, renamed the colony New York. He blithely assumed he could rule the Dutch settlers through his chosen governor without any consultation whatsoever with the residents. He soon learned that such an approach from across thousands of miles of ocean guaranteed disobedience and lawlessness. Thus, when he succeeded his brother as King James II, he did permit the calling of a legislative assembly. Still, his regular disregard of the needs and requests of the New York colonists only generated further discord. The system of semifeudal landholdings of the original Dutch settlers further exacerbated the problem. It produced social, economic, and ethnic tensions between them and the new English arrivals.

James turned over the lower section of his holdings to two friends, Lord John Berkeley and Sir George Carteret. Since Carteret had served as governor of Jersey in the English Channel, the area was named New Jersey in his honor. Berkeley was in charge of the western half of the province and Carteret of the eastern half. Both men later sold their proprietorships, and Puritans, Anglicans, and Quakers settled the divided province until the King united East and West Jersey into a single royal colony in 1702.

One of the more successful attempts at establishing a proprietary colony resulted from a grant of land in the New World from Charles II to William Penn. While studying at Oxford, Penn joined a radical religious sect, the Society of Friends, whose members denounced war, rejected the authority of priests and bishops, abhorred ceremonial worship, and obeyed only what they called the "inner light of conscience." These Quakers even refused to bow to the king or remove their hats when confronted by royal officials. They professed complete equality—none excepted.

William Penn embraced their beliefs with a fervor that landed him in prison and provoked the anger and disappointment of his father, Admiral William Penn. Once released from jail, he took up missionary work in Holland and Germany, where he organized Quaker societies. Since Charles owed Admiral Penn a large sum of money, he agreed to grant the son a tract of land in full payment of the debt. William Penn realized that it could be a haven for persecuted Quakers, and in 1681 he received a charter, which made him the proprietor of what is now the state of Pennsylvania. Young Penn also persuaded the duke of York to cede to him the three lower counties on the Delaware River that the Dutch had seized from the Swedes years earlier. These three counties remained a part of the Penn proprietary domain until the American Revolution, when they asserted their independence and became the state of Delaware.

What is remarkable about Pennsylvania was the liberality with which it was governed. It became a "holy experiment" in which everyone could live in peace and harmony. And that included Indians. In his Frame of Government of 1682, Penn included a governor with an appointed council who originated all laws, along with an assembly, which initially lacked real authority but over time became more self-assertive. Most important of all, Penn advertised in England and on the continent, inviting people of all nationalities to settle in his colony and offering land at extremely low prices. Dutch, Welsh, Swedish, French, German, and English emigrants responded to his appeals, and Pennsylvania soon became the most populous and prosperous of all the American colonies.

In 1732, Georgia was founded, when James Oglethon obtained a twenty-one-year charter from George II to a group of trustees for land between Savannah and Altmaha rivers.

BECAUSE OF CLIMATE variations, soil conditions, the type of settlers, and the reasons that brought them to the different areas of the New World, among other things, a distinctive culture soon evolved within each of three areas: the New England, Middle, and Southern colonies. New England, for example, engaged in shipbuilding because of the sturdy, straight, tall pines that grew throughout the region. Fishing also became an important component of the New England economy. But many settlers built small farms in clusters around a seaport or farther inland near rivers or streams. Each cluster comprised a village, with a section of land held as commons to serve all the nearby inhabitants for such purposes as grazing cattle. Since the settlers were predominantly

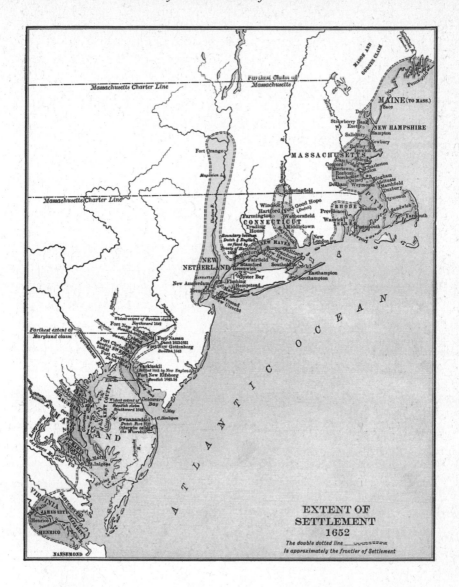

MASON AND GORGES CLAIM

Furthest Claim of Massachusetts

Massachusetts Charter Line

MAINE (TO MASS.)
Saco

Strawberry Bank
Exeter
Salisbury
NEW HAMPSHIRE
Hampton

Fort Orange

Bowley Ipswich Newbury
Concord Cambridge Salem Charleston
Watertown Roxbury Boston
Dorchester
Dedham Weymouth Quincy Hingham
Scituate
Marshfield
Duxbury

MASSACHUSETTS

Massachusetts Charter Line

Springfield

Plymouth

Windsor Fort Good Hope (Dutch)
Hartford
Farmington Wethersfield
CONNECTICUT
Trading & Middletown
House
RHODE Taunton
ISLAND
Providence
Warwick
Sandwich
Yarmouth

Boundary between
Dutch & English
as fixed by
Treaty of Hartford
1650

NEW HAVEN
New
London
Portsmouth
Newport

NEW
NETHERLAND
Stratford
Guilford
Milford
New Haven
Southold
Stamford
Fairfield
Greenwich
Easthampton
New Amsterdam
Oyster Bay
Southampton
Flushing
Brooklyn Hempstead
New
Utrecht

Widest extent of Swedish claim
Northward 1642
Fort New Korsholm
Farthest extent of
Maryland claim
Fort Nassau
(Dutch)
Fort Christina
Swedish 1638
Fort Casimir
Fort New Gottenberg
Swedish 1643
Varkinskil
(Settled 1641 by New Englanders)
Fort New Elfsborg
Swedish 1643-54

MARYLAND

Kent Co.
Widest extent of
Swedish claim
Southward 1643
Delaware
Bay
C. May
C. Henlopen

Swaanandael
Dutch Fort 1631
otherwise called
the Whorekill

St. Mary's
St. Inigo's

VIRGINIA
JAMES CITY
Henrico
HENRICO
James

NANSEMOND

ATLANTIC OCEAN

**EXTENT OF
SETTLEMENT
1652**

The double dotted line
is approximately the frontier of Settlement

Puritan, their lives centered on the local church they built and the minister who preached to them and guarded their moral behavior. The New
England colonies were founded primarily for religious purposes.

In the Middle colonies, farming and commerce developed in which
wheat, corn, and vegetables were grown; while beavers, raccoons, and
other animals provided fur for export. Ships from New York City and
Philadelphia regularly put to sea carrying these commodities not only to

Europe but also to the southern colonies and the West Indies. Most settlers had farms of small or moderate size, except in New York, where the Dutch had laid out enormous estates that extended across an entire county, such as the Van Rensselaer tract that straddled both sides of the Hudson River. The Dutch influence in New York continued after the arrival of the English and had an impact on architecture, language, and customs. Germans in Pennsylvania added a strong flavor to the colony's culture. Although Pennsylvania had been founded for religious and idealistic reasons, the other middle colonies were settled to exploit the wealth of the area. The population of this region tended to be quite diverse.

Because the cultivation and harvesting of tobacco, cotton, rice, and indigo in the Southern colonies necessitated the creation of sizable plantations and a large workforce, life in this section of the New World was distinctly different from that in regions farther north. Initially there was the reliance on indentured servants, individuals who signed contracts to work for a period of four or five years for the holder of their contract in return for passage to America. Then in 1619 a Dutch ship arrived in Virginia with twenty Africans who may have been slaves or indentured servants. It is not clear just what their status was. In any case, slavery soon became institutionalized, as more and more Africans were brought to America. By 1700 there existed in the South a master class and a slave class, and life and death were determined by the former without regard for the rights or needs of the latter. A small middle class that provided services not available on plantations, such as legal assistance, arose in urban centers of the South near harbors and seaports. The people of these Southern colonies tended to be more homogeneous than those of the Middle and New England colonies.

And the governments of these British colonies differed in some particulars, depending on whether they were royal, corporate, or proprietary, but they had several common characteristics. Each colony had a governor who represented the king, the proprietor, or the corporation and was expected to enforce all English laws passed by Parliament or the policies devised by the Privy Council who advised the king. In purely local matters, the governors had wide discretion. They were advised by resident landowners who were appointed to their position. Elected assemblies or legislatures enacted local laws but theoretically had limited power since their actions could be annulled by the governor or the royal authority in England. In actual practice, however, these elected assemblies exerted considerable authority. Since they enacted local taxes they had the power of the purse, which they used to compel the governor to heed their demands. They could deprive him of his salary, for example, or the salaries of his assistants. He, in turn, could dismiss them and call for new elections; but he could not compel them to pass laws they opposed.

James II did attempt to exercise greater control over several northern colonies in 1686, when he created the Dominion of New England, consisting of Massachusetts, Rhode Island, Connecticut, and New Hampshire. Later he added the colonies of New York and New Jersey. He appointed Sir Edmund Andros governor of this dominion, and granted him the power to enact laws, including taxes. The loss of the considerable freedom the colonists had enjoyed engendered resentment and anger. And Andros himself was a mistake. Arbitrary, contemptuous of individual rights and traditions, he exercised dictatorial rule over the settlers and soon came to grief.

King James was hated both in America and in England, especially for his defiance of Parliament and its laws. He was overthrown in the Glorious Revolution of 1688. As a Catholic in spirit if not in fact, he was feared by many Protestants, who revolted when James's wife gave birth to a son who would inherit the throne, most probably as a Catholic. So Parliament invited James's daughter Mary, a Protestant, and her husband, William of Orange, to take the English throne as a pair. When word of James's overthrow reached Boston, the colonists arrested Andros and terminated the Dominion of New England. The colonial governments and local officials were reestablished. The Parliament in England made no attempt to resurrect the dominion.

The action of James II in establishing the Dominion of New England to bring the northern colonies under closer supervision, and the action of his predecessor, Charles II, in creating a Council of Trade and a Council of Foreign Plantations, by which a favorable balance of trade with the colonies could be achieved, were not simply expressions of political ambitions or goals. Actually they reflected economic need. These monarchs hoped to acquire wealth for England, and that meant gold and silver. To achieve such wealth necessitated a favorable balance of trade, wherein the money owed to a nation would be paid in specie.

Colonies were therefore necessary to provide the goods the mother country could sell abroad—selling more to foreigners than it bought and thus producing the favorable balance. The American colonies could supply raw materials such as tobacco, naval stores, cotton, rice, indigo, furs, and sugar, which England could sell to other nations. At the same time the colonies would provide a market for the mother country's manufactured goods. This program was called mercantilism, and through a series of Navigation and Trade Acts, Parliament in the seventeenth and eighteenth centuries acted to monopolize the trade of its colonies and exclude foreign nations from that trade.

In Boston a mercantile class developed, transporting furs, naval stores, and fish to other colonial and Caribbean ports. The Bostonian merchants traded lumber and furs for West Indian molasses, which could be distilled into rum. New England shippers took their wares to England and the European continent and then sailed to Africa, where they acquired slaves to transport to the southern colonies. This triangular trade—Africa, West Indies, and North America—was carried on in violation of the Navigation Acts, but these enterprising merchants were an intrepid lot and managed to get away with it.

They were so successful that they soon acquired sufficient wealth to displace the New England Puritan elite of the earlier generation. The amount of money an individual acquired became the means by which an American rose to the upper class of society. This became the norm throughout America, not simply New England. Money or property determined social rank. Material goods replaced birth and heredity as the most important component in determining one's position in society.

RELIGION HAD ALWAYS been a prime factor in bringing settlers to America. Some colonies were actually founded as a haven for adherents of a particular creed or church. Puritans and Quakers were obvious examples.

Puritans were governed along congregational lines, that is, the congregation formulated the rules of society and its economy. But as the commercial activity of New England expanded, ministers became aware of the threat to their authority and sought to counteract it by holding synods, which spelled out doctrinal errors and demanded conformity in understanding the will of the Almighty. Obtaining membership in the church that would allow a male to vote and hold office involved a lengthy examination to make certain an individual had a genuine conversion and actually experienced the presence of God. At a synod in 1662 the clergy established what they called the Halfway Covenant by which individuals were granted "halfway" status if they were the grandchildren of "saints," thereby conferring on them the right to vote and hold office.

In Quaker-dominated Pennsylvania problems arose over the fact that Quakers refused to take oaths, insisting that oaths violated the Bible. This made testimony in legal disputes difficult to obtain; and it complicated the pledging of allegiance to the crown. Moreover, Quakers were pacifists and refused to engage in warfare against the Indians. Over time the Quaker-domination of the government in Pennsylvania evaporated, and William Penn's "Holy Experiment" came to an end.

A revival of strong religious practice occurred in America in the middle of the eighteenth century with what is known as the First Great Awakening. It began around the 1720s in New England and New Jersey and affected all classes of society and all regions of the country. Ministers such as Jonathan Edwards in Northampton, Massachusetts; Theodorus Frelinghuysen in New Jersey; and the young George Whitefield, who came to this country from England in 1739, preached salvation to all who would repent and place their trust in Jesus Christ. Whitefield toured the colonies, mesmerizing those who heard him. He helped regenerate the revivalistic fervor that swept the country. In Philadelphia he preached to 10,000 who were hungry for salvation.

Jonathan Edwards and other revivalists, called New Lights in New England, likened humans to the lowest of God's creatures who were in desperate need of salvation. In a sermon, "Sinners in the Hands of an Angry God," Edwards declared, "The God that holds you over the pit of hell, much as one holds a spider or some loathsome insect over the fire . . . is dreadfully provoked." Only His mercy stays His hand from allowing the wicked to fall into hellfire. But unless His creatures repent and desist from their sinfulness He will surely and utterly destroy them.

This Great Awakening evoked intense emotional outbursts both from the ministers and from those who heard them. One could hear "screaming, singing, laughing, praying all at once," with people experiencing convulsions and falling into trances. It was not uncommon for an audience to become so aroused that it bordered on frenzy. Many of these preachers were itinerants and insisted that there must be a direct and close connection between the sinner and God, thus undermining the authority of the resident clergy. This individual and personal relationship was necessary for salvation, they argued, not the ministration of preachers. Preachers emphasized the fact that individuals alone were responsible for their final end. Without doubt, the promotion of individualism was one of the important effects of the Great Awakening. Another was its antiauthoritarianism, which permanently altered and diminished the power of resident ministers in both religious and secular affairs. Still another important effect was that it fostered the founding of new colleges to provide an education which would help individuals achieve salvation as well as to train New Light ministers. Such schools as Princeton, Dartmouth, Brown, Rutgers, and Columbia were established, and Jonathan Edwards himself became the president of Princeton.

By the 1770s, the fervor of the Great Awakening began to fade, but it succeeded in convincing Americans that they had a choice in religion and that it was up to them to earn their salvation. Such ideas carried into the political realm as well. Colonists reckoned that their government should be grounded in the will of the people, that they had a choice in the kind of government they wanted, the kind of government that suited their needs.

THE BRITISH ROYAL authority in London failed to provide the colonies in America with regular direction, and as the settlers moved farther west they encountered problems that required immediate solutions. The Indians and the invading French from Canada in the western country resisted English encroachment, and so the colonists were obliged to attend to this problem themselves and conduct their own affairs without outside guidance, instruction, or contradiction. Thus they relied on their own assemblies to address their concerns and pass the necessary legislation to resolve them. Since they believed they were unrepresented in Parliament, they felt justified in raising taxes to operate their local governments, pay the salaries of their officials, and increase the size of the militia to fight the Indians and ward off French intrusion. It was an arrangement by which England followed a policy of "salutary neglect," a policy that suited the needs of the inhabitants and buttressed their sense of their right as Englishmen to conduct their own affairs.

The problem of Indian resistance to the constant need of colonists for land frequently resulted in all-out war. When the Puritans moved into the Connecticut River valley in the 1630s a full-scale conflict broke out with the Pequot in 1637 and resulted in the virtual extermination of that tribe. This was followed by King Philip's War in 1675. The Indian chief of the Wampanoag tribe, Metacom, but dubbed King Philip by the British, launched a war that centered around Plymouth. This tribe had greeted the Pilgrims when they first arrived on Cape Cod and had had friendly relations with the settlers. But these relations soured over time, and the hanging of several Wampanoag, including the brother of Metacom, touched off the war and soon involved many of the other tribes in the surrounding area. It ended with King Philip's death in August 1676, when his severed head was put on public display.

THE FRENCH CONSTITUTED another problem for the English settlers. In their search for furs they had spilled down from Canada into the western regions beyond the Appalachian Mountains and around the Great Lakes. As directed by the French governor of Canada, Marquis Duquesne de Menneville, they built a series of forts from Lake Erie to the Ohio River to ensure their control.

The rivalry for empire between England and France had already developed into a hundred years of warfare, starting in the late seventeenth century, in both Europe and America. It began in Europe in 1689 with the War of the League of Augsburg, called King William's War in America. In that war colonists under the command of Sir William Phips captured Port Royal, Nova Scotia, but it was recaptured by France a year later. The War of the Spanish Succession, which started in 1702, was called Queen Anne's War in the colonies. Then came the War of the Austrian Succession, or King George's War, in 1740. At its conclusion France ceded Newfoundland, Arcadia, and Hudson Bay to

Great Britain. In all these wars both the French and the English allied themselves to Indian tribes, the French arming the Algonquin and the English the Iroquois.

In the final war of this struggle for empire, the Seven Years' War, or French and Indian War, actually started in America. In 1754, Governor Robert Dinwiddie of Virginia dispatched his militia, led by a twenty-two-year-old colonel, George Washington, to construct a fort at the juncture of the Monongahela and Allegheny rivers that forms the Ohio River. Driven off the site of the junction, the Virginians built a stockade fifty miles away, called Fort Necessity. The frontier became a living hell for colonists in the west as the French and their Indian allies ravaged the American settlements in one military defeat after another.

Then the situation made a complete about-face. When William Pitt became prime minister, he completely altered British policy in fighting this war. He left the conflict on the European continent to his Prussian ally, Frederick the Great, and concentrated on the war in the colonies. He sent crack troops and his best generals to America, including generals James Wolfe and Jeffrey Amherst. Amherst had a reputation for gifting the Indians with smallpox-infected blankets. After a series of engagements the French abandoned Fort Duquesne in what is now Pittsburgh. Louisbourg, Ticonderoga, Quebec, and Montreal were captured by the British. In the siege of Quebec both General Wolfe and the French general, Marquis de Montcalm, were killed.

At the peace treaty signed in Paris in 1763, France surrendered Canada to Great Britain. To compensate its ally, Spain, for losing Florida to Great Britain, France ceded Louisiana to her. The acquisition of Canada pleased fur traders because it provided an enormous territory in which to hunt animals, and it pleased the colonists, who no longer feared the presence of the French and their incitement of Indians on the frontier. The French minister, Étienne-François de Choiseul, sagaciously predicted that the colonies would break free of Great Britain once Canada was ceded.

At the outset of the conflict between American colonists and their French opponents on the frontier, particularly at Fort Duquesne, there was an attempt at unified action. Representatives from seven colonies—Massachusetts, Rhode Island, Connecticut, New Hampshire, New York, Pennsylvania, and Maryland—met in Albany in June 1754, along

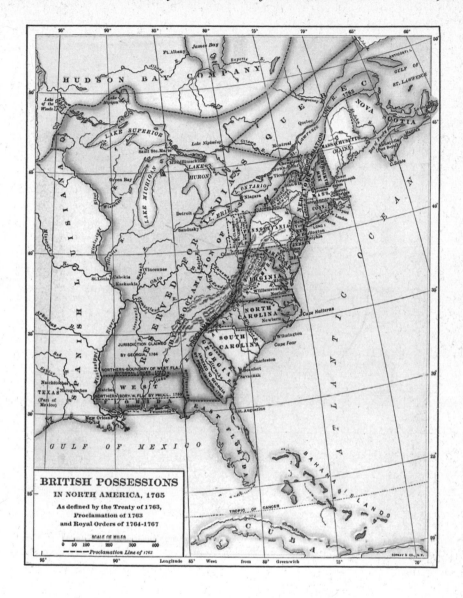

BRITISH POSSESSIONS
IN NORTH AMERICA, 1765
As defined by the Treaty of 1763,
Proclamation of 1763
and Royal Orders of 1764-1767

SCALE OF MILES
0 50 100   200   300   400
– – – – – Proclamation Line of 1763

with 100 Iroquois chiefs, and agreed on a Plan of Union for the common defense. Devised for the most part by Benjamin Franklin of Pennsylvania, the plan recommended the creation of a continental government with representatives from each colony. A president-general appointed by the king would act as the chief executive officer with veto power over all legislation. The single house would meet annually to regulate such matters as Indian affairs, public lands, and a colonial militia. This was the first attempt by American settlers to form a continental government to act for the entire English population within the colonies. But to Franklin's intense disappointment, the king and several colonial legislatures rejected the plan.

Because of their long history of conducting their own local affairs, the colonists believed they were merely acting on their rights as Englishmen. Besides, the policy of "salutary neglect" pursued by Parliament seemed to confirm their claim. They regarded their legislative assemblies as one expression of their right to enact laws commensurate with perceived local needs, not the gift of a temporarily distracted or overburdened Parliament.

Parliament, of course, saw it differently. The colonists were British subjects and therefore obliged to obey the laws enacted by the central government in London. It was all well and good to have local assemblies operating in the colonies, but they were inferior to Parliament, which could alter or nullify what they enacted when and if it conflicted with imperial needs. Such a difference of conception about their position and rights was sure to produce a collision. And it was not long before the collision burst into violence.

Independence and Nation Building

ALTHOUGH THE TITANIC battle for empire between the French and British ended with a total English victory, it created monumental problems in London as to the administration of this vast domain. French forces had been swept from the region west of the Allegheny Mountains, but thousands of Indians lived in the area and resented and resisted the ever-increasing invasion of their hunting grounds by English colonists. The Indians also demanded that the British continue the French practice of supplying them with weapons and ammunition and lower prices on other trading necessities. The British had no intention of imitating French practice, and in the summer of 1763 the Indians finally rose up, under the leadership of the Ottawa chief Pontiac, in an effort to drive the settlers back to the ocean. Tribes from the Great Lakes to the Gulf of Mexico joined the rebellion and destroyed every frontier fort west of the mountains.

The British government not only decided that it must keep a standing army of at least 10,000 troops in North America to maintain order and control, but also issued the Proclamation of 1763, which forbade colonists from settling west of the Appalachian Mountains. It drew a north-south line at the crest of the mountains with the idea of reserving the land west of the line for the Indians. This was meant to pacify the tribes but served only to infuriate the colonists, who refused to be bound by the Proclamation.

Another problem arising from the cessation of hostilities between the British and French involved expense. The national debt in England stood at £147 million, and the Prime Minister, George Grenville, was determined to reduce it. One of his worst headaches was administering this expanded empire. It proved so costly that Parliament abandoned the policy of "salutary neglect" and passed a series of laws levying duties on English imports into America, with part of the revenue to go toward paying the salaries of royal officials in the colonies. The first bill was the Sugar Act, passed in 1764, which established duties on foreign sugar, textiles, coffee, indigo, rum, wine, and several other items. It was the first law approved by Parliament intended specifically to raise money in the colonies. Grenville expected this act to yield at least £45,000 annually if properly enforced. The Sugar Act was not simply a customs duty but a program that threatened to disrupt American trade and the livelihood of thousands.

This act was followed the next year by the Quartering Act, which required the colonies to provide lodging for troops stationed in their communities to protect them. The Stamp Act, which came a few days later, added a tax stamp to be placed on newspapers, legal documents, contracts, playing cards, marriage licenses, land deeds, and a host of other items that involved paper. It was the first direct tax levied by Parliament on the colonies. These acts—the Sugar, Quartering, and Stamp Acts—created quite an uproar in the colonies—the legal class was particularly hard hit by the Stamp Act—and James Otis in Massachusetts proposed that a general meeting of delegates from each of the colonies meet to take action against the Stamp Act. The proposal won a favorable response from the various colonies, and delegates chosen by their constituents met in October 1765 in New York City to protest the despised legislation. All but four colonies were represented at this Congress; in a "Declaration of Rights and Grievances," written chiefly by John Dickinson of Pennsylvania, the delegates insisted that only their own duly elected legislatures had the right to tax them. Parliament in no way represented them, they insisted, and was prohibited from imposing taxes on them. Taxation without representation, they declared, was nothing less than tyranny. In London, Benjamin Franklin, an agent for Pennsylvania, warned Parliament that any attempt to enforce the Stamp Act with troops might lead to rebellion.

Organizations such as the Sons of Liberty and the Daughters of Liberty were formed in 1765, and several riots occurred. The Sons of Liberty did not hesitate to resort to violence. All the stamp agents resigned. The violence, and the disastrous effect on merchants and businessmen, finally prompted Parliament to repeal the Stamp Act in 1766, but again it asserted in the Declaratory Act the government's "full power and authority . . . to bind the colonies and people of America, subjects of the crown of Great Britain, in all cases whatsoever."

But Americans were so delighted that they had forced Parliament to repeal the Stamp Act that they simply disregarded the Declaratory Act. If nothing else, their Stamp Act Congress had demonstrated that by unified action the colonies could compel Parliament to respect their rights. Let Parliament attempt another such tax, and the consequence might be the onset of rebellion.

It is interesting and important that they used the word "Congress" to describe their assembly. The word did not have the same meaning as it does today, namely that of a legislative body. A congress in the eighteenth and nineteenth centuries usually denoted a diplomatic assembly of sovereign and independent states. Thus the delegates to this Stamp Act Congress represented a collection of individual and distinct entities who considered themselves as having rights and powers as Englishmen by which they had full power to enact legislation for the benefit of the people living in their respective colonies.

In Virginia, a young, eloquent lawyer by the name of Patrick Henry, got up in the House of Burgesses and railed against both the king and Parliament. He argued so vehemently and so convincingly for the rights of colonists against the authority in London that someone in the room shouted, "Treason!" He was quick to respond, saying that if standing up for one's rights is treason then the colonists should take advantage of it. He introduced seven resolutions denouncing the monarchy and Parliament. Although the Burgesses passed only four of the less extreme of them, newspapers printed all seven and distributed them to the other colonies.

At this point a change in government in London brought the Chancellor of the Exchequer, Charles Townshend, to the head of government, a man who rejected every argument Americans put forward regarding their rights. To demonstrate his contempt, he persuaded Parliament to impose what he called an "external" as opposed to "internal" taxes on a wide variety of items to be imported from England, including glass, paper, and tea. Worse, part of the revenue to be collected would pay the salaries of royal officials in the colonies. Not only did these duties tax colonists without their consent, but they also eliminated the one lever of power the colonists had over their royal governors: namely, the appropriation of their salaries and the salaries of their advisers and other officials.

In another act the Parliament, on October 1, 1767, suspended the New York assembly for refusing to provide supplies to the troops quartered in the colony. This suspension was an all-out assault on what Americans regarded as their fundamental rights. Suspension could lead to an abolition of legislative assemblies, they contended, and result in virtual enslavement of the settlers. John Dickinson of Pennsylvania spelled out the colonists' complaints in a popular pamphlet, *Letters from an American Farmer.* The suspension of the New York assembly, he wrote, was a damnable "stroke aimed at the liberty of all these colonies. . . . For the cause of one is the cause of all." Moreover, "*Those* who are *taxed* without their own consent are *slaves,*" he cried. "We are taxed without our own consent. . . . We are therefore—SLAVES."

A new prime minister in London, Lord North, took over from Townshend in 1770 and ordered the repeal of the duties, except for a tax of three pennies a pound on tea, which was meant more as a symbol of Parliament's authority than as a producer of revenue.

Radical activists who plotted to bring about a revolution kept stirring up popular resentment against British rule. Sam Adams, a cousin of John Adams, wrote letters and articles in newspapers, summoning "the people of this country explicitly to declare whether they will be Freemen or Slaves." He urged the formation of committees of correspondence and in 1772 set up such committees in every Massachusetts town. The idea prompted Thomas Jefferson of Virginia to aid in the formation of similar committees throughout the colonies.

In 1771 Thomas Hutchinson was appointed governor of Massachusetts. He was not a British nobleman sent by the crown to enforce absolute control of the province. Rather, he was a Harvard-educated fifth-generation American, but a devoted loyalist who had served in the assembly and later became chief justice of the highest Massachusetts court. Because Hutchinson hated and sought to quell public demonstrations and mob action as a way of getting across their demands, Bostonians regarded him as the figurehead of everything they detested about British rule. And although he deplored the stupidity of the Stamp Act, he defended the right of Parliament to tax the colonies. The rage against him grew to such an extent that his house had been ransacked in 1765, when he was the chief justice.

Hutchinson had also defended the use of search warrants, called writs of assistance, in an effort to curb smuggling in the colonies during wartime. James Otis gave a crowd-pleasing tirade against the writs, a speech so powerful that John Adams hailed it as the beginning of the American Revolution. "Then and there," Adams later wrote, "the child Independence was born."

Then, on March 5, 1770, the mounting antagonism between the British authority and the citizenry of Boston erupted in violence. British soldiers guarding the customhouse, commanded by Captain Thomas Preston, were jeered at and heckled by agitators who threw stones and snowballs at them. The soldiers reacted by firing into the crowd, killing five men and wounding six others. A general melee was avoided when Hutchinson, at the insistence of Sam Adams, agreed to withdraw the troops from Boston. Preston and eight of his soldiers were arrested and charged with murder. John Adams and Josiah Quincy accepted the request that they defend the soldiers. Preston and six of his men were acquitted, but two soldiers were found guilty of manslaughter and were released after being branded on the hand. This "Boston Massacre," as it was called, was regularly remembered each year in Massachusetts, and a print of the bloody scene was circulated throughout the colonies.

But it was the tea tax that really set off a series of events that played into the hands of the most radical colonial agitators. The East India Tea Company verged on bankruptcy and turned to the government for help. It had a monopoly on the importation of tea into England and held a surplus of 17 million pounds of tea. But it could not pay the duty required by law, and therefore could not sell the tea in Britain. Parliament responded in May 1773 by passing a Tea Act allowing the company to sell its tea in America, where the tax of threepence per pound of tea would be collected. Under this arrangement the company could undersell American merchants and smugglers and create a monopoly for itself, a situation the colonists fiercely resented. The Sons of Liberty condemned the act and called for a boycott of tea.

Governor Hutchinson was determined to enforce the collection of the tax when three ships arrived in Boston with a large cargo of tea. His two sons and a nephew were among the agents assigned to sell the shipment. Resistance and determination reared on both sides of the issue. Finally, on the night of December 16, 1773, colonists dressed as Mohawk Indians boarded the ships and dumped 342 chests of tea worth £90,000 into the harbor.

The British reacted sharply to this "Boston Tea Party" and labeled it an act of rebellion. They chose to believe that a conspiracy had been hatched in Boston to initiate a rebellion against the crown and win independence for the colony. Angrily, in the spring of 1774 Parliament enacted the Coercive Laws, or, as the colonists called them, the Intolerable Acts, by which the port of Boston was closed to all trade until the tea was paid for; it forbade town meetings; it altered the voting for members of the Massachusetts assembly; and it included a new quartering of soldiers that applied to all colonies. Parliament had gone beyond simple punishment for the Tea Party, according to the colonists. It had now abridged their fundamental freedoms as Englishmen.

Following the Intolerable Acts came the Quebec Act, which was passed on May 20, 1774, and extended the boundaries of Quebec to include the territory west of the Allegheny Mountains. In an effort to conciliate French-speaking Roman Catholic Canadians, Parliament had unwittingly roused fears among Protestant colonists about a "popish" plot to gain greater control of government. More troubling, however, was the fact that it annulled the territorial claims of New York, Pennsylvania, Virginia, Massachusetts, and Connecticut.

At this juncture, in August 1774, Thomas Jefferson published a pamphlet titled *A Summary View of the Rights of British America*, in which he defended the Boston Tea Party as the action of a "desperate people" struggling to protect their basic rights as citizens. So powerful, so well crafted, and so direct were the arguments in this pamphlet that Jefferson overnight became the leading spokesman for colonial rights.

In addition to all the other outrages perpetrated by the crown, Hutchinson was replaced as governor of Massachusetts by General Thomas Gage, accompanied by an army of 4,000 soldiers, who promised to put an end to the colonists' resistance to British law. "The die is cast," King George informed Lord North. "The colonists must either triumph or submit."

Submit they would not. Once more delegates assembled from all the colonies, except Georgia, to agree on demands and devise plans to make Britain acknowledge their basic rights as Englishmen. This First Continental Congress convened in Carpenter's Hall in Philadelphia on September 5, 1774, and included such radical activists as Sam and John Adams of Massachusetts and Patrick Henry and Richard Henry Lee of Virginia. However, moderates led by Joseph Galloway of Pennsylvania preferred a more conciliatory policy. They offered a variation of the Albany Plan of Union, but the Congress rejected it. Instead, the Congress adopted a Declaration written by John Adams, which affirmed the rights of colonists to "life, liberty, & property," and condemned the recent acts of Parliament as "unconstitutional, dangerous, and destructive." Again they used the word "Congress," asserting once more their existence as separate, individual, and sovereign states.

Forthwith, the delegates demanded repeal of the Intolerable Acts, and of all taxes by Parliament. Moreover, they agreed to collective economic action involving nonimportation of British goods, starting on December 1, 1774, and nonexportation of American goods on September 1, 1775. This Continental Association was to be enforced by local committees within each colony. When this Congress adjourned, the delegates truly believed that they had vindicated American rights. They agreed to reassemble the following May.

But events soon developed that pitched the colonies into all-out war with the colonial authorities. On April 18, 1775, General Gage in Massachusetts sent 1,000 troops to seize suspected supplies of guns and ammunition at Concord. Paul Revere rode out of Boston to warn Americans of the approach of the soldiers. At Lexington a company of colonial minutemen tried to block the advance of the British and were fired upon. Eight minutemen died in the clash. The British troops continued to Concord, where they destroyed whatever weapons were found, and then turned around and headed back to Boston. But along the way they were attacked by thousands of colonists, who hid behind trees, bushes, and stone walls. By the time the British arrived back at headquarters they had lost almost 300 men.

The situation escalated when Colonel William Prescott fortified Breed's Hill with 1,600 colonials on the night of June 16, 1775, and General Gage sent his army to dislodge them. It took three assaults and the loss of over 1,000 men before the British finally reached the trenches at the top of the hill where the Americans were hidden. Their powder gone, the colonials abandoned the trenches and fled from their attackers. They suffered about one-third as many casualties as they inflicted on the British, who lost over 1,000 men.

This Battle of Bunker Hill, incorrectly named after a hill nearby, was one of the bloodiest in the entire Revolutionary War. One-eighth of all the British officers who died in the war were killed at Bunker Hill. General Henry Clinton, who—together with Generals William Howe and John Burgoyne—had recently arrived in Boston with reinforcements, wrote a fitting comment on this battle: "Another such victory would have ruined us."

With violence increasing each month, the Second Continental Congress assembled on May 10, 1775, and decided to pursue more radical measures in seeking redress of grievances. The delegates raised an army, appointed General George Washington to command it, issued Continental currency, and opened negotiations with foreign powers to win their support and intervention.

To subdue this rebellion, the British hired 20,000 German mercenaries and shipped them to America, thereby intensifying Americans' determination to seek independence. The publication of *Common Sense* by Thomas Paine in early January 1776, called for immediate independence. He labeled George III the "Royal Brute" and accused the king of instigating all the wretched legislation directed against the colonists. Paine acknowledged that many Americans looked upon Britain as the "parent country," but if true, he said, the recent acts were all the more outrageous: "Even brutes do not devour their young, nor savages make war upon their families." But the "Royal Brute" could and did "unflinchingly hear of their slaughter, and composedly slept with their blood upon his soul." America was destined for a republican form of government, Paine insisted, not a "monarchical tyranny." It has been and will continue to be "the asylum for the persecuted lovers of civil and religious liberty from *every part* of Europe." Paine's pamphlet had such an impact on those who read it that it persuaded many to adopt the cause of independence. More than 100,000 copies of the pamphlet were snapped up by an eager public, and the work enjoyed twenty-five printings in 1776 alone. George Washington referred frequently to its "sound doctrine and unanswerable reasoning."

On April 12, 1776, North Carolina instructed its delegates in Congress to seek separation, and on June 7 Richard Henry Lee of Virginia offered a resolution stating that these colonies "are and of right ought to be, free and independent states." John Adams seconded Lee's resolution, but there were some in Congress who argued for reconciliation with the mother country. Benjamin Franklin of Pennsylvania reminded them, however, that if the members of the Congress did not "hang

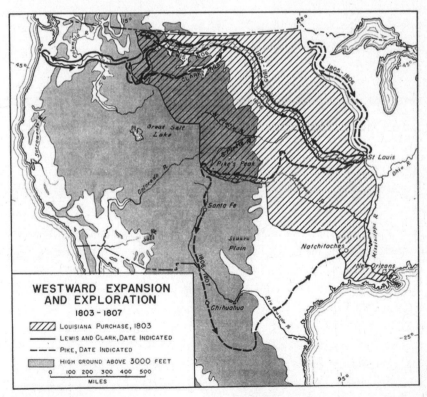

Westward Expansion

together," they would "all hang separately." Ultimately the advocates of independence prevailed. As Jefferson explained, "The question was not whether, by a declaration of independence, we should make ourselves what we are not, but whether we should declare a fact that already exists."

A committee was formed to write a justification of the action to be taken should Congress choose to accept the resolution. Thomas Jefferson, Benjamin Franklin, John Adams, Roger Sherman of Connecticut, and Robert R. Livingston of New York composed this committee, but a subcommittee of Jefferson and Adams was actually assigned the task of writing the document. Because Jefferson was known to be a "felicitous" writer, he was prevailed upon to prepare what turned out to be an eloquent statement about human liberty and equality. Adams and Franklin added some minor amendments. On July 2 Lee's resolution was passed, and on July 4 the Declaration of Independence was adopted without dissent and signed by the president of the Continental Congress, John Hancock.

The Congress also adopted a flag, on June 14, 1777, one consisting of thirteen red and white alternating stripes and thirteen white stars on a field of blue.

As delegates from sovereign, independent states, the members were united in their determination to win freedom from the tyranny of Great Britain, but they had little enthusiasm for creating a controlling central government. Still, they needed some sort of central authority to attend to such matters as providing for military and financial needs in prosecuting the ongoing war. So another committee was chosen to lay out the specifics for a national government that could address these concerns. The document produced by this committee, known as the Articles of Confederation, was chiefly the work of John Dickinson of Pennsylvania. What the document proposed was a Confederation of states, not a Union of people. As a result, the government it projected was doomed from the start. Nevertheless, it was a major breakthrough in the evolution of a representative government that would encompass a collection of thirteen independent political entities.

The Articles declared that the several states were to be joined in a "perpetual union" and a "firm league of friendship." But it also admitted that all the states would retain their "sovereignty, freedom, and independence." A unicameral legislature was established for this "union," representing all the states. And although it could enact laws, it had no authority to enforce them. It relied on the states and the people to obey whatever it decreed, but voluntary compliance proved to be virtually impossible. In addition, the government lacked the power to tax. To support its operation and pay for carrying on the war, it had to rely on contributions from each state as set forth by the national legislature. But few states paid what they owed. If hard-pressed for cash, they would pay less, and there was nothing the central government could do about it.

Two other problems were present in the Articles. First, the unanimous agreement of all the states was required before the document could go into effect. Maryland withheld its consent until all the states ceded their western lands to the central government. That state had no claim to the western country and hoped to share in the largess of more fortunate states, such as Virginia. Not until 1781 did all the states agree to the condition and Maryland finally added its consent. The second problem involved amending the Articles once the government began operation. Again it required unanimous approval by the states, and that proved to be impossible. What the document created was a government subservient to thirteen other governments.

It must be remembered that at the time, the delegates who produced the Articles of Confederation had no experience in establishing a workable central authority that would understand and recognize the sovereignty of each state. It would take a learning experience of almost half a dozen years for others to decide what had to be done to create a permanent Union that could pass and enforce laws to protect liberty and property for its citizens and show proper regard for the rights of the states. In a word, a federal system needed to be erected.

The delegates debated the Articles of Confederation for over a year, and not until November 15, 1777, was it formally adopted. Then, it took another three and a half years before all the states agreed and the government under the Articles was established.

THE WAR ITSELF had begun at Lexington and Concord, but to put down the rebellion the British had to destroy General Washington's ability to remain in the field or militarily occupy the entire country.

The rebels, on the other hand, simply had to get the British to tire of the war and withdraw. They did not need to win battle after battle. If they could maintain an army in the field over an extended period of time, it was very likely that they could obtain their objective.

On July 12, 1776, the British sent reinforcements to New York to link up with Sir William Howe's army, which came down from Halifax. They rendezvoused with other British troops from South Carolina under General Henry Clinton to constitute a powerful force of 30,000 soldiers. Washington had less than half that number and realized he could never hold New York. Still he was determined to put up a fight. On August 27 he challenged the British on Long Island. Following an inevitable defeat, he moved his army under cover of a thick fog across the East River to Manhattan. Howe pursued him up the Hudson River valley, and Washington retreated to New Jersey. New York remained in British hands for the remainder of the war.

Washington crossed the Delaware River at Trenton and tried to keep his army together. But his soldiers shivered in the December cold and began to desert, since the situation looked hopeless. Their general pleaded with Congress to provide supplies and additional troops but had little success. As the situation became desperate, Thomas Paine, from an American camp, wrote the first number of *The Crisis*, in which he declared, "These are the times that try men's souls." Indeed, Washington himself almost lost hope. "If every nerve is not strained to recruit a new army," he wrote, "I think the game is pretty well up."

Then he attempted something truly daring. On Christmas evening, with about 2,500 men, he crossed the ice-filled Delaware River about nine miles northwest of Trenton and attacked the Hessians who had taken the town and were sleeping off their Christmas celebration. The Americans captured more than 900 Hessians. Lord Cornwallis attempted to strike back, but Washington hit the British rear guard at Princeton and forced Cornwallis to retreat to protect his military supplies. What Washington had done by his daring action was restore his army's confidence that it could win and spike the determination of the British to bring the war to a speedy end.

Resolved as ever to put down the rebellion, the British came up with a three-pronged plan. They would bring down two separate armies from Canada, which would meet in Albany and then join a force sent northward by General Howe in New York, thereby cutting off New England. Cutting off New England was an important objective for the British. But the army marching down from the St. Lawrence via Lake Champlain and commanded by General John Burgoyne was surrounded by thousands of Americans from Massachusetts, New Hampshire, and New York led by General Horatio Gates. Recognizing the hopelessness of his situation, Burgoyne surrendered his army of 6,000 at Saratoga on October 17, 1777.

It was quite a disaster for the British and prompted the French to conclude that an alliance with the United States would be to their advantage. On February 6, 1778, American ministers, led by Benjamin Franklin, signed two treaties with the French government. The first was a treaty of amity and commerce in which both countries were granted most-favored-nation status; they further agreed to guarantee forever each other's possessions in the New World. The second was a treaty of alliance whereby neither country would lay down its arms until Great Britain acknowledged the independence of the United States; this second treaty was to become effective when war broke out between France and Britain.

The surrender at Saratoga also convinced Lord North and King George to make concessions, and a bill was introduced in Parliament that granted virtually all the Americans' demands, to wit: Parliament would not levy any tax on the colonies; all unacceptable laws enacted since 1763 would be repealed; and leaders branded as rebels would be pardoned. But the bill did not win passage until nearly two weeks after the alliances with France had been signed, and the Americans had no wish to revert from free states back to dependent colonies. On June 17 France and Britain clashed on the open sea and war was declared between them. That spring Count Charles d'Estaing, commanding twelve French warships and several regiments of troops, headed for America.

Meanwhile, Howe took part of his army and headed south to capture Philadelphia, apparently with the approval of London. Washington hastened to thwart the British move but was outflanked at the battles of Brandywine Creek and Germantown. So while Howe spent the winter in the city enjoying a life of parties and dances, Washington took up a position at Valley Forge, twenty miles northwest of Philadelphia, where he and his men, numbering 12,000, endured a dreadful winter. Men and camp followers sickened and died from lack of proper shelter, food, clothing, blankets, and medicine. Again the general begged for assistance from Congress but received very little.

General Clinton took command in place of Howe and decided to return to New York. Washington followed and met the British at Monmouth, New Jersey, on June 28, 1778, where he managed to turn back Clinton's counterattack. It was the last battle that Washington directed prior to his assuming command of a combined French and American force at Yorktown in Virginia.

The French had planned all along that the fleet under d'Estaing would head for the West Indies in the hope of capturing several British islands, such as Jamaica or one of the sugar islands. The Americans had little naval might to challenge the British fleet patrolling the coastline, but one American ship, commanded by John Paul Jones, captured several hundred British vessels and raided a number of English coastal towns. Jones himself became something of an American hero in this war. The country needed heroes, and there were so few.

Then, when Spain entered the war against Great Britain in the expectation of recapturing Gibraltar and Florida, the ministry in London decided to change its strategy and shift the war to the southern American colonies. It began with the capture of Savannah in December 1778. General Clinton sailed from New York with an army of 8,500; captured Charleston; and compelled the American general, Benjamin Lincoln, to surrender his army of over 5,000. Lord Cornwallis replaced Clinton, who returned to New York, while Congress appointed General Gates to supersede Lincoln. Gates's appointment was a mistake. He suffered the worst American defeat of the war at Camden, South Carolina, when his troops fled the field in disarray. Gates ran too. The British then came to a very wrong conclusion—that untrained, undisciplined American soldiers would drop their weapons and flee when confronted by professional British troops.

Another disaster occurred on September 25, when Benedict Arnold, a splendid general who had participated in the surrender of Burgoyne at Saratoga, turned traitor and deserted to the British. In need of money to pay his many debts, he agreed to turn over West Point, which he commanded, to the enemy. It turned out that he had been spying for General Clinton for the past year. The capture of Major John André, who carried messages between Clinton and Arnold, revealed the treason. Arnold fled. He later became a British general and joined Lord Cornwallis, who had moved his army from the Carolinas into Virginia, where he took up a position at Yorktown.

The urgent call to the French for help resulted in the arrival of 7,000 men aboard a fleet of twenty warships commanded by Admiral François de Grasse. The combined Franco-American army of 16,000 under Washington's command surrounded Cornwallis while de Grasse's fleet blocked the entrance to Chesapeake Bay, thus preventing the British from escaping the net that had been tightly wound around them. On October 18, 1781, the British general surrendered his army of 8,000 regulars and sailors.

For all intents and purposes the American colonies had won their independence. The House of Commons in London voted to end the war and authorized a negotiating team to arrange a peace treaty with the former colonies. Lord North resigned and was succeeded by Lord Rockingham. A year later, on November 30, a provisional treaty was signed in Paris by Benjamin Franklin, John Adams, John Jay, and Henry Laurens for the United States. Commissioner Richard Oswald signed for Britain. On April 15, 1783, Congress ratified the treaty. According to the terms of this treaty U.S. independence was recognized, and its boundaries stipulated—although the treaty failed to include the cession of Canada to the United States as demanded by Franklin. The boundaries ran from the Atlantic Ocean to the Mississippi River and from the forty-fifth parallel in the south to Maine and the Great Lakes in the north. The treaty also called for the cessation of hostilities and the evacuation of British-held territory within the United States. In addition it provided fishing rights for Americans, and that the rights and property of loyalists would be restored. It was a very generous treaty as far as the former colonists were concerned. The French bitterly criticized it because they had not been consulted in arranging the terms. A diplomatic response from Franklin soothed the hurt feelings of the French and prevented the two allies from breaking off relations.

THE NEXT SEVERAL years were difficult for the United States. Individual states quarreled with one another and with the central government. Boundaries between states were one problem; commerce, debts, and currency were others. To make matters worse, a rebellion flared in Massachusetts when economically depressed farmers demanded laws to protect them against farm foreclosures and cheap money. When violence resulted, Governor James Bowdoin called out the militia to restore order. But Daniel Shays, an officer during the Revolution, assembled a force of 1,200 men in the late fall of 1786 and marched on the town of Springfield. After several engagements, the militia, commanded by General Benjamin Lincoln, crushed the rebellion by March 1787. Shays himself fled to Vermont and was later pardoned. The government under the Articles of Confederation did nothing to help the Massachusetts authority despite the fact that Congress authorized the Secretary of War, Henry Knox, to raise a 1,000-man force to fight.

There were a few bright spots during this period of the Confederation. In Virginia on January 16, 1786, the House of Burgesses adopted a statute of religious freedom, written by Thomas Jefferson. It declared that no one could be compelled to join or support a church or suffer discrimination on account of religious beliefs. Jefferson ranked his authorship of this act along with his writing of the Declaration of Independence and the founding of the University of Virginia as his most significant contributions as a public official.

But nationally, things went from bad to worse. Topping off the problems for the central government was an economic recession that lingered for several years during the 1780s. Trade and wages declined, and paper currency issued by the several states mounted to nearly $1 million and its value steadily declined. Some people began to consider amending the Articles but quickly realized what an impossible task it would be.

Congress, however, did enjoy one notable success under the Articles. On July 13, 1787, it passed the Northwest Ordinance, a scheme by which future states could be added to the Union. The Ordinance provided a government for the territory north of the Ohio River which had been ceded by New York, Connecticut, Massachusetts, and Virginia. On the basis of a plan devised in 1784 by Thomas Jefferson, the western region would be surveyed and laid out in townships, six-mile-square with parcels set aside for education. The area was placed under the control of a governor, a secretary, and three judges appointed by Congress. When the number of adult white males in the area reached 5,000, they could elect a bicameral legislature and send a non-voting delegate to Congress. Once the number reached 60,000, they could apply for admission as a state on an equal basis with all the other states. Freedom of religion, trial by jury, and support for public education were guaranteed. Slavery was prohibited. It was expected that three to five states would be created out of this Northwest Territory. Later, the Congress under the Constitution adopted the procedure formulated by the Northwest Ordinance, a process that settled once and for all the method by which new states could be joined to the Union.

But the problems confronting Congress under the Articles grew worse with each passing year, and many Americans recognized that something had to be done. A start in that direction occurred when Virginia and Maryland met at Mount Vernon in 1785 to address the question of interstate commerce, in particular the navigation of the Chesapeake Bay and the Potomac River. It soon developed that Delaware and Pennsylvania also had an interest in the problem and wanted to take part in the negotiations. Whereupon Virginia invited all the states to send delegates to Annapolis, Maryland, in 1786 to see if they could find a solution to the problem of interstate commerce. Nine states accepted the invitation, although only five (New York, New Jersey, Delaware, Pennsylvania, and Virginia) showed up in time to take part in the proceedings. So Alexander Hamilton of New York suggested that they attempt something far more comprehensive than interstate commerce. He wrote a report, adopted by the convention, in which he proposed that the delegates invite the several states to send representatives to attend a special convention in Philadelphia in 1787 for the purpose of devising such "provisions as shall appear to them necessary to render the constitution of the Federal Government adequate to the exigencies of the Union." Put another way, he wanted the Articles thoroughly overhauled to create a truly workable central government with genuine powers that it could enforce.

The Congress under the Articles added its recommendation to the proposal that the delegates had issued and called on the states to appoint delegates to the convention in Philadelphia "for the sole and express purpose of revising the Articles of Confederation."

ALL THE STATES except Rhode Island responded, and dispatched a total of fifty-five representatives to this new convention, which met in May 1787. From this turnout it was clear that most states realized something had to be done if the Union was to last. Not surprisingly, a number of notables attended. First and foremost was General George Washington, who by this time had achieved the status of a national hero and whose presence lent a high degree of legitimacy to the meeting. Others included James Madison of Virginia, who would provide the basic frame for a totally new government; and Alexander Hamilton, who argued effectively for a stronger and more potent national government. Still other distinguished members included Gouverneur Morris and James Wilson of Pennsylvania, Roger Sherman and Elbridge Gerry of Massachusetts, and George Mason and Edmund Randolph of Virginia. William Jackson of Georgia was elected to serve as secretary, but his journal is so substantively thin that it provides little information about what took place at the convention. Fortunately James Madison kept extensive notes, which were published in 1840, shortly after his death.

The first thing the convention did was unanimously elect George Washington president. Next, the members decided to keep their debates secret, as most colonial assemblies did. They agreed on secrecy for the simple reason that they decided, at the start of their deliberations, to scrap the Articles and write an entirely new document. Had this decision been known, several states might well have recalled their delegations.

Once the convention began its serious work, Governor Edmund Randolph of Virginia introduced, on May 29, a suggested form of government prepared by Madison and based on the people rather than on the states. This "Virginia Plan" or "Large State Plan," as it was called, established a government consisting of three independent branches—legislative, executive, and judicial—in which each would have certain powers and could check the others. Checks and balances were the ideal it hoped to create. Congress, the legislative branch—which the founders regarded as the centerpiece of government—consisted of two houses. The lower house (elected every two years by the people) would be proportional to population and would elect the members of the upper house from nominations put forward by individual states. This proposal conferred broad legislative powers on the Congress and could annul state law, a feature that generated immediate criticism. The legislature would also choose the executive, as well as the judiciary, which would include a supreme court and such inferior courts as necessary. Finally, a council of revision composed of the executive and members of the judiciary would exercise a veto over legislative acts.

The Virginia Plan obviously favored the states with the largest population, a fact that troubled small states. Their delegates preferred a different proposal, the one put forward by William Paterson of New Jersey on June 15 and known as the "New Jersey Plan" or "Small State Plan." This proposal imitated the Articles in that it called for a unicameral legislature in which each state would have one vote. The state governments, not the people, would elect the representatives to this Congress and choose a plural executive and a supreme court. The executive would not have veto power. Although the New Jersey Plan granted the government additional authority to tax and regulate foreign and interstate trade and included a statement that the laws of Congress would be the supreme law of the country, it was hardly more than a slight modification of the Articles which everyone knew had proved unworkable. The Virginia Plan, on the other hand, was too lopsided in favoring a proportional system of representation, but it did provide for an entirely new and innovative form of government.

Some members of this convention actually preferred nothing more than a set of amendments to the Articles of Confederation, as difficult as that might be. They did not want to participate in any way in the diminution of states' power and rights, and in the case of several members, like Governor George Clinton of New York, their own individual authority. Clinton and several others withdrew from the convention when they realized that their position found little favor with the other delegates.

The members of the convention spent days arguing and debating the two proposals; and since they were genuinely interested in resolving the governmental problems that beset the country—specifically, maintaining viable states and a strong central authority—they finally resorted to compromise to bring about a solution. When there are opposing views to any problem, let alone a set of problems, they agreed, the only way to resolve them is through compromise. To reach an agreement, both large and small states had to yield something to the other side in order to gain what they felt was important for their particular requirements.

To break the impasse, Roger Sherman of Connecticut suggested what has been called the Connecticut Compromise: that is, a Congress consisting of two houses, in which the lower house would be elected by the people on the basis of population, thereby satisfying the large states, and the upper house would be elected by the states with each state having two representatives, thus providing equality of representation and thereby meeting the demand of the small states. Further compromises included counting three-fifths of the slave population in determining the population for a state's representation in the lower house. And there was to be no interference with the slave trade for twenty years. The convention also agreed to permit Congress to regulate trade, as the North demanded, but forbade the imposition of export duties, which the South insisted upon to protect its exports of cotton and tobacco.

These various compromises were adopted toward the end of July and then submitted to a five-member committee of detail to draft the completed Constitution. The committee finished its work and submitted the result to the convention on August 6. After a monthlong debate the delegates agreed on a two-year term for representatives, a six-year term for senators, and a four-year term for the chief executive. States were forbidden to issue paper money or infringe on the obligation of contracts. The document went on at length in describing the powers delegated to Congress but said little about the other two branches. It obviously meant to imply that the legislature would attend to the needs of the executive and judiciary. What it did say about the other two branches was the manner in which the President would be elected (by a College of Electors chosen in each state) and the justices appointed. It awarded the chief executive veto and appointive powers, and the position of commander in chief of the armed forces. It also decreed the establishment of a Supreme Court and such inferior courts as Congress would from time to time establish. It prohibited bills of attainder and ex post facto laws. It further stipulated that the members of the three branches of government would receive compensation from the national treasury, not from the states.

Having agreed substantially to the important segments of this federal government, the convention appointed a five-man committee on style and arrangement to prepare the final document. Principally written by Gouverneur Morris, the draft included a preamble that declared, "We the people of the United States" establish this Constitution—not "we the states" as stated in the Articles of Confederation. The preamble went on to identify the objectives of this new government: to "form a more perfect Union, establish Justice, insure domestic Tranquility, provide for the common defence, promote the general Welfare, and secure the Blessings of Liberty to ourselves and our Posterity." The document also stated that the Constitution, the treaties, and the laws of the United States "shall be the supreme Law of the Land."

This draft was submitted to the convention on September 12 and reviewed at length. After a few minor changes each of the twelve state delegations voted to approve the Constitution on September 17, 1787. Of the forty-two members present, three refused to sign the final copy: Elbridge Gerry of Massachusetts, and Edmund Randolph and George Mason of Virginia. The signed document then went forth with a letter of recommendation to the Congress under the Articles that the states call special conventions elected by the people to approve or reject the instrument. When nine states ratified it, the Constitution would replace the Articles of Confederation and go into effect in those states.

Delaware was the first state to give its approval to the new document, on December 7, by a unanimous vote. It was followed by Pennsylvania, New Jersey, Georgia, Connecticut, Massachusetts, Maryland, South Carolina, New Hampshire, Virginia, and New York. The approval by New York on July 26 provided the eleventh state to ratify, but Rhode Island rejected the Constitution and North Carolina delayed its approval until November 21, 1789. Rhode Island subsequently reversed itself and ratified the document on May 29, 1790. During the debates in the ratifying conventions there were many complaints about the Constitution's failure to provide a bill of rights, especially a statement that those powers not expressly granted to the national government were reserved to the states. A number of states made recommendations that this deficiency be addressed as soon as possible.

Once the ratification by eleven states had been achieved in July, the Congress under the Articles of Confederation decreed that on the first Wednesday of January 1789, electors would be chosen in the several states who would vote for President and Vice President; that on the first Wednesday of February 1789 those electors would cast their ballots; and on the first Wednesday of March 1789—which happened to be March 4, a date that would mark the beginning of each new administration until passage of the Twentieth Amendment on February 6, 1933, when it was changed to January 20—the newly elected Congress would assemble in New York City, the seat of the American government since 1785, tabulate the ballots, and announce the names of the chosen President and Vice President, thereby completing the election of the legislative and executive branches. Once the individuals of these two branches assembled, they could then begin the process of establishing the judiciary and name the individuals who would sit on the Supreme Court.

There was virtually no question as to who would be elected President. George Washington was universally loved as the military hero who had won the nation's freedom. Without him no Union seemed possible. So the electors unanimously elected him chief executive and John Adams Vice President. Coming from Massachusetts, Adams provided a good balance to Washington, a Virginian—thus both North and South were represented in the executive branch—and his career as a public servant and his contributions in the struggle for independence placed him in the front ranks of American statesmen. He was among the members who had negotiated the treaty that ended the Revolution, and he had represented the new nation at various times in France, Holland, and England.

When these two men were notified of their election, Adams hurried immediately to New York, but Washington endured an eight-day triumphal march from his home in Mount Vernon through Philadelphia and New Jersey to New York City, where on April 30, 1789, he was inaugurated with as much pomp as befitted this incomparable hero. He rode to Federal Hall in a yellow carriage drawn by six white horses and attended by four footmen in livery. Members of Congress marched behind, along with the New York militia. Washington was dressed in a suit with silver buttons embossed with eagles, and he wore white silk stockings and pumps with silver buckles. Strapped around his waist was a ceremonial sword. Thin-lipped and tall, with a prominent Roman nose, the most distinguishing feature of his slightly pockmarked face, he both looked and acted presidential.

Washington was sworn into office by Chancellor Robert R. Livingston, the highest legal officer of New York, as he stood on the open gallery of the second floor of Federal Hall so that an adoring crowd outside could see and applaud him. To deliver his inaugural address, an address composed in large measure by James Madison, he returned to the adjoining chamber, where he told the assembled members of Congress that he had been "summoned" to the presidential office "by my country, whose voice I can never hear but with veneration and love." He then spoke in general terms about virtue and duty and the need for providential guidance. He also called for the passage of a bill of rights as amendments to the Constitution, thereby acknowledging the many complaints heard during the debates in several state ratifying conventions. Madison had resisted such a bill in the Constitutional Convention, since the proposed government enjoyed only delegated powers and therefore would not concern itself with personal rights. But he subsequently learned from his constituents that they felt such a bill was absolutely necessary for inclusion in the Constitution for the protection of their rights.

When the ceremony ended the President walked to Saint Paul's Chapel, a short distance away, where the Episcopal bishop invoked divine blessing on this new administration and government. One representative, Henry Wynkoop of Pennsylvania, said, "The Rooff is now raised & the federal Edifice compleated." A Union of states and people had now been accomplished. But would it endure?

THE FIRST CONGRESS under the Constitution completed a number of important actions that made it one of the most productive in the entire history of the United States. First of all, it raised revenue; established the executive departments of State, Treasury, and War; created the federal judiciary system; and passed a Bill of Rights. President

Washington chose Thomas Jefferson to head the State Department, Alexander Hamilton the Treasury, and Henry Knox the War Department. The Judiciary Act of 1789 organized a Supreme Court with a chief justice and five associates; three circuit courts of appeal; and thirteen district courts. It also established the office of attorney general. John Jay was named the first chief justice, and Edmund Randolph the attorney general. All this in just six months, from April to September 1789.

At the insistence of James Madison, the House agreed to seventeen amendments to the Constitution. They mostly dealt with personal liberties and forbade the government to legislate on any of these. The liberties involved basic freedoms such as speech, press, religion, the rights of assembly and petition, and the right to bear arms. The amendments also guaranteed a fair trial for the accused, and specifically stated that those powers not delegated by the Constitution to the national government were reserved to the "States respectively, or to the people."

In the Senate, through combinations and deletions—a guarantee of protection of the right of conscience and a statement on the separation of powers were deleted—the number of amendments was reduced to twelve and passed. Madison wanted these amendments woven into the text of the Constitution, with a preface that would emphasize the sovereignty of the people and proclaim the principles of republican government. But Roger Sherman proposed that the amendments be grouped together at the end of the Constitution. In this form Congress would create an actual "Bill of Rights."

On September 28, the amendments were submitted to the states for ratification. Not until December 15, 1791, did the states ratify ten of the twelve. Amendments regarding congressional salaries and the apportionment of House seats failed to pass, although the amendment on salaries was approved in 1992 as the Twenty-Seventh Amendment to the Constitution. It declared that compensation to members of Congress, whether increased or decreased, shall not take effect until an election of Representatives shall have intervened.

The first sign of real trouble in the new government developed when the secretary of the treasury, Hamilton, issued a series of reports on the public credit. He proposed that the national debt, which stood at $54,124,464.56, be funded at par, part of which, running to $11,710,378,

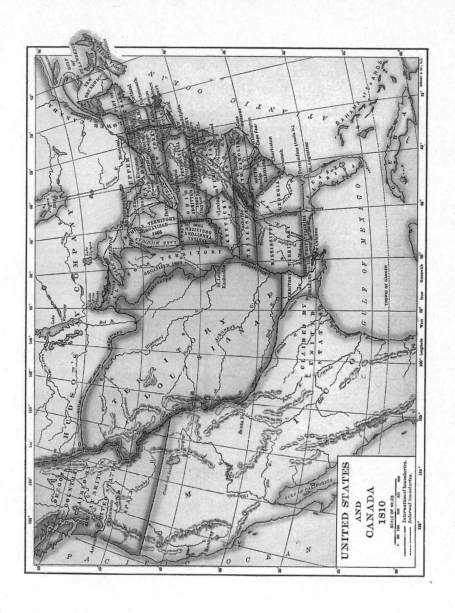

UNITED STATES
AND
CANADA
1810

SCALE OF MILES

International Boundaries.
Internal Boundaries.

was owed to foreigners, mostly French and Dutch. Hamilton also called for the assumption of state debts by the federal government. The assumption of state debts was intended to attract the loyalty and support of business and commercial interests toward the central government. There was little if any opposition to funding the national debt, although James Madison did suggest that allowances be made for the original holders of the debt who had sold their shares to speculators, a suggestion that was rejected. But the assumption of state debts triggered fierce opposition by those states, like Virginia, that had paid part or almost all of their debt by selling their western land. These states felt they were being penalized in having to contribute toward paying off the debts of other states in addition to having paid off their own. The New England states, on the other hand, had amassed heavy debts during the war and generally favored Hamilton's plan of assumption.

But on April 12, after a protracted debate, the House of Representatives rejected assumption by a vote of thirty-one to twenty-nine. The friends of Hamilton were visibly shocked by the outcome, their faces "reddened like Scarlet . . . or [turned] deadly White." Theodore Sedgwick of Massachusetts took the floor and denounced the action. The people of his state had "implored" Congress to "relieve us from the pressure of intolerable burdens—burdens incurred in support of your freedom and independence." Is this the way it is repaid?

Hamilton turned to Jefferson for help. He insisted that assumption must go forward, and if Jefferson could persuade a few of his friends to change their vote, Hamilton would help in fixing the permanent capital of the country in the South, as many southerners decidedly desired. Jefferson held a dinner party attended by both Hamilton and Madison, and the so-called Compromise of 1790 was concluded. As a result the House reversed itself and voted thirty-four to twenty-eight to adopt the assumption plan, and on July 10 the site of the new capital was transferred from New York to a ten-mile square along the Potomac River in Maryland. This capital would be called Washington in honor of the first President, and the district would be named Columbia after one of the symbols regularly used to represent the United States. The government would move from New York to Philadelphia while this new capital was being built and would remain there for ten years.

Another issue that stirred controversy was a request by Hamilton on December 13, 1790, that Congress charter a central banking system for twenty years, with the principal bank in Philadelphia and branch banks in the major cities throughout the United States. The bank would operate with a capital stock of $10 million, of which four-fifths would be subscribed by private investors and one-fifth by the government. Thus it would be a quasi-public, quasi-private institution. Management of the bank would consist of a president and a board of twenty-five directors, of whom twenty would be elected by the subscribers and five would be appointed by the government. This banking system would act as an agent for the collection of taxes and serve as a depository of federal funds. It was authorized to issue banknotes, redeemable in specie and acceptable in the payment of taxes, thereby increasing the money supply with which to finance the nation's economic growth. It was Hamilton's hope that the bank would not only provide sound credit and currency for the country but further unify and strengthen it.

However, Madison, the father of the Constitution, pronounced the bank unconstitutional. The right to grant a bank charter was not one of the delegated powers granted by the Constitution, and therefore was reserved to the states and people. And, as a matter of fact, the issue had been raised in the constitutional convention and rejected.

Despite this serious complaint Congress passed the bill early in 1791, when it was pointed out that the Constitution specifically allowed the legislature to pass "all laws necessary and proper" for the execution of its delegated powers. How else could Congress implement the funding and assumption laws without such a bank? argued its supporters. That argument proved convincing. The bill went to President Washington for his signature, but before approving it he asked the members of his cabinet for their opinion. Jefferson responded with what has been called a strict construction of the Constitution, insisting that unless a power was specifically delegated to the government it was reserved to the states and people. Hamilton, on the other hand, argued a "loose-construction" of the Constitution, citing the "implied powers" clause as the means of enacting legislation that would implement other powers specifically granted to the government. Although still troubled, Washington decided to sign the measure because he felt obliged to support the secretary whose department was directly involved.

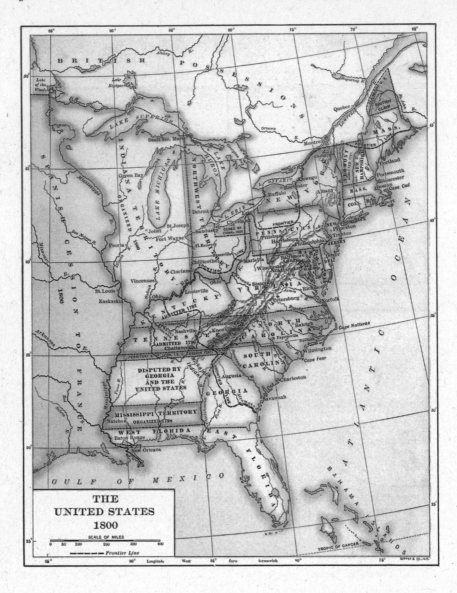

THE
UNITED STATES
1800

SCALE OF MILES

0   50   100   200   300   400

– – – – – Frontier Line

In his second report on the public credit on December 13, 1790, Hamilton had recommended passage of an excise tax on distilled liquor to ease the burden created by the assumption of state debts. It was enacted on March 3, 1791. There were thousands of stills around the country and farmers, especially those in western Pennsylvania, regularly shipped their surplus grain to eastern markets in the liquid form of whiskey. So they refused to pay the tax and attacked the federal revenue officers who tried to collect it. Alarmed that this resistance to law might become another Shays' Rebellion, Washington sent some 13,000 militiamen in 1794 to crush the uprising. Most of these troops came from New Jersey, Maryland, Virginia, and Pennsylvania. It was dubbed the Whiskey Rebellion but quickly evaporated upon the arrival of the troops in western Pennsylvania. A number of individuals were tried for treason, but those convicted were pardoned by Washington. Still it had the excellent effect of reaffirming the authority of the central government, something that had to be visibly demonstrated sooner or later. It proved that this new government had the will and the power to enforce its laws.

The creation of the militia occurred on May 8, 1792, when Congress authorized the states to organize and enroll all white males between the ages of eighteen and forty-five. The militiamen proved to be invaluable during the Whiskey Rebellion.

The growing disagreement between those who favored the Hamiltonian position on the public debt, the bank, the interpretation of the Constitution, the powers of Congress, and the relationship between the states and the central government, as distinct from those who agreed with the Jeffersonian-Madisonian view, initiated the slow evolution of a two-party system in the United States. Hamilton believed in a strong national government, one that would protect property and support the nation's commercial and industrial interests. He distrusted the people's ability to govern wisely and favored rule by the moneyed elite. Jefferson and Madison, on the other hand, believed in local autonomy as the best way of protecting individual rights. They worried about the concentration of power in a central government, arguing that the people should be left to govern themselves as much as possible.

These differences brought about the development of the Hamiltonian or Federalist party, while the Jeffersonians became known as the Democratic-Republican party. The split between the two groups widened over foreign affairs, particularly after France declared war against Great Britain, Spain, and Holland in early February 1793. The French had overthrown their monarchy in a revolution that turned bloody during the Reign of Terror. In place of the monarchy they established a republic. Since France had aided the United States in achieving its independence and since it had now become a republic, there was considerable sympathy toward France in this country, especially among Republicans. But New England merchants and shippers found the British a better market for American products and therefore wished to encourage a deeper friendship with the former mother country in the hope of securing valuable trade concessions.

The United States was still formally allied to France under the Treaty of 1778, signed during the American Revolution; but when war broke out between England and France, President Washington issued a Proclamation of Neutrality on April 22, 1793, in which he declared that this country needed to remain at peace with both of them. He also urged Americans to avoid any action that would jeopardize that neutrality. This policy set a standard that remained in place for generations. In European wars, which did not really concern the United States, it was best to steer clear of any involvement.

But the brilliant, indiscreet, and impetuous French minister to the United States at that time, Edmond-Charles-Édouard Genet, conspired to have Americans attack British vessels along the coast. When Genet's actions became known, Washington promptly demanded his recall. Since the Jacobins had taken control of the French government and had begun the Reign of Terror, Genet wisely decided to remain in the United States as a private person, knowing that the guillotine awaited him in Paris. He became an American citizen and married a daughter of Governor George Clinton of New York. It was obvious that the President took his advice on foreign affairs from Hamilton, resulting in Jefferson's resignation as secretary of state. He was succeeded by Edmund Randolph in January 1794.

The Eleventh Amendment to the Constitution was also proposed in early 1794. It resulted from protests by states over the decision of the Supreme Court in the case *Chisholm v. Georgia*. The amendment stated that the judicial power of the United States shall not "extend to any suit in law or equity, commenced or prosecuted against one of the United States" by a citizen of another state or by citizens of a foreign state. It was ratified on January 8, 1798.

Meanwhile the situation in foreign affairs worsened when the British issued a series of Orders-in-Council in June and November 1793 by which U.S. vessels were seized and American seamen were impressed into service in the British navy. In addition, Britain retained military posts within the territorial limits of the United States—in violation of the peace treaty that had ended the Revolution—and continued to incite Indian tribes in the Ohio Valley to attack American frontiersmen.

In an effort to avoid war, Washington dispatched John Jay, the chief justice of the United States, to Britain as a special envoy to negotiate U.S. grievances. What resulted was a treaty signed on November 29, 1794, with terms humiliating to the United States. The treaty favored British interests across the board, said nothing about impressment, and required the abandonment of American trade in such staples as cotton, sugar, and molasses. Public protests registered the nation's anger, and Jay himself was pilloried. Still, Washington accepted the treaty and submitted it to the Senate for ratification because he feared the possibility of war with Great Britain that would surely jeopardize the nation's independence. The Senate did ratify the document—but just barely—by a two-thirds vote.

The House of Representatives attempted to nullify the treaty by refusing to appropriate the money necessary to implement it. The members also called upon the President to submit all the documents and correspondence relating to the treaty. Washington refused, asserting his executive privilege, thus setting an important precedent. "It does not occur that the inspection of the papers asked for," snapped the President, "can be relative to any purpose under the cognizance of the House of Representatives, except that of an impeachment which the resolution has not expressed."

The stinging tone and manner of Washington's response—especially the reference to an impeachment—jolted the members of the House and they appropriated the funds for the Jay Treaty on April 30, 1796, by the tie-breaking vote of the Speaker, Frederick Mühlenberg.

The furor generated throughout the country by the Jay Treaty provided the final stimulus in the formation of a two-party system in the United States. Each side attacked the other; each held political rallies; and each organized its supporters in an effort to control one or more branches of the government. The sainted Washington was condemned for his role in sanctioning the treaty. According to one report, Jefferson supposedly referred to him as the "Samson whose head was shaved by

that harlot England." At a dinner party in Virginia a toast was proposed for the "speedy death" of General Washington. So offended was
the President by this brutal condemnation of his action that he refused
to run for a third term in office, and in 1796, after a nasty campaign,
John Adams was elected over Thomas Jefferson to replace him. As
runner-up, Jefferson was chosen Vice President.

The rise of political parties, and the introduction of partisan politics
into the operation of the government, was a major turning point in
U.S. affairs. It began a new era in American history.

3

An Emerging Identity

Two major events occurred in the United States to close out the eighteenth century. The first was a conflict that broke out between this country and France in 1797, when the French ministers in Paris attempted to extort a bribe of $240,000 from American diplomats as the price for recognizing them and their mission. Insulted, all but one of these American diplomats returned home, and the country expressed its outrage with the cry, "Millions for defense, but not one cent for tribute." There followed what has been called a "Quasi-War" between the two nations during which their ships attacked one another on the high seas. This naval conflict from 1798 to 1800 might have led to an actual declaration of war save for the determination of President Adams to maintain the peace. In an effort to prepare for the possibility of war Congress authorized the creation of the Department of the Navy and the building of a fleet of warships. It also expanded the size of the army. The war hysteria diminished the popularity of the Republican Party, which was seen as pro-French and therefore as infected with "radical" or Jacobin notions about governing the country.

The genuine fears many Americans felt about Jacobin influence on Republican policy brought about the second major event. The Federalist majority in Congress decided to pass a series of laws that they felt would help combat foreign intrigues and conspiracies in the United States. These were the Alien and Sedition Acts, passed in June and July 1798, which placed restrictions on both citizens and aliens. These laws belied everything the nation professed about liberty and democracy and can be explained only by the fact that Americans were genuinely frightened about their safety. The first of these acts, the Naturalization Act, changed the period of residence required to become a citizen from five to fourteen years. This law was repealed in 1802, and the Naturalization Law of 1795 was reenacted. The Alien and Alien Enemies Acts authorized the President to imprison or deport anyone he deemed a threat to the peace and safety of the nation; they expired in 1800. The Sedition Act imposed fines and imprisonment on both citizens and foreigners convicted of publishing any "false, scandalous and malicious writing" against the government, Congress, or the President. Limited to two years, this act expired in 1801.

Jefferson and Madison responded to these measures by writing a set of resolutions passed by the Kentucky and Virginia legislatures in 1798. These Kentucky and Virginia Resolutions, as they were called, condemned the Alien and Sedition Acts as unconstitutional and affirmed the right of the states to judge for themselves "the mode and measure of redress" whenever the national government assumed powers not specifically delegated to it by the Constitution. Moreover, the states were "duty bound to interpose for arresting the progress of the evil."

Interpose! There were some who genuinely believed that states had the right and obligation to nullify federal law whenever the central government acted improperly—and that states had the right to secede if necessary.

WITH THE BEGINNING of a new century the ten years of residence by the national government in Philadelphia mandated by the Residency Act of 1790 came to an end, and on April 24, 1800, President Adams signed the legislation that directed the relocation of the government to its new site along the Potomac River. On May 13 Congress stipulated that the second session of the Sixth Congress would convene on November 17 in the new Federal City, to be called Washington after the much revered first President.

In June President Adams traveled to Washington to inspect what had been built in the ten-mile square that Pierre Charles L'Enfant had laid out. He found what one congressman later described as a city in "ruins"—at least, that is the way it looked. Very few government buildings had been completed. The Capitol and the Executive Mansion were still under construction. Only the Treasury, a two-story brick building next to the Executive Mansion, was ready for occupancy.

When Congress convened in November 1800, the members gathered in an unfinished Capitol in an unfinished city and learned that their first important decision involved settling an unfinished presidential election. John Adams had run for reelection on the Federalist ticket, along with General Charles Cotesworth Pinckney of South Carolina for Vice President. The Republicans in Congress held their first caucus for nominating their candidates and chose Thomas Jefferson to head their ticket, and Aaron Burr of New York as Vice President. They would continue holding caucuses to name their leaders for the executive branch through the election of 1824, when, after loud criticism that it was undemocratic, the system was finally abandoned. As a substitute, state legislatures at first put forward favored sons, but in 1832 both parties began holding conventions of delegates from every state to nominate their ticket, a practice that continues to this day.

The friends of Alexander Hamilton despised Adams for many offenses, perhaps most importantly his failure to ask Congress for a declaration of war against France. Toward the end of the campaign, Hamilton himself published a fifty-four-page pamphlet excoriating Adams for his public conduct and defects of character, citing his reputed weakness, vacillation, and ungovernable temper. What is more, Hamilton conspired with several Federalist electors to have them withhold their votes for Adams so that the more acceptable Pinckney would be elected President. As a result, Adams lost the election. He struck back by calling Hamilton "that bastard son of a Scotch merchant." Jefferson defeated Adams by winning seventy-three electoral votes to Adams's sixty-five. Pinckney took sixty-three and John Jay one. But Burr ended up with the same number of electoral votes as Jefferson: seventy-three. Republicans, in their desire to capture the executive branch, failed to withhold at least one vote for Burr, and the tie that resulted meant that the election would be determined by the lame-duck House of Representatives, not the new Congress in which Republicans had won sizable majorities in both chambers.

On February 11 Congress met, counted the electoral ballots, declared a tie, and then turned the final decision over to the House to decide whether Jefferson or Burr would become President. It took thirty-seven ballots for the House to finally choose Jefferson on February 17, after an agreement was worked out by which it was promised that the Republicans would not dismantle the Hamiltonian fiscal system and that officeholders who were Federalists would not be arbitrarily removed because of their party affiliation. To prevent a recurrence of this unfortunate election, Congress proposed the Twelfth Amendment to the Constitution in December 1803. This amendment, which provided separate balloting for President and Vice President, was ratified on September 25, 1804.

Just before leaving office Adams appointed a large number of judges to the various federal courts under a recently passed Judiciary Act. John Marshall, then serving as secretary of state, was nominated to preside as chief justice of the United States. Right down to the last day of his administration Adams kept bombarding the Senate with these "midnight" appointments, as the Republicans called them. The Federalists had lost the executive and legislative branches, but at least they could continue to dominate the judiciary branch. But one of the first things the Republicans did when they came into power was repeal the Judiciary Act. They also attempted to impeach several of the "midnight" appointees.

Jefferson took office on March 4, 1801, and in his inaugural address he tried to smooth over the differences and antagonism that existed between the two political parties. "We are all Republicans; we are all Federalists," he said. "If there be any among us who would wish to dissolve the Union or change its republican form, let them stand undisturbed as monuments of the safety with which error of opinion may be tolerated where reason is left free to combat it."

It was a revolutionary moment in U.S. history. Without bloodshed or turmoil, without accusations of fraud and corruption, without any attempt at a conspiracy, the government had been turned over by one political party to another. Once the outcome of the presidential election had become known, Margaret Bayard Smith, the wife of the owner of an important newspaper in Washington, said, "The dark and threatening cloud that had hung over the political horizon rolled harmlessly away, and the sunshine of prosperity and gladness broke forth."

Although the founders had created a government in which the

legislature was the centerpiece and was given specific powers to run the country, President Jefferson sought to control Congress by encouraging certain members of the House and the Senate to serve as the administration's spokesmen. He generally worked through chairmen of powerful committees, such as the House Ways and Means Committee. Like other Presidents before and since he regularly proposed a legislative agenda in his annual messages to Congress, but he also operated clandestinely by giving several dinner parties a week at which his proposals could be explained and support for their passage elicited. John Randolph of Roanoke, who had been one of Jefferson's original spokesmen but later broke away, denounced the President's practice. He revealed and lambasted "the back-stairs influence of men who bring messages to this House [of Representatives], which, although they do not appear on the Journals, govern its decisions." When he heard about this outburst, Jefferson countered by declaring, "We never heard this while the declaimer was himself a backstairs man as he called it." But the President was very effective in imposing his will on the Congress. As Josiah Quincy, a Federalist from Massachusetts, noted, "all the great political questions are settled somewhere else," not in the halls of Congress.

Here, then, is one of the more important political threads of American history: the ongoing struggle between the executive and legislative branches of government to control national policy. Over the past two centuries Presidents have frequently sent military forces into battle without a declaration of war by Congress. And at various times, Presidents have assumed the power of the purse to deal with such problems as economic panics and depressions. Over the years the pendulum of control of national policy would swing back and forth. During much of the nineteenth century control remained with Congress, except during the presidencies of Andrew Jackson and Abraham Lincoln, who both steered the House and Senate in the direction they wished to see the country take. But starting in the twentieth century, as will be seen, the leadership was reversed and many more Presidents assumed greater control of legislative action.

An early example of a President assuming wartime powers occurred when Jefferson decided to end the practice of bribing the Barbary nations of Algiers, Morocco, Tunis, and Tripoli to keep them from seizing American merchant ships in the Mediterranean and holding

American seamen for ransom. The President refused to continue paying the tribute, and the pasha of Tripoli reacted with a declaration of war, by ordering his soldiers to chop down the flagpole at the American consulate. Congress was not in session when this incident was reported; consequently, Jefferson on his own authority dispatched a squadron of warships to the area, but he did so without summoning the legislature into special session. And when Congress did return at its regular time there was no request for a declaration of war and no effort by the legislature to take action. Instead Congress raised import taxes in order to pay for the war. After several years of intermittent fighting, the pasha sued for peace and was paid a ransom of $60,000 for the release of American prisoners. But payments to the other Barbary states continued until 1816.

This high-handed involvement in a war by the President who did not have congressional authorization encouraged Jefferson to expand his powers again after he decided to purchase Louisiana from France.

When he learned that the Spanish had closed New Orleans to American trade and that Napoleon, in his desire to revive the French empire in North America, had pressured the Spanish into ceding Louisiana back to France in the Treaty of San Ildefonso in October 1800, the President recognized it as a threat to the safety of the United States. "There is on the globe one single spot the possessor of which is our natural and habitual enemy," he said. "It is New Orleans." From the moment that France takes possession of New Orleans, he continued, "we must marry ourselves to the British fleet and nation."

Jefferson immediately notified the U.S. minister to France, Robert R. Livingston, to begin negotiations for the purchase of New Orleans, and he dispatched James Monroe as an envoy extraordinary with authority to offer $2 million for New Orleans and West Florida. In the meantime Napoleon had abandoned his plan for a revival of the French colonial empire in the New World when his troops, attempting to put down a slave revolt, were soundly defeated in Haiti by native forces under Toussaint-Louverture. In need of money to further his military ambitions against Great Britain, he decided to sell the entire province of Louisiana. On April 11, 1803, the French foreign minister, Talleyrand, asked Livingston how much the United States would be willing to pay for this vast stretch of territory. At length they finally agreed on

60 million francs, or approximately $15 million, and the treaty was signed on April 30. Of this amount, the French received $11.25 million in six percent stock, not redeemable for fifteen years. The United States assumed a total of $3.75 million to pay claims of its citizens against France.

It was an incredible bargain, and it doubled the size of the nation. But its constitutionality was immediately challenged by the Federalists, who argued that there was nothing in the Constitution to permit this annexation. Moreover, Congress did not have the power to incorporate this vast area and its people into the Union without the approval of the several states. The President had acted unlawfully, they insisted. Even Jefferson had doubts about the legality of his action, not that these doubts stopped him. "The Constitution," he explained to Senator John Breckinridge, "has made no provision for our holding foreign territory, still less for incorporating foreign nations into our Union." But he set aside these doubts in the belief that this acquisition was essential for the future safety of the country.

The Senate quickly ratified the treaty on October 20 by a vote of twenty-four to seven, with all but one Federalist voting against it. The House agreed and, after a long and stormy debate, authorized the certificates of stock to be paid to the French and directed the President to take control of Louisiana. The U.S. flag was raised above New Orleans on December 30, 1803.

Shortly after asking Congress for money to undertake the negotiations regarding Louisiana, Jefferson also requested a small appropriation of $2,500 for an expedition to explore the Missouri River to its source. By the time Meriwether Lewis and William Clark began their celebrated journey westward, Louisiana had been acquired, and the two men now undertook the exploration of a greatly expanded nation. They pushed west to the mouth of the Columbia River, giving the United States a claim to the Oregon country. The Lewis and Clark expedition, from 1803 to 1806, not only brought back significant scientific information but stimulated western settlement of this new expanse of territory.

In another action to broaden executive authority, Jefferson demanded a change in the judicial system. The Judiciary Act of 1802 restored a six-member Supreme Court and established six new circuit courts.

Jefferson also sought the removal of a number of justices who regularly injected politics into their decisions. Perhaps the most famous episode in this regard was the impeachment of an Associate Justice of the Supreme Court, Samuel Chase, which failed to result in his removal.

Jefferson was particularly offended when Chief Justice John Marshall read his decision in the case of *Marbury v. Madison*. Marbury was one of the midnight appointments but had not received his commission to serve as justice of the peace. He therefore sued James Madison, the secretary of state, and demanded that his commission be handed over. In the decision of February 24, 1803, Marshall dismissed Marbury's suit on the ground that he did not have the authority to act. He lacked jurisdiction because Section 13 of the Judiciary Act of 1789, which conferred such authority, was unconstitutional. This was the first time a congressional statute was voided by the high court. The decision pronounced the doctrine of judicial review, and although the doctrine was not used again for fifty years, it had the effect of raising the judiciary to equality with the other two branches of government.

THE FIRST ADMINISTRATION of Thomas Jefferson was an unqualified success in what it achieved, but the second, following his reelection in 1804, brought one failure after another. The basic problem was the continued harassment by the British against U.S. ships at sea and the impressment of American seamen. With the renewal of war between England and France, the British issued a series of orders-in-council that decreed a blockade of the European coast from Brest to the Elbe River and barred all ships from the French coastal trade. Napoleon countered by issuing the Berlin and Milan decrees, by which Britain was blockaded and neutral ships were threatened with seizure if they obeyed the orders-in-council. Caught between these two rivals, Jefferson asked Congress for an embargo that would forbid American ships to leave port for a foreign destination, and forbid foreign ships to leave American ports with U.S. goods. The Embargo Act of 1807 proved to be a disaster for the United States. It mainly affected American trade. Large coastal cities suffered tremendous losses, and New England verged on rebellion.

The obvious failure of the Embargo Act prompted its repeal. It was replaced by the Non-Importation Act of March 1, 1809, which reopened trade with all foreign nations except France and England. And it encouraged Jefferson to imitate George Washington and step down after two terms in office. He was succeeded by James Madison, who also failed to compel the two belligerents to respect neutral rights. Congress tried to help by passing Macon's Bill No. 2, which removed all trade restrictions against France and England but decreed that if either of the belligerents revoked its decrees, the President was empowered to reimpose nonintercourse on the other belligerent. Naturally Napoleon took advantage of this invitation to deception by announcing, falsely, that he would revoke the Berlin and Milan decrees. And Madison believed him. The President announced the continuance of trade with France and its closing with Great Britain. It was not long before Madison realized he had been hoodwinked and made to play the fool. Britain responded by redoubling its impressment of American seamen.

As presidential leadership faltered, a newly elected member of the House of Representatives, Henry Clay, stepped forward and launched his congressional career with such brilliance that other members quickly succumbed to his direction. Elected Speaker on his first day in office—his earlier but brief career in the U.S. Senate provided proof of his outstanding abilities—he had every intention of determining national policy and the legislation to come to the floor of the House for a vote. Unlike his predecessors, who acted more like traffic cops in directing the flow of debate, in imitation of British speakers, Clay became an integral part of House operations and participated directly in the debates on important issues and in influencing their outcome. He appointed chairmen of committees who would assist his efforts to make the House a dominant force in national politics. He enforced the rules of the House and never hesitated to cut off debate when he felt that it was time for a vote. To prevent filibusters, he allowed members to call the previous question. On occasion he muzzled John Randolph and forbade him to enter the House chamber with one of his hunting hounds. Part of his success as Speaker and the reason he was reelected whenever he ran for the office was his eminently fair and evenhanded treatment of his colleagues. Added to this were his quick wit, his ferocious intellect, his sharp tongue, and his mesmerizing talents as an orator and debater. He proved to be the first great Speaker of the House of Representatives.

Under his direction and with the help of like-minded members, known as War Hawks, who felt the British needed to be shown conclusively that the United States would no longer suffer the humiliations imposed by their policy toward neutral nations, Clay moved the House in the direction of seeking immediate redress. Working with the administration as much as possible, he helped persuade the President to ask Congress for a declaration of war. Most likely Madison had already made that decision, and a request for such a declaration came from Madison on June 1, 1812. After a three-day debate, steered by the Speaker, it was quickly passed in the House by a vote of seventy-nine to forty-nine. The Senate took more time but finally gave its consent on June 17. The President signed the declaration the next day and proclaimed that a state of war existed between the United States and Great Britain. Two days later Lord Castlereagh, the British foreign secretary, agreed to suspend the orders-in-council.

At first the war appeared to be a colossal mistake, if not a catastrophe. A three-pronged invasion of Canada by American soldiers ended in defeat on all fronts. The invasion also terminated any thought Canadians might have had about alienating themselves from British rule. Furthermore, General William Hull surrendered Detroit to British invaders out of fear that any resistance could bring a massacre of women and children in the city by Indians allied to the British. Meanwhile England blockaded the east and gulf coasts from New York to the mouth of the Mississippi River. Initially New England was exempt from the blockade in the hope that it would secede from the United States.

To make matters worse, Napoleon abdicated after a failed invasion of Russia, leaving England free to direct its full military force against its former colonies in America. In addition, the Creek Indians in the southeast began a general uprising along the Alabama frontier and massacred hundreds of Americans at Fort Mims, about thirty-five miles north of Mobile. The governor of Tennessee dispatched General Andrew Jackson of the west Tennessee militia to subdue the Creeks. Affectionately dubbed "Old Hickory" by his soldiers, in admiration of his leadership, Jackson defeated the Creeks after a series of engagements at the Battle of Horseshoe Bend on March 27, 1814. As part of the peace treaty, he exacted about two-thirds of Creek land in Alabama and Georgia, which was ceded to the United States.

To crush the Americans and bring the war to a speedy conclusion, the British concocted a major offensive from three areas: Lake Champlain, the Chesapeake Bay region, and New Orleans. General Sir George Prevost headed the invasion from Canada. Commanding an army of over 10,000, he marched from the St. Lawrence River area to the western edge of Lake Champlain, where an American naval force blocked his further penetration into the United States and ultimately forced his withdrawal to Canada.

Veterans of the Napoleonic war were transported to America and on August 24, 1814, an army of 4,000 under the command of General Robert Ross landed in Maryland, marched to Washington, and burned the capital. The executive mansion, the Capitol, and most of the public buildings were put to the torch. Fortunately, a violent storm, which might have been a hurricane, struck during the night, extinguishing the fires and preventing what could have been the total destruction of the city.

The British had intended to take Baltimore but were repulsed by a strong American army that fortified the heights around the city. When the British fleet and army withdrew from the Chesapeake area, they were ordered to seize New Orleans and gain control of the lower Mississippi River valley. By the time they arrived off the coast of Louisiana, General Jackson was waiting for them. He had hurriedly marched to the threatened city after defeating the Creeks and had taken a position behind a millrace or ditch that stretched from the Mississippi River to a swamp about a mile away. The British tried to smash their way through this line of defense but failed. Over 2,000 British soldiers were killed, wounded, or missing in the action that took place on January 8, 1815, about ten miles south of New Orleans, while the Americans suffered only a dozen or so casualties.

The victory represented the first time the United States had demonstrated its will and capacity to defend its independence in a world hostile to its existence. Ordinary citizens had faced and defeated a powerful enemy. The Battle of New Orleans made Americans proud of their country and themselves. "The last six months is the proudest period in the history of the republic," claimed *Niles Weekly Register*, the Baltimore newspaper. "*Who would not be an American? Long live the Republic.*"

American commissioners at Ghent—in what is now Belgium—produced a peace treaty with Great Britain on Christmas Eve 1814, weeks before the New Orleans battle took place. But the treaty would not go into effect until both sides approved it. The Senate received it on February 15, 1815, and ratified it the following day. And that is when the war officially came to a close.

The news of the victory and the writing of a peace treaty reached Washington at the same time that a delegation from a convention of New England states held in Hartford, Connecticut, arrived to demand constitutional changes in the operation of the government. The states represented at the convention had adopted resolutions as the price of their continued allegiance to the Union. But with the country wildly delirious over its military victory at New Orleans and the signing of a peace treaty in Ghent, the delegates realized that their demands would receive short shrift. So they quietly turned around and went home. The Hartford Convention was never controlled by secessionists, but suspicions of treason on the part of its participants lingered for many years. The suspicions were directed mainly at the Federalist Party, which was accused of initiating and participating in this disloyalty. As a consequence, the party lost popular support and steadily declined as a national organization. It staggered on for a few more years in a few New England states but finally disappeared. Its disappearance marked a suspension of political strife between two opposing parties. There was now only one national party—the Republican Party—and the next several years were known as "the Era of Good Feelings."

FOLLOWING THE WAR the country underwent a series of important changes that transformed not only the American people but their culture, their society, and their relations with foreign nations. Nationalism, the sense that a new breed of citizen had emerged, was perhaps the most obvious change. People were proud to call themselves Americans. No longer did they refer to themselves as New Yorkers, Virginians, or

Pennsylvanians, as in the past. They had a new and distinct identity. They were united in their victory over their enemy, and they were united in a republican form of government that was unique in the western world. Americans after the war were markedly different from their predecessors. No longer colonists, no longer British, no longer European, they reveled in the discovery of their special characteristics. Over time they gave up wearing wigs, silk stockings, ruffled shirts, and knee breeches; instead they donned trousers and shirts with neckties and jackets. When they spoke, their accent no longer sounded British but had a distinctly American twang. What is regarded today as the American character slowly emerged after the War of 1812.

The sense of nationhood was spurred on by a series of Supreme Court decisions that favored the central government at the expense of individual states. In *Fletcher v. Peck* (1810), Chief Justice Marshall and the Court struck down one of Georgia's laws; in *Martin v. Hunter's Lessee* (1816) they contradicted the highest court in Virginia, which had claimed the case could not be appealed to the Supreme Court; and in the Dartmouth College case an action by the New Hampshire legislature in changing the charter of the college was reversed as a violation of the U.S. Constitution, which forbade impairing the obligation of contracts. The college's charter, declared Marshall, was a contract and therefore could not be altered. Then, in *McCulloch v. Maryland*, the Supreme Court declared that a tax levied by Maryland on the Baltimore branch of the Bank of the United States, which had been chartered by the federal government, was void. "The power to tax involves the power to destroy," Marshall ruled, and no state may tax or control any institution created by the national government within its borders. Finally, in *Gibbons v. Ogden* the court annulled the monopoly on steamboat traffic that the New York legislature had granted to Robert Livingston and Robert Fulton, declaring that only Congress can control interstate and foreign commerce.

Another expression of nationalism in the period following the War of 1812 was the beginning of a genuine and uniquely American form of literature. Between 1815 and 1830 a number of writers offered works based upon native themes and set in recognizable local places. Washington Irving was one such artist, whose *History of New York ... by Diedrich Knickerbocker* (1809) and *Sketch Book* (1819) led the way in providing stories about people and locales that Americans could recognize and enjoy. James Fenimore Cooper went farther. His works *The Spy* (1821), *The Pioneers* (1823), the first of the Leatherstocking series, and *The Last of the Mohicans* (1826) extolled American history and the life of the frontier. This early beginning of a distinctly American art form was later enlarged upon, and its artistry greatly surpassed, by more distinguished writers.

IN ADDITION TO this nationalistic outburst, the industrial revolution arrived within the country and began the process by which an independent national domestic economy would be achieved to spare the nation the problem of relying on foreign imports for the necessities of life. In New England and the Middle Atlantic states financial capital shifted from commerce to manufacturing, and something like 140 cotton mills began operating. Within a few years 500,000 spindles were said to be functioning throughout New England. Factories turned out iron, woolen, and cotton products, and these industries spread to the Ohio Valley and the Middle West. The market revolution that ensued converted the country in time from a purely agricultural to an industrial society. A transportation revolution witnessed the building of roads, bridges, and canals, the most famous of which was the Erie Canal in New York: it opened in 1825 and connected the Hudson River with Lake Erie, stimulating the growth of such cities as Buffalo, Cleveland, Detroit, and Chicago. New York City thus became the leading commercial center in the United States. The transportation revolution also provided the country with railroads, starting in the 1820s. In the next forty years railroad tracks would stretch 3,000 miles across the continent.

The manufacturing interests of the northern states demanded higher tariffs to protect themselves against foreign—mainly British—competition, and they therefore supported the idea of free immigration to provide the laborers they needed for their mills and factories. They also naturally opposed westward migration, which could empty their establishments of workers; but they favored easy credit and a sound currency and banking system.

The South, on the other hand, turned increasingly toward the cultivation of cotton. With the invention of the cotton gin by Eli Whitney in 1793, it became possible to grow short-fiber cotton, whose seeds could be extracted by the cotton gin more than 300 times faster than removing them by hand. As a result, the plantation system moved steadily westward along the gulf coast and necessitated an ever-larger workforce. Slave labor was essential to the plantation system, and the laws regarding slavery in the South became more restrictive. By 1820 over one-third of the cotton grown in the United States was raised west of the Appalachian Mountains.

The original thirteen states of the early Republic had grown to nineteen by the end of the war, and a new era of expansion took shape. The Louisiana Purchase allowed thousands to seek a better life in the West. By 1818 about 60,000 settlers had crossed the Mississippi River and penetrated deep into the interior along the Missouri River. St. Louis became a bustling city cashing in on the fur trade that had opened up. Steamboats plied the Mississippi River from the upper Midwest to New Orleans. It had taken British colonists 150 years to occupy an inland area of about 100 miles from the coastline. In less than fifty years, following this "Second War for Independence," Americans, bursting with determination, optimism, and self-confidence, would stretch the boundaries of their country south to the Gulf of Mexico and the Rio Grande, north to the 49th parallel, and west to the Pacific Ocean. It was the true beginning of a new nation that by the end of the nineteenth century would rise to become a world power.

Americans of the early nineteenth century were intent on building a materialistic society, one dedicated to business, trade, and the acquisition of wealth. To them, money meant everything. "No man in America is contented to be poor, or expects to continue so," observed one foreign traveler. "Go ahead. Go ahead"—that was the spirit of the age. "The whole continent presents a scene of *scrambling* and roars with greedy hurry," commented another visitor. "Go ahead is the order of the day, the real motto of the country." Senator Daniel Webster of Massachusetts agreed. "Our age," he said, "is full of excitement" and rapid change.

Americans were committed to the work ethic. It had been prevalent in the country since the arrival of the first English settlers, and by the nineteenth century it had taken on a special urgency and new purpose.

"Work," lectured one man, "and at eighteen you shall . . . live in plenty, be well clothed, well housed, and able to save." Other rewards would follow. "Be attentive to your work, be sober and religious, and you will find a devoted and submissive wife; you will have a more comfortable home than many of the higher classes in Europe." Not only will you be better off and more comfortable, he continued, but you will be admired by everyone in your community. "He who is an active and useful member of society, who contributes his share to augment the national wealth and increase the numbers of the population, he only is looked upon with respect and favor."

With such motivation, it is little wonder that these Americans developed a strong and successful economy. Fired by ambition and purpose, committed to the work ethic, and appreciative of the seemingly limitless wealth they discovered in the natural resources surrounding them, they reached, within a relatively short time, the "take off" stage in becoming a powerful industrial society.

GOVERNMENT CHANGED AS well, and Madison initiated the new direction by calling for a different approach in the way Washington operated. In his annual message he urged the Congress to take the lead in safeguarding the economic interests of the nation. He recommended the creation of another national bank to provide sound credit and currency, the imposition of a protective tariff to encourage the establishment and growth of native manufactures, and the financing of internal improvements to promote westward expansion. These were Federalist doctrines, now advanced and supported by ardent nationalists who demanded a more modern concept of the responsibilities of government in protecting the welfare and liberties of the American people and in accelerating the emerging market revolution. "England is the most formidable power in the world," exclaimed Representative John C. Calhoun of South Carolina. "We, on the contrary, are the most growing nation on earth."

Henry Clay, now returned as Speaker of the House of Representatives following his sojourn in Europe as a commissioner who helped draft the peace treaty at Ghent, viewed these economic proposals as essential for the continued life, growth, and prosperity of this country and set about enacting them into law. Using the enormous powers he had earlier built into the office of Speaker, he won support in the House for a series of measures that he later articulated in what he called his American System—that is, a system to approve tariffs, internal improvements, and viable currency and credit. Before President Madison's term in office ended, a number of these proposals had become law. In 1816 the Second National Bank of the United States was created that was similar to the First Bank, but its capital stock was larger and it was obliged to pay the government a bonus of $1.5 million. Calhoun, as chairman of the House Committee on the National Currency, wanted to use the bonus, along with dividends from the government's bank stock, to construct roads and canals that would stimulate commercial development. "Let us then bind the Republic together with a perfect system of roads and canals," he cried in presenting his bill. "Let us conquer space." But Madison had doubts about the constitutionality of the bill after it passed Congress and vetoed it just days before he left office.

On April 27, 1816, Congress also enacted the first protective tariff in U.S. history. It established a twenty-five-percent duty on woolen and cotton goods and a thirty-percent duty on iron products. The whole idea was to encourage manufacturing in this country and block competition from foreign nations, which could easily undercut the price of native products by companies just getting started. Furthermore Congress increased the size of the navy, and created an army of 10,000 men. It was a wholly new approach to governmental operations in that the central government, not the states, was expected to provide the kind of leadership that would advance the interests of the entire nation. It justified Calhoun's claim that the United States, as a single unity, was "the most growing nation on earth."

Madison was replaced as President by James Monroe, the last of the so-called Virginia Dynasty, which included Jefferson, Madison, and Monroe and endured for a total of twenty-four years. Monroe, along with his secretary of state, John Quincy Adams, tended to pursue foreign rather than domestic affairs, and together they acquired Spanish Florida by treaty and formulated the Monroe Doctrine, addressing foreign intrusion in the western hemisphere.

The acquisition of Florida came about because the Seminole Indians in Florida regularly crossed the border into the United States, borders that white men had created that meant nothing to these Native Americans in their pursuit of enemies, food, and adventure. The Seminoles regularly attacked American settlements in Georgia and Alabama and then retreated back into Florida, where they knew the Americans would not pursue them. Monroe decided to put an end to this practice and instructed his newly appointed secretary of war, Calhoun, to direct General Andrew Jackson, now the commander of the U.S. southern army, to halt these Indian invasions and if necessary to cross the border and attack them in their towns in Spanish territory. Jackson, a very aggressive general, decided on a more productive course of action and asked permission to seize Florida from the Spanish. That would be the surest way of dealing with the Indian problem and bringing the incursions along the American frontier to a complete halt. As far as can be determined, Jackson received permission from Monroe himself, or thought he did, although the President's letter was rather guarded, as might be expected. So Jackson slammed across the Florida border, killed a number of Seminoles, and burned their towns. He also captured two British nationals, Alexander Arbuthnot and Robert Ambrister, accused of aiding the Indians, and had them executed: one hanged, the other shot by a firing squad. Finally, Jackson captured St. Marks and Pensacola, the two important seats of Spanish authority in Florida, and turned them over to the United States.

Henry Clay was horrified—or so he said. He harbored a grudge against Monroe for selecting Adams instead of himself as secretary of state, and he used the invasion as an excuse to lambaste the administration. After all, Jackson had invaded Florida, had engaged in hostilities with the Indians and Spanish, and had executed foreign nationals without a declaration of war by Congress. Clay wanted the general punished and his actions repudiated, so he gave a powerful speech in the House of Representatives demanding that Jackson be censured. He failed in this attempt, but he did succeed in making a lifelong enemy of Old Hickory.

Adams defended Jackson's action both within the administration and with Spanish and British officials. After all, he said, Americans had suffered long enough because of the inability of Spain to control the movement of the Seminoles into the United States. It would be best

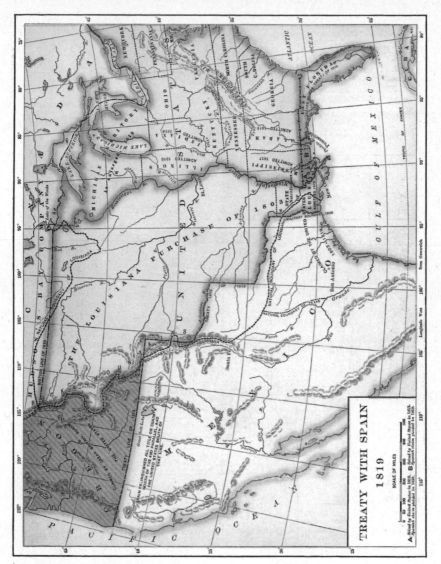

Adam's Onís Treaty with Spain

for Spain to sell us this troublesome territory, he argued. The result was the Adams-Onís Treaty of February 22, 1819, by which Spain ceded Florida to the United States and, in return, the United States agreed to assume the claims of American citizens against Spain to the extent of $5 million. In addition, the western boundary of the Louisiana Purchase was determined and the United States inherited the claims of Spain to the northwest country beyond the Louisiana territory.

Quite obviously the nation was growing in more ways than Calhoun imagined. New states had been admitted to the Union during the past decade: Louisiana in 1810, Indiana in 1816, Mississippi in 1817, and Illinois in 1818. Then, in 1819, Congress took up the requests for statehood from Alabama and Missouri. There was no problem in granting Alabama's admission, but Missouri's unleashed a storm of objections that almost resulted in the breakup of the Union.

The Missouri Territory had been carved out of the Louisiana Purchase, and it sought admission as a slave state. If granted it would be the first state totally located west of the Mississippi River. But it would also upset the numerical balance between free and slave states. This was obviously a situation that called for compromise, but neither the slave nor free states seemed prepared to reconcile their demands with each other's needs. The matter came to a head when Representative James Tallmadge of New York introduced an amendment to the Missouri enabling act which prohibited the further introduction of slaves into the territory and mandated the emancipation of all slaves subsequently born in Missouri when they reached the age of twenty-five.

Southerners were infuriated by this bold attempt to allow Congress to outlaw slavery in the territories. They insisted they had a right under the Constitution to take their slaves anywhere in the territories and were determined to protect that right under all circumstances. After all, the Constitution protected property; and slaves, according to southerners, were property. The debate in Congress grew more and more heated with each passing day. "If you persist," Representative Thomas W. Cobb of Georgia shouted at Tallmadge, "the Union will be dissolved. You have kindled a fire which all the waters of the ocean cannot put out, which seas of blood can only extinguish."

"Let it come," roared Tallmadge in response.

Despite the anger and threats of secession, the amendment passed the House by a vote of 79 to 67. But the Senate, where southerners had greater numerical strength and friendlier sympathizers, defeated the measure 31 to 7. With mounting tension and verbal explosions a daily occurrence in the lower chamber, Speaker Clay feared the worst. "The words, civil war and disunion," he told a friend, "are uttered almost without emotion."

A possible escape from this predicament occurred when Maine, the northern province of Massachusetts, petitioned Congress for admission to the Union as a separate and free state. Thus the admission of both Missouri and Maine would at least maintain the numerical balance between free and slave states. As part of the compromise Senator Jesse Thomas of Illinois offered an amendment to the Missouri enabling act which prohibited the extension of slavery into the Louisiana Territory north of 36° 30' with the exception of Missouri itself.

And that did the trick. Although the House of Representatives rejected a single bill containing all these provisions, it miraculously passed three separate measures that did the same thing, namely admit both states and restrict slavery north of 36° 30' in the Louisiana Territory. Southerners did not take exception to the latter provision, recognizing that slavery could not exist in such a northern clime. Presumably they could take their slaves into the western and southern territories. "The Southern & Western people talked so much, threatened so loudly, & predicted such dreadful consequences," declared Representative William Plumer of New Hampshire, ". . . that they fairly frightened our weak-minded members into an abandonment of their stand against slavery in the territories."

Before opposition could be organized against these measures, Speaker Clay signed them and hurried them to the Senate, where they received quick passage. John Randolph called for a reconsideration of the bills, but Clay ruled him out of order and the House sustained his ruling. It was a close call.

Without question, the Missouri Compromise of 1820 became law because of the parliamentary skills of Henry Clay. From that moment on he was known as the "Great Compromiser" or "Great Pacificator." "The Constitution of the Union was in danger," wrote Langdon Cheves of South Carolina, "& has been Saved," thanks to Henry Clay. Without bloodshed or dismemberment of the country, Missouri entered the Union. But an obvious problem remained. Secession may have been avoided; still, the central question of whether Congress had the right to prohibit slavery in the territories had not been resolved to the satisfaction of either the North or the South. It would plague the country for the next forty years. But as Abraham Lincoln noted years later, Henry Clay made the difference. As long as Clay remained alive, Lincoln said, he could always find the compromise to keep the country from rushing into civil war and the dissolution of the Union.

President Monroe signed the several bills that admitted Maine and Missouri as the twenty-third and twenty-fourth states comprising the United States, but he had little to do with bringing about this historic settlement. He left domestic affairs pretty much to Congress, where Clay played the most dominant role. This freed the President to concentrate on foreign affairs, in which he scored several successes. He recognized the independence of those Latin American nations that had escaped Spanish rule and gained the approval of Congress. The Republic of Colombia was recognized on June 19, 1822; Mexico on December 12, 1822; Chile and Argentina on January 27, 1823; Brazil on May 26, 1824; the Federation of Central American States on August 4, 1824; and Peru on May 2, 1826. He approved the treaty signed with Russia that fixed the southern boundary of Alaska, a Russian possession, at 54° 40'; he agreed to the acquisition of Florida and the settlement of the western boundary of the Louisiana Purchase; and in his annual message to Congress on December 2, 1823, he announced what has been called the Monroe Doctrine. In justice it must be pointed out that his secretary of state, John Quincy Adams, served as the principal negotiator in all these successes.

When the members of the Quadruple or Holy Alliance (France, Austria, Prussia, and Russia) agreed in 1822 at the Congress of Verona to restore King Ferdinand VII of Spain to full authority after he had surrendered and accepted the demands of those who insisted on a constitutional monarchy, Great Britain became concerned about such a policy and especially fearful that the Holy Alliance might attempt to restore Spanish control of its lost possessions in South America. England enjoyed economic advantages in dealing with independent South

American states and did not want to see a return to the previous arrangement, which favored Spanish interests. George Canning, the British foreign secretary, suggested to Richard Rush, the U.S. minister to England, that their two countries jointly agree to oppose any intervention by European powers in the New World. The suggestion was forwarded to Washington, where all the cabinet officers, except Adams, favored a joint Anglo-American declaration. Adams, on the other hand, supported the action but not as a joint undertaking. He wanted the United States to make the statement independently. We have "a very suitable and convenient opportunity," he said, ". . . to take our stand against the Holy Alliance and at the same time to decline the overture of Great Britain. It would be more candid, as well as more dignified, to avow our principles explicitly to Russia and France, than to come in as a cock-boat in the wake of the British man-of-war."

A cock-boat in the wake of the British man-of-war! That is precisely the way it would be perceived by the world. We must not go that route, argued Adams. We have to stand up and declare our own position as a sovereign, independent nation. The United States, he insisted, should openly declare the principles on which this government was founded; it should reject the notion of spreading those principles elsewhere by force of arms; and it should state emphatically that this nation also expects Europe to refrain from propagating its principles in this hemisphere or from subjugating "by force any part of these continents to their will."

These doctrines of non-intervention and non-colonization in the New World by any European country, or any other country, formed the core of the Monroe Doctrine and were presented by the President to Congress in his annual message rather than in diplomatic dispatches, as Adams initially suggested. Much of the message as drafted was written by Adams, and it advanced four important doctrines: first, the American continents were no longer to "be considered as subjects for future colonization by any European Power"; second, in "wars of the European powers in matters pertaining to themselves, we have never taken any part, nor does it comport with our policy, so to do"; third, the United States would consider any attempt by Europeans "to extend their system to any portion of this Hemisphere, as dangerous to our peace and safety"; and fourth, with "existing Colonies or dependencies of any European power, we have not interfered, and shall not interfere."

Secretary Adams enunciated one other doctrine dealing with foreign affairs that is not as well known. He used the occasion of a Fourth of July oration in 1821 to announce it. He delivered his remarks from the rostrum of the House of Representatives and faced his audience dressed in the academic robe of a university professor. Staring pointedly at his audience, he declared that the United States would always be "the well-wisher to the freedom and independence of all" nations but that it must not go "abroad in search of monsters to destroy" by enlisting under banners other "than our own." Such a departure by the United States from a rational foreign policy would unhappily inaugurate America's reach for "dominion and power" in the world and would ultimately result in the loss of its own "freedom and independence."

FOLLOWING THE WAR of 1812 the United States experienced not only a surge of nationalistic pride and the advent of an industrial revolution but a marked advance in the development of a democratic society. Universal white manhood suffrage was quickly achieved after 1815, prompted by the arrival of many new, western states that placed no property or religious restrictions on adult white males. This breakthrough in the qualifications for voting encouraged the older, eastern states to convene conventions that altered their constitutions and broadened suffrage. These actions were the first important steps in moving the country from a republican to a democratic government. Several more such moves remained—such as providing voting and citizenship rights to those of a different race and sex. But the country was headed in a new direction, although it would take time and even bloodshed to achieve a more perfect Union.

Another dynamic force impacting the growth of democracy in the United States was the rise of a self-conscious working class, resulting in large part from the growth of factories and the arrival of ever larger numbers of immigrants from Europe. They knew what they needed and did not hesitate to express their wishes, demanding social, economic, and even political legislation to satisfy their wants. For one thing, they demanded the abolition of imprisonment for debt; they demanded free public education for their children; and they demanded that employers pay the wages that were owed and not seek to escape their obligations when faced with economic difficulties. They even formed a Workingmen's Party in Philadelphia and put up candidates for public office who would advance the rights of the laboring classes. They organized strikes in support of higher wages and a ten-hour workday. In 1840 the federal government adopted the ten-hour workday for its employees, and two years later Chief Justice Lemuel Shaw of the Massachusetts supreme court ruled in *Commonwealth v. Hunt* that it was legal for workers to form unions and go on strike to gain their economic goals.

Now that the people of the United States had achieved a new identity, which was not British, foreign, or European but distinctly American, changes became apparent in the presidential election of 1824. Where in the first election, back in 1789, George Washington took the oath of office wearing a powdered wig, knee breeches, silk stockings, and pumps with silver buckles, a ceremonial sword strapped around his waist, the candidates in 1824 wore trousers, shirts, and neckties. No wigs, no breeches, no swords. The sharp changes that had taken place in the country were revealed not only in the clothes the candidates wore but in the way they looked and behaved. Washington was an aristocrat to his fingertips and acted as such. Andrew Jackson, one of the candidates in 1824, played the role of an ordinary citizen, a democrat, even though he clearly belonged to the upper class in his home state, Tennessee.

In this presidential election, Monroe did not name a successor, and since only one party—the Republican Party—existed, the person chosen by the traditional congressional caucus would automatically be elected. For that reason, many objections were raised about continuing the traditional method. In effect it took the election away from the people and handed it over to a small group of politicians in Congress. Thus in 1824, a number of candidates were put forth by the state legislatures, insisting that "King Caucus," as they called the traditional method, "was dead."

Nevertheless, despite these objections, a caucus was held—although it was sharply reduced in number. It was called by Senator Martin Van Buren of New York, who believed that a party system was essential for the furtherance of a republican society. The founders berated parties and described them as cabals of greedy men seeking their own private interests, not the interests of the people at large. But the realistic Van Buren understood that men holding particular principles should join together in order to advance those principles. It could not be done any other way. So he summoned the caucus to meet on February 14, 1824, in the House chamber, but only sixty-six members put in an appearance. To the "heavy groans in the Gallery," packed with friends and enemies of the caucus, William H. Crawford, the secretary of the treasury, was nominated as the Republican Party's presidential candidate. He received sixty-two votes, while two were given to John Quincy Adams, and one apiece to Andrew Jackson and Nathaniel Macon.

The Speaker of the House, Henry Clay, had long proved his talents as an elected official, so Kentucky put forward his name in nomination; this was the first of Clay's many attempts to be elected President. Since the office of secretary of state had been considered a stepping-stone to the presidency for the past twenty-four years, Massachusetts advanced the name of John Quincy Adams. Another cabinet officer, Secretary of War John C. Calhoun of South Carolina, decided to run but soon found his northern supporters more inclined toward Andrew Jackson, so he withdrew as a presidential candidate and accepted a nomination as Vice President. Of all the candidates in this election Andrew Jackson was the least qualified in terms of public service in administrative positions. But his successful military career made him the most popular among the electorate, and with so many more Americans exercising the vote in 1824 he had no trouble in winning the largest number of popular and electoral votes. Jackson garnered 152,901 popular and ninety-nine electoral votes; Adams came second with 114,023 popular and eighty-four electoral votes. Even though Crawford had suffered a debilitating stroke during the campaign, he won 46,979 popular and forty-one electoral votes. Still, his electoral votes were more than what Clay accrued, thirty-seven. Nonetheless Clay's popular vote was higher than Crawford's: it reached 47,217. Since no one had a majority of electoral votes, as the Constitution required, it was up to the House to choose the next President. Unfortunately for Clay the Twelfth Amendment to the Constitution stated that only the top three candidates with the highest electoral votes could be considered by the House of Representatives in making its decision, and these included Jackson, Adams, and Crawford.

As Speaker and as a man popular among his colleagues, Clay would most certainly have won the contest. Now he was in a position to decide who would be named the chief executive. He let out a sigh. "I only wish I could have been spared such a painful duty," he declared in a letter to a friend. But it proved easier than he let on. First, he dismissed Jackson as a possible choice because he, Jackson, was a "military chieftain" who defied any law that he disliked and gave promise of developing into an American Napoleon. Besides, Clay's attack on Jackson's invasion of Florida had created an unbridgeable chasm between the two men. The Speaker also dismissed Crawford, who was physically incapacitated and could not assume the duties of the President. So that left Adams, and although he and the secretary had clashed previously—especially in Ghent, where they both served as commissioners in arranging the treaty that ended the War of 1812—they were ardent nationalists, and Adams would certainly endorse Clay's American System.

On Sunday, January 8, 1825, Clay visited Adams at his home and following a three-hour conversation he made it clear that he would support the secretary for President. Their meeting became known, and the rumor spread that they had entered a bargain in which Adams would be chosen chief executive and would in return appoint Clay secretary of state. It was supposedly a quid pro quo agreement.

The election took place on February 9 during a heavy snowstorm. The two houses of Congress met, counted the electoral ballots, and announced that no candidate had a majority. Whereupon the Senate withdrew from the chamber and the House proceeded to choose the next President. Each state had one vote, determined by its delegation.

The gallery of the House was packed with spectators as the balloting began. And the choice was decided on the very first ballot. Adams received the votes of thirteen states, Jackson seven, and Crawford four.

The result infuriated Jackson. The people had obviously preferred him among the several candidates, but their will had been turned aside by what was called a "corrupt bargain" between Clay and Adams. Then when Adams chose Clay as his secretary of state that action provided supposedly irrefutable proof that the election had been rigged by two scheming, power-hungry "poltroons." "So you see," raged Jackson, "the Judas of the West"—Clay was frequently referred to as "Harry of the West"—"has closed the contract and will receive the thirty pieces of silver. . . . Was there ever witnessed such a bare faced corruption in any country before?"

The Adams-Clay team shrugged off the accusations and set to work to enact a program that they hoped would advance the welfare of the American people, a program based to a large extent on Clay's American System. But they never had a chance of getting it through Congress. The opposition, who were mainly Jacksonians, regarded the pair as having unlawfully connived their way to power. Thus when Adams, in his first annual message to Congress in December 1825, requested the building of a system of roads and canals, the founding of a national university and a naval academy similar to West Point, and the "erection of an astronomical observatory" to observe the "phenomenon of the heavens," Congress laughed at him. In a burst of nationalistic enthusiasm, Adams declared that the "great object of the institution of civil government is the improvement of the condition of those who are parties of the social contract." He asked the members not to be "palsied by the will of their constituents."

Palsied by the will of their constituents! Forget the will of their constituents is what Adams seemed to be saying, just as he and Clay had done in cheating Old Hickory out of the presidency. Furthermore, Jacksonians thought Adams was mad to offer such proposals. Not only did they declare them unconstitutional but financially preposterous. Only a corrupt administration spawned by a "monstrous union" between what John Randolph called "the puritan and the black-leg" would propose such outlandish nonsense. Clay took offense at Randolph's remark and challenged him to a duel. Neither man was injured in the ensuing exchange of fire, although Clay's bullet tore through Randolph's trousers.

Dueling in the United States, said Alexis de Tocqueville, the French author of *Democracy in America*, had become a deadly practice. In Europe participants intended a duel to be no more than a show of honor, which could be achieved without inflicting mortal wounds. Not so in America. In the United States, Tocqueville said, the participants meant to kill each other. For some southerners, such as William Yancey of Alabama, "a duel was only a pleasant morning recreation."

Over the next several years the differences widened between the nationalistic administration and the Jacksonians. The era of rule by a single party ended. New parties formed and the two-party system re-emerged. Under the direction of Senator Martin Van Buren of New York, with the help of Vice President John C. Calhoun, the opponents of the administration aligned themselves in support of the candidacy of Jackson for President in the upcoming election of 1828. They soon took the name Democratic-Republicans, or Democrats, and emphasized states' rights and fiscal conservatism. The friends of Adams and Clay advocated a more active role for the government in addressing domestic issues and were known as National Republicans. Thus the ill-termed "Era of Good Feelings" passed into history.

One object of the Adams administration was the imposition of high tariffs in order to advance the manufacturing segment of the country. The tariff had been increased in 1824 but it did not satisfy its proponents. So the House Committee on Manufactures, chaired by Rollin C. Mallory of Vermont, a strong protectionist, set about concocting a new set of duties. But Mallory and his allies were outnumbered and outmaneuvered in the committee by Jacksonians, headed by Silas Wright Jr. of New York, a close associate of Van Buren.

The new tariff recommendations, as finally put forward by this committee, startled and then outraged the friends of the administration. Here was not a bill to encourage manufactures, but rather, as John Randolph rightly described it, a measure to "manufacture a President." The committee, explained Wright to his political friends in New York, jacked up the rates on all products from those states Jackson needed to win election in 1828. At the same time it limited protection on items produced by industries from states supporting Adams, particularly New England. Consequently woolen goods, produced mainly in Massachusetts, failed to get the rates necessary to contend against British competition. How had this happened? Well, explained Wright, the committee raised the rates upon "all kinds of woolen cloths" as "high *as our own friends* in Pennsylvania, Kentucky & Ohio would vote them." Then he jumped the rates on molasses, flax, hemp, and lead to attract votes from western states where these products were produced. And the high duty on iron, he explained, was "the Sine qua non with Pennsylvania." Thus raw materials would be favored by this tariff whereas New England's manufactures would not.

But these duties would hurt southerners, who were among Jackson's strongest and most loyal supporters. They wrongly believed that the tariff had caused the decline in the price of cotton on the world market. Furthermore, they argued, tariffs favored the industrial interests of the north, which meant that southerners had to buy their manufactured goods on a closed market while selling their tobacco and cotton on an open market, and this was unfair. Obviously, the framers of this bill felt that they did not have to worry about southern support for Jackson—it was inconceivable that southerners would vote for Adams in the next election—and therefore these framers had no need to gratify their demands to win their allegiance. In self-defense southerners worked out a scheme to kill the measure. They agreed among themselves that if they voted *in favor* of the provisions advanced by the committee, the New Englanders and their supporters would coalesce to defeat the bill on the final vote.

A series of amendments were offered to make the measure less odious by raising rates on manufactured goods and lowering those on raw materials. But they went down to defeat, thanks to the scheme hatched by southerners. They had no intention of making the bill more acceptable to northerners. When the amendments failed, many of the southerners burst out with loud cheers of jubilation, convinced that the bill was now lost. But by their shouts they foolishly revealed their plot to all the other members of the House. It was obvious, said one, that they had "voted for molasses, & some other articles with a view of making the Bill odious" to all protectionists, especially New Englanders. Such overt expressions of victory were stupid. "We have not only disclosed our plan," groaned Augustine H. Shepperd of North Carolina, "but defeated its success."

That started the New Englanders wondering. "Can we go the *hemp*, iron, spirit and molasses," asked Daniel Webster of Massachusetts, "for the sake of any woolen bill?" After many discussions among themselves they decided that indeed they could, and on final passage in the House on April 22 the measure received a vote of 105 to 94. In the Senate the rates were adjusted to increase the woolen rate to forty percent ad valorum with a five percent increase each year until it reached fifty percent. The Senate, then, on May 13, approved these changes, 26 to 21, and sent them back to the House, where, after a heated debate, they were sustained, 85 to 44. Adams signed it, and in their fury southerners called it a "Tariff of Abominations."

Vice President Calhoun returned home when Congress adjourned and set to work on a document that expressed not only his outrage but his argument that the states may nullify any federal law they believed violated their basic rights. This "Exposition and Protest" was submitted anonymously to the South Carolina legislature, where it was passed. The document advanced the doctrine of nullification, which Calhoun hoped would be the means by which states could protect their interests without resorting to secession.

Adams also announced in his first annual message that a congress of the newly independent states of Latin America had been called by Simon Bolivar, the great liberator of South America, and would be held in Panama to discuss matters of common concern and interest. He further announced that the United States had been invited to attend and that he had accepted the invitation. Democrats took sharp exception to the information, insisting that the conference departed from the established foreign policy of the United States. Furthermore, they planned to reject the nominations of the two ministers to the Panama Congress that the President had sent to the Senate for confirmation. In setting forth the advantages of participating in the conference, Adams underscored the importance of promoting "liberal commercial intercourse" with Latin American countries. Most particularly, he said, the mission would demonstrate to South American countries "the interest that we take in their welfare" and provide the foundation on which could be built "the most cordial feelings of fraternal friendship."

The Jacksonians would have none of it. Confirmation of the two ministers was delayed so long that the Panama Congress had adjourned before they arrived. One of the ministers died en route; the other had only reached Mexico City when the conference ended.

It was a lost opportunity, a chance that a long history of cooperation and interaction between the North and South American continents could have been initiated. Politics, as would happen again and again over the years, canceled the makings of something that might have advanced the welfare of all the parties involved.

Because of politics, the Adams administration left a very thin record of achievements when placed against the things it had hoped to achieve at the outset. Tagged as corrupt, Adams and Clay could not silence or disprove these accusations to the satisfaction of most Americans. In running for reelection in 1828 Adams went down to defeat in one of the filthiest elections in American history. Jackson was accused of stealing another man's wife when he had married Rachel Donelson Robards, who thought she was divorced from her first husband, Lewis Robards, but was not. She was still married to Robards at the time she married Jackson and was therefore technically a bigamist. Also, Jackson's mother was accused of being a prostitute who had been brought to this country to service British soldiers. Adams, on the other hand, was called a pimp. Supposedly, he had procured an American girl for the czar when he served as U.S. minister to Russia.

It was all very ugly and ended when Jackson swept the South, West, and Northwest for a total of 178 electoral votes to Adams's 83 votes, almost all of which came from New England. Out of a population of approximately 13 million, 1,155,340 went to the polls, an increase of 800,000 voters over the last election. Of that number Jackson received 647,276 votes and Adams 508,064.

The country had changed. The Republic was evolving into a democracy, but the process would be long, difficult, and even bloody.

4

The Jacksonian Era

THOUSANDS OF PEOPLE crowded into Washington on March 4, 1829, to witness the inauguration of President Andrew Jackson. It seemed "like the inundation of the northern barbarians into Rome, save that the tumultuous tide came in from a different point of the compass." Many could not understand what was happening. Daniel Webster was positively shocked. "I never saw such a crowd here before," he said. "Person have come five hundred miles to see General Jackson, *and they really seem to think that the country is rescued from some dreadful danger.*"

Actually they had come to celebrate the inauguration of their hero, a man like so many of them who had achieved success in America. Born in poverty, without an immediate family for the first part of his life, he had risen to the highest office in the country. To ordinary citizens, he represented what was exceptional and exciting about America. He was a "self-made man," a term invented at this time to describe those who had achieved fame and fortune through their own efforts without the assistance of family or wealth. Ambition and determination could guarantee success to anyone who made the effort.

The crowd shook the ground with screams and applause as the hero appeared on the east portico of the Capitol and took the oath of office. And when the ceremony ended, the people pursued him as he made his way to the Executive Mansion. They poured into the building—men, women, and children "scrambling, fighting, romping." The *"Majesty of the People* had disappeared," wrote Mrs. Samuel H. Smith, wife of the editor of a leading Washington newspaper, and in its place there appeared a rabble herd of the lowest society. "The President, after having been *literally* nearly pressed to death & almost suffocated & torn to pieces by the people in their eagerness to shake hands with Old Hickory, had retreated through the back way or south front & had escaped to his lodgings at Gadsby's."

Refreshments had been prepared for the reception, but each time the waiters attempted to enter a room to serve the guests, a mob rushed forward to seize the drinks. An orange punch, laced with hard liquor, was pitched to the floor moments after being brought through the pantry door. Cut glass and china were smashed in the melee. The general destruction had reached such a level that tubs of punch, wine, and ice cream were finally taken to the garden outside in the hope that they would draw the crowd out of the mansion. And it worked. Men dived through the windows in hot pursuit, and children wrestled and fought with each other in their effort to grab the ice cream and other refreshments. In their distress on witnessing such behavior, women fainted. "We had a regular Saturnalia," exclaimed one congressman. The mob was "one uninterrupted stream of mud and filth. . . . However notwithstanding the row Demos kicked up the whole matter went off very well thro the *wise neglect* of that great apostle 'of the fierce democracy,' the Chairman of the Central Committee, which body corporate so far from being defunct by the election of Old Hickory seems now to have gathered fresh vitality and has I believe even taken the old man under their parental guardianship."

The Central Committee. It was a new age, a democratic age. Many more people—that is, white males—had won the suffrage, and now politicians formed committees to guide and direct them to the polls so that large majorities could be built for favored candidates. Politics encouraged the use of parades and barbecues to attract public interest. Hickory poles were erected in town squares to salute and celebrate the accomplishments of the "Hero of New Orleans." Newspapers were not only a source of information about local, national, and world events and a means of defining party doctrine, be it Democratic or National Republican, but a way of assisting the formation of organizations to advance the parties' political goals. Hundreds of new journals had appeared during the election of 1828, so that about 600 newspapers circulated in various parts of the United States: fifty of them dailies, 150 semiweeklies, and 400 weeklies. "I had a meeting of 12 to 15 friends   at my house last evening," bragged William L. Marcy, one of Van Buren's most trusted lieutenants in New York, "& arrangements were made to publish and distribute extensively some of the best things that have appeared against the [Adams] administration and in favor of Genl Jackson."

So efficient were these editors and writers that after Old Hickory's victory they descended on Washington like vultures, looking for their reward. Among them were Isaac Hill from New Hampshire, Nathaniel Greene from Massachusetts, Gideon Welles from Connecticut, Mordecai Noah from New York, and Amos Kendall from Kentucky. They became party spokesmen, and for their efforts they received political appointments or lucrative contracts for public printing, or both.

Everything about politics changed in this Jacksonian era. When the government first got under way in 1789 most, if not all, congressmen spent only one or two terms in public service, after which they returned to their regular professions back home. By and large, government was not a means of making money; nor was it regarded as a lifetime career. That changed after the War of 1812. Now congressmen served longer terms and fashioned their service into a profitable career. But this necessitated winning elections—every two years in the case of representatives in the House—which could best be achieved by creating strong political organizations within the states or districts and making certain that one's constituents were pleased with one's performance. Not surprisingly, these needs produced a number of unfortunate consequences: the pork barrel, conflicts of interest, and wholesale bribery. True, these practices probably occurred early in legislative history, but with the advent of democracy they developed rapidly over a long period of time. Lobbyists became more apparent and more insistent in representing their clients.

The type and character of the individuals who ran for office also changed—and not necessarily for the better. A wider-based electorate encouraged the candidacy of many men who really lacked the education and knowledge and background to serve in Congress. Alexis de Tocqueville, the author of *Democracy in America*, attended sessions of both the House and the Senate and was appalled by what he witnessed.

"On entering the House of Representatives at Washington," he reported, "one is struck by the vulgar demeanor of that great assembly. Often there is not a distinguished man in the whole number. Its members are almost all obscure individuals, whose names bring no associations to mind. They are mostly village lawyers, men in trade, or even persons belonging to the lower classes of society." Indeed, the *New York Tribune* reported that Representative William Sawyer of Ohio was one such member of the lower class. He regularly left his seat in the House at one o'clock in the afternoon and went to a window with a recess, opened a bundle wrapped in newspaper, and pulled out a sausage for lunch. He would devour the sausage, then brush away the crumbs, dispose of the newspaper, and return to his seat. A man of rustic manners, declared the *Tribune*, from "some backwoods benighted region in Ohio"—this was the new type of legislator that now sat in Congress and framed the nation's laws. Contrast Sawyer with such men as Madison, Ames, Sedgewick, and Mühlenberg et al. who sat in the House earlier and helped establish the government under the Constitution, and the marked change in the operation of the government becomes immediately apparent. Such a change in just a few years, marveled some. Contemporaries worried that the increase in the suffrage had lowered the standards for running for elective office.

The most obvious change was Jackson himself. He followed a distinguished line of public servants from Washington to Adams, all men of outstanding public service. And Jackson had a nickname: Old Hickory. None of his predecessors possessed such a nickname—but many of the Presidents who followed him did, such as Martin Van Buren, known as the "Little Magician"; or William Henry Harrison, dubbed "Tippecanoe"; James Knox Polk, called "Young Hickory"; and Zachary Taylor, known as "Old Rough and Ready." To many commentators at the time, this use of a new kind of nomenclature surely marked a decline, in their minds, in the caliber of men who served as President of the United States. With the possible exception of Polk, none of them could be regarded as first-rate statesmen.

Still, Andrew Jackson proved to be one of the most outstanding chief executives in U.S. history. He had a reform program that he asked Congress to enact into law. In his first message he proposed a constitutional amendment to replace the electoral system with a popular vote, so that the "fair expression of the will of the majority" would decide who serves as President. As a firm believer in democracy, he preached a simple definition of what that meant. "The people are the government," he said, "administering it by their agents; they are the Government, the sovereign power." In this message he reiterated his claim that "*the majority is to govern.*" Amending the Constitution to abolish the College of Electors would ensure that the disastrous election of 1824–1825 would never be repeated.

He also hoped to settle existing differences with foreign countries, in particular the money due to Americans for property depredations during the Napoleonic Wars. These obligations by Europe had been disregarded for decades and he had every intention of collecting what foreign nations owed American citizens. He also expected to root out the corruption that he believed had seeped into the government during the previous administration. To accomplish this he applied a reformed policy of appointment to office, a policy his opponents called a "spoils system." "Rotation in office," is what he called it. "There has been a great noise made about removals," he declared. Those who have been in office for a few years think they have a vested right to it. "In a country where offices are created solely for the benefit of the people no one man has any more intrinsic right to official station than another." It is by a periodic rotation of men in office that we can "best perpetuate our liberty."

Furthermore, he thought the tariff should be readjusted to a more "middle and just" level so that all sections of the country might benefit. Obviously the Tariff of Abominations had created considerable controversy, especially in the South, and Jackson believed that appropriate "adjustments" could and should be undertaken. Most particularly he believed that the Indian tribes should be moved beyond the Mississippi River for their own safety—to escape probable annihilation—and more particularly for the safety of the nation. As far as he was concerned the presence of Indians in certain parts of the country, especially the Southeast, jeopardized the ability of the nation to defend itself. Finally, he wanted changes in the operation of the Second Bank of the United States inasmuch as it had failed, he said, to establish "a uniform and sound currency." Only with such changes would it be possible to "prevent our liberties" from being "crushed by the Bank & its influence."

After an unfortunate interlude in which a constitutional crisis resulted from the ostracizing of Peggy O'Neale Eaton, the wife of his secretary of war, John H. Eaton, because of her reputation as a "scandalous woman," the President shuffled his cabinet to gain the kind of support he needed to enact his reforms. He defended Peggy, as he had his wife, seeing her as a victim of malicious troublemakers within the administration who would use an innocent woman to gain whatever advantage they could to control the operation of government.

The first important bill to be enacted under Jackson's guidance was the Indian Removal Act of 1830. Because Native Americans were a threat to the safety and security of the nation—the Creek War during the War of 1812 was a prime example—they had to be relocated to an area where they could do no harm. He also believed that unless they were removed they would be exterminated by white settlers who wanted their land and were prepared to wage an exterminating war to obtain it. The disappearance during the past 100 years of such tribes as the Yamassee, the Delaware, and the Mohicans and others convinced him that the same fate would befall the Creek, Chickasaw, Cherokee, Choctaw, and Seminole, the so-called Five Civilized Nations, if they remained where they were.

The Removal Act provided funds to negotiate with these tribes and relocate them to the West. It called for the creation of an Indian Territory, which later became the state of Oklahoma, and within which each tribe would occupy a select area and govern itself without interference from the United States. The removal would involve the signing of treaties in which there was an exchange of equivalent amounts of land—eastern land where the tribes now resided for western land beyond the Mississippi River. The federal government would provide transport, food, and some tools to ease the transition of the Indians to their new homes. Some tribes submitted without a fight. But others did not—notably the Cherokee who were undoubtedly the most "civilized" of the Indians, boasting schools, a written language, a newspaper, and a constitution. So civilized were they that, like white men, they even held slaves. Ultimately they took their complaint to the U.S. Supreme Court, insisting that they were a sovereign, independent nation.

The case developed when the state of Georgia imposed its laws on

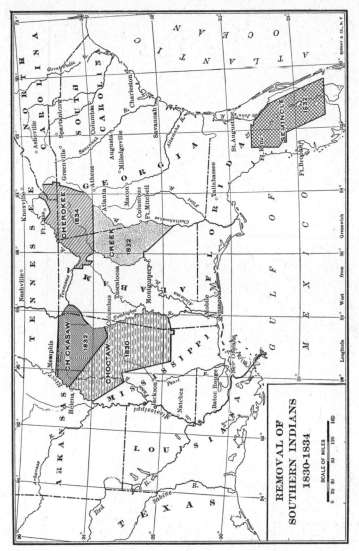

Removal of the Five Southern Indian Tribes, 1830-1834

the Cherokee living within its boundaries. In *Cherokee Nation v. Georgia*, Chief Justice John Marshall decreed that the tribe was not subject to state laws, but he also denied that it was sovereign and independent. Rather, the Cherokee were wards of the federal government. They were, he declared, "domestic dependents in a state of pupilage."

Georgia, of course, paid no attention to the ruling and had the implicit approval of President Jackson. The Georgia legislature followed through by prohibiting white men from entering Indian territory without the state's explicit permission. Two missionaries—Samuel Worcester and Dr. Elizur Butler—refused to comply and were imprisoned. They sued and in the case *Worcester v. Georgia* the Supreme Court ruled against the state and ordered it not to interfere. Whereupon Jackson stepped in and pressured the governor of Georgia, Wilson Lumpkin, to free the missionaries at the same time he urged the Indians to move. Through fraud and chicanery, a removal treaty—the Treaty of New Echota—was approved by the Cherokee Nation and the tribe was rounded up, its members held in stockades while they awaited transport, and then hurried westward along what the Indians called a "Trail of Tears." It was an 800-mile journey of sickness, misery, and death. Some 18,000 Cherokee were removed from their homeland, and 4,000 of them died along the way.

One reason Jackson was anxious to settle the quarrel with Georgia was the fact that a greater crisis had developed with South Carolina, and the President wanted to bring it to a speedy conclusion without provoking civil war. The last thing he needed was a confrontation with Georgia when he was about to face down the nullifiers in South Carolina.

The quarrel began over passage of the Tariff of Abominations and the doctrine put forward anonymously by Calhoun that the states could reject federal laws which violated their rights. This notion of "interposition" would protect minority rights, declared Calhoun, and prevent the tyranny of the majority, always a danger in a democratic society. States must remain strong so that they can block the central government from assuming absolute authority. It was an additional check in a federal system of checks and balances. It was the only way of protecting liberty and individual rights.

These views received a thorough airing in January 1830, at the very start of Jackson's administration, when Daniel Webster of Massachusetts and Robert Y. Hayne of South Carolina got into a fierce debate on the Senate floor over the nature of the Union. Hayne defended the Calhoun doctrine and argued that the Union could last only if the rights of the states—including their right to hold slaves—were respected and protected. The national government was nothing but the agent of the states. States were sovereign, and the Union was simply a compact of states.

Webster countered in his famous second reply to Hayne, in which he denied that the Union was a confederation of states. Rather, it was a Union of people. "I go for the Constitution as it is, and for the Union as it is," he thundered. "It is, Sir, the people's Constitution, the people's government, made for the people, made by the people, and answerable to the people." As for the argument that liberty can be safeguarded only by strengthening the states, Webster insisted that individual liberty depended on the perpetuation of the Union. "Liberty and Union," he cried, "now and forever, one and inseparable."

Jackson thoroughly agreed. At a commemorative celebration to honor Thomas Jefferson on April 13, 1830, many dignitaries were present, including Calhoun. Several toasts were offered, and Jackson proposed the first. According to tradition he looked squarely at Calhoun and said, "Our Union, *it must be preserved*." Calhoun responded with, "Our Union, next to our liberty, the most dear; may we all remember that it can only be preserved by respecting the rights of the States and distributing equally the benefit and burden of the Union." Jackson later allowed the word "federal" to be added to his toast, so that it declared, "Our federal Union, *it must be preserved*."

Congress attempted to settle the problem by passing the Tariff of 1832, which removed some of the abominations of the Tariff of 1828. But it merely modified—it did not appreciably lower—the rates, and the effort proved unsatisfactory to the nullifiers. Whereupon the governor of South Carolina called a special session of the state legislature, which in turn ordered an elected convention to meet on November 19, 1832, to take appropriate action. When this convention assembled, the nullifiers proposed and obtained passage of an Ordinance of Nullification on November 24 by a vote of 136 to 26, declaring the tariff laws of 1828 and 1832 to be "null, void, and no law, nor binding" on South Carolina, its officers, or its citizens.

This was quite a challenge. The convention further decreed that after February 1, 1833, it would be unlawful to collect the tariff duties imposed by the nullified law, and warned the federal government against attempting to force compliance, threatening secession and the establishment of a "separate Government."

Jackson responded immediately with a Proclamation on December 10, 1832, in which he reminded the people of South Carolina, his native state, that as President he had the duty and responsibility of enforcing the laws of the United States. "Those who told you that you might peacefully prevent their execution deceived you. . . . Disunion by armed force is *treason*. Are you really ready to incur its guilt? . . . On your unhappy State will inevitably fall all the evils of the conflict you force upon the Government of your country."

More importantly, Jackson declared, "I consider . . . the power to annul a law of the United States, assumed by one State, *incompatible with the existence of the Union*." The people, not the states, he went on, formed the Union. The people are the sovereign power, and the Union is perpetual. Jackson was the first President to announce publicly that the Union is indivisible, a position endorsed by some Americans at the time but certainly not by all. To southerners especially, the right of secession was fundamental in a free society.

In the interim Calhoun resigned as Vice President and had himself elected to the Senate, where he hoped to block any action the government might attempt against his state. Henry Clay, now a senator from Kentucky, was also anxious to prevent bloodshed, and through his skillful handling of a new tariff bill succeeded in satisfying the nullifiers. The Tariff of 1833 provided a ten-year truce during which rates would slowly fall until, at the end of that period, duties would stand at a uniform twenty percent ad valorum rate and remain there. Jackson signed both this Compromise Tariff and a Force Bill that gave him the authority to deploy the military to put down any attempt at armed rebellion.

South Carolina quickly convened another convention and expressed its approval of the Compromise by repealing its Ordinance of Nullification. But it showed its defiance by nullifying the Force Bill. "If this is to be no more than a swaggering conclusion of a blustering drama," snorted the *Washington Globe*, the administration's mouthpiece, "it will speedily be consigned to the contempt of an enlightened and patriotic public."

"Nullification is dead," Jackson rightly concluded. But the danger inherent in the controversy still lingered on. "The next pretext," he warned, "will be the negro or slavery question."

AT THE TIME he issued his Proclamation of December 10, Jackson had just won reelection as President over Henry Clay. The major issue of the campaign involved the rechartering of the Second National Bank of the United States (BUS). It had developed when the President, in his first annual message to Congress, had asked for changes in the operation of the BUS. Headquartered in Philadelphia with twenty-six branches throughout the country, the institution was run by a board of twenty-five directors, of whom five were appointed by the government and the rest were chosen by stockholders. But the actual manager of the Bank's affairs was its president, Nicholas Biddle, a well-educated, extremely intelligent scion of a wealthy and socially prominent Philadelphia family.

Congress paid no mind to the President's call for changes, because his claim that it had failed to provide the nation with sound credit and currency was patently untrue. But a more important reason for Jackson's hostility arose from his distrust of speculation and paper money, a distrust that emanated from a horrible experience he endured as a young man, when he almost landed in debtors' prison. And lately he began to notice that the BUS used its influence and money to arrange the election of individuals who were friendly toward it and would support its interests. Furthermore, as someone totally dedicated to the sovereignty of the people, he felt that the Bank tended to serve the interests of the wealthier classes in America at the expense of ordinary citizens.

The matter finally came to a head when Henry Clay proposed that Congress renew the Bank's charter four years before it was due to expire. He had a political objective. He thought this might provide the issue by which he could defeat Old Hickory in the presidential election of 1832. He figured that if Jackson signed the legislation it would end all the nonsense about improving the institution. But if he vetoed it, then Clay could challenge Jackson in the election and accuse him of destroying a necessary financial institution, one that provided the people with sound credit and currency. Clay was certain that citizens would never permit the destruction of the BUS; that they would chose him over Old Hickory; and that he, as President, would then sign a new rechartering bill.

So a bank bill was introduced in January 1832, and by July it had passed both houses of Congress. On July 10 Jackson sent it back with a ringing veto, one of the most important presidential vetoes in American history. What it did was open new ground for a President to reject a bill. Previously, all vetoes cited a constitutional reason for rejection of a bill. In the present veto, Jackson did include his constitutional objection, but he also went far beyond that. He cited political, economic, and social reasons for his action. He argued that by this charter the government had granted the Bank monopolistic advantages, where by right it should act as an honest broker among all classes and all interests. He accused the BUS of interfering in the electoral process by favoring certain candidates over others, and thus tampering with the democratic system of government. Moreover, some of its investors were foreigners, which meant that they were enriched from the profits provided by American taxpayers. He also challenged the decision of the Supreme Court about the Bank's constitutionality. In *McCulloch v. Maryland*, Chief Justice John Marshall agreed with Alexander Hamilton's contention that Congress possessed an implied power to create the Bank inasmuch as it was "necessary and proper" to fulfill the legislature's enumerated responsibilities. "To this conclusion," said Jackson in his veto message, "I cannot assent." Both Congress and the President "must each for itself be guided by its own opinion of the Constitution. . . . The authority of the Supreme Court must not be permitted to control the Congress or the Executive when acting in their legislative capacities, but to have only such influence as the force of their reasoning may deserve."

He ended his message with a dynamite passage. "It is to be regretted that the rich and powerful too often bend the acts of government to their selfish purposes." When the laws attempt to make "the rich richer, and the potent more powerful," he continued, "the humble members of society—the farmers, the mechanics, and laborers—who have neither the time nor the means of securing like favors to themselves, have a right to complain of the injustice of their Government." Government must treat all equally, rich and poor, and this Bank bill constitutes a "wide and unnecessary" departure from that principle.

What Jackson did was put Congress on notice that he was a participant in the legislative process. Since he could invalidate a bill for any reason—not simply the dubious constitutionality of a measure—it behooved legislators to check with the President to see if he had any objection to their intended action. If they did not, if they disregarded his authority in the matter, they risked a veto, which, under ordinary circumstances, is extremely difficult to override, since it needs a two-thirds vote from both houses of Congress.

Friends of the BUS were appalled. It was a "manifesto of anarchy," snarled Nicholas Biddle, "such as Marat and Robespierre might have issued to the mobs" during the French Revolution. Senator Daniel Webster was incensed. Jackson, he thundered, "claims for the President, not the power of approval, but the primary power of originating laws." Naturally, Clay agreed. The message, he said, was "a perversion of the veto power."

The founders of this country, in writing the Constitution, had attempted to make Congress the centerpiece of government. Here Jackson attempted to alter that arrangement by making the President the head of government. "Congress is the *democratic* branch of the government," said the *National Intelligencer*, not the executive. "If power is safe anywhere in a Republic it is safe with the representatives."

Madison's claim that the executive was the weaker branch of government had suddenly changed. The reverse was now true. "We have arrived at a new epoch," declared Webster. "We are entering on experiments with the government and the Constitution, hitherto untried, and of fearful and appalling aspect."

Shortly after Jackson defeated Clay in the presidential election of 1832, he decided to remove the government's deposits from the BUS. When his secretary of the treasury refused to carry out his order and refused to resign, Jackson fired him, the first cabinet officer to be so removed. And this was an important first. It meant that the President had absolute control over the entire administrative apparatus.

In the process of withdrawing government funds from the BUS, the administration drew out the money it needed to operate while new revenues were deposited in selected state banks in the major cities, called "pet" banks by the opposition. In retaliation, Biddle ordered a general curtailment of loans throughout the banking system. He refused to increase discounts, and he restricted discounted bills of exchange to ninety days. "This worthy President thinks that because he has scalped Indians and imprisoned Judges"—this was a reference to Jackson's imprisonment of Judge Dominick Hall for issuing a writ of habeas corpus to release a journalist in defiance of Jackson's order establishing martial law in New Orleans in 1815—"he is to have his way with the Bank. He is mistaken." As a result of Biddle's actions the country was pitched into a sharp recession in the winter of 1833–1834.

Meanwhile the Senate, under the prodding of Henry Clay, passed a resolution on March 28, 1834, censuring Jackson for assuming "upon himself authority and power not conferred by the Constitution and laws, but in derogation of both." The vote was 26 to 20. Outraged, the President fired back a "Protest" on April 15, denying the Senate's right under the Constitution to "take up, consider, and decide upon the official acts of the President." Impeachment is the exclusive right of the House of Representatives, he went on, and the Senate cannot attempt what in effect is a resolution of impeachment. He then added something that had been implicit in many of his previous actions and messages: that he was the direct representative of all the people and responsible to them.

Along with many other senators, Daniel Webster denounced Jackson's "outrageous contentions." Where is the "authority for saying the President is *the direct representative of the People?* . . . I hold this, Sir, to be a mere assumption, and dangerous assumption." If he is allowed to claim that he is the "SOLE REPRESENTATIVE OF THE AMERICAN PEOPLE, then, I say, Sir, that the government . . . has already a master. I deny the sentiment . . . and protest the language."

It was during this prolonged controversy over the BUS, the transfer of government deposits to pet banks, and the censure motion that a new party arose from the remnants of the Federalist and National Republican parties, along with some nullifiers and those who abominated Jackson's policies and conduct. They called themselves Whigs, a reference to those in their colonial past who opposed the king and supported republican rule. They dubbed Jackson "King Andrew," and vowed to overturn all his works.

Jackson, during his two terms in office, actually redefined the role of the President, placing him squarely at the head of the government. And this redefinition won immediate acceptance by the electorate. Sighed one senator, "Until the President developed the faculties of the Executive power, all men thought it inferior to the legislature—he manifestly thinks it superior; and in his hands the monarchical part of the Government (for the Executive is monarchical . . .) has proved far stronger than the representatives of the States." The President, not Congress, had become the instrument of the popular will.

BIDDLE'S ACTION IN initiating a financial panic proved to the American people that they did not want an unelected controller of the nation's finances with power to dictate to the government and force it into submission. The House of Representatives agreed. Under Democratic leadership, it passed a series of resolutions that condemned the Bank for calling in loans and attempting to force a recharter by financial pressure. The House rejected rechartering, advised that government funds be kept in the pet banks, and called for an investigation of the operations of the BUS and the causes of the financial panic. And that about killed the bank. "The Bank is dead," ventured one cabinet officer. It had proved itself unworthy of trust. Jackson, of course, was delighted. "I have obtained a glorious triumph," he exulted. The House resolutions "has put to death that mammoth of corruption and power, the Bank of the United States."

To a very large extent this "Bank War," as it has been called, was a power struggle between Andrew Jackson, who represented democratic government as he understood it, and Nicholas Biddle, who represented privilege and financial control. And the issue was whether elected officials or captains of industry would determine the direction and future course of the country. In a real sense it was a question of whether this nation could survive as a democracy if private, unaccountable concentrations of wealth were more powerful than democratically elected officials of the government. And this power struggle has influenced reformers and progressives throughout the history of the United States. Again and again, it has happened that individuals and groups have attempted to use the government to advance their special interests, and at times they have gotten away with it. Only a vigilant electorate can prevent this. Today lobbyists regularly corrupt congressmen to better serve their clients, and the people suffer as a result.

In addition, Jackson's action and claims altered the relationship between the executive and the electorate. Insisting on his position as representative of all the people, Jackson created a national power base on which presidential authority could securely rest. When he opted to destroy the BUS and Congress thwarted his will, he turned to the people and asked for their support. This was the first time in American history that a major issue was taken to the people for resolution. That is rarely done, even today. People hate to decide issues. They are not always certain they are competent to decide momentous questions. Members of Congress are chosen to perform this duty and are paid accordingly. But in 1832 the future of the Bank rested on whether the electorate would choose Jackson or Clay. In favoring Old Hickory so decisively, the people rallied to him and give him a mandate to destroy the BUS, or so he claimed, despite fierce congressional opposition. Presidential power had been buttressed by mass support. The executive office would never be the same again. All it takes is a President with determination, popular support, and leadership skills to direct both domestic and foreign policy and decide the future course of American history.

Unfortunately, pet banks did not and could not replace a functioning central bank so that the nation's currency and credit would be respected throughout the world. For almost 100 years the nation did without central banking, until passage of the Federal Reserve System during the administration of Woodrow Wilson. Out from under the control of the BUS, state banks enjoyed considerable freedom and took advantage of it by irresponsibly issuing paper money without adequate security. To stop this inflation of the currency, Jackson issued his Specie Circular in 1836, which required gold and silver for the purchase of land from the government. One of the most important components of the economy was the sale of public land. Nevertheless, the continued flood of paper currency helped sustain and augment industrial growth and the expansion of the country.

But disaster soon struck. Jackson was not two weeks from leaving the presidency to his successor, Martin Van Buren, who won election over such Whigs as Daniel Webster, Hugh L. White, and William Henry Harrison, when the nation suffered a financial collapse. On March 17, 1837, the I. and L. Joseph Company of New York, one of the largest dealers in domestic exchange, went bankrupt because of the failure of the New Orleans cotton market. This set off a chain reaction in which many banks and a variety of commercial and mercantile enterprises collapsed. Over the next several months many other bankruptcies followed, and this Panic of 1837 was so severe that it lasted for the remainder of the decade and well in the 1840s.

VAN BUREN SPENT his entire administration trying to cope with this depression, but the best he could do was win passage of the Independent Treasury—a "divorce" or subtreasury plan—which required that public money be managed by the government itself without the assistance of private banks. Deposits of cash would be stored in subtreasury buildings in the leading cities of the country and withdrawn as needed by the government. This plan was repealed in John Tyler's administration, which followed Van Buren's, but was reenacted in the administration of James Knox Polk. The Independent Treasury remained the basic banking system for the next seventy years.

The Panic of 1837 also toppled Van Buren from office when he ran for reelection in 1840. General William Henry Harrison, presumably another version of the military hero who had defeated Indians at the Battle of Tippecanoe Creek in 1811; and his running mate, John Tyler of Virginia, overwhelmed the Little Magician, in a rollicking campaign of songs, parades, noise, and nonsense. "Tippecanoe and Tyler, Too," shouted the Whigs; "Van, Van is a used up man." Complete with hard cider, coonskin hats, rolling balls, and other such paraphernalia, this campaign was one of the liveliest and funniest in American history. Was this another result of a democracy run wild? Another effect of Jacksonian Democracy? Had the nation abandoned rationality and statesmanship for bombast and mindless buffoonery? Many Whigs thought so, and feared that this development would in time destroy the Republic. Still they won.

In the election, Harrison captured nineteen of the twenty-six states for a total count of 214 electoral votes to Van Buren's 60. A third party that favored the abolition of slavery, the Liberty Party, nominated James G. Birney, who garnered a little over 7,000 popular but no electoral votes.

The appearance of the Liberty Party as an instrument for ending slavery in the United States was only one expression of a general feeling around the country that horrible conditions existed in society and needed to be reformed. This zeal for reform—or, as Ralph Waldo Emerson called it, "the demon of reform"—had infected a population in every section of the nation. It was not abolition alone that stirred people to action but a wide range of causes that were expected to revitalize and humanize social institutions.

Much of this enthusiasm carried forward from the Enlightenment into a new age of Romanticism. Americans of this era believed in the perfectability of man and the inevitability of improvement. They preached the need to improve the conditions in which men and women worked and lived—the need, as one reformer declared, "to raise the life of man by putting it in harmony with his idea of the Beautiful and the Just." Emerson expressed this romantic notion when he said that "one day all men will be lovers; and every calamity will be dissolved in the universal sunshine."

Improve society. Reform what is wrong. Fix what is broken. This, insisted these Romantics, was an obligation upon all, and human beings had the capacity to achieve these goals because they could "transcend" experience and reason and through their intuitive powers discover universal truths. A group of men and women in New England, including Bronson Alcott, George Ripley, Nathaniel Hawthorne, Orestes Brownson, Margaret Fuller, Henry Thoreau, and Emerson, espoused this "Transcendental" idea by proclaiming that man was not only good but divine. The old Puritan notion about man's sinfulness was replaced by a belief in his divinity. "Pantheism is said to sink man and nature in God," wrote one Transcendentalist; "Materialism to sink God and man in nature; and Transcendentalism to sink God and nature in man."

Transcendentalists saw beauty in nature but ugliness in a materialistic society full of greed and avarice. "I know of no country, indeed," declared Alexis de Tocqueville, "where the love of money has taken stronger hold of the affections of men" than in the United States. Still, man had it in his power to change this because he was "endowed with an infinite faculty for improvement." This faculty emanated from an American belief in equality, Tocqueville insisted. Clergymen who were at the forefront of the Transcendentalist movement put it another way, a more romantic way. For example, Emerson declared, "What is man born for but to be a Reformer, a Re-Maker of what man has made, a renouncer of lies, a restorer of truth and good, imitating that great Nature which embosoms us all?"

At first these Transcendentalists met at George Ripley's home in Boston to discuss their beliefs and ideas, but then a few of them founded a community called Brook Farm in West Roxbury, Massachusetts, where they could live together and put their ideas into practice. The farm never numbered more than 150, but they were visited by thousands who came to hear what they had to say. This experiment in communal living attracted many Americans, although Brook Farm died out after a disastrous fire in 1847.

But communitarianism itself enjoyed a remarkable spurt when any number of communities were established to create cooperative units whereby individuals would be provided with a more harmonious way of life. They were called "phalanxes" and were first introduced by Charles Fourier, a French socialist. Members of these phalanxes would live together and work at tasks they enjoyed and found fulfilling. Presumably such an environment would result in a productive society in which all the members would benefit equally. Fourier's ideas were propagated in this country in 1840 by Albert Brisbane of New York, whose book *Social Destiny of Man* described the "vast and foolish waste which results from our present social mechanism and . . . the colossal economics and profits which would arise from Association and Combination in industrial interests."

Another, and different, communal experiment was founded by Robert Owen, a successful Scot manufacturer, known for his humanitarian activities. He founded his community in New Harmony, Indiana. Through collective ownership of property and cooperative labor, New Harmony was expected to flourish as a model society in which everyone would lead a happy and productive life and poverty and crime would be extinguished. But within two years this experiment failed. Owen's rather strange ideas about "free love," among other things, generated internal discord and conflict.

Much more successful attempts at communal living had a religious basis. The most notable, perhaps, was the Shaker movement, founded by Mother Ann Lee, an Englishwoman who came to the United States in 1776 and settled in Albany, New York. She taught that God had a dual personality: male as exemplified by Christ; and female, which her followers believed she epitomized. She preached the evil of sexual lust and insisted that her followers practice celibacy, which meant that their society continually needed converts to survive. Her disciples were known as Shakers because of the religious dance they practiced. They would form lines, three abreast, and race around the room in a wild gallop, presumably shaking sin from their bodies, and singing as loudly as possible. By the 1840s some 6,000 Shakers resided in over two dozen communities that had been established from Maine to Indiana. The Shaker movement continued well into the twentieth century but finally died out.

Perhaps the most remarkable and certainly the most distinctively American and important religious group to appear during the Jacksonian era were the Mormons, members of the Church of Jesus Christ of Latter-Day Saints, founded by Joseph Smith. He claimed he was visited and instructed by an angel, Moroni, to dig up and transcribe a book written on golden plates and buried in a stone box. The resulting Book of Mormon, published in 1830, purported to provide an account of the lost tribes of Israel. And the name Mormon was derived from a prophet who lived among the early settlers of America. Smith gathered followers to his new faith and led them from New York, where he was born, to Ohio, then Missouri, and finally Nauvoo, Illinois. At age thirty-eight he was murdered in Carthage, Illinois, because of the hostility to his faith among neighbors in the surrounding towns and the fact that some Mormons, including Smith, practiced polygamy. Brigham Young then assumed leadership of the Mormon community and moved it to a desert region near the Great Salt Lake in Utah, where the church flourished and steadily grew in wealth and number. Over the past 150 years it has spread around the world because of the missionary efforts of its young people. By the middle of the twenty-first century membership in the church is expected to exceed fifty million and will rank among the top five Christian denominations in the United States.

The Shaker and Mormon phenomena was one expression of a remarkable outburst of religious frenzy that swept across much of the country in the late eighteenth century and the early nineteenth. This was the Second Great Awakening, and it is one of the most important reasons for the reforming zeal of the Jacksonian era. It influenced almost every aspect of American thought and activity. It was the beginning of an evangelical movement that started with a series of revival meetings at the turn of the nineteenth century and reached its zenith in the 1820s and 1830s. Itinerant preachers who had little formal theological education but mesmerizing theatrical talents summoned worshippers to repent their sins and reform their lives. Their words, their own deep commitment, and their physical involvement resulted in emotional orgies, with men and women tearing their hair, beating their breasts, rolling on the ground, begging God's forgiveness, publicly confessing their sins, and promising to devote themselves to doing good and improving society.

It is no surprise that many of the reforms during the Jacksonian age were initiated and advanced by religious leaders. They called on their followers to band together and establish organizations to improve society and ameliorate human suffering. Charles Grandison Finney was the most prominent preacher of his day and the originator of modern evangelical Protestantism in America. "The evils have been exhibited," preached Finney, "the call has been made for reform. . . . Away with the idea that Christians can remain neutral and keep still, and yet enjoy the approbation and blessing of God." So men and women like Horace Mann, Dorothea L. Dix, Frances Wright, Neal Dow, Lucretia Mott, William Ladd, Susan B. Anthony, and Elizabeth Cady Stanton, along with many others, responded to these pleas and set about improving penal institutions and insane asylums, ending slavery, providing equal rights and better education for women, promoting temperance, assisting the poor, advocating better working conditions, and fostering peace around the world. Horace Mann shared his creed with the graduating class of Antioch College in Ohio just a few weeks before his death. "Be ashamed to die until you have won some victory for humanity," he said.

The improvement in public education to which Mann devoted his life also stimulated the improvement of textbooks. Virtually all the early manuals were of poor quality, and not until Noah Webster introduced his *Spelling Book* and *Reader* did education improve substantially. In 1836 William H. McGuffey's *Eclectic Reader* was published and had an immediate and tremendous impact on elementary school instruction. The book emphasized cultural and moral standards and preached a patriotism that exactly fitted the country's growing sense of nationalism. There is little doubt that McGuffey had a greater influence on American life than any other writer or politician of the age.

How did this happen? What could have brought on this strange and wonderful phenomenon, this Age of Reform, this Second Great Awakening? As with most important events in history, there are a number of reasons. For one, Americans were in the midst of a series of enormous changes, and the changes came with a staggering number of sudden jolts to the body politic. It has been argued that the United States changed more profoundly during the thirty years from 1790 to 1820 than during any other period in its entire history. It should be remembered that Americans had just concluded a Revolution in which they cast off monarchical rule and established a republican government. Then, in the midst of their "experiment in freedom" under the Constitution, political parties formed to run the government. But the experiment elicited contempt from European powers, and ultimately resulted in a war with England. Only the incredible victory at New Orleans by General Jackson and his troops spared the United States from utter humiliation.

Additional changes followed the war. The industrial revolution began and would eventually convert the nation from an agricultural to an industrial society. It was followed by a Transportation Revolution in which communication between sections and regions advanced the expansion of the nation. Most profoundly, the evolution from a republican government to a democratic government brought a new and different generation of leaders into power. Washington, Franklin, Adams, Jefferson, Hamilton, and Madison had been replaced by Old Hickory, the Little Magician, Tippecanoe, Young Hickory, and Old Rough and Ready. Small wonder, then, that Americans who were caught up in these many changes turned to religion to find stability and purpose in life and meaningful activities that could reform society and make it better.

THIS GENERATION OF romanticists also produced a flowering of a national literature. A large number of creative artists flourished during the Jacksonian era. Nathaniel Hawthorne, for example, experienced the ideas of Transcendentalism while living in Concord, Massachusetts, and conveyed them in *Twice-Told Tales* and his novels *The Scarlet Letter* and *The House of the Seven Gables*. Henry Thoreau, a close friend of Emerson's and another prominent Transcendentalist, spent two years at Walden Pond before producing his masterpiece, *Walden*, which expressed his philosophical, religious, and economic views and the joy of living close to nature. "I went to the woods," he wrote, "because I wished to live deliberately, to front only the essential facts of life, and to see if I could learn what it had to teach, and not, when I came to die, discover that I had not lived." He refused to pay a Massachusetts tax to support a war and preferred to go to jail rather than allow a sovereign state to coerce his free will. He wrote the vastly important "Civil Disobedience," a work that had an enormous influence on Mahatma Gandhi and Dr. Martin Luther King, Jr.

Probably the most gifted writer of this generation was Herman Melville, whose monumental novel *Moby-Dick* grappled with the problem of man's eternal struggle with evil. He even included in this work a tribute to Andrew Jackson and the democracy that bore his name:

If, then, to meanest mariners, and renegades and castaways, I shall hereafter ascribe high qualities . . . then against all mortal critics bear me out in it, thou just Spirit of Equality, which hast spread one royal mantle of humanity over all my kind! Bear me out in it, thou great democratic God! . . . Thou who didst pick up Andrew Jackson from the pebbles, who didst hurl him upon a warhorse, who didst thunder him higher than a throne! Thou who, in all Thy mighty earthly marchings, ever cullest Thy selectest champions from the kingly commons, bear me out in it, O God.

No one writer epitomized romanticism in his works more than Edgar Allan Poe, who created the detective novel in such books as *Murders in the Rue Morgue* and *The Purloined Letter*. His poetry, "The Raven," "The Bells," and "Annabel Lee"; his short stories, such as "The Gold Bug" and "The Fall of the House of Usher," proved him to be a singularly inventive and exciting writer. Other poets of the Jacksonian age include Henry Wadsworth Longfellow, James Russell Lowell, and John Greenleaf Whittier. Longfellow romanticized Indians, Lowell satirized the Mexican War, and Whittier attacked slavery. But the outstanding poetic genius of the antebellum era was Walt Whitman, whose *Leaves of Grass* emphasized the Transcendental themes of man's goodness and the beauty of nature. His work is a landmark of American literature.

Although the South did not produce literary masterpieces comparable to those from the North, several southern writers produced works of more than common interest and value. William Gilmore Simms wrote a number of romantic novels about the old South, such as *The Yemassee* and *The Partisan*. Both Augustus B. Longstreet, who wrote *Georgia Scenes*; and Joseph Baldwin, who penned *The Flush Times of Alabama and Mississippi*, sought to capture the rawness and vitality of backwoods life. But as Simms so graphically said, "The South don't give a d—d for literature or art." And certainly not for genuine American literature, which described southerners' surroundings.

A different kind of artist, but a major one nonetheless, John James Audubon, produced magnificent paintings in *Birds of America*, capturing the beauty and variety of these creatures and demonstrating the lush and gorgeous background of the American forest.

Americans also showed a preference for applied scientific techniques over pure scientific theory. They were pragmatists and sought what could be useful and profitable. One foreign observer commented, "Where in Europe young men write poems or novels, in America, especially Massachusetts and Connecticut, they invent machines and tools." Indeed. During the Jacksonian era several important machines and techniques were invented, including the mechanical reaper for harvesting grain, invented by Cyrus McCormick in 1831; the revolver, a weapon developed by Samuel Colt in 1835; the vulcanization of rubber, produced by Charles Goodyear in 1839; the telegraph, the work of the artist Samuel F. Morse in 1844; and the sewing machine, by Elias Howe in 1846; and many other discoveries of such lesser renown as the discovery of anaesthesia by William T. G. Morton, a dentist, in 1842.

A further result of this creativity was the establishment of new businesses and new markets. Americans became experts at converting inventions into marketable commodities and then selling them around the world. What happened was that these new Americans of the antebellum era possessed characteristics that set them apart from Europeans. Some of those characteristics included an intensely pragmatic outlook on life and a burning desire to get ahead and improve their position in society.

Of the many economic, religious, and social reforms that occurred during this Jacksonian period, none was more eventful than the increasingly determined demands by northerners that slavery be abolished throughout the country. After all, a free, supposedly civilized, Christian people holding slaves and profiting from the institution of slavery seemed to many a contradiction of everything the nation espoused about freedom and democracy.

There was a long tradition of opposition to slavery in the United States, especially among religious groups such as the Quakers. But as a result of the reform impetus following the War of 1812, the demand for abolition intensified. A striking example was the debate in Congress over the admission of Missouri into the Union: secession and even civil war were threatened by southerners if their "peculiar institution" was jeopardized in any way. A series of compromises spared the Union a possible breakup. But they prompted Jefferson, now in retirement, to warn that the conflict was "a speck on our horizon" that might well "burst on us like a tornado." It was frightening, he said, like hearing "a fire-bell in the night."

Another frightening sound came in 1822, when Denmark Vesey, a free mulatto, led a small army of followers (whites exaggerated the number by claiming that it reached 9,000) in preparing for a general revolt to win their freedom in Charleston, South Carolina. This "servile insurrection" was brutally suppressed by five companies of the South Carolina militia, and some thirty-five slaves were hanged and another thirty-seven were banished from the state. But the fear of future insurrections lingered in the minds of southerners. They convinced themselves that blacks would rise up one day and indiscriminately murder whites, just as blacks on the island of Santo Domingo in the Caribbean had done a short while before. "Let this never be forgotten," warned one man, "that our NEGROES . . . are the *anarchists* and the *domestic enemy*; the *common enemy of civilized society*, and the barbarians who would, IF THEY COULD, become the DESTROYERS *of our race.*"

An even worse incident occurred less than ten years later. Nat Turner's rebellion is undoubtedly the worst slave insurrection in American history. It probably knocked all southerners into a permanent state of fear and terror with respect to their relationship to African-Americans. Turner was driven by the horrors regularly visited on his race because of their servitude. Some say he was a religious fanatic intent on leading his people to freedom. In any event, on August 22, 1831, at a place called Jerusalem in southeast Virginia, he and about 100 slaves slaughtered sixty whites, including some women and children. They continued their murderous rampage throughout the day and virtually wiped out the entire white community.

The local constabulary rushed to the scene and began a systematic massacre of every black they could find, guilty or not. Several of these bloodthirsty avengers swore that they would kill "every black person they saw in Southampton County." Some slaves were beheaded, their heads hoisted on poles and publicly displayed. It is uncertain how many blacks were executed in this mad act of revenge, but the figure surely ran to several hundred.

The Turner Rebellion sent shock waves across the entire South. "Fear was seen in every face," reported one Southerner. And what made it worse was the growing presence of abolitionists, who demanded the outlawing of the institution or at least a decision by Congress to ban the importation of slaves into the territories. The founding in 1833 of the American Antislavery Society provided organizational structure to the movement, and the establishment of a network of stations on the "underground railroad" assisted runaway slaves in their flight to freedom. This abolitionist activity was augmented by a number of northern states that passed "personal liberty laws," forbidding state officials from assisting in the capture and return of these fugitives.

To make matters worse, race riots regularly occurred in a number of cities, including Washington. What triggered the outbreak in the capital was the attempt by an abolitionist to distribute "incendiary publications among the negroes of the district" which were "calculated to excite them to insurrection and the bloody course" that had resulted in the Turner Rebellion. The rioting in Washington went on for days and necessitated the calling out of armed troops to restore order and protect public buildings. The *National Intelligencer* commented, "We could not have believed it possible" that such violence could occur in the capital of a free people.

Neither the Whig Party nor the Democratic Party would adopt a platform calling for the abolition of slavery or the prohibition of its expansion into the territories. Democrats argued that the situation of the black man had been decided by the Constitution in a compromise that called for the counting of three-fifths of slaves in determining each state's representation in the lower house of Congress. That was the agreement. To change it by freeing the slaves would void the contract and lead to disunion. The Whigs were torn between those in the South who decried any interference in their right to hold slaves and to take them into the territories and those in the North who recognized the need to address the problem but could not agree on a single solution. Many of these northerners later drifted away from the party in the 1850s and eventually formed the Republican party.

Petitions flooded into Congress demanding that some action be taken to limit slavery. But southerners would have none of it, and on May 26, 1836, in the House of Representatives the members voted to table (in effect, to kill) any petition that related "in any way or to any extent whatsoever to the subject of slavery or the abolition of slavery." John Quincy Adams, now a member of the House, defended the "right of petition" and over the next several years fought to have this "gag resolution" rescinded. Year after year the "gag" was reimposed, until December 3, 1844, when it failed to win passage by a vote of 108 to 80. Northern members were at last responding to the increased demands of their constituents to protect the right of petition. "Blessed, forever blessed, be the name of God," pronounced Adams on finally winning this battle.

The right of petition had been sustained, but the basic problem remained: slavery. And the continuance of the Union lay in the balance.

THE WHIGS HAD triumphed in the election of 1840, and with both houses of Congress and the office of the chief executive in their control, they expected to dismantle Jackson's program, charter a new bank, and raise the tariff once the ten-year truce ended in 1843. But President William Henry Harrison died a month after his inauguration in 1841. Now John Tyler succeeded him, and Tyler reverted to his old loyalty to the Democratic Party. He not only vetoed the Whig-sponsored measures to revive the national bank and raise the tariff, but he sought the annexation of Texas, which won its independence from Mexico in 1836. This reaching out for additional territory in the west inaugurated a new concept in American thinking, one John L. O'Sullivan, editor of *The Democratic Review*, called Manifest Destiny. His essay in the *Review* stated that it is "the right of our manifest destiny to overspread and to possess the whole of the continent which Providence has given us for the development of our great experiment of liberty and federated self government entrusted to us."

Years earlier, Jackson had encouraged expansion. He said it was essential for American security, especially in the Southwest along the Gulf of Mexico. It was dangerous, he declared, "to leave a foreign power in possession of heads of our leading branches of the great mississippi." Expansion was "necessary for the security of the great emporium of the west, Neworleans." Besides, he went on, "the god of the universe had intended this great valley to one nation." And that nation—obviously—was the United States. Which is why he regarded the presence of the British, the Spanish, and Native Americans to be a constant threat to the safety of the American people and why he was determined to get rid of them. One by one he had defeated all of them militarily. But that was not enough. Jackson was simply repeating what he had said just before the War of 1812: that he sought the acquisition by the United States of "all Spanish North America."

Manifest Destiny quickly captured the imagination of the American people and their government, and it is small wonder that when Tyler proposed a joint resolution of both houses of Congress (an earlier attempt at a treaty of annexation, which required a two-thirds vote, was defeated in the Senate) that required only a majority vote from each house, it passed. The President signed it on March 1, 1845, a few days before he was succeeded by James Knox Polk, who had defeated Henry Clay in 1844 in a very close presidential election. Texas ratified the annexation on July 4, 1845, and was admitted as a slave state on December 29, 1845.

But Polk, a protégé of Andrew Jackson, was not satisfied with Texas. Like Jackson, he lusted after "all Spanish North America." In particular he wanted California, with its incomparable seaports fronting the Pacific Ocean and the possibility of an expanded trade with the Orient. During the presidential campaign of 1844, the Democrats not only demanded all of Texas to the Rio Grande but raised the cry of "54°40' or Fight," by which they meant the reoccupation of Oregon—that is, all the territory of the extreme northwest, right up to the border of Russian Alaska. The area in dispute—roughly from the Rocky Mountains to the Pacific Ocean and from the northern border of California to 54°40'—was jointly occupied by Britain and the United States. Polk's victory over Clay encouraged Tyler to move forward on Texas, but he made no move toward the Oregon country. When Polk succeeded to the presidency, he was more concerned about acquiring California and the area west of Texas than challenging Great Britain over Oregon, so he readily agreed to establish the 49th parallel as the border separating Canada and the United States. A treaty was speedily arranged with Great Britain on June 15, 1846, and the Senate hastily ratified it.

Mexico regarded the annexation of Texas as a clear indication of the United States' ever-expanding lust for additional territory, and it insisted that the Nueces River, not the Rio Grande, separated the two countries. Furthermore, Mexico rejected offers by the United States to buy California. Whereupon Polk ordered General Zachary Taylor, commander of about 3,500 troops stationed on the Nueces River, to advance to the Rio Grande, a sort of no-man's-land between the United States and Mexico. This action virtually invited a Mexican attack, which not surprisingly occurred on April 25, 1846, when a detachment of Mexican troops crossed into the "no-man's-land," ambushed an American scouting party of sixty-three soldiers, killed sixteen of them, and captured the others.

When word of this engagement reached Washington, Polk immediately prepared a war message. He told Congress that Mexico had "shed American blood on American soil," and he asked the House and Senate to "recognize the existence of war" between the two countries. A bill appropriating $10 million and authorizing the President to call for 50,000 volunteers prompted the protests of Whig congressmen, who claimed they were being asked to vote on providing volunteers before war had been declared, an act of outright aggression. To resolve the problem the administration's leaders in Congress attached a preamble to the bill stating that war already existed by virtue of the invasion of Texas by Mexico. The measure passed and the President signed it on May 13, 1846.

The war itself provided one military victory after another for the United States. General Taylor defeated a superior force of Mexicans at Buena Vista in February 1847; and General Winfield Scott led an expe-

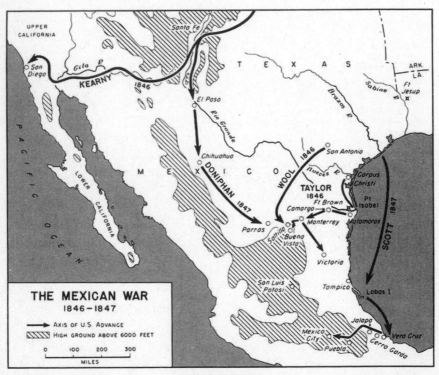

Military operations during the Mexican War

dition that landed at Vera Cruz and swept inland to Mexico City. On September 14, 1847, American troops captured the capital and Scott accepted its formal surrender by the city council. Meanwhile John C. Frémont, captain of an engineering corps, arrived on an exploring expedition in California and upon hearing that the United States had declared war against Mexico helped a band of frontiersmen proclaim the independence of California. At first they set up the Bear Flag Republic, but then they raised the Stars and Stripes.

At about the same time Colonel Stephen W. Kearny, stationed at Fort Leavenworth, Kansas, was ordered to invade New Mexico. He arrived at Santa Fe in August, forced the retreat of a Mexican force that was more than twice the size of his own army, and proclaimed New Mexico a territory of the United States. He then proceeded west, where he joined Frémont and completed the conquest of California.

In an effort to end the war as quickly as possible, Polk dispatched a clerk in the State Department, Nicholas Trist, to Mexico as his peace commissioner. Trist succeeded in producing the Treaty of Guadalupe

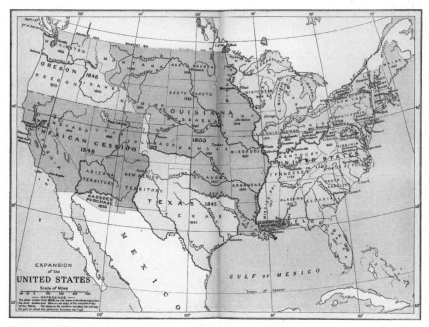

Continental expansion of the United States

Hidalgo on February 2, 1848, and the Senate ratified it on March 10 by a vote of 38 to 14. By the treaty the United States received title to over 500,000 square miles of territory, including the present states of California, Nevada, Utah, New Mexico, and Arizona; the western slope of Colorado; and a corner of Wyoming. Mexico also recognized the Rio Grande as the boundary of Texas. In return, the United States paid Mexico $15 million plus $3.25 million in assumed claims by its citizens against Mexico. American casualties in the war came to 1,721 from combat, and 11,550 from disease. Both Daniel Webster and Henry Clay, who had opposed the war, lost sons in the conflict. Mexican casualties amounted to 50,000.

Manifest Destiny had brought the nation to a new era in its history, one that generated pride in what had been accomplished, especially the acquisition of a territorial empire. But the consequences of the Mexican War also brought a series of crises during the next decade that ended in secession and civil war.

5

The Dispute over Slavery, Secession, and the Civil War

ALREADY THE NATION was reeling. On August 8, 1846, a young, impetuous, ruddy-complexioned freshman member of the House of Representatives by the name of David Wilmot, rose in the chamber and proposed a Proviso to an appropriations bill. The Wilmot Proviso took everyone by surprise. It stated "that, as an express and fundamental condition to the acquisition of any territory from the Republic of Mexico . . . neither slavery nor involuntary servitude shall ever exist in any part of said territory." Wilmot claimed that he did not oppose slavery where it already existed, as in Texas; but free territory, such as the territory received from Mexico, was totally different. "God forbid," he declared, "that we should be the means of planting this institution upon it."

All hell broke loose in the House. Southerners expected to take their slaves into a territory they had done so much to acquire. They raved and ranted in the heated debates over passage of the Wilmot Proviso, threatening secession. The House became one continuous riot of angry and frustrated men who frequently ended their outbursts with challenges to meet on the dueling ground.

Southerners tried to block passage of the Proviso, but it passed in the House by a vote of 80 to 64. In the Senate, however, where southerners had greater voting strength, they killed it. Session after session during the next several years the Proviso won passage in the House and defeat in the Senate. "As if by magic," editorialized the *Boston Whig*, the Proviso "brought to a head the great question which is about to divide the American people." Still, the issue could not be left hanging indefinitely, especially after the Mexican War ended and the country received millions of acres in the Southwest that seemed ripe for the introduction of the "peculiar institution."

With a presidential election approaching, Polk decided to step down after one term as chief executive, and the Democrats nominated Lewis Cass of Michigan to replace him. Cass supported the doctrine of popular sovereignty, whereby local government, not the national government, should decide whether or not to allow slavery within its borders. As his running mate, William O. Butler was chosen.

Because of the growing controversy, a number of Democrats split off from the party, nominated Martin Van Buren for President, and endorsed the Wilmot Proviso. The Liberty Party, which supported abolition, joined these dissenters, and together the two groups met in Buffalo, where they formed the Free Soil Party in support of Van Buren and Charles Francis Adams, the son of John Quincy Adams, for Vice President. Their platform called for "free soil, free speech, free labor, and free men." The Whigs decided to try another general as their candidate and picked Zachary Taylor to head their ticket, along with Millard Fillmore.

In another extremely close election Taylor defeated Cass by winning 163 electoral votes to Cass's 127. The popular vote was 1,361,000 for Taylor; 1,222,000 for Cass; and 291,000 for Van Buren. The former President received no electoral votes, but he deprived Cass of enough popular votes to give New York, and with it the election, to Taylor. Had New York or Pennsylvania voted for Cass, he would have won the election.

Then, an event in California necessitated immediate congressional action concerning the territories acquired from Mexico. Shortly after the Treaty of Guadalupe Hidalgo was signed, ending the war, workmen constructing a mill for John Sutter, a Swiss immigrant, discovered gold in the foothills of the Sierra Nevada in the Sacramento valley. Sutter tried to keep the discovery secret, but word of it quickly spread and a mad rush to the gold fields began. Thousands flooded into the region, crossing the plains by wagon, or sailing around Cape Horn at the tip of South America, or fighting their way through the jungle of the Isthmus of Panama. These were the forty-niners, northerners for the most part, and their numbers swelled within a year so that the population of California skyrocketed from 6,000 to over 85,000. When delegates met in September 1849 to write a constitution, they excluded slavery. And they demanded admission into the Union as a state, not as a territory.

It was the intention of the new President, Zachary Taylor, to bring California and New Mexico into the Union quickly and if possible sidestep any fight in Congress. But the plan was hopeless. As soon as Congress convened in December 1849, the two sections of the country, North and South, began accusing each other of actions that they found intolerable and that, if pursued, would likely shatter the Union. In one exchange, Representative Robert Toombs of Georgia, "a stormy petrel . . . and always intolerant, dogmatic and extreme" shouted his protest. "I . . . avow before this House and country, and in the presence of the living God, that if by your legislation you seek to drive us from the territories of California and Mexico . . . thereby attempting to fix a national degradation upon the States of this Confederacy, *I am for disunion* and . . . I will devote all I am and all I have on earth to its consummation."

Northerners sneered. They had heard it all before, many times over. How often can you threaten to leave the Union, only to find an excuse to remain? But other southerners reiterated Toombs's threat. Alexander H. Stephens of Georgia jumped to his feet. "I tell this House that every word uttered by my colleague meets my hearty response. . . . I would rather that the southern country should perish . . . than submit for one instant to degradation."

At one point the quarreling in the House became so intense that it resulted in a melee. Members physically attacked one another. "Had a bomb exploded in the hall," reported the sergeant at arms, Nathan Sargent, "there could not have been greater excitement." It seemed as though the nation was headed toward dissolution unless some compromise could be found that would be satisfactory to both sides.

Fortunately, the "Great Compromiser" himself sat in the Senate, and on January 29, 1850, Henry Clay proposed a series of resolutions that he believed both the North and the South would find satisfactory.

These resolutions included the admission of California as a state without reference to slavery; the establishment of territorial governments for New Mexico and Utah based on popular sovereignty; settlement of the boundary of Texas and the assumption of Texas's debt on condition that Texas relinquish all claim to any part of New Mexico; passage of a more effective fugitive slave law; agreement to the "inexpediency" of abolishing slavery in the District of Columbia without the approval of the people living there and the "expedience" of abolishing the slave trade within the District; and the denial of congressional authority to interfere in the interstate slave trade.

During the debates Senator Daniel Webster delivered his famous 7th of March speech, in which he said: "I wish to speak today not as a Massachusetts man, not as a Northern man, but as an American. . . . I speak today for the preservation of the Union. Hear me for my cause." On the other hand, the dying John C. Calhoun (his speech had to be read by a colleague) blamed the North for all the nation's problems and demanded the restoration of southern rights through a constitutional amendment. "Disunion is the only alternative that is left us," he warned. Shortly thereafter, on March 31, 1850, he died. Clay appealed for mutual concessions, which, he said, were the only basis for compromise. Each side must give something and each must gain something. Neither can win or lose. Both must yield to the needs to the other.

This debate is arguably the most celebrated in American history. When it came time to vote, the eight proposals were offered as a single package, an Omnibus Bill, and as such it went down to defeat on July 31. A single package gave the senators no choice. It was approval for all eight resolutions or nothing. Fortunately, after the defeat, Senator Stephen A. Douglas of Illinois unraveled the Omnibus Bill and arranged to bring each one of the proposals up for a separate vote. He realized that the senators could not be expected to vote across the board in favor of the entire measure. By separating them he gave each senator the option of voting for one and against another. As it turned out there was a majority for every one of the proposals, and they passed the Senate in August and September 1850. The House of Representatives also approved, and the bill was signed by Millard Fillmore, who had succeeded to the presidency upon the sudden death of Zachary Taylor on July 9.

The Compromise of 1850 ranks among the greatest and most important legislative acts in the entire history of the United States. If nothing else, it postponed secession and civil war by ten years, a period that made possible the salvation of the Union. During those ten years the North underwent rapid industrialization that would enable it to pummel the South into submission; and the ten years also provided the time necessary to bring about the political rise of Abraham Lincoln, the sole figure most responsible for saving the Union.

THE IMPORTANT CHANGES occurring in the United States were augmented by a great new wave of immigrants. During the Jacksonian era the number of immigrants arriving in this country steadily increased from approximately 8,000 a year to 80,000. Then, between 1840 and 1860, that number climbed to 4.2 million—six times what it had been over the previous twenty years. England, Scotland, and Wales provided 500,000 people in the antebellum period, but far and away the largest number of immigrants came from Ireland. The widespread famine during 1845 and 1846, resulting from a disease that destroyed Ireland's potato crop—its chief food supply—caused the death of 1 million men, women, and children. Another 2 million abandoned their homeland and came to America between 1846 and 1860. Although for the most part they were farmers, they did not have the money to purchase land in the West, so most of them settled in the cities, especially Boston, New York, Philadelphia, and other port cities along the coast. They tended to cluster together for support and thus created the first American ghettos. They found employment as domestic help, factory workers, and construction laborers on the railroads and slowly advanced their status in society. They also turned to politics to protect their interests, and since they spoke English, they did not encounter the problems that other, non-English-speaking immigrants faced. In fact it did not take long for them to assume political leadership in the many cities where they settled.

Another national group to migrate to the United States at this time were the Germans. Following the revolution of 1848 thousands of political refugees fled Germany. Some of them were intellectuals, but most of these immigrants were peasants who had more money than the

Irish and therefore tended to move to the farming communities along the frontier or to western cities.

There were artisans and skilled craftsmen among these immigrants, and they helped advance the industrial development of this country. Once the United States recovered from the prolonged Panic of 1837, the rate of economic growth, especially in the manufacturing sector, accelerated rapidly. About 1.3 million skilled, semiskilled, and unskilled workers found jobs in industry. The opening of rich coal mines in Pennsylvania allowed companies to switch from wood-burning to coal-burning sources of heat. This was particularly true in the iron manufacturing industry. Steam power, applied to steamboats and railroads, also transformed transportation. The demand for railroad construction intensified in the 1850s, so that by the end of the decade 30,000 miles of track had been laid in the United States, and railroads such as the Erie, the New York Central, the Pennsylvania, and the Baltimore and Ohio connected cities in the Midwest, especially Chicago, to eastern cities. The machine-tool industry in America developed quite rapidly, and more and more products sold at home and abroad were the result of machine labor.

There was some manufacturing in the South, but nothing compared with what developed in the North. The South remained primarily an agricultural area, although it did have merchants, lawyers, and other professionals. The overwhelming number of southerners were farmers, raising cotton, tobacco, hemp, sugar, and rice, depending on their location. Of the 8 million southern whites in 1860, only a third owned slaves. The rest worked small farms themselves, with members of their family. Most of those who did own slaves had only a few, perhaps one or two. The idea of the South as a vast collection of huge plantations manned by hundreds of slaves, where the master lived in a large colonnaded mansion and the slaves resided in small shacks behind the big house, is totally false. There were few such plantations, although some did exist in each state. These plantations usually consisted of about 1,000 acres, with fifty slaves, and their owners constituted the upper class of society in the South. Andrew Jackson, for example, owned 150 slaves at one time, but that was quite extraordinary. On these particularly large 1,000-acre farms—Jackson always called his property "the farm"—the owner would normally hire an overseer to supervise the work of the slaves. Overseers were usually poor whites who would administer the workforce by dividing the slaves into smaller units directed by trusted and able blacks called drivers. "Mammies" were the domestic equivalent of drivers and had charge of maintaining the big house where the owner and his family lived. Smaller plantations of from 300 to 500 acres were worked by maybe ten or twelve slaves. Yet although most southerners owned no slaves at all, it was the slave culture that defined life from Virginia to Texas. The "peculiar institution" of slavery informed the legal, political, and economic framework of society throughout the South in the antebellum period.

Slaves were considered property, chattel. They could be bought and sold at the pleasure of the master. Indeed, slave families could be broken up: wives separated from husbands, children taken from parents. In sum, the slave had no rights. Although it was a crime in most southern states to kill a slave, still, when such a killing occurred, the perpetrator invariably escaped punishment. Slaves could not go to court, or bring charges or testify against whites. They depended almost totally on the goodwill and decency of their owner. Naturally, the relationship between slave and master varied from place to place. It was complex and has been described by many historians as paternalistic, with both master and slave having responsibilities.

Despite this cruel and oppressive system, black men and women did manage to carve out a space in which they could maintain a degree of dignity. Some even learned to read and write. Many were craftsmen who built the mansions that housed their owners. Family and religion became the center of black culture. Frequently adopting Evangelical Protestantism as their religion, the slaves combined it with remnants of their west African heritage that energized, enlivened, and humanized their religious services.

The harshness of slavery varied according to location and type of plantation operation. It was undoubtedly harsher in the deep South than along the border states of Maryland, Kentucky, and Tennessee. There were five basic types of plantations, and they varied in size, organization, and operation. The first type, the cotton plantation, employed about two-thirds of the slaves from North Carolina to Texas. Long-fiber cotton had been grown on the southern Atlantic coast, but with the invention of the cotton gin in 1793 it was possible to profitably grow short-fiber cotton farther west. After the War of 1812 the cultivation of cotton spread into Alabama, Mississippi, Arkansas, Louisiana, and Texas, so that by the 1850s southerners could boast that "cotton is king." The second type of plantation involved the cultivation of tobacco. It began in eastern Maryland, Virginia, and North Carolina and then spread in the nineteenth century to Kentucky, Tennessee, and Missouri. The third type was the rice plantations, which were located in the swampy coastal areas of North and South Carolina, in Georgia, and along the banks of the Mississippi River in southern Louisiana. These rice plantations required large capital investments and were relatively few. The fourth type, the sugar plantations, existed almost exclusively in Louisiana. These plantations not only grew sugarcane but refined it into basic sugar, thus combining manufacturing with agriculture. Like the rice plantations, they required a large outlay of capital. For example, the smallest sugar plantation had an investment of $40,000. The fifth type was the hemp plantation, which was limited to Kentucky and parts of Missouri. It was the smallest operation that required slaves and therefore the smallest in number.

Make no mistake, slavery was the most basic and most financially rewarding economic operation in the United States prior to the Civil War. And although it was profitable for individuals, it did not encourage the creation of the infrastructure of an industrial economy as was happening in the North. But since individual southerners were profiting from the slave system, they were not about to see it abolished, even if perpetuating it meant dissolving the Union.

As SLAVERY CONTINUED to expand westward with the acquisition of Texas, the demand for its abolition also intensified. Indeed, at one time there had even been antislavery societies in the South, and many of these supported the American Colonization Society, which succeeded in founding a colony of free blacks in Liberia in the 1820s. But with the religious fervor of the Second Great Awakening, the abolitionists of the Jacksonian age breathed a hatred for the peculiar institution that was far more intense than anything earlier. Many of them were evangelists who could recognize sin from great distances, and to them, slavery was sin writ large. One zealot, William Lloyd Garrison, published a newspaper called *The Liberator* in which he even denounced the Constitution of the United States. It was, he wrote, "a covenant with death and an agreement with hell."

In 1852, Harriet Beecher Stowe published a novel, *Uncle Tom's Cabin*, graphically depicting the cruelties of the slave system. It begged "the Christian and humane people of the North" to block the implementation of the Fugitive Slave Act, which had been passed as part of the Compromise of 1850 and authorized federal marshals to return runaway slaves to their masters. Stowe's book sold widely and had a tremendous impact on the thinking of Americans about the institution of slavery. Some, like Abraham Lincoln, declared that it helped start the Civil War.

Runaway slaves had always been a problem for southerners, especially when the Underground Railroad system was set up. This consisted of "stations" (usually private homes or barns) along which "conductors" could help slaves escape to freedom. Harriet Tubman, a runaway herself, escorted several hundred slaves to safety. It was estimated that by the 1850s the Underground Railroad helped 1,000 or more runaways a year escape their servitude.

THE COMPROMISE OF 1850 brought about a period of relative political calm, but it did not last long. It was shattered in December 1853, when a bill was introduced to organize the territory of Nebraska without mentioning slavery, since Nebraska was north of 36°30' as established by the Missouri Compromise. A great deal of politicking took place in the passage of the measure, and because many of the leading figures in the discussion favored popular sovereignty for the region, it was finally decided to split the territory in two and establish Nebraska to the north and Kansas to the south. In addition, the Missouri Compromise was declared "inoperative." Another reason for organizing this territory was the desire of northern congressmen to facilitate the building of a railroad through the northern tier of states and territories that would eventually reach the Pacific Ocean. Building a railroad across organized territory with a governmental apparatus in place was far better than building one across unorganized territory. More particularly, a number of congressmen had invested heavily in real estate in the surrounding states and were anxious to protect their investment. In addition, the bill extinguished Indian titles to the land, which also helped win approval for the entire measure.

But the Kansas-Nebraska Bill set off a titanic battle in Congress. Still, after the screaming and fighting ended in late May 1854, it became law through the healthy application of the "whip & spur" by the party leadership, especially by Stephen A. Douglas in the Senate and Alexander H. Stephens in the House. Douglas claimed full responsibility. "I passed the Kansas-Nebraska Act," he later bragged. "I had the authority and power of a dictator throughout the whole controversy in both houses. The speeches were nothing. It was the marshaling and directing of men, and guarding from attacks, and with a ceaseless vigilance preventing surprise." But Stephens helped. "If I had not been here the Bill would never have been got through. I took the reins in my hand and drove with whip & spur until we got the 'wagon out of the mud.'"

To make the measure more acceptable to southerners, it specifically repealed the Missouri Compromise and established two territories: Kansas to the west of slaveholding Missouri, and Nebraska to the west of the free states Minnesota and Iowa. The many southerners who voted for it clearly intended that Kansas would become slave (they would see to that) and Nebraska free. But the legislation was a fatal mistake. It annihilated the peace brought by the Compromise of 1850 and sent the country spinning toward disunion.

It also refashioned the party system. For one thing, sectional loyalty had replaced party loyalty. With the slow decline of the Whig Party, southerners were steadily drifting into the Democratic Party. Northerners too. Furthermore, on February 24, 1854, a number of Free-Soilers, northern Whigs, and antislavery Democrats met in Ripon, Wisconsin, and recommended the formation of a new party, which they called the Republican Party. Months later, after passage of the Kansas-Nebraska Act, a meeting was held in Jackson, Michigan, on July 6 that formally adopted the new name and demanded the repeal of the Kansas-Nebraska Act along with that of the Fugitive Slave Act.

Another party to appear in the middle of the 1850s was the Know-Nothing or American Party. It developed as a result of the large number of Irish and German immigrants who entered the country. By

1860 there were about 4 million immigrants, and native-born Americans suddenly became conscious, and resentful, of this large number of foreigners in their midst. In addition, many of these aliens were Roman Catholic. So the new party evolved into an anti-immigrant, anti-Catholic, and antislavery party whose members responded with "I know nothing" when asked about the purposes and policies of their organization.

Thus, in the election of 1854, according to Senator Douglas, the anti-Nebraska movement became "a crucible" into which Know-Nothings "poured Abolitionism . . . and what was left of Northern Whiggism, and then the Protestant feeling against the Catholic, and the native feeling against the foreigner." And they won a great many seats in Congress, as did the newly organized Republican Party. Of the forty-three northern Democrats who voted for the Kansas-Nebraska Act, only seven won reelection. So successful were the Know-Nothings that some predicted they would win the presidency in 1856. "How can anyone who abhors the suppression of negroes be in favor of degrading classes of white people?" remarked Abraham Lincoln. "As a nation, we began by declaring that '*all men are created equal.*' . . . When the Know Nothings get control, it will read, 'All men are created equal' except negroes, *and foreigners, and catholics.*" But the Know-Nothing Party was short-lived. Internal divisions over slavery and the Kansas-Nebraska Act led to its demise by 1860.

Meanwhile in Kansas, violence erupted between free men and slaveholders that degenerated into a local civil war known as Bleeding Kansas. An investigation of the situation in that territory reported that in its present condition Kansas could not conduct a free election without a new census, impartial judges, and the presence of U.S. troops at every polling station. And the bloodshed in Kansas was reflected in Congress when, on May 19, 1856, Senator Charles Sumner of Massachusetts gave a speech in the upper house titled "The Crime against Kansas," in which he accused "hirelings picked from the drunken spew and vomit of an uneasy civilization" of invading Kansas in an attempt to impose a proslavery legislature upon the citizens by force and violence. He singled out the senior senator from South Carolina, Andrew Pickens Butler, as the personification of that "uneasy civilization" and verbally assaulted him in a personal attack that was one of the most abusive speeches ever delivered in Congress.

Retaliation came swiftly. On May 22, 1856, Representative Preston S. Brooks, a nephew of Senator Butler, strode into the nearly empty Senate chamber, where he found Sumner sitting at his desk franking copies of his "Crime Against Kansas" speech. "Mr. Sumner," barked Brooks in a threatening voice, "I have read your speech twice over carefully. It is a libel on South Carolina and Mr. Butler, who is a relative of mine." And with that, he raised a large, heavy gutta-percha cane and struck Sumner repeatedly over the head. The badly mauled senator tried to escape. He was sitting close to his desk, so he tried to push back his chair, but the desk was firmly screwed to the floor and the rug underneath made it impossible to move the chair. So Sumner simply rose with a mighty heave, using all his strength, and in the process ripped the desk from its moorings as he toppled to the floor. "Bully" Brooks, as he came to be called, continued raining blows about Sumner's head and shoulders until the cane broke in two. "Every lick went where I intended," Brooks later boasted. "I wore my cane out completely but saved the Head which is gold."

Brooks resigned from the House, but his constituents reelected him overwhelmingly. To them he was a hero. Five months later he died of a liver disease at the age of thirty-seven. Sumner survived the attack and after his recovery had this to say about Brooks: "Poor fellow, he was the unconscious agent of a malign power."

DURING THIS PERIOD of crisis, when the nation desperately needed a strong, wise leader at the head of the government, one of the worst Presidents in the nation's history was elected. James Buchanan, the Democratic candidate, won election in 1856 over the Republican, John C. Frémont, and the Know-Nothing candidate, Millard Fillmore. Buchanan received 174 electoral votes to Frémont's 114 and Fillmore's 8. It was a remarkable showing for the young Republican Party, and had Pennsylvania and either Illinois or Indiana voted for him, Frémont would have been elected.

Straight off, Buchanan demonstrated his stupidity in his inaugural address, by announcing that the Supreme Court was about to hand down a decision which would settle the problem of slavery. The question immediately arose as to how he knew beforehand what the court would decide. In point of fact he was not mistaken, but he foolishly thought that his announcement of it would calm fears and quiet strife. Two days later Chief Justice Roger B. Taney delivered the Dred Scott decision, which declared the Missouri Compromise unconstitutional because the Fifth Amendment to the Constitution stated that no one could be deprived of their property without due process of law. Taney also denied that Dred Scott, a slave suing for his freedom by virtue of his residence in a free state and free territory, was a citizen. As a slave, Scott was not entitled to sue in a federal court. The decision solved nothing, as Buchanan had predicted in his inaugural, and the reputation of the court plunged to its lowest level in its history.

Meanwhile, a rigged convention held in Lecompton, Kansas, wrote a constitution that protected slavery and prevented the electorate from outlawing the institution. Voters were given the choice of approving slavery or forbidding its *further* introduction into the territory. Either way Kansas would become a slave state.

Despite this obvious ploy to prevent a fair vote on the Lecompton constitution, President Buchanan asked Congress to admit Kansas as a state under that constitution. And this action set off a brouhaha in both houses of Congress. In the House it was a wild free-for-all with fifty or more members wrestling and punching one another. This outburst was the largest such melee in the entire history of that body. During the fracas, John F. "Bowie-Knife" Potter of Wisconsin reached for the hair of William Barksdale of Mississippi and tore off his toupee. "I've scalped him," cried the startled Potter, and everyone burst into laughter.

A compromise bill was finally reached by which voters in Kansas could accept or reject the Lecompton constitution. On August 2, 1858, the electorate defeated the constitution. Kansas remained a territory until after the secession of southerners in 1860–1861. It was admitted as a free state on January 29, 1861.

IN 1857 SOUTHERNERS were further outraged by the publication of a book by Hinton R. Helper, *The Impending Crisis of the South, and*

How to Meet It. He argued from statistics that many southern whites were impoverished by slavery and that the institution was detrimental to their economic welfare. What increased southern anger was the fact that Helper was a southerner himself, from North Carolina. But the book itself provided the kind of ammunition that abolitionists used to attack slavery in both the northern and the southern sections of the country.

The Lincoln-Douglas debates in the summer of 1858 also infuriated southerners in that Lincoln asked Douglas to reconcile the doctrine of popular sovereignty with the Dred Scott decision. Douglas replied that slavery could not "exist a day or an hour anywhere, unless it was supported by local police regulations." Since he was the leading candidate of the Democratic Party for the presidency in 1860, that remark lost him the South at the nominating convention. Southerners said they could not support a candidate who held this view. However, the debates did elevate Lincoln to national attention.

Then in mid-October 1859, at Harpers Ferry, John Brown led a raid that he hoped would ignite a slave insurrection. He seized the federal arsenal there, and after two days of fighting he was captured, tried for treason against the state of Virginia, and hanged on December 2. Brown became a martyr to northern abolitionists but a frightening figure of madness run amok to southerners. Throughout the South there was a feeling that this kind of horror would be repeated because of the propaganda of abolitionists and the political diatribes of Republicans.

In Congress the madness surfaced in the fistfights that broke out on the floor and the bitter words of recrimination that the members continually hurled at one another. "We will never submit to the inauguration of a Black Republican as President," stormed a Democrat from Georgia. "I speak the sentiment of every Democrat on this floor from the State of Georgia." And this remark was repeated when the Democrats held their nominating convention in Charleston on April 23. Northern delegates were unwilling to satisfy the demand of the South that slavery be allowed in the territories, whereupon members from the eight southern states walked out of the convention. The party split, and northern Democrats held their convention in Baltimore on June 18 and nominated Douglas and Herschel V. Johnson of Georgia for President and Vice President. Southern Democrats also held their convention in Baltimore, on June 28, and nominated John Breckinridge of Kentucky and Joseph Lane of Oregon.

The Republicans met in Chicago on May 16. Senator William H. Seward had been the leading candidate for the presidency until he gave a speech in Rochester, New York, on October 25, 1858, in which he said: "It is an irrepressible conflict between opposing and enduring forces, and it means that the United States must and will, sooner or later, become either entirely a slaveholding nation or entirely a free-labor nation." That "irrepressible conflict" speech frightened a great many Republicans, and he lost their support. Lincoln, on the other hand, gave a more conciliatory but carefully worded speech at Cooper Union in New York City, known as the "House Divided" speech, in which he avoided any suggestion of conflict but did appeal for sectional understanding. On the third ballot the Republican convention named Lincoln for President and Hannibal Hamlin for Vice President. Remnants of the Whig and Know-Nothing parties formed the Constitutional Union Party in Baltimore and chose John Bell of Tennessee and Edward Everett of Massachusetts as their nominees.

Crippled by the split in its ranks, the Democratic Party went down to defeat. Lincoln won eighteen free states for 180 electoral votes, a clear majority. Breckinridge carried eleven slave states for a total of 72 electoral votes. Bell captured three border states for 39 votes. Douglas won only one state (Missouri) and scattered votes from a second (New Jersey) for a total of 12 electoral votes. In the popular contest Lincoln garnered 1,865,593 votes; Douglas 1,382,713; Breckinridge 848,356; and Bell 592,906.

Many southerners had sworn that they would never remain in a Union with a "Black Republican" President. So as soon as the results of this election became known nationally, the South Carolina legislature summoned a state convention to consider a course of action. The convention met on December 20, 1860, and formally dissolved South Carolina's ties to the other states "comprising the United States of America." This action was soon followed in the rest of the lower South: Mississippi seceded on January 9, 1861; Florida on January 10; Alabama on January 11; Georgia on January 19; Louisiana on January 26; and Texas on February 1. These states held a convention in Montgomery, Alabama, on February 8, and their representatives adopted a constitution closely resembling the U.S. Constitution. The document established the Confederate States of America and recognized the independence and sovereignty of each state. Naturally, it protected the "peculiar institution." The following day the members elected Jefferson Davis as provisional President of the Confederacy, and Alexander H. Stephens as Vice President.

There were attempts to forestall this horrendous break. A peace convention made up of members from northern, southern, and border states met behind closed doors in Washington on February 4, 1861, with John Tyler, the former chief executive, presiding. But the participants failed to find an agreement acceptable to both sides. On February 28, another effort failed to turn back secession when Congress considered a joint resolution to amend the Constitution and guarantee slavery in the states where it already existed. But some sixty-five Republicans, led by Thaddeus Stevens of Pennsylvania, opposed it. Still the amendment passed the House (133 to 65) and the Senate (24 to 12), but the states did not ratify it.

In his inaugural address on March 4, 1861, President Lincoln tried to reassure southerners that their rights, especially their right to hold slaves, would be protected: "I have no purpose directly or indirectly to interfere with the institution of slavery in the States where it exists." And he endorsed President Jackson's claim that the Union was indivisible, that no state had the right to separate itself from the others. "Physically speaking," he declared, "we cannot separate." No state, acting on its own, "can lawfully get out of the Union." Like Jackson, he also reminded citizens that he was under oath to enforce the laws, and that duty required him to maintain federal property throughout the United States. His decision to provision Fort Sumter in the Charleston harbor, therefore, prompted the Confederates, under the command of General Pierre G. T. Beauregard, to attack the fort, which surrendered on April 12 after more than a day of constant bombardment. And by this military action, the Civil War began.

Once the fighting started, Lincoln summoned 75,000 volunteers to defend the Union, and he called Congress into special session to begin on July 4. As commander in chief he felt he had the authority to expand the military, authorize the purchase of armaments, and suspend the writ of habeas corpus wherever necessary. He also directed the states to increase the size of their militias so they could best serve the interests of the nation. When Congress convened, he told the members that he had done nothing they could not legislatively approve. By the summer of 1861 the Union had 186,000 men under arms. Jefferson Davis also summoned southerners to defend their homeland and within a few months some 112,000 recruits responded to his call.

Once armed conflict erupted, the upper South seceded: Virginia on April 17, Arkansas on May 6, Tennessee on May 7, and North Carolina on May 20. Four other slave states—Delaware, Maryland, Kentucky, and Missouri—remained loyal to the Union, despite strong sentiment for the Confederacy in certain sections of these states. On the other hand, the western half of Virginia remained loyal to the United States, and seceded from the state and was admitted into the Union as West Virginia on June 19, 1863.

When Virginia seceded, the capital of the Confederacy was moved from Atlanta to Richmond, and in no time rebel troops appeared across the Potomac within sight of Washington. Hurriedly, troops were rushed to the Union capital and were housed in the halls and chambers of the House and Senate. Once Congress met for its special session on July 4, the soldiers were bivouacked in other parts of the city.

Under the strong leadership of Thaddeus Stevens, chairman of the Ways and Means Committee, the House within five days approved legislation that permitted the secretary of the treasury to borrow $250 million over the next twelve months. By the time Congress adjourned on August 6 it had passed sixty-six bills, all but four of which dealt with the war. In a little over a month it set a record for productivity, mainly because of vigorous leadership and a determination by a majority of its members to cope with a crisis of staggering proportions. This record of achievement continued for the next several years.

In the belief that the Confederate capital at Richmond could be captured with a sudden and unexpected blow, pressure from politicians and the press prompted Lincoln to overrule Winfield Scott, the commanding general, who argued that the troops in Washington needed additional training before going into battle. Accordingly, Lincoln ordered General Irwin McDowell, with a force of 30,000 troops, to advance and attack Confederate forces under General Beauregard at a place called Manassas Junction, a little town on Bull Run, or creek, about thirty-five miles southwest of Washington. On July 21 the two forces met, and at first the battle went well for the Union. But Confederate reinforcements, under General Joseph E. Johnston, arrived from the Shenandoah Valley and routed the Union forces, who panicked and fled back to Washington. During the engagement General Thomas J. Jackson earned the nickname "Stonewall" because of his heroic stand during the battle. Lincoln now realized the wisdom of General Scott's insistence on further training for the Union troops. McDowell was replaced by General George B. McClellan, who had won several skirmishes in western Virginia and who became general in chief upon the retirement of General Scott.

A crisis with Great Britain was narrowly avoided when an American warship stopped the British steamer *Trent* and removed James M. Mason and John Slidell, two Confederate commissioners bound for England. Secretary of State Seward ordered the men released, thus preventing the crisis. He declared that the American warship acted improperly in not bringing the *Trent* and the two commissioners to port for adjudication by an admiralty court.

The Union suffered another military defeat on October 21, at Ball's Bluff near Washington, which stiffened demands by the more radical Republicans for an increased prosecution of the war and the abolition of slavery. Led by senators Benjamin Wade of Ohio and Zachariah Chandler of Michigan, and Representative Thaddeus Stevens, they called for the creation of a Joint Committee on the Conduct of the War, presumably as a response to Lincoln's assumption of authority in conducting it. The joint committee was approved on December 9, 1861, immediately after Congress convened for its regular session. It was given broad investigatory powers to summon persons to testify and demand papers to document the progress of the war. The committee included three senators—Chandler; Wade; and Andrew Johnson, a Democratic Unionist from Tennessee—and four representatives: George W. Julian of Indiana, Daniel W. Gooch of Massachusetts, John Covode of Pennsylvania, and Moses Odell, a Democrat from

New York. Wade chaired the committee, which was dominated by Radical Republicans. None of these men knew much about conducting the war, but all shared distrust, if not disdain, for the military. They sought any opportunity to embarrass or humiliate top-ranking generals.

And they abused their authority. They investigated the War Department for allegations of fraud and incompetence, and delved into the problem of government security, including rumors that the President's wife, Mary Todd Lincoln, was a Confederate spy. Worse, they harassed the President about his reluctance to proceed with immediate emancipation of the slaves and his failure to find the necessary person or persons to bring the conflict to a speedy and successful conclusion. The committee was, said one, "a mischievous organization, which assumed dictatorial powers." It summoned generals to testify and then asked them inane questions, such as, "What do you know about war?" A number of obsequious and incompetent generals "scolded and carped and criticized, and caviled, told half truths and solid lies, and the August and astute Committee listened with open ears." Such testimony was just the sort of thing the members wanted to hear—anything that belittled the military. In the course of its benighted history, it issued eight volumes of reports on a succession of military defeats. It also provided documentation that severely damaged the reputations of a number of unfavored generals, particularly General McClellan, whom the members loathed for failing to move his army and provide victories in the field.

The committee met with Lincoln and his cabinet on January 6, 1862, and, with malicious intent, reported that "neither the President nor his advisers seemed to have any definite information respecting the management of the war, or the failure of our forces to make any forward movement."

Since the cost of the war quickly mounted to $2 million a day, Congress passed a bill on February 6, 1862, authorizing the issuance of "greenbacks" or paper money as legal tender. It was the first paper currency ever issued by the national government. Two months later, on April 16, Congress outlawed slavery in the District of Columbia, with compensation to those who would free their slaves, thereby initiating the first step in legislating the end of slavery. Republicans shouted their approval when the bill passed. "A few of the radical members," sneered one critic, "indulged in excessive and quite undignified manifestations of this delight, hurrahing in the corridors [of Congress], and seizing every negro they met and overwhelming them with congratulations." Lincoln regarded the action as a ploy to force him to take a stand on the issue. Despite his reluctance, he signed the bill, and it became law. Later Congress also abolished slavery in the territories, without compensation.

Of enormous importance to the steady expansion of the population in the west, Congress passed the Homestead Act on May 20, 1862, which provided 160 acres of public land to any person who would reside on it and farm it for five years. Within two years some 25,000 settlers staked claims to over 3 million acres of land. Similarly, the Morrill Land Grant College Act, passed on June 17, 1862, provided 30,000 acres of land to each member of Congress to finance the establishment of public agricultural and mechanical institutions within the states and territories.

One of the most important actions taken by Congress was the passage of the Internal Revenue Act of 1862, which taxed a wide range of items, few of which survived the war. But the Bureau of Internal Revenue created by this measure did become a permanent fixture of the federal government. And passage of the Pacific Railroad Act provided land and funds for the building of what would become a transcontinental railroad from Omaha, Nebraska, to Sacramento, California.

ALTHOUGH THE GOVERNMENT achieved a number of legislative successes, there was nothing but defeat on the military front. General McClellan, who was relieved of supreme command, except for the Army of the Potomac, was ordered to begin an advance on Richmond, and he took a route along the peninsula between the James and York rivers rather than lead a frontal attack from Washington that would relieve the pressure on the nation's capital. This peninsula campaign came to an abrupt end in the early summer of 1862, with the Seven Days battle, in which nearly 20,000 men on both sides were killed or wounded. Major General Henry W. Halleck was put in command of the Union army. And a significant battle occurred on March 8, 1862, when two ironclads, the *Merrimac* and the *Monitor*—their hulls were shielded in metal—engaged in a five-hour battle on the James River that resulted in a draw. The age of wooden fighting ships effectively ended on that day.

A naval squadron under David G. Farragut ran the Confederate defenses below New Orleans in April 1862 and bombarded the city, whereupon it was occupied by Union troops under General Benjamin F. Butler. For his success, Farragut was named a rear admiral, the first to be accorded that rank.

At the Second Battle of Bull Run in late August, the Union army suffered another humiliating rout by a Confederate army now commanded by General Robert E. Lee, who succeeded General Johnston after Johnston was severely wounded at the Battle of Seven Pines in late May. Lee then invaded the North in an attempt to isolate Washington by cutting the major rail lines leading to the city. At Antietam the Union and Confederate armies met in another bloody engagement. Over 3,000 on both sides were killed and another 18,000 wounded. The battle ended in a draw when McClellan failed to deploy his reserves, but Lee withdrew to Virginia and so the Union could claim a "technical" victory.

It was enough of a victory for President Lincoln to issue his Preliminary Emancipation Proclamation on September 22. Although at the beginning of the war he insisted that the conflict involved preserving the Union, by this time slavery had become the defining issue. In this Preliminary Proclamation, Lincoln declared that on January 1, 1863, he would free all the slaves in Confederate areas still in rebellion against the United States. "I wish it were a better time," he told his cabinet. "I wish that we were in a better condition. The action of the army against the rebels has not been quite what I should have best liked." Even so, it was time to bring the question of slavery to an end.

The "technical" victory at Antietam also halted any possibility of recognition of the Confederacy by Great Britain and France. Those two countries had been on the verge of recognition, but now they held back, and this danger to the Union cause passed without further difficulty. However, Great Britain continued building raiding ships for the Confederates, allowing the *Alabama* to slip out of Liverpool and inflict heavy damage on American shipping. Not until the U.S. minister to

England, Charles Francis Adams, pointed out to the British ministry in April 1863 that it was engaged in an act of war against the United States did the government halt the further building of these raiding ships.

And early in 1863, the emperor of France, Napoleon III, proposed mediation of the conflict, which Congress and Secretary of State Seward rejected out of hand. Over protests from the United States, Napoleon intruded in Mexican affairs, occupied Mexico City with a French army, and installed Archduke Maximilian of Austria on the Mexican throne. Not until the Civil War ended did Napoleon heed the protests of Secretary Seward and withdraw his troops from Mexico. Maximilian was subsequently executed by Mexican partisans under Benito Juarez.

Two days after issuing the Preliminary Proclamation, the President announced that at his discretion the writ of habeas corpus could be suspended anywhere in the United States. That was quite a leap of executive authority and really required the approval of Congress. But this was war, and the President felt that there could and probably would be circumstances in which he must exercise extraordinary power to safeguard the liberty of the American people. Congress obliged in March 1863 by passing the Habeas Corpus Act, which allowed the President to suspend the writ for the duration of the war.

Democrats, led by Clement Vallandigham, denounced this "imperial military despotism." Called "Copperheads" by their opponents because they wore "copper penny" badges to signify their willingness to pursue a conciliatory policy toward the South, these Peace Democrats engaged in antiadministration activities that only succeeded in discrediting their cause because they adversely affected the war effort. When the Confederates inflicted one of the worst military defeats of the war on Union forces, now commanded by General Ambrose Burnside, at Fredericksburg, Virginia, on December 13, 1862, Copperheads were horrified by the carnage and demanded to know when the butchery would end. Over 10,000 Union soldiers were killed or wounded in this engagement. Lincoln replaced Burnside with General Joseph Hooker.

To assist the military operation, Congress passed both a bill for the recruitment of 150,000 black soldiers in early January 1863 and the

Conscription Act on March 3, by which all men between the ages of twenty and forty-five were subject to a draft. However, it exempted those who paid a commutation fee of $300 or hired a substitute to enlist for three years. Opposition to this law exploded in the draft riots in New York City in mid-July 1863, violence that actually masked a race riot.

The Confederates also resorted to a draft. On April 16, 1862, they passed a Conscription Act that applied to all white men between the ages of twenty and thirty-five. Certain occupations were exempted, and substitutes were permitted. But the manpower problem in the South became more acute as the war continued year after year.

Although Confederate forces won a stunning victory over a Union army that was twice their size at the Battle of Chancellorsville in May 1863, the war began to shift toward an ultimate Union victory. At Chancellorsville, Lee lost over 10,000 troops killed and wounded. This loss, which he could ill afford, included "Stonewall" Jackson, who was shot by his own men on May 2.

General Ulysses S. Grant captured Vicksburg, Mississippi, in July, thereby slicing the Confederacy in two and bringing the entire Mississippi River region under Union control. Lee's second attempt at invading the North was turned back at Gettysburg, Pennsylvania, by numerically superior Union troops under the command of Major General George G. Meade. However, Meade allowed Lee to escape into Virginia without attacking him. Some 50,000 men were killed or wounded at Gettysburg, and on November 17, 1863, the cemetery at the battlefield was dedicated, in a ceremony in which the main speaker was Edward Everett. But it was the brief comments by Abraham Lincoln that are still remembered. We cannot dedicate or consecrate or hallow this ground, he said. The brave men, living and dead, did that far better than we can ever attempt. Rather it is for us to be "dedicated to the great task remaining before us," that we here resolve that "these dead shall not have died in vain—that this nation, under God, shall have a new birth of freedom—and that government of the people, by the people, for the people, shall not perish from the earth."

A new birth of freedom! That is precisely what the war produced, and Lincoln found the noble language to convey that miraculous vision.

With these victories and those at Lookout Mountain and Mission-ary Ridge around Chattanooga, which routed the Confederates in late November 1863, thereby opening a route through Georgia to the sea, Lincoln issued a Proclamation of Amnesty and Reconstruction on December 8, 1863, that declared that when ten percent of those persons in the seceded states who voted in the presidential election of 1860 swore an oath of loyalty to the United States, they might then form a government without slavery, which he would recognize, and reestablish themselves within the Union. It was the first effort to bring about a reconstruction of the fractured nation. And it was a relatively mild plan, one Radical Republicans strongly opposed. In their view Congress must administer the restoration of the Union, not the President.

Meanwhile the war ground to an inevitable end. General Ulysses S. Grant, promoted to the rank of lieutenant general and given supreme command of the Union forces, assumed control of the Army of the Potomac, now numbering over 100,000. On May 5, 1864, he began his monthlong Wilderness campaign in which he planned to pursue his line of attack if it took all summer and thereby shred Lee's army of 60,000 to bits. But the slaughter was horrendous. It is estimated that in the battles of Spotsylvania and Cold Harbor, Grant's losses added up to nearly 60,000, as against half that number suffered by Lee. But there was no way the Confederates could replace their losses. The Confederacy was bleeding to death. Grant then swung his army south to Petersburg, about twenty miles below Richmond, expecting to cut Lee's supply lines. He was unable to capture Petersburg and so laid siege to the city in June 1864; the siege lasted nine months.

Meanwhile, General William T. Sherman set out with 100,000 troops from Chattanooga, Tennessee, and headed toward Atlanta, Georgia. As Vicksburg had sliced the Confederacy vertically, east from west, the Chattanooga victory allowed Sherman to initiate an invasion that would bisect the South horizontally, upper from lower. On September 2 he oc-cupied Atlanta, and after destroying whatever supplies or materials that might prove helpful to the enemy, he headed for the sea.

In Congress, Radical Republicans responded to Lincoln's ten-percent plan by passing the Wade-Davis bill, which required a majority of the electorate—not ten percent—to swear to past and present loyalty before any government could be formed. It demanded the abolition of slavery and stipulated that no one could vote who had held a state or Confederate office or who had borne arms against the United States.

Lincoln, who had already recognized Louisiana and Arkansas as restored to the Union under his ten-percent plan, pocket-vetoed the Wade-Davis bill. He said he was not committed to any single plan of reconstruction. He also denied that Congress had the authority to abolish slavery in the states. That would require a constitutional amendment.

Radicals shot back with the Wade-Davis Manifesto, in which they asserted the absolute authority of Congress to deal with the rebellious states and instructed the President to execute the laws of the country, not legislate them. As commander in chief, Lincoln's job was to put down the rebellion, the document declared, and leave the political reorganization of the seceded states to Congress.

Despite their differences the Radicals supported Lincoln's renomination for President at the Republican convention in Baltimore on June 7, 1864, and were delighted with the choice of Andrew Johnson, the loyalist military governor of Tennessee, as Vice President because Johnson had been a particularly vociferous critic of secessionists when he served as a member of the Joint Committee on the Conduct of the War. The purpose behind nominating Johnson was obvious: the formation of a National Union ticket that might attract Democratic voters and symbolize the restoration of the Union.

The Democrats met in Chicago in late August and nominated General McClellan and George H. Pendleton of Ohio. Under Copperhead control, the convention adopted a platform that called for the immediate cessation of hostilities and the establishment of peace on the basis of a federated union of states, a platform that McClellan repudiated.

The National Union ticket was strengthened by Sherman's capture of Atlanta and his continuing march toward the sea. That victory may well have made the difference as to which party would win. Lincoln was overwhelmingly reelected in November, with an electoral vote of 212 to 21 and a popular vote of 2,206,938 to McClellan's 1,803,787.

When Congress reconvened, the President asked that an amendment ending slavery throughout the United States be adopted and sent to the states for ratification. The Senate had already passed it the previous spring. It was now up to the House. On January 31, 1865, the vote was called. The galleries were packed, and in the chamber sat the Chief Justice of the United States, Salmon P. Chase; several associate justices; a number of senators; several members of the cabinet; and a group of foreign ministers. And the amendment passed, 119 to 56. With the announcement of the result, the entire House burst into a storm of screams, shouts, applause, and stamping of feet. Women waved their handkerchiefs; men threw their arms around each other; "and cheer after cheer, and burst after burst followed." For ten minutes the noise level did not abate. Finally adjournment was moved "in honor of the sublime and immortal event." On December 18, 1865, three-fourths of the states ratified this Thirteenth Amendment.

By late 1864 the war was clearly coming to an end. Sherman cut a 60-mile-wide, 300-mile path to the sea, destroying homes, public buildings, factories, cotton gins, railroads, and bridges, or confiscating anything that might be regarded as contraband or assist the rebels in their effort to stay the course. Looting was commonplace. Savannah fell on December 22, after which Sherman headed north through the Carolinas, burning towns and cities in his wake. Columbia, the capital of South Carolina, was a prize target, and its destruction on February 17, 1865, predictable, although retreating Confederate soldiers were later blamed by Sherman for the tragedy. A determined Sherman plowed straight ahead, and an increasingly demoralized Confederate force could not bar his way.

Lincoln made clear how he now intended to proceed with reconstruction. In his second inaugural address on March 4, 1865, he said, "With malice toward none, with charity for all, with firmness in the right . . . let us strive on to finish the work we are in, to bind up the nation's wounds . . . to do all which may achieve and cherish a just and lasting peace among ourselves and with all nations."

At the same time, Grant pressed forward in Virginia, and Lee was forced to retreat from Petersburg and Richmond in the hope of joining forces with a Confederate force in North Carolina, commanded by the very capable General Joseph Johnston. But Grant blocked his path and on April 7 asked for Lee's surrender. His army now numbering only 30,000 and practically surrounded, Lee had little choice. At Appomattox Court House the two men met on April 9 and arranged the terms of surrender. Lee's troops were paroled so they could return home, and his officers were permitted to keep their sidearms. In addition, all the rebels were allowed to retain their own horses and mules. All other equipment was surrendered to Union forces. Grant did not ask for or receive Lee's sword in surrender.

After four harrowing years of murderous combat the war had ended. The South was totally defeated in a lost cause. The numbers of dead on both sides were staggering. The Union suffered 359,528 dead and 275,175 wounded; the Confederates lost approximately 258,000 dead and 100,000 wounded.

In the North people shouted their gratitude when they heard the news of Lee's surrender. Washington was "delirious with gladness" when General Grant and his troops came marching through the town. April 13 was "a day of general rejoicing. . . . The stars and stripes waved over the public and many of the private buildings. . . . As night came on . . . bonfires blazed in the streets, and fireworks lit up the sky. In the forts and camps around the city blazed huge bonfires, while the heavy siege guns thundered their joyful approval of peace." It was the same in many other cities. The horrible war had ended.

Then tragedy struck. Lincoln had visited Richmond, and only upon his return to Washington did he learn of Lee's surrender. Once more, at a cabinet meeting, he reiterated the need for conciliation and a swift return to a reunited country. In his last public address on April 11, he spoke from the balcony of the White House to a crowd celebrating the Union victory. "We meet this evening, not in sorrow, but in gladness of heart. The evacuations of Petersburg and Richmond, and the surrender of the principal insurgent army, give hope of a righteous and speedy peace. . . . Let us all join in doing the acts necessary to restore the proper practical relations between these [seceded] states and the Union."

On April 14 Lincoln attended a performance of *Our American Cousin* in Ford's Theater, where John Wilkes Booth, a distinguished if crazed actor, entered the President's box shortly after ten PM and shot Lincoln at point-blank range. The dying man was carried across the street to a lodging house where he succumbed at seven-thirty the following morning. He had saved the Union, only to die before completing the task of reconstruction.

"Now he belongs to the ages," intoned Edwin Stanton, the secretary of war. And now Andrew Johnson was President, and would in the following months and years bring about a titanic battle between the executive and legislative branches of the government, a battle that would have repercussions for generations to come.

6

Reconstruction and the Gilded Age

THREE HOURS AFTER Lincoln died, Andrew Johnson took the oath of office as President, and the Radical Republicans were ecstatic. They thought they would have no difficulty determining the course by which the rebellious South would be reconstructed. They reckoned that they could control this Tennessean and that he would summon them to a special session of Congress or wait until they reconvened in December 1865 before initiating any presidential action.

They thought wrong. With the final surrender of the Confederate forces, President Johnson basically adopted Lincoln's plan and recognized the governments already established in Arkansas, Louisiana, Tennessee, and Virginia by the late President. Johnson also issued two proclamations in which he appointed provisional governors in the remaining seven southern states for the purpose of calling state conventions that were expected to nullify the ordinances of secession, repudiate their Confederate debt, and ratify the Thirteenth Amendment. He granted amnesty to all rebels who took an oath of allegiance, but he exempted those who had held high office in the Confederate government or the military. He also exempted from amnesty those who owned $20,000 or more in property, a prejudice against the rich and upper classes of southern society that reflected his bitterness over the poverty he suffered as a youth. However, those exempted could apply directly to him for individual pardons, and only those with amnesty or pardons could participate in reconstructing their states.

Immediately, the Radicals recognized not only that the President planned to undertake the Reconstruction of the South on his own but also that he intended to complete it before the Thirty-Ninth Congress reconvened. This realization greatly angered those who believed that Congress, not the President, was the lawful, constitutional body to re-unify the country.

Thaddeus Stevens wasted no time challenging Johnson's actions. From Philadelphia he wrote the President and expressed his displea-sure. "I hope I may be excused for putting briefs on paper," he declared; "what I intended to say to you orally. Reconstruction is a delicate ques-tion. . . . It is a question for the Legislative power exclusively."

Exclusively! That stated the Radical position exactly. "Better call an extra session," Stevens instructed, "than to allow many to think that the executive was approaching usurpation." He also advised the Presi-dent to stop the wholesale pardoning of former rebels. The presump-tion of Stevens in speaking this way and dictating to the chief executive what he should or should not do was unbelievable. Stevens followed through on his return to Washington by confronting Johnson and insisting that if he, the President, persisted in executing his plan of Reconstruction, he could expect no support or cooperation from Re-publicans in Congress.

Johnson remained calm throughout the interview. He appealed for understanding and harmony. The people of this nation need to put the war behind them in order to restore peace, he said. And that was what he was trying to do. Indeed by December every one of the remaining seven Confederate states, except Texas, had done exactly what he had instructed them to do, and he had recognized them. Four months later Texas complied with the requirements.

When Congress convened on December 4, Johnson informed the members in his first message that the Union was restored, but they re-sponded by disregarding his announcement and establishing a Joint Committee of Fifteen on Reconstruction with nine members from the House and six from the Senate to report on whether the rebel states should be represented in Congress. Moreover, until this committee issued its report and was approved by Congress, "no member shall be received into either house from any of the said so-called confederate states." Whereupon the representatives from several of the southern states who had shown up when this Congress convened quietly withdrew from the House chamber. Although the Joint Committee had Stevens as one of the members, it was essentially moderate in composition and was chaired by Senator William P. Fessenden of Maine. During their meetings together the committee members heard repeated testimony from an assortment of witnesses hostile to the Johnson amnesty policy and insisted that if representatives from the rebel states were readmitted "the condition of the freedmen would be very little better than that of the slaves."

As a matter of fact, several Confederate states had already passed a series of "Black Codes" defining the condition of the freedmen in such a way as to keep them bound to the land. Although they were freed, these codes virtually restored them to slavery. In the House of Representatives Thaddeus Stevens railed against these codes, insisting that the South should be treated as "conquered provinces." "We have turned over, or about to turn loose, four million slaves without a hut to shelter them or a cent in their pockets. The infernal laws of slavery have prevented them from an education, understanding the commonest laws of contract, or of managing the ordinary business of life. This Congress is bound to provide for them until they can take care of themselves."

In the Senate, Charles Sumner, having recovered from the beating inflicted by Bully Brooks, essentially agreed with Stevens, only he interpreted secession as an act in which the South had committed "state suicide." As such only Congress could set the conditions by which these states could be admitted back into the Union.

In approaching the problem of Reconstruction, Congress faced a section of the country that lay in ruins: cities and plantations burned, transportation wrecked, and billions invested in slavery wiped out. Stevens expected to transform the South through a redistribution of land in an effort to destroy the power structure of the planter aristocracy, and provide the former slaves, now freedmen, with enough land from the forfeited property of the enemy so that they could support themselves and their families. Congress rejected this proposal. Instead, it passed the Freedmen's Bureau on March 3, 1865 (and repassed the measure on July 16 over a presidential veto), and a supplementary act in

February 1866, that made permanent a bureau to provide for the freedmen and southern refugees, both white and black. The act also granted judicial power to the bureau to protect the freedmen against discrimination. It was sponsored by a number of moderate Republicans, such as Fessenden and Lyman Trumbull of Illinois, chairman of the Senate Judiciary Committee, who sought to work with the President to counteract the Black Codes. Unfortunately for Johnson, he chose not to seek an alliance with moderates and declared that this new bill was nothing less than a gigantic pork barrel and prohibitively expensive. The House overrode his veto, 109 to 40, but the Senate sustained it when five moderate Republicans agreed about the cost.

Other moderates were dismayed by the President's action. They tried again by passing the Civil Rights Act of 1866, a bill that "embodied the moderates' position" and granted civil rights to all persons born in the United States, except Native Americans. It spelled out rights to be "enjoyed equally without regard to race," such as initiating lawsuits and contracts, giving testimony in court, and obtaining "security of person and property." It authorized federal officers to bring suit in federal courts against violators, and it imposed fines and imprisonment on anyone who deprived citizens of their rights. To placate the President it did not grant political rights to freedmen. That was made very explicit by Trumbull.

This civil rights legislation was "the first statutory definition of the rights of American citizenship" and "reflected how ideas once considered Radical had been adopted" by a large number of Republicans. And it applied to the North, where discriminatory laws had been enacted and were still operative, as well as to the South. As such it was not strictly a Reconstruction measure.

Nevertheless, Johnson vetoed it. He claimed that it violated "all our experience as a people" and constituted "a stride toward centralization and the concentration of all legislative powers in the national Government." Furthermore, in an outburst that was blatantly racist, Johnson said that he doubted blacks could qualify for citizenship and insisted that the states had the right to discriminate on the basis of race.

Both houses of Congress erupted. Moderates were appalled—and completely alienated. They wanted to cooperate with Johnson but now felt totally rejected. The *New York Herald*, on March 28, 1866, called the veto "a declaration of war." Clearly, cried the outraged Trumbull on the Senate floor, the President will approve no bill that would protect "the freedmen in their liberty and their property." Both the House and the Senate promptly overrode the veto. The Civil Rights Act of 1866 was the first major piece of legislation in American history to be enacted over the objections of the President.

It was important in another way. In effect it announced that the national government had the responsibility of protecting the rights of citizens, not the states. The concerns about states' rights that had plagued the nation for generations were swept away. From now on, equality before the law would be enforced by the national government.

By his veto, Johnson lost whatever support he had once enjoyed among moderate Republicans. They quietly drifted over to the side of the Radicals. Any future vetoes were sure to be overridden. What the President had done was commit political suicide.

Still, a genuine concern for the constitutionality of the Civil Rights Act bothered many members, so the Joint Committee of Fifteen proposed the Fourteenth Amendment to the Constitution, which defined citizenship in a manner that included black males and forbade any state from infringing the rights of citizens without due process of law. It abrogated the three-fifths clause of the Constitution in calculating representation in the lower House of Congress, which thereby added twelve southern seats when these states were readmitted.

Since this amendment specifically introduced the word "male" into the Constitution, feminists such as Susan B. Anthony and Elizabeth Cady Stanton felt betrayed. Men protected their own rights, they complained, but not the rights of females. Very well, women would now rely on their own efforts, and in 1869 they formed the National Woman Suffrage Association, which admitted only women. But the American Woman Suffrage Association, formed immediately thereafter, welcomed both men and women. The two groups subsequently merged under Stanton's leadership and became the National Woman Suffrage Association. The fight for suffrage equality now began in earnest.

Tennessee ratified the Fourteenth Amendment and was immediately readmitted to the Union on July 24, 1866. But the other southern states refused, in the hope that the midterm election in 1866 would result in a defeat of the Radicals and the election of a Congress that would provide a milder form of Reconstruction. As a result of their rejection, Congress made ratification of the Fourteenth Amendment a condition for the southern states to win readmission to the Union.

Conditions in the South worsened. Race riots broke out in Memphis and New Orleans in the spring and summer of 1866. In Memphis an altercation between white and black drivers of horse-drawn hacks on May 1 started a free-for-all that ended with forty-eight persons dead (all but two were blacks); five black women raped; and many schools, churches, and homes burned to the ground. Twelve weeks later, New Orleans erupted in violence on the opening day of a constitutional convention that had been summoned to enfranchise freedmen. A massacre of blacks in the convention hall resulted, even though white flags of surrender were raised. These unfortunate incidents only proved to northerners that the South was unregenerate, that it was still arrogant and defiant. It proved that the rebel states were not ready to be restored to full membership in the Union.

In an effort to turn the situation around in this election year, President Johnson undertook a speaking tour of the North, stopping off at Philadelphia and New York and then swinging around to Cleveland and St. Louis—a tour that was laughingly called a "swing around the circle." Accompanied by General Grant, Admiral David Farragut, and Secretary of the Navy Gideon Welles, Johnson stumped the North; but during his speeches he frequently lost his temper, giving his opponents additional ammunition with which to ridicule and demean him. At times he seemed hysterical, wild, certainly unpresidential. "I have been traduced," he ranted. "I have been slandered. I have been maligned. I have been called Judas Iscariot. . . . Who has been my Christ that I have played the Judas role? Was it Thad Stevens?"

The tour was a disaster, and the electorate showed its disgust by trouncing the Democrats at the polls. Republicans now had a two-thirds majority with which to override any future presidential veto. Johnson was completely neutralized. "The President has no power to control or influence anybody," claimed Senator James W. Grimes of Iowa, "and legislation will be carried on entirely regardless of his opinions or wishes."

"It is now our turn to act," declared Representative James A. Garfield of Ohio. The Confederate states "would not co-operate with us in rebuilding what they destroyed. We must remove the rubbish and build from the bottom." George Julian of Indiana agreed. The South does not need oaths of loyalty that invite men to perjure themselves. What they need is "government, the strong arm of power, outstretched from the central authority here in Washington."

And that arm of power struck with the return of Congress after the election. On January 3, 1867, Thaddeus Stevens introduced the first Reconstruction Act, which after several amendments became known as the Military Reconstruction Act. It divided the South into five military districts and gave the commander of each district the right to declare martial law in order to preserve order, protect blacks, and begin the process of restoring the former Confederate states to the Union. The process involved calling new constitutional conventions, elected by blacks and those whites who had not participated in the rebellion. These conventions must guarantee black suffrage and ratify the Fourteenth Amendment. Naturally, Johnson vetoed the bill, and Congress overrode it on March 2, 1867.

Congress then proceeded to add Supplementary Reconstruction Acts, which directed the military commanders to begin the enrollment of voters, and after a proper constitution had been written and approved by the reformed electorate, to put it into operation. Congress, of course, reserved to itself the exclusive right to review each new constitution, end military rule at the proper time, and accept states back into the Union and seat their representatives. It also passed the Army Appropriations Act, which directed that the President, in his capacity as commander in chief, must issue all military orders through the General of the Army, U. S. Grant, whose office could not be moved from Washington without Senate approval. In the Tenure of Office Act, Congress further restricted presidential authority from removing officials approved by the Senate without first obtaining the consent of the Senate. "Though the President is Commander-in-Chief," ranted Stevens, "Congress is his commander; and God willing, he shall obey. He and his minions shall learn that this is not a Government of kings and satraps, but a Government of the people, and that Congress is the people."

In the South the provisional governments established by Johnson were swept away, and the registration of blacks and acceptable whites began. Those white southerners who cooperated with Radical Reconstruction were labeled "scalawags" and those northern whites who traveled into the military districts to advance the Radical cause were called "carpetbaggers." It was not surprising that when eligible voters were tabulated, at least five southern states—Louisiana, Mississippi, Alabama, Florida, and South Carolina—had a majority of blacks. There were over 700,000 black registered voters, compared with 60,000 white registered voters.

Over the next several months these southern conventions met and prepared constitutions as required. By June 1868, six of the former Confederate states were admitted, and with their approval the Fourteenth Amendment was ratified on July 28, 1868. The six included Arkansas (June 22), Florida (June 25), North Carolina (July 4), Louisiana (July 9), South Carolina (July 9), and Alabama (July 13). Georgia had been restored on July 21, but Congress did not seat its representatives. It was readmitted on July 15, 1870, and its members took their seats the following January.

President Johnson tried to block Radical Reconstruction by removing those officers and commanders who he felt were particularly ardent in enforcing the Reconstruction Acts. Accordingly, he removed several military commanders, and on August 12, 1867, he dismissed Secretary of War Edwin Stanton, a holdover from the Lincoln administration, and replaced him with General Grant. In complying with the Tenure of Office Act, Johnson submitted to the Senate his reasons for suspending Stanton, which the upper house rejected, 36 to 6, in January 1868. Grant was persuaded by the Radicals to relinquish his office, and Stanton resumed his position.

Undaunted and still defiant, Johnson sacked Stanton a second time on February 21, 1868, accusing Grant of treachery, and appointed Adjutant General Lorenzo Thomas to take Stanton's place. That same day, Representative John Covode of Pennsylvania offered a motion on the House floor that "Andrew Johnson, President of the United States, be impeached for high crimes and misdemeanors in office." The motion was referred to the Joint Committee on Reconstruction, which in turn brought the motion to the floor for a vote with its approval. After an intense debate, the House, by a vote of 126 to 47, gave its approval on February 24, 1868; a committee was formed to prepare the articles of impeachment; and on March 2 the committee brought in nine charges. These articles dealt mainly with alleged violations of the Tenure of Office Act, but they also included accusations of a conspiracy by intimidation and threats to prevent Stanton from holding office. The following day the House added two more articles: one accusing the President of "violent utterances" and the other a catchall called the omnibus article. Seven members were appointed to prosecute the charges in the Senate; the most prominent of these were Ben "Beast" Butler, Thaddeus Stevens, George Boutwell, and John A. Bingham.

Opening statements by the members before the Senate began on March 30 with Chief Justice Salmon Portland Chase presiding. But the prosecutors merely harangued the senators and assumed that the ultimate verdict was a foregone conclusion. They did not offer tangible evidence of "high crimes and misdemeanors."

On May 16 the senators voted the omnibus article first, and Johnson escaped removal by a vote of 35 in favor to 19 opposed, just one vote shy of the required two-thirds necessary for conviction. The nineteen included seven Republicans and twelve Democrats. Senator Edmund G. Ross of Kansas, a Radical Republican, showed courage and conviction by voting for acquittal. When several more articles failed to convict Johnson, the Senate on May 26 adjourned as a court of impeachment. When Stevens was informed of the verdict, he cried out, "The country is going to the devil." He died shortly thereafter. When asked about the court's decision, Senator James Grimes of Iowa declared that they had been asked to make a decision based on politics. "I can not agree to destroy the harmonious working of the Constitution for the sake of getting rid of an unacceptable President."

The decision marked the end of the kind of presidential power exercised by Abraham Lincoln. Johnson had tried and failed to control Reconstruction. By its actions, Congress had assumed command of national policy in restoring the Union. This is the way it should be, insisted Senator John Sherman of Ohio: the executive "should be subordinate to the legislative branch," just as the founders intended.

SHORTLY AFTERWARD, THE Republican national nominating convention met in Chicago and on the first ballot chose Ulysses S. Grant as its presidential candidate, along with Schuyler Colfax, the Radical Speaker of the House of Representatives, as his running mate. The Democrats nominated Horatio Seymour, former governor of New York; and Francis P. Blair of Missouri, who were defeated by a lopsided vote in the electoral college (80 to 214) by the Republican ticket.

The strength and determination of the Radicals were again demonstrated by the passage of the Fifteenth Amendment to the Constitution on February 26, 1869. This amendment forbade any state to deny a citizen the right to vote on account of race, color, or previous condition of servitude. All unreconstructed states had to ratify this amendment before they could be considered ready for readmission to the Union. Virginia was restored on January 26, 1870; Mississippi on February 23; and Texas on March 30. The Fifteenth Amendment was declared ratified on March 30, 1870.

These reconstructed southern states sent the first of a long line of African-Americans to Congress as both representatives and senators. Hiram R. Revels, a Republican from Mississippi, won election to the Senate. A Methodist-Episcopal minister, he had served as chaplain of a black regiment during the Civil War. He took his seat on February 25, 1870. In the House, the first African-American to gain election was Joseph H. Rainey, a Republican from South Carolina, who was sworn in on December 12, 1870. He had been a barber on a Confederate blockade runner and was the first black man to preside over the House when Speaker James G. Blaine of Maine turned the gavel over to him in May 1874.

Other African-Americans who were House members during these years included Benjamin S. Turner of Alabama, Robert C. De Large and Robert B. Elliott of South Carolina, Josiah T. Walls of Florida, and Jefferson F. Long of Georgia—all Republicans. A total of sixteen African-Americans served in Congress during Reconstruction, but each served only one or two terms.

Throughout Reconstruction military courts were employed to carry out the directives of the various laws passed by Congress. But in *Ex parte Milligan*, the Supreme Court ruled that martial law was unconstitutional where civil courts were in operation. Fearful that the court might invalidate the Reconstruction Acts, Congress passed legislation in March 1868 that denied it jurisdiction in the matter. Still, the Court upheld the right of Congress to reconstruct and in *Texas v. White* affirmed the argument by Andrew Jackson and Abraham Lincoln that the Union was indissoluble. More important, through a number of decisions over the next several years it slowly gained recognition as the final interpreter of the Constitution, a claim not specifically stated in the document itself.

Although the Fifteenth Amendment forbade states from denying citizens the right to vote on account of race, it did not forbid states from enacting literacy, educational, and property tests that whites would later invoke when military reconstruction ended. With these instruments they effectively disenfranchised African-Americans and ultimately restored white rule in the South. They claimed to have "Redeemed" their states from what they called "Black Reconstruction."

But one of the more effective ways of preventing blacks from voting was by intimidation. The Ku Klux Klan, founded in Pulaski, Tennessee, in 1866, with the former Confederate general Nathan Bedford Forrest as the first Grand Wizard, aimed specifically at restoring white rule through violence and lawlessness by striking terror among blacks if they dared to vote. Lynchings and beatings became daily occurrences, especially during elections, and it has been estimated that approximately 400 hangings of African-Americans occurred between 1868 and 1871.

This resort to violence only convinced northerners that enforcement of federal law by federal troops in the South was necessary and justified. Accordingly, Congress passed three Enforcement Acts in 1870–1871, the first two of which outlawed the use of force or intimidation to prevent citizens from exercising their right of suffrage and provided federal supervisors to oversee the registration of voters. The third Enforcement Act, also called the Ku Klux Klan Act, empowered the President to use the military to protect black voters from intimidation and violence and to suspend the writ of habeas corpus when necessary. Not until the Democrats returned to power some twenty years later were these "Force Acts," as they called them, repealed. But the Grant administration slowly moved away from employing the military and the courts to carry out Congressional Reconstruction, and consequently whites gradually "Redeemed" their states from Republican rule. More and more ex-Confederates were elected to Congress, including the former Vice President of the Confederacy, Alexander H. Stephens; six cabinet officers; fifty-eight members of the Confederate Congress; and nine high-ranking army officers. The South was slowly being reclaimed by its former ruling class.

But Congress did attempt to protect certain rights of African-Americans from infringement by whites. The Civil Rights Act of 1875 prohibited racial discrimination in public accommodations, public transportation, and jury selection. The bill was passed and signed by President Grant on March 1, 1875.

It was a landmark event. It culminated what was a constitutional revolution. Together with ratification of the Thirteenth, Fourteenth, and Fifteenth amendments, this Civil Right Act extended equality under the law to millions. Democracy in America had made a noticeable advance. It only remained to grant these privileges to all persons regardless of gender.

AND A NEW age began, an age that extended to the end of the century, an age Mark Twain and coauthor Charles Dudley Warner described in a book depicting American society. This society was profoundly corrupt. The main characters in their book are involved in a railroad bribery scheme in which the government is a participant. It was a "tale of today," the coauthors wrote in 1873, because it typified business operations throughout the nation following the Civil War. The book was titled *The Gilded Age*.

Henry Adams, an historian of note and a contemporary, described this era as "poor in purpose and barren in results. One might search the list of Congress, Judiciary, and Executive during the twenty-five years, 1870–1895, and find little but damaged reputations." There was more than simply damaged reputations, but the damage was quite extensive and reached right up the political chain of command.

The industrialization of the country, stimulated by the Civil War and continuing unabated to the end of the nineteenth century, resulted in large measure from the direct and indirect support and subsidy given it by government, especially the national government. The railroads throughout the nation expanded from over 30,000 miles of track to an estimated 200,000, and this expansion involved extensive public assistance, particularly land grants. Protective tariffs were another form of support and stimulated such manufactures as steel, copper, and wool. In addition, federal banking and monetary policies attracted both foreign and domestic investors.

Money flowed, bringing unheard-of wealth to those individuals who knew how to obtain privileges that would advance their goals. Of course, it came at a price. Bribery, conspiracy, conflict of interest, blackmail, and other assorted crimes were commonplace during the Gilded Age. It was a matter of recognizing the appropriate targets. Quite obviously, for the railroads and those needing tariff protection the targets were congressmen and officers of the national administration. As it turned out, during this era such targets proved to be willing recipients of whatever largess was offered. Congressmen chose to accept them as gifts in appreciation and recognition of their status and importance. They liked to believe there was nothing wrong in providing favors through legislative action and then receiving appropriate acknowledgment for their efforts.

Railroads offered free passes, stock in the company, and even cash to appropriate legislators, especially chairmen of key committees. Some congressmen even held executive positions or served on railroad boards. Representative Grenville Dodge, for example, held the position of chief engineer of the Union Pacific all the while he represented his Iowa district in the House of Representatives. The so-called financier of the Civil War, Jay Cooke, regularly conferred financial favors on congressmen and even held the mortgage on the home of Speaker James G. Blaine.

Sooner or later these cozy and usually improper arrangements were certain to explode into public print, and in the decade of the 1870s they did. The first and perhaps most notorious was the Credit Mobilier scandal. It was uncovered by Charles A. Dana's *New York Sun* on September 4, 1872, and exposed the involvement of not only the former Speaker of the House and current Vice President of the United States, Schuyler Colfax, but Henry Wilson of Massachusetts, who succeeded Colfax as Grant's running mate in the presidential election of 1872. Also included were George Boutwell—the secretary of the treasury and one of the prosecutors of the Johnson impeachment trial—and at least a dozen congressmen, including James A. Garfield, chairman of the Committee on Appropriations; Henry L. Dawes, chairman of

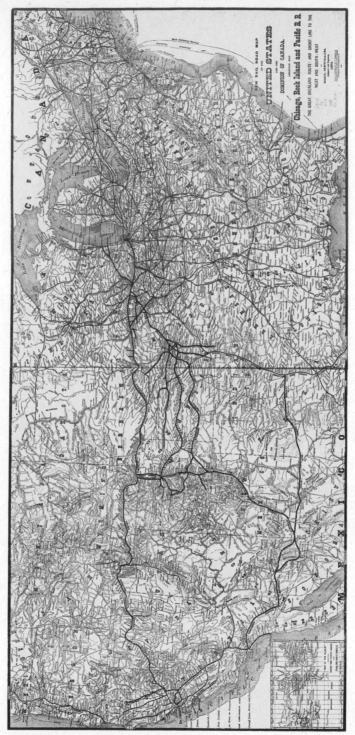

The extent of the railroads in the United States in 1880

Ways and Means; William D. ("Pig Iron") Kelley, chairman of the Civil Service Committee; John A. Bingham, chairman of the Judiciary Committee and another of Johnson's prosecutors; and Glenn W. Scofield, chairman of the Naval Committee. Quite a group!

Credit Mobilier was a dummy construction company formed by the Union Pacific Railroad to provide profits from the building of the line which were distributed to worthy congressmen in return for political favors. Republican Representative Oakes Ames of Massachusetts sold the stock to select members of the House, who were expected to use their political influence to benefit the company. It was alleged that to show their appreciation these congressmen helped kill a bill that would have regulated the Union Pacific's railroad rates.

These revelations came late in the presidential election of 1872 and therefore had little effect on its outcome. Grant was reelected, and his running mate, Henry Wilson, won the Vice Presidency. They defeated the Liberal Republican ticket of Horace Greeley, editor of the *New York Tribune*, and B. Gratz Brown. This Liberal Republican faction had developed within the Republican Party in 1871 in an effort to provide needed civil service and tariff reforms. It was led by the German-born Senator Carl Schurz, a former Union general.

The Democratic Party chose to endorse Greeley and Brown rather than name its own candidates. A Prohibition Party selected James Black and John Russell as its ticket. Throughout the campaign, Republicans "waved the bloody shirt" as a reminder of the recent rebellion and successfully linked the Liberal Republicans, who opposed further federal intervention in the South, with unreconstructed southern rebels. Greeley himself was a feeble candidate and died a few weeks after the election.

Once Congress reconvened following the election, a committee was immediately formed to investigate the Credit Mobilier scandal. The accused testified before the committee, and Ames denied that he had ever bribed a member. All he did was sell stock to his colleagues as a sound investment. It was business, nothing more. But the committee found Ames "guilty of selling to members of Congress shares of stock in the Credit Mobilier of America, for prices much below the true value of such stock, with the intent thereby to influence the votes and decisions of such members in matters to be brought before Congress for action." It also recommended his expulsion from the House. But the House, demonstrating genuine concern for a colleague, by a vote of 115 to 110 and 15 abstentions, chose merely to "condemn" his conduct. When the decision was announced, something strange and unbelievable happened: Republicans who had just voted to condemn Ames crowded around him and asked his pardon. "We know you are innocent," they babbled, "but we had to do it in order to satisfy our constituents."

As for the other members mentioned in the scandal, the committee declared that they might have been "indiscreet" in accepting stock in the company, but that they were not guilty of criminal intent. In fact most of them returned the stock as soon as the scandal came to light and denied making any appreciable financial gain.

Although Ames was not expelled from the House, his term in office was due to expire momentarily, and he died shortly thereafter. As for the others implicated in the scandal, most of them survived, except Schuyler Colfax who had contradicted himself so often during his appearances before the committee that the public turned against him and his career ended in disgrace.

Revelations of other scandals soon followed. Congress busied itself setting up committees to investigate several charges initiated by newspapers, such as the *St. Louis Democrat*, that exposed the "Whiskey Ring" in the spring of 1875. And, as it turned out, President Grant's personal secretary, General Orville E. Babcock, allegedly directed the "Ring," by which the government was defrauded of millions of dollars in taxes through the sale of forged revenue stamps. Indictments of more than 200 individuals resulted, many in the Treasury Department. Although indicted himself, Babcock escaped imprisonment through the intervention of the President.

The Secretary of War, William W. Belknap, was impeached by the House on March 2, 1876, for accepting bribes for the sale of trading posts in the Indian Territory. He resigned to avoid a trial in the Senate. But the Treasury and War departments were not the only ones to dabble in embezzlement and fraud; the Freedmen's Bureau, the Navy Department, the Interior Department, the Post Office, and the attorney general's office helped themselves to whatever largess they could identify, resulting in numerous indictments, resignations, and, on occasion, convictions.

One disgrace followed another, and it seemed as though few governmental agencies could resist the temptation to put their hands in the till. Congress itself plundered the Treasury in March 1873 by passing the so-called "Salary Grab Act," by which the President's salary was doubled to $50,000 and the salaries of representatives and senators were raised from $5,000 to $7,500. Worse, the raise for congressmen was awarded retroactively, thereby giving each member a $5,000 bonus. But the public reacted so vehemently that Congress promptly repealed the law at its very next session, except for the President's increase and that of the judges of the Supreme Court.

And the former Speaker of the House of Representatives, James G. Blaine, now the minority leader and favored candidate for the Republican presidential nomination in 1876, was also accused of offering worthless bonds as collateral for a loan of $64,000 which he had received from the Union Pacific Railroad and which he had never been asked to repay. Supposedly he had used his influence as Speaker to obtain for the railroad a generous land grant. In a dramatic speech from the floor of the House he denied the charges, and his effort was so convincing that his audience broke out in wild applause.

The consequences of these scandals and the involvement of Congress with big business were bad enough for the administration and the Republican Party, but the onset of the Panic of 1873 proved devastating. This was an economic depression that hit hard and lasted from 1873 to 1879. Triggered by the wild speculation in railroads, dishonest banking practices, overexpansion in industry, commerce, and agriculture, and the failure of Jay Cooke's banking firm, the Panic generated widespread suffering. Three million workers lost their jobs over the next five years, the stock market collapsed, banks closed, farm prices fell, and one in four railroads defaulted on its bonds.

To counter the depression, Congress released $26 million in greenbacks. Previously, in February 1873, before the Panic struck, it had passed the Coinage Act, which eliminated silver coins from circulation and designated gold as the only coin to be minted. Then, when the country went bust in September with this devastating depression, those who favored soft (paper) money such as greenbacks denounced the Coinage Act as the "Crime of '73." They demanded a further increase in the money supply through the coinage of silver. They insisted that millions of silver dollars be minted and circulated at a ratio to gold of sixteen to one. They claimed that the recent discovery of silver in the mines of Nevada, Colorado, and Utah could easily provide the means of achieving this end.

So in January 1875, Congress enacted the Specie Resumption Act, which increased the supply of greenbacks and made them redeemable in gold, starting in January 1879. But advocates of soft money kept demanding the free and unlimited coinage of silver. Whereupon Richard P. ("Silver Dick") Bland of Missouri introduced a bill in the House providing for the free and unlimited coinage of silver at the ratio of sixteen to one. But the Senate added an amendment, introduced by William B. Allison of Iowa, that the Treasury coin not more that $4 million and not less than $2 million in silver monthly. This passed, over a presidential veto, and only partially satisfied the advocates of soft money.

BUT THE GILDED Age was not all moral depravity. There were some bright spots, such as the technological advances in industry and agriculture, the growth of big business, the availability of money, the continued attraction of foreign capital, and the increased number of immigrants into the United States. All these developments, and more, changed the nation dramatically. The telegraph stretched across the continent, as did the railroads. The telephone and typewriter were invented, and a cable was successfully laid across the Atlantic Ocean, providing quicker and cheaper communication between the continents. The Edison Electric Illuminating Company constructed the first electric plant in New York City in 1882, and soon homes and city streets were illuminated by electricity. Technological advances in agriculture allowed farmers to grow enough crops not only to feed the nation but to export the surplus abroad.

As a result, the nation expanded at the same time that it engaged in reconstructing the Union. Both these major events—Reconstruction and the industrialization of America—occurred simultaneously. Not surprisingly, northern states were constantly distracted from the problems of Reconstruction and the need for reform. They focused instead on making money and those capitalistic developments that were transforming American life. As the Republican governor of South Carolina remarked, "The North is tired of the Southern question."

But the Grant administration ended on a happy note in 1876. The nation celebrated the centennial year of the Republic—one hundred years of independence under a government that had continued to evolve as a democracy in which adult male suffrage had been achieved and a society created that was undergoing rapid industrialization.

It was also a presidential election year. The Republicans decided against nominating James G. Blaine, because of the suspicions recently raised against him. Instead, they chose Rutherford B. Hayes of Ohio for President and William A. Wheeler of New York for Vice President. The scandals of the Grant administration, to say nothing of the Panic of 1873, did not bode well for a Republican victory at the polls, and that is why the party picked someone untainted by scandal. Hayes enjoyed an "unblemished reputation" and so he won the nomination.

The Democrats decided on Samuel J. Tilden of New York, one of the richest corporate lawyers in America, who had prosecuted and broken up the Tweed Ring. They named Thomas A. Hendricks of Indiana as his running mate. And the November election pretty much validated what had been predicted. Tilden received 250,000 more popular votes than Hayes. He also won the "Redeemed" southern states along with New York, New Jersey, Connecticut, and Indiana for a total of 184 electoral votes.

Florida, Louisiana, and South Carolina still lingered as Republican enclaves, but the white population was determined to reassert control. There was a good deal of fraud and intimidation in the voting in these states, and consequently two sets of electoral returns were reported from each: one declaring Tilden the winner, the other Hayes. The results from the Oregon contest were also in dispute. Of all these disputed votes Tilden only needed a single electoral vote from one of these states to win the presidency. Hayes needed them all.

So Congress decided to allow a special committee to decide which votes should be counted. This Electoral Commission would consist of five members from the House and the Senate and five justices from the Supreme Court. Of these fifteen, seven would be Republican and seven Democratic. The fifteenth member was expected to be Justice David

Davis, an independent. But this intended arrangement was foiled when the Illinois legislature elected Davis to the U.S. Senate and he was replaced on the Electoral Commission by Justice Joseph P. Bradley, a Republican.

The commission began its hearings in early February 1877, and on February 7 it voted to give all the disputed votes to Hayes. The vote was 8 to 7, along strict party lines. The Democratic-controlled House threatened to prevent, by filibustering, the formal and constitutional requirement that Congress count the ballots. As March 4, the day of the inauguration, approached, there was fear that the Grant administration would expire without anyone constitutionally qualified to take its place. Southern congressmen were lobbied to vote for Hayes with promises that as President he would withdraw all federal troops from the South, appoint at least one southerner to the cabinet, and provide a generous share of federal patronage and sufficient funds to rebuild the South's shattered economy.

And that did it. On March 2, 1877, at four AM, Rutherford B. Hayes was declared the new President by an electoral vote of 185 to 184. The result was predictable. The Democrats, and Tilden in particular, failed to provide leadership in settling the dispute. They failed to undertake a public protest for the justice of their cause. They failed to encourage southerners to denounce what was declared in dispute. They failed to ask Hayes to concede at the very beginning of the contest, when he might have done so. And by their failures they encouraged the opposition to pursue an admittedly unlikely course of action that ultimately led to Hayes's victory.

Because March 4 fell on a Sunday, Hayes was inaugurated privately in the Red Room of the White House, with Chief Justice Morrison R. Waite administering the oath of office. On Monday, March 5, the public inauguration took place without demonstrations or trouble. On the same day, Hayes appointed David M. Key of Tennessee as postmaster general, thus fulfilling one part of the bargain involved in his election. One month later the President withdrew all federal troops from the South, bringing Reconstruction to a close. It had taken exactly twelve years to finally stitch the Union back together again.

But any number of people regarded this election as one more example of the political corruption that existed in Washington and was so prevalent during the Gilded Age. As a matter of fact, there were scandals beyond the nation's capital. In New York the Tweed Ring had robbed the city of millions until Tilden broke it up. William Marcy Tweed was the boss of Tammany Hall, the city's Democratic machine, and his henchmen raided the municipal treasury and took anywhere between $100 million and $200 million through kickbacks, fake vouchers, padded bills, and other fraudulent devices. Tweed was arrested, convicted of these assorted crimes, and died in prison, although several other hoodlums in the ring escaped to Europe with their loot.

And there was considerable corruption in the South, where the rebuilding of a shattered economy and society allowed scalawags, carpetbaggers, and the criminally minded to arrange contracts and bids for social services that resulted in higher taxes and increased state indebtedness. In some instances the debt was tripled in just a few years. There were also many opportunities to cheat, defraud, steal, and commit bribery. Even after the South was "Redeemed" these criminal activities continued, and in some instances grew worse. But it should be pointed out that during "Black Reconstruction" a good deal of the money was spent on hospitals, public education, and various asylums that benefited the poor and disabled.

An important source of corruption in the nation's capital emanated from the abuse of the patronage system. Civil service reform was desperately needed. Senator Roscoe Conkling of New York sneeringly referred to it as "snivel service." "During the last twenty-five years," commented Representative James Garfield, "it has been understood by the Congress and the people, that offices are to be obtained by the aid of senators and representatives, who thus become the dispensers, sometimes the brokers of patronage." Frankly, he continued, the Tenure of Office Act "has virtually resulted in the usurpation, by the senate, of a large share of the appointing power." This measure "has resulted in seriously crippling the just powers of the executive, and has placed in the hands of senators and representatives a power most corrupting and dangerous."

President Hayes tried to regain control of appointments by challenging one of the most powerful figures in Congress, Senator Conkling, the leader of the "Stalwart" or Radical faction of the Republican

Party, by ordering an investigation into the allegedly corrupt patronage operation in the New York Custom House, the political power base of Conkling's organization. Chester A. Arthur was its collector and Alonzo B. Cornell its naval officer. President Grant had conferred control of the patronage of the Custom House on Conkling, but Hayes was determined to terminate it and did so by firing both Arthur and Cornell and naming their replacements, who were subsequently confirmed by the Senate. This victory weakened the Stalwart faction within the Republican party and strengthened the "Half Breed" faction, so called because they were supposedly not full-blooded Republicans. This faction was headed by James G. Blaine.

During the ongoing struggle between these two factions, the Republicans held their national nominating convention in Chicago to choose the next President. Hayes had previously pledged not to seek a second term. To try to bridge the gulf between the opposing factions within the party, the convention chose a "dark horse" after thirty-six ballots. They nominated James A. Garfield for President, and as a sop to the Stalwarts and a means of securing New York's electoral vote, they named Chester A. Arthur as Vice President.

The Democrats chose Winfield Scott Hancock, a Civil War general, and William H. English of Indiana to head their ticket. A third party also appeared. This was the Greenback Party, whose platform advocated money inflation, including the free and unlimited coinage of silver. It also supported federal regulation of interstate commerce, women's suffrage, and a graduated income tax. This party nominated James B. Weaver of Iowa and B. J. Chambers of Texas for President and Vice President. And a fourth party, the Prohibition Party, put forward Neal Dow of Maine and A. M. Thompson of Ohio.

Because of the return of prosperity following the disastrous Panic of 1873, and the enormous financial support the Republican Party received from business, Garfield won an extremely close election by an electoral count of 214 to 155. He was the first candidate to go directly from the House of Representatives to the White House. The Greenback candidate polled a little over 300,000 popular votes, and the Prohibitionist got 10,000. Hancock carried the "solid South," something the Democratic candidates would enjoy for nearly 100 years. Unquestionably, the "solid South" was created through intimidation and various discriminatory laws regarding suffrage by which southern states effectively nullified the Fifteenth Amendment with respect to voting by African-Americans. But this election proved that the Republicans could win the White House without southern support.

After his inauguration in March 1881, Garfield clashed repeatedly with the Stalwart faction of his party over distributing the patronage. And he infuriated them further by appointing James G. Blaine his secretary of state. Several months later, on June 2, 1881, the President was shot by a disgruntled and unstable office-seeker, Charles J. Guiteau, who wanted Garfield replaced by Arthur as President, an action that went a long way in destroying the Stalwart faction. Garfield lingered for two months before dying on September 19.

As a result of the assassination, and with President Arthur's strong endorsement, Congress passed the Civil Service Reform Act on January 16, 1883, which established a permanent three-man Civil Service Commission to conduct competitive examinations and make appointments based on merit. This had been one of the urgent demands by reformers who felt that the patronage system was thoroughly corrupt and detrimental to the public good. During Arthur's term of office, something like 14,000 out of 100,000 government positions were filled by civil service examinations. It was an admirable beginning, but further reform of the civil service was necessary if the patronage system was ever to be completely controlled. Some independent Republicans felt that further reform preceded all other issues, and they were called Mugwumps because they were seen as fence-sitters with their mugs on one side of the political fence and their wumps on the other. Three of the more prominent Mugwumps were Carl Schurz, Charles Francis Adams, and E. L. Godkin.

IN ADDITION TO the Greenback and Prohibition movements during the Gilded Age, a group known as the Patrons of Husbandry, or Grangers as they were more popularly known, developed, as early as 1867. It was a secret society that at first sought to advance the interests of the farmer. It was organized in Washington and called for action against monopolies because they prevented competition and the establishment of maximum railroad rates for shipping goods and charging passenger fees. Members were particularly angry over the rates charged by the railroads. The movement soon spread to the Midwest under the leadership of Ignatius Donnelly. Illinois was the first state to enact legislation that created a commission to set maximum rates to be charged by railroads and warehouses. Wisconsin and Iowa followed by enacting laws which maximized railroad freight rates. These Granger laws were immediately challenged in the courts, but the Supreme Court upheld them in *Munn v. Illinois* in 1877, arguing that they were within a state's police power to protect the public interest. It said that the way to appeal was through the polls, not through the courts.

As a further measure to unravel the effects of Reconstruction, southern states began to enact Jim Crow laws. Tennessee passed the first such law in 1881, when it segregated railroad coaches, followed by Florida in 1887, Texas in 1889, and Louisiana in 1890. Again appeals reached the Supreme Court, which in 1896 upheld these state laws in the case *Plessy v. Ferguson*, so long, the Court said, as equal accommodations existed.

The rise of monopolies and trusts to eliminate competition was another important development during the Gilded Age. In 1882, the Standard Oil Company formed a trust with a number of other oil producers and refiners to create a company that controlled ninety percent of all the oil produced and refined in the United States. Investment bankers financed consolidations in railroads, utilities, and other industrial enterprises. The number of these trusts that were chartered by the states reached nearly 300, with investments ranging close to $250 million. The perpetrators of this rapaciousness won the inelegant title "Robber Barons," and these moguls used their money to control legislators and legislation, especially anything that would regulate or control their operations. The use of lobbyists to corrupt congressmen became more extensive. They were journalists and former congressmen who hovered around the Capitol building like "birds of prey." They also included women who were widows or daughters of former congressmen and could not be "shaken off as readily."

States with farming communities also witnessed heightened political activity to gain advantages denied them because of the growing number of business monopolies. Alliances were formed to protect farmers against railroads, industrial monopolies, and advocates of hard money (specie). Two of the more important regional groups were the Southern Alliance and the National Farmers' Alliance of the Northwest.

But monopolies and trusts were not the only problem. Corruption seemed to seep into every conceivable activity involving money, and it took a variety of forms. Political machines in the cities chose candidates for office who would perform as directed, and these machines then rigged the elections. As more and more immigrants crowded into the cities, they became easy targets not only for political bosses seeking to build mass electorates, but also for industrial tycoons who operated sweatshops and rarely paid a living wage.

In Congress there was continual disagreement over which issues and reforms needed to be addressed, and which should take priority. At first their main concerns involved hard money versus soft money, and tariff protection. Among themselves, Democrats often divided over tariff reform, most of them favoring a tariff for revenue, not for protection, but some, like those in Pennsylvania, argued in favor of protection. The Republicans split over civil service reform, and the Mugwumps took offense when the Republican National Convention nominated Blaine for President in 1884 and John A. Logan of Illinois for Vice President. The Mugwumps did not believe that Blaine would support reform. Worse, he was tainted with corruption involving a railroad. So they supported the Democratic candidate, Grover Cleveland, a reform mayor of Buffalo and former governor of New York, along with Thomas A. Hendricks of Indiana. In a hotly contested campaign both candidates were vilified: Blaine because he had allegedly lied about his involvement in the railroad scandal—"Blaine, Blaine, James G. Blaine, the Continental Liar from the State of Maine," sang Democrats—and Cleveland because he had allegedly fathered an illegitimate child: "Ma, Ma, Where's My Pa? Gone to the White House, ha, ha, ha," laughed the Republicans.

But what really damaged Blaine in this contest was a remark by the Reverend Samuel D. Burchard that the Democratic Party was a party of "Rum, Romanism, and Rebellion." The remark was made in a New York hotel room in Blaine's presence, and he failed to disavow it. New York's vast number of Irish-American Catholics took offense, and he lost many popular votes. Cleveland won 219 electoral votes to Blaine's 182, becoming the first Democratic President since James Buchanan.

As corruption mounted and monopolies abounded, the electorate became more vocal in their demands for governmental action. The farmers constantly complained about railroad abuses, such as discriminatory rates and rebates. Their alliances threatened retaliation at the polls, and their complaints eventually resulted in a congressional probe that finally produced federal regulation of interstate commerce. In 1887 Congress passed the Interstate Commerce Act, which prohibited discriminatory rates by railroads, rebates, and a higher charge for a short haul than for a longer one. Railroads were required to post their rates and not change them without giving advance notice. The act also established a five-member Interstate Commerce Commission (ICC), the nation's first regulatory agency. Still, the cleverness of railroad lawyers in finding loopholes in the law, combined with the skill of lobbyists and the favorable decisions toward railroads by the Supreme Court, all but rendered the ICC powerless in its attempts to curb abuses.

Manufacturers not only sided with the railroads but employed lobbyists and contributed to political campaigns to win greater protection of their products from foreign competition. And Republicans responded favorably. Year after year the tariff rates were raised, bringing the government greater revenue and a mounting surplus that encouraged larger pork barrels. President Cleveland pleaded for tariff reduction, but he succeeded only in alienating some members of his own party, especially those from Pennsylvania. What he did achieve was a new record in the number of vetoes he issued, a total of 414, mostly dealing with pensions, at least a fourth of which were probably fraudulent. All of Cleveland's predecessors vetoed only 205 bills. He more than doubled that number.

Cleveland's position on the tariff and his vetoes provided the Republicans with adequate ammunition to attack his record of four years and bring about his defeat in the presidential election of 1888. The Republicans put forward Benjamin Harrison of Indiana (the grandson of William Henry Harrison) and Levi P. Morton of New York. Cleveland lost a great many popular votes when a letter by the British minister to the United States, Sir Lionel Sackville-West, advised a naturalized Englishman (a California Republican, as it turned out) to vote for Cleveland. The letter was subsequently published. This apparent foreign intrusion into American affairs outraged many voters, especially

Irish-Americans. Harrison took 233 electoral votes to Cleveland's 168. But the popular vote proved far different: 5,540,000 for Cleveland to 5,440,000 for Harrison.

TRADITIONALLY, REPUBLICANS SUPPORTED higher tariff rates while the Democrats felt the rates needed to be lowered, especially since the surplus was getting out of hand. With Thomas Brackett Reed as Speaker, a man who exercised tight control on the proceedings in the House of Representatives— in fact he introduced new rules to force the House to attend to business and was dubbed "Czar" Reed by Democrats—the Republicans rammed a bill through the lower chamber that raised duties on virtually every import that competed with American products. On average the rates jumped by 49.5 percent. William McKinley of Ohio, the chairman of the Ways and Means Committee, introduced the measure. He was a staunch advocate of protection and a man of principle who was an excellent speaker and a congenial colleague. He was a favorite among Republicans. The bill passed by a vote of 164 to 142, but it ran into stiff opposition in the Senate, and western senators promised to defeat it unless a more acceptable coinage bill, allowing for the free and unlimited coinage of silver at the ratio of sixteen to one with gold, was passed. And southern senators threatened to join their western colleagues if a House-approved Federal Election Bill, or Force Bill, as they called it, was enacted. This measure was intended to protect black voters in the South by providing federal supervision of federal elections. It specified that when 100 voters in any district applied for an investigation, federal officials would inspect and verify or question the results.

Fearful that the McKinley tariff would fail, the leadership of the Republican Party jettisoned the Force Bill and suggested a compromise on silver. What became the Sherman Silver Purchase Act found favor with the western senators because it required the Treasury to purchase 4.5 million ounces of silver each month at the market price, which was more than double the amount bought under the Bland-Allison Act, and pay for it with legal tender notes redeemable in specie (gold or silver). It was estimated that the amount to be purchased was approximately the total U.S. production of silver. This legislation was passed on July 4, 1890, whereupon the Senate approved the McKinley Tariff Act and President Harrison signed it on October 1. Naturally, manufacturers raised the prices on their products without fear of being undercut by foreign competition. It did not take long for the tariff to be seen as a tax on the poor to benefit rich industries.

This bill also included an interesting provision that allowed the President to raise duties without obtaining congressional approval, in order to encourage reciprocal tariff agreements with foreign nations. This was an important surrender by Congress of one of its most jealously guarded prerogatives: the power to levy taxes and control the purse strings.

An even more important piece of legislation was passage of the Sherman Anti-Trust Act. The need to curb and control the proliferation of monopolies in basic industries, such as oil, sugar, and beef, had for many years been demanded by reformers and those who recognized that the elimination of competition hindered the formation of small and middle-size companies. It also meant higher prices for the consumer, and that struck hardest at middle-class people and the poor. Public concern about the growth of monopolies had already prompted twenty states and territories of the United States to pass antitrust legislation. But to really get a handle on the problem required federal action. Although the Republican Party generally opposed such legislation, it saw the need to accede to popular demand, and in July 1890, it passed the Sherman Anti-Trust Act, whereby "every contract, combination in the form of trust or otherwise, or conspiracy in restraint of trade . . . is hereby declared to be illegal."

But this act was inherently weak. It was ambiguous. It failed to define the meaning of such words as "trust," "restraint," and "combination." And was unclear whether unions and railroads were covered by this legislation. Thus, the act was not vigorously enforced, and monopolies continued to grow under other names.

The record of achievement by this Congress in passing 641 bills, many of which were important, came as something of a shock to the American people when it learned that $1 billion had been appropriated. A billion dollars! It struck many as unbelievable. They therefore demanded an explanation of this "Billion-Dollar Congress." Speaker Reed supposedly responded: "It is a billion-dollar country."

That explanation hardly satisfied the electorate, who showed their displeasure by voting Democrats back into office. The Democrats now held a majority in the House of Representatives, although the Senate remained under Republican control because of the many holdovers who were not up for reelection. The unpopularity of the McKinley Tariff was especially significant in understanding the size of the Republican defeat. Indeed, McKinley himself lost his bid for reelection in 1890.

THE BITTERNESS MANY Americans felt about the direction of the country was reflected in a number of violent incidents that occurred within a few years. For example, the Haymarket Massacre in Chicago in May 1886 occurred when agitation over conditions of labor in the city ended in clashes with the police that resulted in the hanging of four anarchist labor leaders. This episode was followed by a violent strike at the Carnegie steel plant in Homestead, Pennsylvania, in July 1892; and by an equally violent strike in Illinois in 1894, called when George Pullman, the inventor of the Pullman railroad car, discharged one-third of his workforce and cut salaries. It took the intervention of federal forces to bring the violence and these strikes to an end. Obviously, the growing economic distress among the laboring poor had increased to the point where they resorted to violence as the only way to make the nation and the government aware of the terrible conditions that existed, especially in the cities. Labor unions such as the American Federation of Labor organized many of these outbursts to publicize the wretched working conditions in industry.

Agriculture, too, suffered an economic turndown in the 1890s, and farmers recognized that their concerns mirrored the problems of labor and that they needed to unite to get them resolved. Representatives from the farmers' alliances met in St. Louis in December 1889 with leaders of the labor unions and the Granger and Greenback organizations, to form the People's Party, better known as the Populist Party. This party held its first national nominating convention in Omaha, Nebraska, in July 1892, with such leaders as Ignatius Donnelly, "Sockless Jerry" Simpson, Mary Elizabeth Lease, and Senator James Kyle of South Dakota in attendance. They nominated James Weaver of Iowa for President, and James G. Field of Virginia for Vice President. Their platform called for the free and unlimited coinage of silver at the ratio of sixteen to one, government ownership of all transportation and communication facilities, a graduated income tax, the direct election of senators, adoption of a secret ballot, a shorter day for industrial workers, and the right to effect legislation through initiative and referendum procedures.

The cruel social and economic injustices that developed at the close of the nineteenth century not only forced ordinary people to band together to form the People's Party but, a few years later, initiate the Progressive movement. A wide spectrum of people in all sections of the country now shouted their demand for better working conditions involving hours and wages, woman and child labor laws, and strict codes to protect the health and safety of workers in factories. These economic demands emphasized the fact that the United States had become a nation divided by class on the basis of wealth.

In the presidential election of 1892 the Democrats once more put forward Grover Cleveland for President and Adlai Stevenson of Illinois for Vice President while the Republicans nominated Harrison for a second term, along with Whitelaw Reid of New York. There were also a Socialist ticket and a Prohibition ticket in this election. But Cleveland won over 5.5 million popular and 277 electoral votes to Harrison's 5 million popular and 145 electoral votes. The Populist candidate, Weaver, garnered over a million popular and 22 electoral votes. His party also won eight seats in the House of Representatives. And for the first time since the Civil War, the Democratic Party controlled both houses of Congress and the presidency.

But no sooner had the Democrats taken over the government than a financial panic hit the country, and it hit hard. Triggered by a run on gold reserves by the British banking house of Baring Brothers in unloading American securities, by the McKinley Tariff, which reduced U.S. revenues; and by the depletion of the government's surplus through the many pensions awarded to Civil War veterans, widows, and orphans by the Harrison administration, the Panic struck in May 1893, when the stock market crashed. Five hundred banks collapsed, hundreds of businesses failed, and unemployment soared. By the end of the year the gold reserve had plunged to $80 million.

To stanch the hemorrhage of gold, Cleveland called Congress into special session and asked for the repeal of the Sherman Silver Purchase Act. Congress agreed and acted quickly. But the hemorrhaging continued and the depression got worse. An "army" of unemployed workers, led by Jacob S. Coxey of Ohio, a Populist, marched on Washington and demanded jobs and an increase in the money supply. Coxey and several other leaders were arrested and Coxey's army was forced to disband.

The Democrats in the House succeeded in reducing the tariff, but the Senate added 634 amendments which jacked rates back up. This Wilson-Gorman Tariff passed on August 27, 1894, but Cleveland refused to sign it. One important feature of the act was a two percent flat rate on personal and corporate income over $4,000. But the Supreme Court, in the case of *Pollock v. Farmers Loan and Trust Company,* declared this provision unconstitutional because it was a direct tax, and direct taxes can be apportioned only according to the population of each state.

To resolve the problem of the continued depletion of the gold reserve, the administration worked out a $62 million loan from a banking group headed by J. Pierpont Morgan and August Belmont whereby 3.5 million ounces of gold would be purchased with government bonds, half the gold to come from abroad. For their assistance, the bankers raked in a profit of $1.5 million.

Maintaining the gold standard became an important issue in the presidential election of 1896, although the depression and the fact that it persisted throughout the Cleveland administration did not bode well for the Democrats. Under the dexterous management by Marcus A. Hanna, a Cleveland mining and shipping magnate, the Republican Party nominated William McKinley for President at its convention in St. Louis in mid-June and Garret A. Hobart of New Jersey for Vice President on a platform that advocated the single gold standard, a high protective tariff, and an aggressive foreign policy.

At their convention in Chicago on July 8, the Democrats adopted a platform that demanded the free and unlimited coinage of silver at the ratio of sixteen to one, and an end to high protective tariffs and the use of injunctions against labor. William Jennings Bryan gave an electrifying speech at the convention, in which he answered the Republican call for a gold standard "by saying to them: You shall not press upon the brow of labor this crown of thorns, you shall not crucify mankind upon a cross of gold." And that speech won him the nomination for President. Arthur Sewall of Maine was nominated for Vice President. The platform also condemned the Supreme Court's ruling against the income tax.

The campaign was a "Battle of Standards," that is, the gold versus the silver standard. The Populist Party endorsed Bryan but nominated the fiery Thomas E. Watson of Georgia for Vice President. Its failure to put forward its own candidate for President demoralized the members, and it ceased to function thereafter as a viable party.

Although Bryan traveled around the country giving mesmerizing speeches to enthusiastic crowds in twenty-nine states, he lost the election to the superbly managed and well-financed Republican organization run by Marcus Hanna. McKinley conducted his campaign from the front porch of his home in Canton, Ohio. At Hanna's call, industrialists contributed around $16 million to the campaign, which was used to portray Bryan as a radical who would destroy the government's fundamental institutions. McKinley captured 271 electoral votes to Bryan's 176. In the popular vote McKinley won over 7 million to Bryan's 6.5 million.

Both houses of Congress remained in Republican hands. A new era was about to begin and would reshape the course of American politics.

7

Manifest Destiny, Progressivism, War, and the Roaring Twenties

A S THE UNITED States experienced the rapid growth of business and the accumulation of wealth, it recognized that it had come a long way in a relatively short period of time. Prior to the Civil War there were few great fortunes. Most industries were small, although there was growth throughout the antebellum period. Indeed, a few men made enough money so that a new word had to be devised to describe them. "Millionaire" was the word, and it applied to such men as John Jacob Astor, for example, who built his fortune from fur trading.

But the great business boom resulting from the Civil War revolutionized the size, methods, and marketing of industrial enterprises. The rise of big business in the United States produced giant companies in the making of steel and the refining of oil and sugar. Even farming became mechanized with the invention of the McCormick reaper. Such inventions as the telephone by Alexander Graham Bell in 1876, the electric lightbulb by Thomas Edison in 1879, the linotype machine by Ottmar Mergentheber in 1886, and many others created entirely new companies. As mentioned earlier, railroads, which had first appeared in the 1820s, now stretched across the continent. By 1900 there were several hundred thousand miles of railroad track connecting urban centers with remote towns and villages. And, as the economic historian Alfred D. Chandler

Jr., has shown, this expanded railroad system required professional managers, engineers, and other specialists to provide for its construction and maintenance, as well as the billing, collection, the preparation of timetables, and other services. Consequently, a new class of managerial professionals had arisen, enabling railroad companies to expand rapidly in size and productivity.

What happened with railroading—that is, the appearance of managerial professionals—soon spread to other industries. The robber barons, obsessed with maximizing their profits, set about converting to a managerial form of capitalism by which they could better dominate their industry and form monopolies to maintain control. Branches of a particular company would be established in various sections of the country, directed by professional managers who supervised thousands of workers and salesmen. Some of these robber barons, such as John D. Rockefeller and Andrew Carnegie, earned so much money that they set up foundations to give it away. Without an income tax, many of them became billionaires.

Because of the enormous wealth generated by the expansion of big business, the United States became more conscious of its increased power in the world—not that it wished to involve itself with the problems of foreign nations or exert any influence in world affairs. Isolationism seemed to provide many people with a sense of security by simply following a policy of neutrality first enunciated by President George Washington. Still, there lurked the pride of knowing that Americans' "experiment in freedom," resulting from a republican form of government, could be attractive to other nations and imitated. If other countries wished to achieve what the United States had acquired in terms of wealth and power they need only convert from monarchy to democracy. Americans had a desire to see their "experiment" take root across the globe and, when necessary, to assist it themselves by direct or indirect action.

THE PROGRESS OF the United States seemed miraculous. Its steady, unrelenting development began with the arrival of Europeans searching for land and with their conquest of a wilderness teeming with native tribes. After the Revolution and the establishment of a unified government under the Constitution, the United States continued its westward expansion with the purchase of the Louisiana Territory in 1803, followed by the acquisition of Florida in 1821, the acquisition of Texas in 1845, and the seizure of territories from Mexico following the Mexican War in 1848, including the Gadsden Purchase in 1853, when the United States paid "conscience money" of $10 million for a strip of land south of the Gila River in Arizona and New Mexico that had been seized four years earlier. Then, in 1867, William Seward, secretary of state under Presidents Lincoln and Johnson, negotiated a treaty with Russia by which Alaska was acquired for $7.2 million. To all these acquisitions there was spirited opposition: Federalists denounced the Louisiana Purchase as unconstitutional, Jackson was denounced for his seizure of Florida, Whigs fulminated against war with Mexico, and Seward suffered personal abuse for the outrageous cost of Alaska. The acquisition of Alaska was called "Seward's Folly." But the discovery of gold and later oil and gas more than justified the purchase of Alaska as far as cost was concerned.

The physical expansion of the nation continued with the annexation of the Hawaiian Islands in July 1898. American missionaries, merchants, and planters had established economic and cultural ties with the islands starting in the 1830s. But in a successful revolt Americans deposed the reigning monarch, Queen Liliuokalani, in 1893 and erected a government that lasted until Congress, during the McKinley administration in 1898, passed a joint resolution annexing the islands, despite the strong opposition of anti-imperialists in both the Republican and the Democratic parties. One of the great attractions in possessing these islands, aside from their being a lucrative market and a source of exotic fruits, such as the pineapple, was the fact that they provided refueling bases and naval facilities for the United States at a time when it was continuing to reach across the seas and bring its supposedly enlightened system of government to a needy and eager world. Two years later Congress granted Hawaii territorial status.

By the end of the nineteenth century the United States had such a congratulatory sense of its success in developing an industrial society committed to individual freedom and democratic rule, combined with its genuine humanitarian regard for the suffering of those living under impoverished conditions and dictatorial rule, that it slowly renewed its belief in its mission to spread freedom and democracy around the globe. This was Manifest Destiny revisited. The idea was first enunciated in

1845 by John L. O'Sullivan, editor of the *Democratic Review*, who said that "Providence" had chosen this country "by the right of our manifest destiny" to spearhead a drive throughout the entire North American continent for "the development of the great experiment of liberty and federative self government entrusted to us." What had begun as an argument "to overspread and possess" the continent had now become a global mission, at least with regard to disseminating the blessings of liberty and democracy. The nation forgot the warning of John Quincy Adams, who had declared that the United States should be "the well-wisher to the freedom and independence of all" nations but that it must not go "abroad in search of monsters to destroy." To do so would inaugurate America's search for "dominion and power" in the world and would ultimately result in the loss of its own "freedom and independence."

Disregarding this sage advice, the United States at the tail end of the nineteenth century, spotted its first "monster to destroy": Spain. Rebels in Cuba had initiated an insurrection against Spanish rule on the island in an effort to obtain their independence. This revolution had resulted in part because of a failed economy brought on by the tariff policies of the United States, which had imposed heavy duties on raw sugar, the island's principal export. Spain's brutal response in crushing the rebellion evoked sympathetic outcries of protest from the United States. The horror stories of the treatment of Cuban civilians by Spanish officials involving rape, assault, and torture were just the sort of juicy material some American journalists loved to feed to a lurid-hungry reading public in the United States. Such "yellow journalistic" newspapers (so called because of a cartoon titled the "Yellow Kid" that appeared in them) such as William Randolph Hearst's *New York Journal* and Joseph Pulitzer's *New York World* published detailed accounts of alleged Spanish depredations committed against Cuban nationals. These made for irresistible reading. As though responding to the public mood, Congress passed a concurrent resolution in February 1896 favoring recognition of Cuban belligerency. The situation heated up when, on February 15, 1898, the USS *Maine*, on a visit to Havana, was sunk by an explosion in which 260 officers and sailors perished. The finger of guilt was pointed directly at Spanish officials. Jingoists had a field day trumpeting what the nation would do in retaliation—as though proof of Spain's guilt already existed. Growled one Congressman on the floor of the House of Representatives, "It ought to be understood in Spain and it ought to be understood in every country on the globe, that while this great country sincerely desires to be at peace, it is prepared for war, if war becomes necessary."

A reply from Spain about the sinking was eagerly awaited, but in April 1898 Congress passed another resolution recognizing Cuban independence and demanding the immediate withdrawal of Spanish authority from Cuba. The President was authorized to use military force to implement this resolution if necessary. The Teller Amendment to the resolution stated that the United States had no intention of annexing Cuba but would "leave the government and control of the island to its own people" once peace had been established. President McKinley signed the resolution on April 20. Immediately, Spain broke off diplomatic relations with the United States, and on April 24 declared war, whereupon Congress responded with its own declaration on April 25.

Most Americans felt a sense of honor and national pride, along with a desire to share the blessings of liberty and democracy, and so they eagerly engaged in what came to be called "a splendid little war." The Spanish-American War provided the United States with a series of naval and land victories in Cuba as well as the Philippine Islands, another Spanish possession. In May, Commodore George Dewey entered Manila Bay in the Philippines and completely destroyed what little Spanish navy was present to guard the islands. In Cuba some 17,000 American troops descended on the island, the most prominent of which was one regiment, known as the Rough Riders, commanded by Colonel Leonard Wood and Lieutenant Colonel Theodore Roosevelt, who had resigned as assistant secretary of the navy to participate in the invasion.

Spain suffered one humiliating military disaster after another and lost an army and its fleet. A young, wealthy, powerful, emerging giant had provoked a poor, weak, decrepit ancient and brought it to its knees. Spain sued for peace in July, and a preliminary treaty was signed in Washington on August 12. The final peace treaty was negotiated in Paris on December 10, 1898. Spain recognized Cuba's independence and ceded Puerto Rico and Guam to the United States as a war indemnity. It also surrendered the Philippine Islands in return for $20 million.

President McKinley claimed that he had been troubled over what to do about the Philippines and had prayed for divine guidance. "I walked the floor of the White House night after night until midnight," he remembered. "I went down on my knees and prayed Almighty God for light and guidance." The answer came in the middle of the night: "that we could not give them back to Spain—that would be cowardly and dishonorable . . . that we could not leave them to themselves—they were unfit for self-government . . . that there was nothing left for us to do but to take them all, and to educate the Filipinos, and uplift and civilize and Christianize them, and by God's grace do the very best we could by them."

Uplift and civilize them! Even Christianize them, despite the fact that most "Filipinos" were Roman Catholics. Bring them the blessings of Americanized freedom and democracy so that some day Filipinos would become wealthy and powerful. Any number of Americans actually believed it was their moral duty to bring an "enlightened society" to the benighted Filipinos, while certain business interests lusted after expanding trade with Asian countries as they looked westward to develop new markets.

In demanding the Philippine Islands the United States had foolishly and needlessly embarked on an imperialistic course that not only divided the nation politically but set into motion forces that would later provoke a bloody war. By thrusting itself into Asian affairs, where it had little real interest or concern, the country courted catastrophe—and it came on December 7, 1941, at Pearl Harbor.

The decision of the United States to purchase the Philippines came as quite a shock to the people of the islands, and they rose up in rebellion. They had expected independence and now, under the leadership of Emilio Aguinaldo, they were prepared to fight to achieve it. American troops put down the insurrection, an action that contradicted everything this nation professed about liberty and democracy. President McKinley appointed a commission—headed by William Howard Taft, a federal circuit court judge—to establish a government in the Philippines. It would take almost fifty years before the Philippine people would achieve their freedom. In 1916 the Jones Act provided self-government for the islands and promised early independence. But it took several more decades before that independence was granted. And in 1917 the United States purchased the Virgin Islands from Denmark for $25 million.

THE TWENTIETH CENTURY began with several momentous events. First, on March 14, the Currency or Gold Standard Act, by which gold—and only gold—became the standard unit of currency, was passed, thus marking the end of a two-decade struggle to make silver equal to gold. Then the following November the nation reelected McKinley as President, along with Theodore Roosevelt as Vice President, a selection that Marcus Hanna, the skillful manager of the 1896 campaign, strongly opposed because of Roosevelt's reform record as governor of New York. The Democrats nominated William Jennings Bryan and Adlai E. Stevenson on a platform of anti-imperialism, anti-trust, and free silver. A Socialist Party nominated Eugene V. Debs of Indiana and Job Harriman of California. A Prohibition Party and a People's Party also put forward candidates for the presidential office.

Less than a year later, on September 6, 1901, President McKinley was shot by Leon Czolgosz, an anarchist, at the Pan-American Exposition in Buffalo, New York, and he died a week later, on September 14. The new President, Theodore Roosevelt, tried to reassure the nation by promising to "continue, absolutely unbroken the policy of President McKinley," but he was known to champion such progressive causes as child labor laws, food and drug regulation, conservation, railroad reform, and trust busting. A number of party leaders expressed concern about what he might do as chief executive. "Now look," exclaimed Marcus Hanna, "that damned cowboy is President of the United States."

Indeed, these leaders had good reason to feel concern. Populists and all manner of social reformers from the East and West joined Roosevelt under the banner of what was called Progressivism, a movement formed to further popular government and progressive legislation. They insisted that the nation needed labor laws regarding women and children, legislation regulating wages and hours, and statutes that defined safety and health conditions in factories. Trusts and railroads were high on the list of what needed reform, along with certain business practices known to violate ethical and moral standards. Of particular concern was the unrelenting drive of industries to form trusts.

Using what he called the "bully pulpit," that is, his position as chief executive of the nation, Roosevelt sought popular approval of his crusade against trusts. The formation of the U.S. Steel Company, the first billion-dollar corporation in the country, and the Northern Securities Company, a railroad holding company, inaugurated Roosevelt's drive to bring an end to industrial abuses. Under prodding by the President to expedite federal prosecution of antitrust suits in federal courts, Congress passed the Expedition Act on February 11, 1903, giving these suits precedence in circuit court proceedings. A few days later, on February 14, 1903, the Department of Labor and Commerce was established which included a Bureau of Corporations that had authority to investigate and subpoena testimony on activities by corporations involved in interstate commerce. The Elkins Act of February 19, 1903, sought to eliminate rebates on freight charges and regulate shipping by railroads. And in 1906 the Hepburn Act reinforced the Interstate Commerce Act by granting it the authority to set maximum railroad rates.

As a President committed to conservation, Roosevelt pressured Congress to pass the Newlands Act, which directed the proceeds from the sale of arid and semiarid lands in the West to be used for the construction of dams, irrigation, and other reclamation projects. This legislation has been compared to the Homestead Act in shaping the development of the western region of the country.

In foreign affairs, Roosevelt decided that the ever-burgeoning interests of the United States necessitated playing a larger role in world events. He summed up his philosophy by what he said was an African proverb: "Speak softly and carry a big stick, and you will go far." The destiny of America, as far as Roosevelt was concerned, dictated that new opportunities should be explored to enhance the reputation, wealth, and prestige of this country. One way to do that was to achieve something which had been contemplated for many decades and revived as a result of the Spanish-American War, namely, the building of a canal that would link the Atlantic and Pacific oceans.

Roosevelt encouraged Panama, then a province of the nation of Colombia, to seek its freedom in order to allow the building of a canal across the Isthmus of Panama. When native Panamanians, aided by foreign promoters of a canal, rose up in rebellion in November 1903, American troops were used to block Colombia's effort to crush the rebellion, and Roosevelt was quick to recognize the independence of the new Panamanian republic. The Hay-Bunau-Varilla Treaty, signed on November 10, 1903, granted the United States control of a ten-mile zone across the isthmus. The United States also agreed to guarantee the independence of Panama. Furthermore, it obtained the right to intervene at any time to protect the sovereignty of this new Republic, and it agreed to pay $10 million and an annual fee of $250,000 to operate a canal after it had been built.

Manifest Destiny had now moved south across the border. Army engineers under Colonel William C. Gorgas set to work on the canal, and on January 7, 1914, the first ship passed through it. Later, Roosevelt would boast, "I took the Canal Zone." The canal not only aided world trade but provided a vital means by which the United States could move its fleet to protect its Pacific and Asian possessions. Much later, during the administration of President Jimmy Carter in 1977, treaties were negotiated by which the United States would continue to operate the canal until the year 2000, after which ownership of it would be turned over to Panama. with the understanding that its neutrality would be guaranteed even during periods of war.

ONCE ROOSEVELT WON election as President in 1904 against the Democrat Alton B. Parker, the Socialist Eugene Debs, the Prohibitionist Silas C. Swallow, and the Populist Thomas E. Watson, he felt more comfortable about urging additional social and economic reforms. In his first message to Congress, after his election on November 4, he proposed several measures regarding child labor, slum clearance, and the strengthening of investigative agencies. These proposals resulted in some of the most important legislation of his administration, starting with the Pure Food and Drug Act, passed on June 30, 1906. This measure forbade the manufacture, sale, and distribution of adulterated drugs and food in interstate commerce, and it prohibited fraudulent labeling of these products. Congress also enacted the Meat Inspection Act, but it took the publication of Upton Sinclair's book *The*

Jungle to expose the filthy conditions in meatpacking houses and neutralize opposition to its passage. The law required sanitary conditions and federal inspection of meatpacking facilities in any operation involved in interstate commerce.

To a very large extent the President's efforts reflected a larger Progressive movement that had developed within the country which demanded an end to the abuses of greedy corporations and machine politics. Several states had already initiated such reforms by requiring more accountability from business, and by returning government to the electorate. Wisconsin, for example, enacted railroad legislation and an income tax during the governorship of Robert M. La Follette. Other states joined the push toward progressivism, by adopting the direct primary and the initiative and referendum to allow voters a greater voice in deciding legislation. To a large extent the movement was advanced by a number of writers, such as Sinclair, Ida Tarbell, Henry Demarest Lloyd, Lincoln Stephens, and David Graham Phillips, who exposed corruption and greed in business and in both state and national politics. Magazines, including *Cosmopolitan*, *McClure's*, and the *American*, which had national circulation, published their reports, and these stories became more and more sensational as they delved deeper into the activities of such monopolies as the Standard Oil Company, the beef trust, and the Chicago stockyards, as well as corruption in city governments and the United States Senate. Roosevelt called them "muckrakers," comparing them to the man with the muckrake in John Bunyan's *Pilgrim's Progress*, who never sees what is around him because he is forever looking down at the filth he is raking.

The Progressive movement was an important development in the evolution of American democracy. It urged legislation that would allow the electorate to have a voice in initiating legislature that would benefit them; it urged legislation that would permit the public to approve or disapprove measures passed by state legislatures; and it urged legislation that would permit voters to recall elected officials who, for one reason or another, did not serve the public well-being. The electorate did not always take advantage of the proposed reforms, however. Indeed, compared with citizens of other democracies around the world, Americans have a poor record of exercising their voting rights. The percentage of qualified men and women who regularly go to the polls rarely exceeds a little more than fifty percent, compared to eighty and ninety percent in other countries.

During the first fifteen years of the twentieth century, many of these reforms were put forward as part of the platforms of the various political parties: Democratic, Republican, Populist, Socialist, Socialist Labor, Progressive, Prohibition, Independence, and United Christian. In 1908, Roosevelt stepped aside—he could have run for another term but chose to abide by the example of George Washington by serving only two terms—and recommended William Howard Taft to succeed him as President. Taft, with a platform that called for stricter enforcement of the antitrust laws and further tariff protection, defeated William Jennings Bryan. The Mann-Elkins Act, passed on June 18, 1909, added telephone, telegraph, and cable companies to the jurisdiction of the Interstate Commerce Commission (ICC) and permitted it to suspend rate increases or to reduce rates if necessary, subject to judicial review.

Republicans also passed the Payne-Aldrich Tariff Act of 1909, which raised duties to an average forty percent ad valorum, which Taft signed, declaring it "the best tariff bill the Republican party ever passed." A number of Insurgent Republicans sharply disagreed and joined Democratic efforts to reduce the tariff, but Taft vetoed those efforts. On January 21, 1911, these Insurgents formed the National Progressive Republican League in Washington, under the direction of Senator Robert M. La Follette, and demanded that the Republican Party directly support progressive legislation, such as the direct election of senators; the initiative, referendum, and recall reforms by the states; direct election of delegates to the national nominating convention; and direct primaries for the nomination of elective officers. Stalwart Republicans resisted these demands and renominated Taft for President in 1912.

Insurgent Republicans in the House of Representatives, led by Representative George W. Norris of Nebraska, stripped Speaker Joseph Cannon of his dictatorial powers in controlling legislation. They also faulted Taft for failing to support and defend the conservationist views of his predecessor. When Theodore Roosevelt returned from a hunting trip to Africa, he broke with Taft, who he felt had betrayed his policies, and expounded on what he called the "new nationalism," which supported an income tax, workmen's compensation, labor laws for women and children, and stricter regulation of corporations. He then accepted the nomination of the Progressive Party in the election of 1912, declaring that he felt as strong as a "Bull Moose."

After a long and difficult struggle at the Democratic convention held in Baltimore between the forces of Beauchamp (Champ) Clark of Missouri, Speaker of the House of Representatives, and Governor Woodrow Wilson of New Jersey, a former president of Princeton University, the delegates chose Wilson on the forty-sixth ballot with a platform supporting political and economic reform. Wilson himself put forward a program known as the "New Freedom." It called for a reduced tariff, a reform of banking and currency, the strengthening of the Sherman Anti-Trust Act, and the end of special privileges for business that had been granted by the federal government.

The election ended with the total triumph of the Democrats. The Party swept to victory in forty states. Wilson won 435 electoral votes to 88 for Roosevelt and 8 for Taft. He polled 6,286,214 popular votes to 4,126,020 for Roosevelt and 3,483,922 for Taft. For the first time in American history, African-Americans voted in large numbers for Wilson because he had promised them fair treatment and greater police protection. He won the support of W. E. B. DuBois, who had founded the National Association for the Advancement of Colored People (NAACP) in 1909 to aid black people in their quest for economic and social equality. The Democrats also won control of the House of Representatives and elected more than two dozen governors, including several from traditionally Republican states, such as Massachusetts, Ohio, and New York.

Clearly, the Progressive movement had profoundly affected the course of American politics. It also helped bring about the passage in Congress of two important constitutional amendments: the Sixteenth, by which the income tax was legalized (it was adopted in February 1913); and the Seventeenth, which provided for the popular election of senators (and was ratified in April 1913).

One of the first things Wilson did on taking office was to call for the lowering of the tariff. He actually appeared before the members of Congress in giving his State of the Union address, thus reviving a practice of Presidents Washington and Adams that had been discontinued by President Jefferson. Wilson informed the members that he wished to act as a partner in their legislative work, not as "a mere department of the Government hailing Congress from some isolated island of jealous power." As a result the Underwood-Simmons Tariff passed on October 13, 1913, which reduced rates on nearly 1,000 items, including wool, sugar, iron ore, leather, hemp, wood, coal, and many foods. It also levied a one percent tax on incomes over $2,000 with a $1,000 exemption for married men, and a graduated tax from one to six percent on incomes from $20,000 to $500,000. It was the first such income tax under the recently ratified Sixteenth Amendment to the Constitution.

Following an investigation by a Banking and Currency subcommittee, chaired by Arsene Pujo of Louisiana, into the monopolistic practices of the banking establishment, the Federal Reserve Act was passed on December 23, 1913. It established twelve regional banks, each owned by private member banks and authorized to issue federal reserve notes to member banks. A Federal Reserve Board of seven members, appointed by the President with the consent of the Senate, controlled this decentralized system. The act also authorized the board to raise or lower the discount rate of member banks, thereby enabling the board to command the availability of credit throughout the nation.

Two more pieces of Progressive legislation were approved: the Clayton Antitrust Act, passed on October 15, 1914, which strengthened the Sherman Antitrust Act by including practices not covered by the original legislation; and the Federal Trade Commission Act, enacted on September 26, 1914, which struck at business practices that were deemed to be unfair or in restraint of trade.

To strengthen his support from farmers and thereby his bid for reelection in 1916, Wilson signed the Federal Farm Loan Act, which divided the country into twelve districts, each having a Farm Loan bank that would provide farmers with long-term, low-interest credit. He also signed the Keating-Owen Child Labor Act in September 1916 which forbade the sale in interstate commerce of any product made by children under the age of sixteen.

A EUROPEAN WAR had broken out in the summer of 1914, and the attention of the nation was abruptly turned to it when a German submarine torpedoed the RMS *Lusitania* on May 7, 1915, and 128 American lives were lost. Wilson protested the action, and when Germany announced its intention of attacking without warning all merchantmen found in the vicinity of the British Isles, Wilson cautioned Americans against doing anything that would violate the nation's neutrality. Instead, he signed the National Defense Act, passed on June 3, 1916, which expanded the regular army to 175,000 and, over the next five years, increased its size to 223,000 and directed the enlargement of the National Guard to 450,000. It also established the Reserve Officers' Training Corps at colleges and universities.

In seeking reelection for Wilson, the Democrats emphasized his desire to maintain peace. "He kept us out of war," they contended. But the election of 1916 proved to be a very close race. The Republicans put forward the Supreme Court Justice Charles Evans Hughes, who had once served as governor of New York. The Progressives tried to induce Roosevelt to run again, but he refused and urged his followers to support Hughes. Not until the results of the California vote came in was it clear that Wilson had been reelected by an electoral count of 277 to 254 for Hughes. The Democrats retained control of the Senate, but they lost the House. Still, the number of representatives of both major parties was so close that Progressives and Independents held the balance of power. With the support of Independents, the Democrats were able to reelect Champ Clark as Speaker.

One of the new members was Republican Jeannette Rankin of Montana, a thirty-six-year-old suffragist and social worker. She said that she would represent everyone in her state but added that she felt "it was my special duty to express also the point of view of women and to make clear that the women of the country are coming to a full realization of the fact that Congress deals with their problems." It should be remembered that the Constitution had not yet been amended to grant the suffrage to women, but Montana, like many other states, had already moved in this new, progressive, direction. Not until 1918 did both houses of Congress agree to a resolution providing women's suffrage. This was the Nineteenth Amendment to the Constitution, which was ratified on August 26, 1920.

Rankin was also a dedicated pacifist and strongly opposed any action that would involve the United States in the ongoing war in Europe. President Wilson hoped to bring about a conclusion to the war without victory for either side, one that would include an international organization dedicated to maintaining peace. But events took a sudden and unexpected turn. Early in 1917, Germany unleashed unrestricted submarine warfare in an effort to bring the conflict to a speedy conclusion, even though this risked involving the United States in the war. Submarines would sink all ships, both neutral and hostile, without warning. Wilson immediately broke off diplomatic relations with Germany on February 3, 1917, and asked Congress for authority to arm merchant vessels. Congress agreed. At the same time the President revealed to the nation a telegram intercepted by the British, written by Arthur Zimmermann, the German foreign secretary, to the German minister in Mexico in which it promised to return Texas, New Mexico, and Arizona to Mexico in the event of war between the United States and Germany—that is, if Mexico declared war against the United States.

After the sinking of three American merchantmen by German submarines—in one of these sinkings, there was a heavy loss of American lives—Wilson summoned Congress to a special session on April 2 and before a joint meeting of both houses asked for a declaration of war. It is a "fearful thing," he said, "to lead this great peaceful people into war. . . . But the right is more precious than peace, and we shall fight for the things which we have always carried nearest our hearts." After a heated debate the Senate approved the resolution on April 4 by a vote of 82 to 6. The House engaged in an even longer struggle, but on the morning of April 6, by a vote of 373 to 50, it passed the declaration, Jeannette Rankin voting against it. At 1:18 PM the same day, Wilson signed the resolution and the United States entered World War I.

One of the first things Congress did was pass the Selective Service Act on May 18, 1917, which called for the registration for military service of all men between the ages of eighteen and forty-five. Of the more than 24 million men enrolled in the draft, almost 3 million were called up for service. Congress also passed the Espionage and Sedition Acts in 1917 and 1918, establishing fines and imprisonment for those convicted of aiding the enemy or committing other disloyal acts. It gave the postmaster general the right to exclude from the mails any materials deemed seditious or treasonable. The constitutionality of this measure was upheld by the Supreme Court in 1919 in the case *Schenck v. United States*.

The war effort at home developed through two stages: the first, from the outset of war to the end of 1917, relied principally on volunteer efforts; the second, from 1918 to the end of the conflict, brought the administration into exercising full control. Using the authority provided by Congress, Wilson mobilized farmers and housewives through the Food Administration program, headed by Herbert Hoover, widely recognized as an expert because of his success in directing the Belgium Relief Commission. The Food Administration succeeded in increasing the food supply so that it tripled the amount of food shipped overseas. Railroads were regulated, and Bernard Baruch headed a War Industries Board, which hastened the steady supply of equipment necessary to conduct the war. To pay for the war, which ultimately cost $33.5 billion, income taxes on individuals and corporations were increased to approximately sixty-five percent, excess profit taxes were enacted, and estate taxes were increased.

Not until the late spring of 1918 did the U.S. military forces, commanded by General John J. Pershing, join the Allied forces in France and take up a position just east of Verdun. Meanwhile the Germans had signed a harsh peace treaty with the new government of the Soviet Union, which had toppled the Romanov dynasty in Russia, executed the czar, and established a communist state. Then Germany launched an all-out assault against the Allies. On June 3, several American divisions joined the French in turning back a German drive at Château-Thierry. And at the battle of the Marne, during the last two weeks of July, the German offensive was brought to an end.

Wilson had already begun planning for the aftermath of the war, and early in 1918 he addressed Congress and outlined "Fourteen Points" that he hoped would be the basis for a just and lasting peace, once Germany had been defeated. These points included general disarmament, freedom of the seas, open covenants openly arrived at, restoration of national boundaries, establishment of an independent Poland with access to the sea, the formation of a League of Nations, removal of artificial barriers to international trade, an impartial settlement of colonial claims, self-determination for Russia, the restoration of Belgium, the return of Alsace-Lorraine to France, and autonomy for the subject people of the

Austrian-Hungarian empire. What the United States was attempting to do by the Fourteen Points was to establish a new world order, something Wilson and the country would soon learn was impossible.

The beginning of the disruption of Wilson's hopes and plans commenced with the Allies' decision to intervene in the civil war that had broken out in Russia between the Bolsheviks and more conservative Russians called Whites, and although Wilson believed the action was wrong and counterproductive he reluctantly agreed to it under pressure from the Allies. Then the President foolishly asked the American people to return a Democratic Congress in the midterm election of 1918 in order to forestall Europe from interpreting a defeat of his party as a repudiation of his leadership. His request and his presumption offended the electorate who responded by sending a majority of Republicans to both houses of Congress. And just as he feared, Wilson's leadership was seriously undermined by the Republican triumph. Meanwhile, the European war ended abruptly with the defeat of the German army and the collapse of the German government. By the time the armistice was signed on November 11, the Kaiser, William II, had abdicated and fled to Holland.

In late December 1918, Wilson traveled to Europe with a large body of experts to attend the Versailles Peace Conference and work for a just peace. To his surprise and chagrin there were no representatives at the conference from the defeated powers or from Russia. As matters turned out, it was Wilson (not the defeated powers) against the Allied leaders—Prime Minister David Lloyd George of Great Britain, Premier Georges Clemenceau of France, and Prime Minister Vittorio Orlando of Italy—who were determined to divide the territories of the conquered nations and make Germany pay for the cost of the war. By threatening to withdraw from the conference and leave Europe to stew in its own mess, Wilson did achieve a number of important concessions. An independent Poland with access to the sea was established, Alsace-Lorraine was returned to France, Belgium was restored, the peoples of the Austrian-Hungarian empire won independence and self-determination, and the Allies agreed to the establishment of a League of Nations. But Germany was saddled with an impossible $56 billion in reparations, and the Allies divided German colonies among themselves, virtually inviting future retaliation.

The overthrow of the czarist regime in Russia, the ultimate victory of the Bolsheviks over the Whites, and the establishment of a communist state unleashed a wave of isolationist sentiment throughout the United States. The American people were in no mood to involve themselves any further in European affairs, and this hostile attitude reinforced the opposition of those in the Senate who were incensed by Wilson's failure to invite a congressional delegation to accompany him to Paris to attend the conference. And these senators, led by Henry Cabot Lodge of Massachusetts, chairman of the Senate Foreign Relations Committee, were determined to block ratification of the Versailles Treaty. They contended that the treaty jeopardized American security and the nation's traditional foreign policy of neutrality. In addition, it did not exclude internal affairs from the jurisdiction of the League, and it contained no recognition of the Monroe Doctrine. Lodge therefore tied the treaty up in committee for six weeks in order to arouse public opposition against it.

To counter his opponents, Wilson took his case directly to the people in September 1919 and pleaded his cause. He traveled nearly 10,000 miles by railroad and gave dozens of speeches. But his health broke and, after attending a rally in Pueblo, Colorado, he collapsed. A few days later, on October 2, he suffered a massive stroke and could no longer continue the fight.

Meanwhile Lodge offered fourteen reservations, one of which rejected the obligation of the United States to preserve the independence and territorial integrity of member nations. This obligation, said Wilson, was the heart of the treaty, and he refused to delete it. The public expected the two sides to agree on a compromise, but the President would not hear of it and thereby lost public support. Instead, he called on Democrats to defeat these reservations. Thus, on November 19, 1919, when the treaty came up for a vote in the Senate with Lodge's reservations attached, it was rejected. Then, a motion by Democrats to ratify the treaty without reservations also went down to defeat, 53 to 38. To a large extent, Wilson killed his own treaty. Not much later Congress adopted a resolution declaring the war with Germany at an end. Wilson vetoed it, and the House failed to pass it over his veto.

Isolated and incapacitated, Wilson announced that the approaching presidential election of 1920 should be a "great and solemn referendum" on the League. The Republicans, lacking an outstanding candidate, eventually chose Senator Warren G. Harding of Ohio to head their ticket, after he first assured the leadership that he had not been involved in any scandal or improper behavior. Handsome and intellectually vapid, he managed to hide his numerous extramarital affairs. His genius, argued the historian John D. Hicks, "lay not so much in his ability to conceal his thought as in the absence of any serious thought to reveal." The nominating convention also chose Calvin Coolidge of Massachusetts for Vice President. His outstanding achievement as governor, according to his supporters, was breaking a strike by Boston policemen.

Democrats also floundered in naming their ticket. It took forty-four ballots before the exhausted delegates chose James M. Cox, governor of Ohio, and Franklin D. Roosevelt of New York, assistant secretary of the navy in the Wilson administration. Cox and Roosevelt did attempt to focus the campaign on the League, but Americans had had enough of European involvement and were attracted by Harding's "back to normalcy" and "America First" appeals. Not surprisingly, the election produced a landslide for the Republicans. They captured the presidency, 404 electoral votes to 127, and both houses of Congress.

In his inaugural address, Harding went out of his way to kill any hope that the country would join the League of Nations, declaring that the United States would "seek no part in directing the destinies of the world." The gravely ill Wilson pronounced Harding's remark a retreat into "sullen and selfish isolation which is deeply ignoble because manifestly cowardly and dishonorable." When Congress passed a resolution similar to the one vetoed by Wilson that ended the war with Germany, Harding signed it on July 2, 1921. It signified not only the country's disengagement from active participation in European conflicts but a withdrawal into isolationism.

As the nation entered the 1920s—known later as the Roaring Twenties—it soon became obvious that profound changes had taken place since the turn of the century. First, the census of 1920 revealed that most Americans now lived in or near cities—not on farms as was generally believed. More than 13 million people moved from rural to urban centers in the 1920s. They became city folk and worked in factories and offices or ran local service establishments. Their manner, clothing, and style of living also reflected the many changes that had taken place. The long, trailing dresses that women wore earlier in the century slowly gave way to shorter skirts revealing more and more leg. Large, plumed hats that required pins to keep them in place were no longer fashionable and were discarded altogether or replaced by smaller, more comfortable ones.

The most important exception to the generalization about the urbanization of the country was the South, which looked no "different than it had at the end of Reconstruction in the 1870s." Southerners planted and harvested crops as they had for decades, and suffered chronic agricultural depression. The grinding poverty inflicted on African-Americans because of racial bigotry and discrimination sent 500,000 of them northward to industrial cities following World War I. They became an essential part of the population migration that so characterized the 1920s. Their number continued to rise during the decade when another million blacks deserted the South and headed north to find employment in factories and packinghouses.

A postwar economic boom was one basic reason for this migration. And the boom developed because of a revolution in technology. New products were developed, new machines were invented, new methods were devised to increase productivity, and new industries were founded, in turn stimulating the nation's economy. A good example of what was happening was the invention of the "horseless carriage." Automobiles by the millions rolled off assembly lines in American factories in the 1920s. Henry Ford applied the assembly-line technique in producing his cars, and the Model T Ford became the favored means of transportation. By the end of this decade the automobile industry provided employment for nearly 4 million individuals.

The electrification of the nation also grew at a tremendous pace, with nearly seventy percent of American homes receiving electric power. The increase in the demand for power resulted in the expansion of the industry, and it soon became the second most important economic activity in the country. Consequently, the production of home appliances, motorized machines, and electric turbines also expanded. Radio transmitters and receivers, which had been invented prior to the

Great War, became another popular commodity, resulting in a broadcasting system that enveloped the nation. The motion picture camera had been invented by Thomas Edison in 1896, but not until the beginning of the twentieth century did the motion picture industry emerge as an art form, especially with the production of *The Birth of a Nation* in 1915. Motion picture theaters were opened in thousands of cities and towns, and by the 1930s the industry enjoyed an investment value of $2 billion and employed nearly 500,000 people.

Perhaps the most spectacular technological development of this period in U.S. history was the growth of the airplane industry. It started at Kitty Hawk, North Carolina, on December 17, 1903, when Wilbur and Orville Wright made the first successful flight aboard a heavier-than-air plane. During World War I, aviation began to show its value and importance. Stimulated by the war, the airplane industry took off, and twenty-four plants were established, producing more than 20,000 planes a year. Aviation became an integral part of the nation's army and navy, and soon airplanes carried mail, passengers, and cargo around the world. Journeys that had once taken days, weeks, or months to complete now took only hours. Then, on May 21, 1927, in a solo flight, Charles A. Lindbergh flew his monoplane *The Spirit of St. Louis* from New York to Paris in thirty-three hours nonstop. The age of flight had truly arrived. In time, especially after the introduction of jet-powered planes, members of Congress would fly home to their districts for the weekend, going as far away from Washington as Alaska and Hawaii.

AMERICAN SOCIETY CHANGED in many other ways following World War I. The Eighteenth Amendment to the Constitution, introduced in 1917 and ratified in 1919, prohibited the manufacture, sale, and transportation of intoxicating liquors. The Volstead Act, passed over Wilson's veto on January 16, 1920, was intended to implement the Eighteenth Amendment. Prohibition had become law, but many Americans had no intention of changing their drinking habits. To obtain liquor, they relied on bootleggers, or they made it themselves in their bathtubs. This acceptance of illegal activities corrupted the thinking of Americans throughout the country and encouraged a carefree disregard for the law. Even in Washington, among the very men who voted for Prohibition, the law was ignored. Congressmen even had their own bootlegger, a man by the name of George L. Cassiday, who operated out of the House Office Building on Independence Avenue. When Prohibition "first came in," declared Alice Roosevelt Longworth—the daughter of Theodore Roosevelt and the wife of the Speaker of the House of Representatives, Nicholas Longworth—"we grumbled, shrugged our shoulders, decided to use the stock we had, and when that was gone turn our attention to wine making and distilling in the home, thinking that undoubtedly supplies would trickle in from one source or another. I don't think that we foresaw in the slightest degree the great bootlegging industry that was to develop, the complete and organized violation of law and order."

Because of the number of customers and the profits involved in the illegal transportation of liquor from foreign countries, such as Canada, criminals were drawn to the operation. Organized crime became rampant. The Mafia, an offshoot of a Sicilian criminal organization, controlled not only bootlegging but gambling and prostitution in the major cities.

Many ordinary citizens frequented "speakeasies," where they could purchase illegal liquor. In these dark, crowded places young women, called flappers, could be seen dancing the Charleston or listening to jazz and the blues. Jazz began among black musicians in New Orleans but quickly spread north and reached Chicago just before World War I. Fundamentally African in its rhythms and tradition, jazz drew from black ragtime, but also included French, Spanish, and English elements. In the 1920s it circled the globe and attracted the attention of serious composers. A number of popular musicians, such as Cole Porter, Jerome Kern, Irving Berlin, and George Gershwin, provided songs that became classics and were sung worldwide. These songs marked the beginning of an American musical tradition that was innovative and unique and extremely popular.

In this jazz age flappers wore short dresses, cut their hair short, and smoked cigarettes. Having lost husbands, brothers, and boyfriends in the war, and parents in the influenza epidemic of 1919–1920, they exhibited a carefree wildness and independence that represented an entirely new version of the American woman. They had the vote and a sense of freedom that encouraged a boldness never expressed before.

In American literature a number of distinctive, talented voices were heard. The most important literary trend provided venturesome styles of writing in the novels of Ernest Hemingway, F. Scott Fitzgerald, John Dos Passos, Theodore Dreiser, and Sherwood Anderson. They completed the full development of the naturalistic school of literature. In drama Eugene O'Neill virtually single-handedly created the American theater tradition. And such writers as T. S. Eliot, Ezra Pound, e. e. cummings, Robinson Jeffers, Robert Frost, and Carl Sandburg added outstanding and uniquely American works of poetry. A celebration of black culture known as the Harlem Renaissance, by such gifted writers as Langston Hughes, W. E. B. DuBois, James W. Johnson, Alain Locke, and Claude McKay emphasized both the joy and the pain of being African-American. Painters like Georgia O'Keeffe produced works that had a definite American cast, and Frank Lloyd Wright's "prairie-style" architecture was so distinctive that it drew international attention.

The Roaring Twenties generated an economy that seemed unstoppable in its growth and strength. Actually, it was headed for a resounding crash. In addition, this period witnessed the renewed growth of the Ku Klux Klan throughout the South; then it migrated northward and established itself in many northern states. A "Red Scare," emanating from a fear of communism and foreign influence in American life and culture, not only increased isolationism throughout the country but resulted in the arrest of hundreds of individuals suspected of subversive activities. The Red Scare intensified after June 2, 1919, when an assassin attempted to kill the U.S. attorney general, A. Mitchell Palmer. The courts dismissed any concern they should have had about the legality of such arbitrary arrests as they too were caught up in the excitement over fear of foreign radicals. Such disdain for the law and the rules of society engulfed the nation and seeped into the operation of government on the local, state, and national levels. Corruption became widespread.

In Washington this corruption reached monumental heights. At its head was the President himself, Warren Gamaliel Harding. His personal tastes ran to booze, gambling, and sex—not necessarily in that order. His immoral behavior was soon reflected in the many scandals that permeated his administration. The most notorious of these scandals occurred in 1921, when two naval oil reserves, at Teapot Dome in

Wisconsin and Elk Hills in California, were transferred from the Navy Department to the Interior Department and subsequently leased, without competitive bidding, to private oil companies. The secretary of the interior, Albert B. Fall, received hundreds of thousands of dollars in bribes while the lease was still being negotiated. When an investigation revealed the extent of the fraud, Fall fled to Europe, but he was caught, brought home, tried, convicted, and sentenced to prison. He was the first cabinet officer in American history to be fined and imprisoned for his crimes. Other members of the Harding administration also went to the penitentiary. Some committed suicide rather than face an investigation.

The nation's isolationism and xenophobia manifested themselves very distinctly in passage of the First Immigration Quota Act, on May 19, 1921, limiting the number of immigrants to be admitted to the country. Accordingly, the number of aliens of any nationality was not to exceed three percent of the number of persons of that nationality listed in the 1910 census; also, the act set a limit of 357,803 immigrants per year.

Just as the scandals of his administration were about to burst into public view, President Harding died suddenly of a heart attack on August 2, 1923. The Vice President, Calvin Coolidge, was immediately sworn in, taking the oath at 2:47 on the morning of August 3. A determined conservative, he pressured Congress to amend the Immigration Act so that certain nationalities that he deemed unworthy of entering the United States would be discriminated against. As it turned out, he had considerable vocal support in Congress. "I think this chamber here," pontificated Representative J. N. Tincher of Kansas, "is a place where we ought to think, act and do real Americanism." By permitting more immigrants to enter this country, he argued, the day may come when a member of the House will have to say "Mr. Speaker in Italian or some other language."

Responding to the President's request, Congress agreed to another immigration bill on May 26, 1924; this one lowered the quota of each nationality to be admitted to two percent, based on the 1890 census. Furthermore, only 150,000 immigrants would be admitted each year, and Japanese citizens were excluded altogether. But at least Native Americans were finally granted citizenship. On June 2, 1924, the Indian Citizenship Act was passed, providing equality in American society to the native population. These two laws—the Immigration Act and the Indian Citizenship Act—stood in marked contrast to each other: the one restricted admission; the other extended citizenship rights. Because of the Immigration Act it was believed in some quarters that within a generation or so the foreign-born would cease to be a major factor in American society. But this generalization did not take into account the number of illegal immigrants who would daily violate the border with Mexico and seek a new life in the United States. There was a large and eager market for unskilled laborers, especially in the farming industry. Fruit and vegetable growers in the Southwest chose not to ask probing questions of their workers about their legal status.

Congress also passed the National Budget and Accounting Act on June 10, 1921, that created for the first time a Budget Bureau in the Treasury Department to regulate and supervise the expenditures of the national government. Later, during the Great Depression, President Franklin D. Roosevelt moved this bureau from the Treasury Department to the White House in order to better control and regulate the sources and disbursement of funds.

During the 1920s there was a considerable effort to provide social and economic improvements. Progressives in both parties—including such men as Senators Robert La Follette of Wisconsin, George Norris of Nebraska, William E. Borah of Idaho, and Burton K. Wheeler of Montana, along with Representatives Fiorello La Guardia of New York, John M. Nelson of Wisconsin, and Victor Berger, a Socialist, of Wisconsin—held a conference in Chicago in May 1923 in which they agreed upon a wide program of reform. They proposed child labor limitation, lower railroad rates, farm relief, freedom for the Philippines, excess profits taxes, and limits on the power of injunctions which were issued by the courts to halt labor strikes. It would take time—more time than they expected or wished—but eventually most of these reforms were enacted into law.

The xenophobia and isolationism so prevalent during the 1920s were reflected in the presidential election of 1924. Naturally, the Republicans nominated Coolidge, but a number of Insurgent Republicans formed a new Progressive Party and nominated Senator Robert La Follette. During the campaign they attracted Socialists, Bull Moosers, and Single Taxers. They proposed the nationalization of the railroads, public development of hydroelectric facilities, and the right of Congress to override decisions of the Supreme Court. At the Democratic convention northern delegates who represented Jews, Catholics, and the foreign-born demanded the condemnation of the Ku Klux Klan and repeal of the Eighteenth Amendment, but southern delegates, controlled to a large extent by the KKK and representing religious fundamentalists, objected. After a protracted struggle between Governor Alfred E. Smith of New York, a "wet" on Prohibition, a Catholic, and a chieftain of New York City's Democratic stronghold, Tammany Hall, and a former secretary of the treasury, William G. McAdoo, who supported southern "drys," the convention gave the nod to John Davis, a New York lawyer with strong ties to banking and industrial interests. But it took 103 ballots to produce this candidate.

An important innovation occurred during the campaign. For the first time the conventions were broadcast over the newest form of communication, radio. Radio stations in New York, Washington, and sixteen stations in twelve cities across the country, carried the proceedings. Some politicians had a natural flare for this new medium, such as Franklin D. Roosevelt. His speech for nomination of Governor Smith, wherein he dubbed him "the Happy Warrior of the political battlefield," electrified the audience and made him an instant celebrity.

This new method of communication became immediately popular and necessitated the establishment of the Federal Radio Commission, with five members appointed by the President to issue and revoke licenses for the operation of radio stations and to regulate programming. The name of this commission was later changed to the Federal Communications Commission (FCC), and granted additional power over television after its invention.

Not unexpectedly, Coolidge and the Republican Party enjoyed a stunning victory. Coolidge himself garnered over 15 million votes, compared with 8 million for Davis and almost 5 million for La Follette. Both houses of Congress were also captured by the Republicans.

THE ROARING TWENTIES were rightly named. And how they roared. American songs, jazz, the shimmy (a dance), and illegal drinking gave the 1920s a special and uniquely American quality. In addition, everyone seemed to be making money, one way or another. The stock market soared; investors found all sorts of ways to increase their wealth, including buying on margin, that is, putting down only a fraction of the cost of a stock with the idea of selling when the price rose and reaping a tidy profit. It seemed so easy.

Only farmers were excluded from this rich harvest. They continued to experience economic depression. Farm prices went into a steady decline following World War I, and conditions on the farm became dire. This should have been a warning of what might happen to the rest of the country. Farmers appealed to the government for help but received little. They formed a farm bloc and demanded subsidies to underwrite the unloading of farm surpluses overseas. But what few bills passed in Congress were quickly vetoed by Coolidge on the ground that the measures constituted price fixing for a special interest. Still, the lingering farm depression might easily spread to the industrial and commercial sectors of the country, and that could produce a major catastrophe.

It came soon enough.

IN THE PRESIDENTIAL election of 1928 the Republicans chose Herbert Hoover to head their ticket, along with Charles Curtis, while the Democrats fielded Alfred E. Smith and Joseph T. Robinson, a senator from Arkansas. During the campaign Hoover promised to provide relief for the despairing farmers, and this promise undoubtedly helped him to win the election overwhelmingly. He captured forty of the forty-eight states for a total of 444 electoral votes while Smith won the remaining eight states with 87 electoral votes. This election also brought the first African-American from outside the south to Congress. Republican Oscar S. Priest of Illinois took a seat in the House of Representatives and served with distinction from 1929 to 1935. Because Washington was so racially segregated, he was forced to dine in the basement of the Capitol next to the kitchen rather than in the all-white dining room for congressmen on the first floor.

Hoover called Congress into special session to deal with the economic problems facing farmers and suggested raising the tariff on all imported agricultural products. Despite many problems, which took more than a year to resolve, Congress finally enacted the Smoot-Hawley

Tariff and the President signed it on June 17, 1930. It was the highest tariff ever passed by Congress and raised import duties on agricultural items to forty-five percent, with special protection awarded to sugar, cotton, and citrus fruits. These increases were so excessive that twenty-six foreign countries retaliated by raising their rates, and American exports took a nosedive. To aid the farmers even further, Congress passed the Agricultural Market Act in June 1929, which established the Federal Farm Board of eight members plus the secretary of agriculture and created a revolving fund of $500 million for low-interest loans to cooperatives to build warehouses and sell surplus crops.

But these efforts came too late. On October 23, 1929, the stock market crashed, and thus began the worst economic depression in the nation's history.

Christopher Columbus

Amerigo Vespucci

Boston Massacre

Jonathan Edwards

Washington addressing members of the Constitutional Convention

Thomas Paine

Alexander Hamilton

James Madison

George Washington

Thomas Jefferson

John Marshall

Lewis and Clark expedition

Battle of New Orleans

Inauguration of Andrew Jackson

Andrew Jackson

The County Election,
painted by
George Caleb Bingham

John C. Calhoun

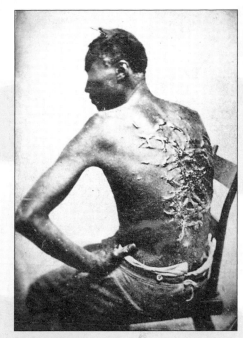

The brutality of slavery

Elizabeth Cady Stanton

Susan B. Anthony

Daniel Webster

Charles Grandison Finney

Henry Thoreau

James Fenimore Cooper

Herman Melville

John J. Audubon

Walt Whitman

Henry Clay addressing the Senate about his Compromise of 1850

Abraham Lincoln

New York artillery, Arlington, Virginia, 1865

Jefferson Davis

Union soldiers in trenches at Petersburg, Virginia, 1864

Thaddeus Stevens

Devastation in Atlanta, 1865

Devastation in Richmond, 1865

Hiram R. Revels

Joseph H. Rainey

Thomas Edison

Theodore Roosevelt

Woodrow Wilson

Kitty Hawk, North Carolina

Jeanette Rankin

Ernest Hemingway

George Gershwin

Eugene O'Neill

The Great Depression, New York City, March 1933

Franklin D. Roosevelt

Pearl Harbor and the sinking of the USS *Arizona*

Stalin, Roosevelt, and Churchill at Tehran, 1943

Senator Joseph McCarthy

Harry S. Truman

John F. Kennedy

Reverend Martin Luther King Jr.

Lyndon B. Johnson

Civil rights demonstration, Washington, D.C., 1963

Landing on the moon,
Apollo 11, July 20, 1969

Vietnam

Watergate Senate Judiciary Committee, 1973

Ronald Reagan

Watergate House Judiciary Committee, 1973

House Impeachment Committee, 1998

William Jefferson Clinton

Speaker Newt Gingrich

Terrorist attack, September 11, 2001

8

The Great Depression, the New Deal, and World War II

WITHIN ONE DREADFUL month the stock market continued its descent until something like $30 billion in the market value of listed stocks was wiped out. This economic collapse would continue for ten years. Businesses by the hundreds went bankrupt, unemployment soared, deflation resulted, and the price of commodities hit an all-time low.

There were many causes for this disaster, besides those already suggested. The Federal Reserve banking system had not been properly run, allowing all manner of improper procedures to generate profits; abuse of credit invited investors to buy stocks without paying the full price; a high incidence of criminal dishonesty had seeped through the business community; and the inflexibility of the gold standard system.

To address the growing agony, President Hoover called for a relief program that would initiate federal leadership to assist voluntary efforts at the state and local levels. He also requested funds in the amount of $100 million to $150 million for a program of public works. But by the summer of 1931 conditions had worsened, and the depression intensified for the next five years. Approximately 2,300 banks, with deposits of over $1.5 billion, failed that summer. The number of unemployed increased from 7 million in 1931 to 14 million by 1936. People migrated from the cities back to the countryside in the hope of scratching out a living. People starved, they lost their homes through foreclosures; they took charity where they could find it; they begged for help. There was a profound loss of confidence in both business and government. A number of congressional investigations turned up evidence that bankers had misappropriated the funds of depositors and had manipulated the stock market in a gamble for greater returns. Investment bankers were seen as villains who, by their actions, had brought on the depression, and Americans blamed Herbert Hoover for failing to bring it to an end. The secretary of the treasury, Andrew Mellon, argued that somehow the normal operations of the business cycle would come into play and bring about an upswing in economic conditions. It was simply a matter of waiting it out. "Let the slump liquidate itself," he declared. "Liquidate labor, liquidate stocks, liquidate the farmers. . . . People will work harder, live a more moral life. Values will be adjusted, and enterprising people will pick up the wrecks from less competent people." Small wonder the American people came to loathe the Hoover administration.

Strangely, Americans did not lose confidence in the capitalist system. Communism did not attract them, nor did fascism—unlike citizens of several European nations. And although there were some hunger marches and riots, the actual number of violent incidents was relatively few. Perhaps the most spectacular display of organized marches was the "Bonus March" on Washington that occurred in 1932, when 12,000 to 15,000 unemployed war veterans descended on the capital and demanded immediate payment in cash of the bonus promised them in 1924 when Congress authorized it over Coolidge's veto. It was meant to compensate veterans for their low-paying service during the last war compared with the high wages earned by civilians. The act provided compensation to all veterans on the basis of $1.25 a day for overseas service and $1 a day for service in the United States. Unfortunately the bonus was not to be paid until 1945. But these veterans and their families were starving. They needed the money now, and they demanded that the government give it to them. To bolster their spirits they sang war songs and displayed placards that read: "Cheered in '17, Jeered in '32." Just outside the capital, on Anacostia Flats, they built shelters that constituted little more than a shantytown. Then violence erupted, causing two deaths, whereupon President Hoover summoned the army, under the command of General Douglas MacArthur, then chief of staff, to restore order. Using excessive force, which was hardly necessary, the army dispersed the veterans with tear gas and then burned the shantytown. The incident only led to further bitterness toward the government.

The Hoover administration did propose a Reconstruction Finance Corporation (RFC) that would create a government lending agency with a capital of $500 million and authority to borrow up to an additional $1.5 billion. Some Democrats and Progressives dubbed it a "millionaires' dole." What was needed, they insisted, was a national system of unemployment insurance. Despite this criticism, the RFC passed Congress on January 22, 1932, and the agency subsequently extended credit to banks, corporations, life insurance companies, building and loan associations, farm mortgage societies, and railroads. However, it did not assist small businesses or individuals threatened with the loss of their homes; nevertheless, it did prevent the largest banks throughout the country from going bankrupt. Then, on July 21, 1932, an Emergency Relief and Construction Act passed, broadening the scope and authority of the RFC to aid construction and agricultural agencies and provide funds to states that were unable to ameliorate economic distress within their jurisdiction.

On February 27, 1932, Congress also enacted the Glass-Steagall Bill, permitting the Federal Reserve Bank to sell $750 million from the government's supply of gold, which had been used to support the currency in order to meet the continuing foreign withdrawals. This measure was also designed to counteract the hoarding of gold by citizens. In July the Federal Home Loan Bank Act established a series of eight to twelve banks around the country by which savings banks, insurance companies, and building and loan associations might join and thereby have the capital to provide home mortgages for home buyers. The act was intended to prevent foreclosures.

Two Progressives in Congress—Senator George W. Norris and Representative Fiorello La Guardia—sponsored the Norris–La Guardia Act, which recognized labor's right to unionize. It outlawed "yellow dog" contracts, which obliged workers to promise not to join a union, and it limited the power of the federal courts to issue injunctions against labor's right to organize.

But efforts to provide federal money for relief and public works were resisted by Hoover, who insisted that the government should help end the depression by balancing the budget and should cease enlarging the pork barrel. A proposed $900 million for public works, he argued, was an outright "raid on the public treasury." Nevertheless, a $2 billion relief measure passed Congress, only to be vetoed by the President. He particularly opposed a feature that allowed the RFC to make loans to individuals and small businesses. He also vetoed a bill for the construction of a hydroelectric facility, at Muscle Shoals on the Tennessee River in northern Alabama, which would provide electrification for a vast area of the Southeast. The President called the measure a gigantic leap by the government into private business. To him it smacked of socialism.

THE DEVASTATING ECONOMIC collapse gave Democrats unbounded confidence that they could achieve a monumental victory in the upcoming presidential election. They held their convention in Chicago in June 1932, and since expectations ran high, the contest for the nomination turned into a battle royal between the forces of Al Smith, supported by Tammany Hall, and the Governor of New York, Franklin D. Roosevelt, who had won reelection in 1930 by the largest majority ever received by a gubernatorial candidate in the state's history. A Harvard graduate who had studied law at Columbia University, an assistant secretary of the navy during the administration of Woodrow Wilson, FDR suffered an attack of polio in 1921 but through determined efforts had achieved partial recovery by 1928. Although he enjoyed the backing of a majority of delegates, he lacked the necessary two-thirds for nomination. Not until the fourth ballot, after the very conservative John Nance Garner of Texas, the Speaker of the House of Representatives, threw his support to Roosevelt, was he nominated to head the Democratic ticket. In return, Garner received the vice presidential nomination, which would remove him from his much more powerful position as Speaker, something reform-minded Democrats had hoped to do. Disregarding the tradition by which a candidate normally waited until he was formally notified of his nomination, Roosevelt flew from Albany, New York, to Chicago to personally deliver his acceptance speech. His flight electrified the entire nation. And on his arrival at the convention he made a solemn vow to the delegates: "I pledge you, I pledge myself, to a New Deal for the American people."

The party platform demanded repeal of the Eighteenth Amendment and promised a reduction of federal expenditures to balance the budget and a removal of the federal government from all areas of private activity "except where necessary to develop public works and natural resources." It further promised to send money to the states in order to provide relief for the unemployed, to reduce tariff levels, and to reform the banking system so as to maintain a sound currency.

The Republicans renominated Hoover on the first ballot, and Vice President Charles Curtis; and they put forward a platform calling for a balanced budget, reduced government spending, loans to the states for relief, the repeal of the Eighteenth Amendment, and continuation of a protective tariff, among other things. Except for the tariff, the two platforms were exactly alike in many respects.

This election also produced an especially large number of political parties offering candidates for the presidency and vice presidency, including the Prohibition, Communist, and Socialist parties. The Prohibition Party nominated William D. Upshaw and Frank S. Regan; the Communist Party, William Z. Foster and James W. Ford; and the Socialist Party, Norman Thomas and James H. Maurer. All told, there were eight parties in this race.

Strangely, both major parties during the campaign seemed more concerned about getting rid of Prohibition than about finding jobs for the unemployed. Perhaps they felt that repealing the Eighteenth Amendment would be easier than solving the nation's economic problems. "Here we are, in the midst of the greatest crisis since the Civil War," sniffed the philosopher and educator John Dewey, "and the only thing the two national parties seem to want to debate is booze."

Actually, Roosevelt gave any number of radio addresses in which he outlined a program of social and economic reforms. With the assistance of a group of Columbia professors, known as the "brain trust," and including such men as Adolph A. Berle, Raymond Moley, and Rexford G. Tugwell, he said, it was the duty of government to adapt existing economic organizations to the needs of the people, and to find the means by which the distribution of wealth and products would be more equitable. Naturally, Hoover savaged FDR's goals as a radical departure from traditional American values and practices. He called for the decentralization of government in order to allow private business to expand. But his mood and tone sounded depressing, whereas

Roosevelt exuded confidence that he was the man who could rescue the nation from this terrible disaster. He scored many points with the American people by alluding to Hoover's supposed callousness toward the starving and his seeming unwillingness to aid those in distress.

The results of the election of 1932 completely reversed the political fortunes of the two major parties. Roosevelt swept the cities and rural areas outside New England for a total of nearly 23 million popular and 472 electoral votes. Hoover carried Maine, New Hampshire, Vermont, Connecticut, Delaware, and Pennsylvania with almost 16 million popular and 59 electoral votes. The Socialist, Thomas, won almost 900,000 popular votes; the Communist, Foster, won 100,000; and the Prohibitionist, Upshaw, 80,000. And both houses of Congress were won by the Democrats.

The lame-duck Congress did nothing to address the worsening economic conditions in the country. Its members simply did not know what to do. They let everything slide until the new administration could take office on March 4, 1933. Industrial construction had plunged from $949 million to a disastrous $74 million. Depositors attempting to withdraw their money from banks caused runs on these institutions, and many of them went bankrupt. Some 50,504 banks closed from 1930 through February 1933. Fourteen million people were out of work. There was talk that what the nation desperately needed was a dictatorial direction of the government. "A genial and lighthearted dictator might be a relief," editorialized one publication, "from the pompous futility of such a Congress as we have recently had." In Germany, such a dictator had already emerged, but he was hardly genial and lighthearted. Adolf Hitler was chosen chancellor in January 1933 and would later plunge Europe and the world into further chaos.

FRANKLIN D. ROOSEVELT was sworn into office on March 4, the last President to take the oath of office four months after his election. On February 6, 1933, the Twentieth Amendment was ratified which directed that henceforth the members of Congress who were elected the previous November would take office on January 3 and the President and Vice President on January 20 instead of March 4. In his inaugural address, Roosevelt tried to restore confidence in the ability of the government to successfully address the dreadful conditions that existed throughout the country. Again, he pledged that he would provide a dynamic program of action to restore prosperity. "This great nation," he exclaimed, "will endure, as it has endured, will revive and prosper. So, first of all, let me assert my firm belief that the only thing we have to fear is fear itself."

It was exactly what Americans needed to hear. And the New Deal, as FDR's program was called, began to function immediately. First, Roosevelt shut all the banks in the country for four days. Next, he summoned Congress to a special session on March 9. As members of the House were still finding their way into the chamber on the designated day, the Speaker, Henry T. Rainey of Illinois, started reading the only available copy of the administration's Emergency Banking Relief bill, which contained last-minute corrections written in pencil. After thirty-eight minutes of supporting speeches, the bill passed the House sight unseen by a unanimous voice vote. Within the first four hours of the session Congress enacted a banking bill that authorized the secretary of the treasury to investigate the financial conditions of every bank in the country and permit only those banks that proved sound to reopen. The bill also declared illegal the ownership of gold and instructed the treasury secretary to call in all gold and gold certificates. By midsummer at least three-quarters of all banks in the country had reopened and resumed normal operations. Confidence had been restored, if slowly, and the runs on banks virtually ceased.

This special session, which lasted until June 16 and was known as the "Hundred Days," succeeded in enacting a comprehensive corps of legislation involving banking, agriculture, labor, industry, and unemployment relief. Indeed, this First New Deal aimed specifically at addressing the problems of relief and recovery.

Even before the New Deal got under way, Congress had begun the process of responding to popular demand for the repeal of the Eighteenth Amendment. The Twenty-First Amendment passed both houses on February 3, 1933, and won ratification by the states on December 5, 1933. At the same time this amendment made its way through the states, FDR asked Congress to end Prohibition by legalizing beer. Within a week the bill passed, and the President signed it on March 22. Beer and wine of 3.2 percent alcoholic content were now legal.

Prohibition proved to be an excellent example of what not to do in tampering with the Constitution. It needs to be remembered that the document outlines the structure of government and its responsibilities. It is not meant to reflect each and every passing fancy, many of which are social fads of limited value or duration.

As the congressional session progressed it became clear that party leadership had shifted to the White House. Because of the crisis facing the nation, the need for quick and decisive action, as well as the popularity of the President, Congress willingly abdicated its authority. Roosevelt himself had no strong commitment to a particular economic program but was willing to experiment to find the means with which to combat the depression. He quickly established direct contact with the electorate through regularly held press conferences and especially through his radio talks, called "fireside chats." But he was deficient as an administrator, frequently dividing authority and responsibility among subordinates in the hope of maintaining his own control.

And control legislation is exactly what he did. "I have seen the Congress of the United States," commented one Republican Representative from Tennessee, "absolutely abdicate its authority to the Executive. I have seen a dictatorship spring up which must have made the noses of Herr Hitler, Stalin, Mussolini and Mustapha Kemal of Turkey turn green with envy."

During the first Hundred Days an avalanche of legislation descended on Congress and was immediately enacted. These included the Civilian Conservation Corps (CCC), the Federal Emergency Relief Act (FERA), the Agricultural Adjustment Act (AAA), the Tennessee Valley Authority (TVA), the Federal Securities Act, the Gold Standard Repeal Act, the National Employment System Act, the Home Owners Refinancing Act, the Banking Act of 1933, the Farm Credit Act, the Emergency Railroad Transportation Act, and the National Industrial Recovery Act (NIRA). These measures provided employment for 250,000 jobless male citizens between the ages of eighteen and twenty-eight (CCC); allowed outright grants to states to initiate work relief (FERA); created an agency to control surplus crops so as to raise farm prices (AAA); established an independent public agency to build dams and power plants and develop rural electrification (TVA); required full disclosure to investors of information about securities; removed the United States from the gold standard and made all contracts and public obligations payable in legal tender; authorized a national employment system; set up the Federal Deposit Insurance Corporation to guarantee individual bank deposits under $5,000 (FDIC); created the Home Owners Loan Corporation to refinance home mortgages for owners who were not farmers (HOLC); refinanced farm mortgages for long terms at low interest; and instituted a better rule of rate-making to improve the operation of railroads. The NIRA established the Public Works Administration to stimulate the economy by constructing huge public works, and it guaranteed the right of workers to organize and bargain collectively through representatives of their own choosing.

By the time this Hundred Day Special Session of Congress ended, an extraordinary variety of economic reforms had been enacted. Farmers, laborers, and industrialists were affected. By this legislation the nation had committed itself to assist the unemployed, guarantee bank deposits, protect individual homeowners and farmers, and undertake vast public works projects.

Still, the depression persisted. By the end of 1933 the income of most Americans had declined by half. A million or more individuals had been evicted from their homes when they could not pay the rent or meet their mortgage payments. Some 9,000 banks and 86,000 businesses had failed. A farmer received ten cents for a bushel of oats, several pennies below what it had cost him to raise the crop. Approximately 20 million Americans during this awful time needed some form of federal relief to stay alive.

The growing reliance by Congress on the chief executive to move the country out of the depression was demonstrated most forcefully when the administration proposed a Reciprocal Trade Agreement Act that permitted the President to raise or lower existing tariff rates up to fifty percent for countries that would reciprocate with similar concessions. Republicans in the House of Representatives strongly objected to the proposal, claiming that it violated the Constitution because all bills raising revenue must originate in the lower house. So the Democrats amended the bill to limit the President's negotiating power to three years and to terminate any agreement after three years. The measure then passed, and Roosevelt signed it on June 12, 1934. By this action Congress surrendered to the executive a power it had jealously guarded for more than 150 years.

This Congress also established the Securities and Exchange Commission on June 6, 1934, to prevent price manipulation of stocks and curb speculation and unfair practices in the securities market. The Corporate Bankruptcy Act, passed on June 7, attempted to assist in the reorganization of corporations that could not meet their financial obligations. And the Federal Farm Mortgage Foreclosure Act extended loans to farmers on favorable terms so as to prevent foreclosures.

In the midterm election of 1934, when traditionally the party in power loses seats, the results came as a blow to the Republicans. They had expected to increase their membership in Congress, but this time they lost seats in both the House and the Senate. As one historian has pointed out, never in its history had the Republican Party taken such a loss. In the House they now had only 103 members, whereas the Democrats had 322 and the Independents 10. The situation in the Senate was just as bad. The Democrats held 69 seats, the Republicans 25, and Independents 2.

But an opposition to FDR's policies had arisen in the country not only among conservative businessmen who felt that he coddled labor and was spending the country into bankruptcy but also among more radical-thinking leftists. Senator Huey P. Long of Louisiana, for example, proposed to divide the wealth of the country and give every family a guaranteed annual wage of $2,500. Father Charles E. Coughlin, a priest in Detroit who had a large radio audience, attacked Roosevelt as a tool of Wall Street, while Dr. Francis E. Townsend of California demanded a $200 monthly pension for every person over sixty years of age.

In his annual address to Congress, delivered on January 4, 1935, FDR jettisoned much of the First New Deal and outlined a program of social reform that historians have called the Second New Deal. First came a $5 billion work-relief program authorized by the Emergency Relief Appropriation Act of April 8, 1935, which set up the Works Progress Administration (WPA). Roosevelt invited Harry Hopkins, a leading advocate of the welfare state, to head this agency. Jobs were created for professionals such as musicians, actors, writers, and historians as well as college students, clerks, secretaries, and other unemployed workers. Over the next six years the WPA spent more than $11 billion and gave employment to millions of Americans.

Hard on the heels of this Emergency Relief Act came the Soil Conservation Act (April 27); the Rural Electrification Administration (May 11); the National Youth Administration (June 26) established by executive order granted by the Emergency Relief Act; and perhaps most important of all, the Social Security Act (August 14). The Social Security Act established a federal-state system of unemployment compensation and old age pensions, thereby transferring to the federal government functions that once had been the responsibility of families and of state and local governments. It imposed a tax on employees' wages and employers' payrolls beginning on January 1, 1937, but would not begin to pay retirement benefits until 1942, a date later advanced to 1940 by amendments passed in 1939. But it failed to provide coverage for domestic servants, agricultural workers, public workers, and certain professionals. Later the act was amended to cover many more employees.

Also important was passage on August 23 of the Banking Act of 1935, the only fundamental revision of the Federal Reserve Act since its inception. By this act a new board of governors had direct and complete control over interest rates, reserve requirements, and the open market operations of the Federal Reserve banks.

Earlier, on July 5, the National Labor Relations Act, better known as the Wagner Act after one of its sponsors, Senator Robert Wagner of New York, created a board with authority to oversee collective bargaining by labor and management. It placed government in support of the right of labor to bargain collectively, and it required employers to permit the peaceful unionization of their companies. The Wagner Act and the Social Security Act were probably the most radical of the bills of the Second New Deal. In addition, the Holding Company Act (August 28) broke up the large electric and gas holding companies and placed the financial operations of these companies under the supervision of the Security and Exchange Commission (SEC). The legislation ultimately abolished holding companies.

Despite FDR's numerous victories in Congress, by the close of his first term as President he faced growing opposition from conservative Democrats and Republicans. He also, unexpectedly, faced the opposition of the Supreme Court. On "Black Friday," May 27, 1935, in a unanimous decision, the court struck down the industry code provisions of the NIRA in the case *Schechter Poultry Corp. v. United States.* The court declared that Congress had improperly delegated power to private industry and interfered in businesses engaged in intrastate activities; and that Congress had also delegated legislative authority to the executive that was unwarranted by the Constitution. The following January, in *United States v. Butler,* the court declared unconstitutional the Agricultural Adjustment Act that authorized payment to farmers to keep land out of production, because this law invaded state power over intrastate commerce. Then in May 1936, in the bituminous coal case, the court invalidated the Coal Conservation Act, declaring that coal mining was a local activity. The Supreme Court had effectively paralyzed the ability of the President and Congress to deal with the depression. In some of these cases the decision resulted from a bare majority, and critics accused the court of attempting to legislate by judicial decree.

Critics insisted that the Supreme Court had to be curbed by removing its right of judicial review, or by requiring unanimity to declare a law unconstitutional, or by allowing Congress to override a court ruling with a two-thirds vote, the same procedure and authority it had in overriding a presidential veto.

Matters came to a head when Roosevelt won another landslide victory in the presidential contest of 1936 over the Republican Alfred M. Landon of Kansas. During the convention the Democrats abolished the traditional two-thirds vote necessary for nomination—which had been the rule since the first Democratic convention in 1832—and replaced it with a simple majority. In his acceptance speech Roosevelt decried the new "despotism wrapped in the robes of legal sanction." The Republican platform denounced the New Deal as a gross violation of the Constitution and accused Roosevelt of usurping the powers of Congress.

But FDR's extraordinary popularity with the electorate won him 60.4 percent of the popular vote and every state in the Union except Maine and Vermont. He carried with him a great number of Democrats running for federal and state offices. In the House of Representatives there was an overwhelming majority of 333 seats, compared to 89 for Republicans; in the Senate the count was 76 to 16. Encouraged by this strong show of support, Roosevelt unwisely decided to remake the membership of the Supreme Court. He planned to ask Congress for authority to appoint a new judge for each judge who had served on the court for at least ten years and did not retire within six months after reaching the age of seventy. Among the nine members of the Supreme Court (the "nine old men," as they were derisively called), six justices had already passed the age of seventy. It was clear to everyone that FDR was seeking revenge for the recent court decisions striking down essential programs of the New Deal. If such a plan ever won congressional approval, it would mean that the court would be expanded to fifteen members. And since FDR would name six of them, he would be certain to form a majority of pro–New Deal justices. The President chose not to inform the party's leadership in Congress in advance of his intentions for the simple reason that, in the words of Speaker William Bankhead, "he knew that all hell would break loose."

And it did. The inviolability of the court had long been acknowledged. Its tradition of standing above politics and partisanship was generally understood and appreciated by the American people. But FDR saw only its conservative bent and its apparent opposition to social and economic reforms. So he insisted on going ahead with his "court-packing" scheme. Many Americans saw his plan as an unconscionable attempt to destroy the independence of the judicial system. And his efforts only further alienated many members of Congress who had resented his assumption of legislative authority and had kept quiet for fear of reprisals from their constituents. Now that the election had passed, they were less hesitant about demonstrating their displeasure. In fact, a split within the Democratic party had already begun along regional and ideological lines. A new conservative bipartisan coalition emerged among southern Democrats and northern Republicans. They no longer feared popular reprisals, because they knew that the electorate would resist any tampering with the Supreme Court. The chairman of the House Judiciary Committee, Hatton Summers of Texas, rejoiced. "Boys," he cried, "here's where I cash in my chips."

FDR's decision was also badly timed, because in March 1937 the Court had already indicated its recognition of and sympathy with some of the purposes of the New Deal and had approved several important pieces of legislation. A minimum-wage bill was upheld (*West Coast*

Hotel v. Parris), as was the National Labor Relations Act (*NLRB v. Jones and Loughlin Steel Corp.*). Most important, the justices approved the Social Security legislation in *Steward Machine Co. v. Davis*. By these decisions the Court ended the quarrel with the President. FDR lost the battle but won the war. Instead of his court-packing bill, he was forced to accept a weaker measure, the Judicial Procedure Reform Act, on August 26, 1937. This legislation permitted federal judges to retire at full pay after they reached age seventy, but did not authorize the appointment of new federal judges. In time, with the retirement of many of the "nine old men," the President filled the Supreme Court with New Dealers, and this "Roosevelt Court" upheld the constitutionality of every important New Deal measure.

The failure of the court-packing scheme had one beneficial result: it helped restore a better balance between the executive and legislative branches. No longer could FDR expect Congress to accede to his every wish. A proper respect for the prerogatives of Congress was necessary if the President expected to win approval for his more controversial measures. Henceforth he found it beneficial to consult with congressional leaders beforehand and try to accommodate their needs and wishes.

One important success came on September 1, 1937, with passage of the National Housing Act. Senator Robert Wagner had been trying for years to get it enacted, but the House defeated it. Henry Steagall, chairman of the House Housing Committee, considered the measure financially reckless and socialist. Roosevelt then stepped in and used his charm to persuade Steagall to allow the bill out of his committee so it could be voted on by the members, knowing full well that a majority of them would approve it. Out of a sense of party loyalty, Steagall agreed. The Wagner-Steagall Housing Act, as passed, created the United States Housing Authority as a public corporation under the Department of the Interior and made available $500 million in loans for low-cost housing. By 1941 the authority had provided funds for building more than 500 low-rent buildings containing 161,000 apartments, at a cost of $767,526,000.

A SHARP RECESSION early in 1938, resulting in part from Roosevelt's efforts to balance the budget at the same time that the new Social

Security tax was imposed, brought a decline of industrial production, higher unemployment, and another stock market decline. Several additional New Deal measures were enacted by which billions of dollars were pumped into the WPA and AAA. The Minimum Wage and Hours Act of 1938 not only prohibited child labor but mandated a minimum wage of twenty-five cents an hour, to be increased to forty cents, and limited a workweek to forty-four hours the first year and forty hours thereafter. Almost 1 million workers benefited by this measure.

The Food, Drug, and Cosmetic Act won approval in June 1938, widening the Pure Food and Drug Act of 1906. It required the manufacturers of food, drugs, and cosmetics to list the ingredients on labels, and it prohibited false and misleading advertisements. Violations would incur heavy fines.

One important aspect of the New Deal was its revolutionary stimulation of the labor movement. Labor had gained the right of bargaining on more or less equal terms with management in most industries. The American Federation of Labor (AFL), founded in 1886 by Adolph Strasser and Samuel Gompers of the Cigar Makers' International Union of New York, consisted mostly of skilled workers. Gompers was elected president and served every year·but one from 1886 until his death in 1924. He chose to lead the union toward higher wages and shorter work hours, rather than the more radical wing of the labor movement, which aimed to bring about wholesale reform of the movement to include unskilled workers. By 1936 certain labor leaders, notably John L. Lewis of the United Mine Workers Union and Sidney Hillman and David Dubinsky, presidents of the garment workers' unions, demanded that the AFL organize industries, irrespective of the work performed by their laborers, so that the still unorganized industries, such as automobiles, steel, and rubber, could be unionized. The old, conservative leaders of the AFL refused, whereupon Lewis and others, in 1937, formed the Committee for Industrial Organization (CIO), which became a separate and independent labor organization. It soon unionized the steel and automobile industries and others, although the workers sometimes had to resort to sit-down strikes in which they refused to leave their factories until management agreed to meet and negotiate fairly with their representatives. Roosevelt aided labor by refusing to send in troops to end the sit-down strikes. With his active encouragement this new labor organization expanded rapidly. By 1941 the CIO had a membership of nearly 5 million, and the AFL a membership of a little over 4.5 million. Later, in 1955, the two organizations merged.

FOR ALL INTENTS and purposes the New Deal program came to an end largely because of events transpiring both inside and outside the United States. Europe had become a powder keg because of the economic crisis that brought Adolf Hitler to power in Germany. Earlier, Benito Mussolini had established a fascist dictatorship in Italy, and Joseph Stalin had begun a tyrannical reign in the Soviet Union. These three dictators chose to intervene in a civil war that had broken out in Spain. Hitler and Mussolini provided military aid to the fascist army of General Francisco Franco, who had launched a war against Spain's Republican regime. Stalin threw his support to the loyalists, and there was fear that this struggle between fascism and communism could widen into another world conflict. Roosevelt seemed anxious to initiate some action by which collective security (that would "quarantine" nations that threatened international stability) could be established. But a strong sense of isolationism still permeated the United States, and any movement toward collaborative action with Europe guaranteed an immediate and hostile response from a concerned electorate. The fear of communism was widespread, and any thought of radical ideas infiltrating this country and undermining fundamental American values brought demands for strengthening national defenses. So FDR scrapped any idea of collaborating with Europeans and instead focused his attention on the military preparedness of the United States. In addition, he asked Congress to appropriate $1 billion for defense and the building of a two-ocean navy.

As the result of the mounting fear of communism, the House of Representatives established a committee on May 26, 1938, to investigate "the extent, character, and objects of un-American propaganda activities in the United States." Martin Dies Jr., a Democrat from Texas and a rabid xenophobe and anti–New Dealer, headed this committee. He claimed that the Roosevelt administration was swarming with "Communists, Socialists, and the 'ordinary garden variety crackpots.'" Secretary of the Interior Harold Ickes responded by calling Dies "the outstanding zany of American political history."

The hearings of the Dies Committee began in the summer of 1938 and concentrated on communist infiltration into the country, completely neglecting any threat of fascism. Witnesses made many unsubstantiated accusations, and the accused rarely had the right of rebuttal. During the first few days of the hearings something like 640 organizations, 483 newspapers, and 280 labor unions were cited as having communist connections. At first this committee was limited to eight months' duration, but ever-increasing concern around the country about the communist menace caused representatives to extend the committee each year until 1945, when it was renamed the House Committee on Un-American Activities.

By the winter and spring of 1938–1939 Congress began to halt the further expansion of the New Deal by cutting the administration's requests for additional relief appropriations, defeating a housing bill, and abolishing a profits tax. "For God's sake," several congressmen told the President's press secretary, "don't send us any more controversial legislation." And since FDR was not expected to run for a third term in 1940, congressmen no longer feared that he could harm them at the polls or command their loyalty through control of patronage. So rather than remain silent as they had done in the past, they now challenged him when they opposed his requests.

The New Deal was also affected by developments in Europe. Chancellor Hitler denounced the Treaty of Versailles, and in violation of that treaty began to rearm Germany. Great Britain and France did nothing to stop him. He then sent troops into the demilitarized German Rhineland and concluded a military alliance with Italy and Japan. Furthermore, he invaded and occupied Austria, and signed a Nazi-Soviet Pact with Stalin. This pact allotted western Poland to Germany, and Russia gained Estonia, Latvia, eastern Poland, Bessarabia, and later Lithuania. Then Hitler threatened to invade Czechoslovakia if it did not surrender the Sudetenland, which had more than 3 million inhabitants of German ancestry. No doubt encouraged by the criminal actions of his German ally, Benito Mussolini invaded Albania. Prime Minister Neville Chamberlain of Great Britain and Premier Edouard Daladier of France met with Hitler and Mussolini in Munich on September 28, 1938, and agreed to the dismemberment of Czecho-slovakia. Chamberlain returned to Britain believing he had a guarantee of "peace in our time."

It is interesting but useless to contemplate what might have happened had Britain and France together stood up to Hitler and challenged his foreign adventures. But they feared provoking another world war, so they remained silent, which only encouraged further assaults on the peace and stability of Europe.

In the United States there was a feeling that this country should remain aloof from any involvement in European affairs. America's priority was achieving economic recovery, not "seeking monsters in the world to destroy." There were organized peace efforts around the country, reminding the nation's leaders that the electorate opposed war and any entanglement with Europe. The spirit of isolationism still persisted, and the message was clearly understood in Washington.

Then the situation suddenly changed. Hitler invaded Poland on September 1, 1939, and Britain and France declared war against Germany two days later. Stalin attacked Poland on September 17 as part of his agreement with Hitler, and on September 29 these two vultures partitioned that hapless country. Stalin then invaded Finland on November 30. To everyone's surprise, the Soviet Union could not defeat and absorb Finland, and so a peace treaty was signed between the two countries on March 12, 1940. Meanwhile Roosevelt called Congress into special session on September 21, 1939, and asked that the arms embargo of the Neutrality Act of 1937, which forbade the sale of U.S. armaments to belligerent nations, be repealed so that Britain and France could purchase military equipment from America. The danger of this spreading conflagration in Europe had become so acute that Congress acceded to FDR's request and passed the Neutrality Act of 1939, by which it authorized "cash and carry" purchases of arms and munitions to belligerents.

A quiet period in the European war followed, as Hitler prepared for a spring offensive. Newspapers called it the "phony war." Then, suddenly, on April 10, 1940, fighting burst out in explosive violence as Germany launched a blitzkrieg, or lightning war, in which tanks, dive-bombers, airborne troops, and motorized infantry raced across neutral countries and overran Denmark, Norway, Holland, Belgium, Luxembourg, and France. British troops in France were hurriedly evacuated from the port city of Dunkirk in late May. Over 300,000 British and French troops were rescued by 861 ships of all sizes and types. Chamberlain resigned his office and was succeeded on May 11 by Winston Churchill. Germany now occupied much of the European continent, including all of northern and western France, since Paris had fallen on June 16 and the French government had asked for an armistice. What was left of France was turned over to a hastily formed government centered in Vichy under a rabid anticommunist, the aged Marshal Henri-Philippe Pétain. Italy declared war against France and England, and it was feared that the Nazis would launch an all-out invasion of Great Britain from France and Norway. But Hitler turned his attention to the Balkans, overran Romania and Bulgaria, and swept up Yugoslavia and Greece.

Fearing that the United States would soon be drawn into the conflict, Roosevelt asked Congress for an appropriation of $1.2 billion for defense and signed the first Revenue Act of 1940, which raised the federal debt limit to $4 billion. He also asked for and received passage of the Selective Service Act (or draft) on September 16, the first enacted in peacetime. This legislation provided for the registration of all males between the ages of twenty-one and thirty-five for a one-year training program. The first draftees were selected on October 29.

It was obvious that the United States was sympathetic to the Allies' cause, and Roosevelt acted accordingly. In September he transferred fifty old but still serviceable American destroyers to Britain so that the Royal Navy could hunt Nazi submarines and convoy merchant ships safely across the oceans. In return the United States received the use of eight naval bases from Newfoundland to British Guiana.

With a presidential election approaching in the fall of 1940, both major parties actively advocated increased aid to Great Britain. The Republicans had expected to nominate a staunch midwestern anti-interventionist, such as Senators Arthur H. Vandenberg of Michigan or Robert A. Taft of Ohio. But Americans panicked over the demonstration of German military might as it powered its way across Europe and brought about the collapse of the French government. So, at their convention, the Republican delegates chose instead Wendell L. Willkie of New York, who was the president of an important utilities company and a former Democrat, who actively advocated additional aid to Britain. His running made was Senator Charles L. McNary of Oregon.

FDR let it be known that he would accept nomination for a third term, even though it would violate the two-term tradition begun by George Washington. The Democrats really had little choice. The extremely popular President enjoyed national support and could not be denied. He was nominated unanimously on the first ballot. He then chose the left-leaning Secretary of Agriculture, Henry A. Wallace, to run for the vice presidency.

At first there was little difference between the two presidential candidates during the campaign, in both domestic and foreign policy. In fact, Willkie approved the draft and the transfer of the destroyers to Great Britain. Not until he accused Roosevelt of leading the country into war did he attempt to differ with FDR's record. The President responded by assuring the American people that he would not send Americans into any foreign wars.

The election brought another triumph for Roosevelt. He won a third term by capturing a plurality of nearly 5 million popular votes (down from 11 million in 1936) and a majority of 449 electoral votes. Willkie won forty-five percent of the popular vote but carried only ten states, for a total of 82 electoral votes.

IN EARLY DECEMBER 1940, FDR received a request from Winston Churchill. The letter explained Britain's urgent need for munitions, airplanes, and other military supplies to carry on the war but admitted that the British government did not have the money to pay for them. Because of the mounting submarine attacks by the Germans, Britain desperately needed American help in order to keep the North Atlantic supply lines open. Roosevelt solved the problem by devising a lend-lease program. He held a press conference on December 17, followed by a fireside chat over the radio twelve days later, in which he explained to the American people the absolute need to lend or lease equipment and supplies to Britain for victory over the forces of fascism. "We must be the great arsenal of democracy," he declared. He concluded his fireside chat by saying, "I call upon our people with absolute confidence that our common cause will greatly succeed." He made it clear that by this action this country fully committed itself to the defeat of Germany.

The Lend-Lease Bill was introduced in Congress in early January 1941, and after a long and full debate it passed both houses overwhelmingly by March 11. Roosevelt signed it immediately and then asked for $7 billion to purchase the materials; his request was approved. The Lend-Lease Act of 1941 allowed any nation whose defense the President deemed vital to American interests to receive arms, munitions, and any other supplies and equipment by sale, transfer, exchange, or lease. The President also asked Congress for support of those nations who were fighting in defense of what he called the Four Freedoms: freedom of speech, freedom of religion, freedom from want, and freedom from fear.

Although Roosevelt still hoped to keep the United States out of the war, he was certainly willing to do whatever was necessary to ensure Germany's defeat. Even when German U-boats attacked and sank American destroyers with a loss of lives, he did not go to Congress and ask for a declaration of war. But he did publicly denounce the "piratical" acts of German submarines, and he ordered American naval vessels to shoot on sight any U-boat that appeared in waters west of Iceland. Furthermore, when Germany invaded the Soviet Union on June 21, 1941, he immediately assured the Soviets that they would receive lend-lease assistance with all due dispatch. Roosevelt gave Hitler every excuse possible to declare war against the United States, but the dictator did not have the will or the armies to take on such an adversary. His forces were fully occupied elsewhere.

In August 1941, Roosevelt and Churchill met aboard the USS *Augusta* off the coast of Newfoundland and agreed on eight principles that would form a better future for mankind. This Atlantic Charter, as it was labeled, called for a restoration of the people's right to govern themselves without dictators. It also called for freedom of the seas, a peace with justice, equal access to raw materials for all nations, and an end of the armaments race.

AS EARLY AS 1931 Japan began its military aggression against China and took control of the southern region of Manchuria. It then set up a puppet regime in September 1932 called Manchukuo. After entering an alliance with Germany and Italy (the Triple Alliance), thereby becoming a member of the Axis powers, it pledged mutual assistance in the event of war. With designs on French Indochina, Japan then signed an agreement with the Vichy government in France that allowed the Japanese to establish military bases in Indochina.

The renewed aggressiveness of the Japanese in Asia prompted Roosevelt to issue a sharp warning to Japan on July 26, 1941, by renouncing the Japanese-American Commercial Treaty of 1911 and halting all shipments of steel and scrap iron to countries outside the western hemisphere, except Great Britain. This embargo was aimed directly at Japan, and it was deeply resented. Indeed, General Hideki Tojo and other Japanese militarists regarded it as a hostile act. Since half the oil, steel, and iron that Japan needed to maintain its economy came from the United States, something had to be done to restore trade relations between the two countries if Japan was to remain a viable modern, industrial state. It tried negotiating, offering one concession after another, such as promising not to attack the Soviet Union and giving assurances that it would not be bound by the Triple Alliance to declare war against the United States if America went to war with Germany. But Secretary of State Cordell Hull demanded more. He wanted Japan out of China, which was totally unacceptable. In turn the Japanese insisted that the United States cease giving aid to the new Chinese leader, Chiang Kai-shek, something Hull refused to do.

An impasse ensued, whereupon the Japanese turned to violence as a solution. On November 20, 1941, an aircraft-carrier strike force under the command of Admiral Isoroku Yamamoto set out from Japan and headed for the Hawaiian Islands, maintaining radio silence for the entire journey. On Sunday morning, December 7, three waves of aerial bombers from the carriers attacked the American naval base at Pearl Harbor. Taken completely by surprise despite several warnings that the Japanese might launch an assault, the administration failed to notify army and navy commanders in Hawaii of the possibility and as a result American forces on the island suffered crippling losses. Nineteen ships were sunk or disabled, including eight battleships. Over 100 airplanes were destroyed, and more than 2,000 men killed. The Japanese also struck naval and air bases in the Philippines, Guam, Midway, Hong Kong, and the Malay Peninsula. Indeed, the American air force in the Philippines was virtually annihilated when its planes on the ground were hit at their base near Manila. Clearly, neither the leaders in Washington nor the commanders in the field understood the military capability of the Japanese. Roosevelt, Hull, and General Douglas MacArthur, commander of the armed forces in the Philippines, had no idea of the intentions of the Japanese, and as a consequence the United States suffered the most devastating military defeat in its entire history up to that time.

Roosevelt had just finished lunch when Secretary of War Henry L. Stimson informed him of the attack at Pearl Harbor. The President immediately summoned the leaders in Congress to meet with him that evening. The next day he appeared before a joint session. He mounted the rostrum, supported by his son James, a member of the lower chamber, and addressed the assembled members, cabinet officers, Supreme Court justices, and a large number of men of the foreign diplomatic corps.

"Yesterday," the determined-toned President began, "December 7, 1941—a date which will live in infamy—the United States of America was suddenly and deliberately attacked by naval and air forces of the Empire of Japan. . . . I ask that Congress declare that since the unprovoked and dastardly attack by Japan on Sunday, December seventh, a state of war has existed between the United States and the Japanese Empire."

When the joint session ended at 12:40 PM, the Senate returned to its chamber and unanimously voted for war. In the House the resolution would have been unanimous save for the negative vote of Jeannette Rankin of Montana, who had also voted against a declaration of war in 1917. The resolutions from both houses were rushed to Roosevelt, who signed them at 4:10 PM. Three days later, on December 11, both Germany and Italy, in compliance with the Triple Treaty, declared war on the United States. On the same day Congress replied with similar declarations, and this time Rankin simply voted "present."

General George Marshall, who had been serving as Army Chief of Staff since 1939, continued in the position until the end of the war. Admiral Ernest J. King was chosen Chief of Naval Operations. Later Marshall and King each received the new five-star rank of General of the Army and Admiral of the Fleet, respectively.

THE ANGER, OUTRAGE, and thirst for revenge by Americans against the Japanese on account of the "dastardly" attack on Pearl

Harbor were so intense that Japanese-American citizens living principally along the West Coast suffered the same fate that befell Native Americans over a century before. They were removed. Congressmen from California, Oregon, and Washington joined other public officials, newspapers, and various pressure groups and complained that the West Coast of the United States was vulnerable to invasion and demanded that Japanese aliens and Japanese-American citizens be expelled from their homes and relocated to the interior. Roosevelt responded by issuing an executive order in February and March 1942, authorizing the secretary of war to designate certain areas as restricted military zones from which "unacceptable" individuals would be excluded. More than 100,000 people of Japanese descent, including Japanese-American citizens, living along the West Coast and in Arizona were removed to what can only be described as concentration camps in the interior. This disgraceful action caused these people to lose homes, businesses, farms, and most of their possessions. On March 21, 1942, Congress approved the action. Without debate, both houses unanimously passed a measure making it a crime to violate military orders in restricted military zones, thus becoming an accomplice to this massive violation of the basic rights of American citizens. The Supreme Court also became a party to this move. It upheld the action as a means of ensuring national security, the same argument Andrew Jackson had given for the removal of American Indians.

Nonetheless, thousands of Japanese-American men in these camps volunteered to fight against Japan and Germany. Taking no chances, the administration sent most of them to Europe. However, when they returned home as decorated war veterans many of them could not recover their lost property or jobs.

Mexican-Americans also suffered, especially those in California. They were victims of urban violence, culminating in the so-called "Zoot-suit war" of 1943 in Los Angeles, when mobs of servicemen roamed and assaulted and robbed at will young Mexican-Americans. Wartime can bring out not only the best but frequently the worst characteristics of any society, and in both areas the United States was no exception.

There was a sense throughout America that the war was justified and right. Fighting the evil of Nazism, Fascism, and militarism in the world so that people could live freely under governments they themselves chose prompted many young men to enlist in the armed services after Pearl Harbor. The Selective Service boards around the country registered about 31 million, of whom 10 million were inducted into service. And the Women's Army Auxiliary Corps Act, sponsored by Representative Edith Nourse Rogers of Massachusetts, passed in May 1942 and created up to 150,000 noncombatant positions (mostly nurses) for women within the army. This corps was intended, said Rogers, to give "women a chance to volunteer to serve their country in a patriotic way." Almost 350,000 women served in the WAACs, the WAVEs, and similar groups in other military branches. A total of more than 15 million American men and women participated in World War II, of whom 10 million served in the army, 3.5 million in the navy, nearly 600,000 in the marines, and 240,000 in the Coast Guard. This was the largest mobilization of manpower in U.S. history. Sadly, some 253,573 died during the war, and 651,042 were wounded, 253,573 missing, and 114,205 taken prisoner.

Of necessity, the war vastly increased the powers of the chief executive. His involvement in and control of foreign and domestic policy was expected by both the electorate and Congress. On December 16, 1941, the First War Powers Act was approved, followed on March 22, 1942, by the Second War Powers Act, which authorized the President "to make such redistribution of functions among executive agencies as he may deem necessary" to prosecute the war. The cost of the war ran into the billions, and the Secretary of the Treasury Henry Morgenthau in March 1942 asked for $56 billion for defense out of a budget of $59 billion. The Revenue Act of 1941 had raised taxes to a level that brought in revenues of $13 billion, the largest single revenue bill in the nation's history up to that time. But the Revenue Act of 1942 went farther, raising the excess profit tax from sixty to ninety percent and the income tax from four to six percent and imposing a "victory tax" of five percent on those with a gross income over $624. Furthermore, it lowered exemption levels to the point where they produced millions of new taxpayers. In fact, this act has been described as the income tax that transformed a "class tax" to a "mass tax." Between 1941 and 1945, the cost of the war came to $321 billion, a little over half of which was borrowed. Consequently, the national debt rose from $49 billion in 1941 to $259 billion in 1945.

On January 13, 1942, Roosevelt appointed Donald M. Nelson to head the War Production Board, which would mobilize the nation's vast resources so that the war could be brought to a speedy conclusion. The Office of Production Management, under William S. Knudson, had been established on December 29, 1941, to coordinate defense production to supply Great Britain and its allies with needed materials, as well as the Office of Scientific Research and Development on June 28, 1941. Price controls and rationing were established along with the Offices of Economic Stabilization, Censorship, War Information, and Strategic Services.

And it is truly amazing what American industry produced in terms of wartime matériel, resulting from unlimited governmental credit, the high demand for these products, and the effective organization necessary to achieve the desired results. American factories produced 75,000 tanks; 275,000 military aircraft; and 650,000 pieces of artillery. American shipyards built 55.24 million tons of merchant shipping. Perhaps no other national economy was managed so efficiently and successfully. In addition, as a result of the Office of Scientific Research and Development, American scientists, with the help of their British colleagues, invented radar, by which ships and planes could be detected from afar.

Most important of all was the development of the atom bomb. The Manhattan Project, under the direction of Brigadier General Leslie R. Groves, was set up to secretly build this crucial weapon. It was a crash program to create the atomic bomb before the Germans perfected one. Considering the long head start the Germans enjoyed in perfecting advanced weaponry, it is astounding that the Americans succeeded in their quest and the Germans did not. Had the Germans succeeded, the war might have ended differently. The three bombs produced by the Manhattan Project cost $2 billion. The first of them was tested on July 16, 1945, at Alamogordo, New Mexico, and a whole new world began.

MEANWHILE, THE WAR in Europe expanded when Hungary and Romania joined the Axis powers, and Italy had invaded Greece with German help and forced its capitulation on April 27, 1941. England endured an agony of daily air raids forcing Londoners to seek shelter in subways and other underground facilities. Germany penetrated deep into the Soviet Union and laid siege to Leningrad. Far worse, the yet generally unknown but systematic extermination of Jews had begun in the gas chambers of Auschwitz, Poland.

The first massive European operation in which American troops participated was the command in North Africa to drive out the Italians and Germans. Hitler's Afrika Corps, under Field Marshal Erwin Rommel, fought the British for control of Egypt, and American tanks arrived just in time to stop the Nazis from advancing. Then, in October 1942, the British general Sir Bernard Montgomery and his army launched a counteroffensive and defeated Rommel at El Alamein. The following month a massive Anglo-American army under General Dwight D. Eisenhower brought about a surrender by the Germans on May 12, 1943, after a long and bitter struggle. The entire Mediterranean area from Gibraltar to the Suez Canal was now under Allied control. Meanwhile the Russians captured an entire German army at Stalingrad and lifted the siege of Leningrad.

From Africa, an Anglo-American force consisting of General Montgomery's Eighth Army and General George S. Patton's Seventh Army invaded Sicily on July 10, 1943, and after heavy fighting subdued the island on August 17. Then, on September 3, 1943, the Allied force crossed the strait and landed on the toe of the Italian peninsula. They also struck at Salerno, below Naples, and Anzio, near Rome, again encountering fierce resistance by the Germans. Not until June 4, 1944, did the Allies capture Rome. Mussolini was overthrown and captured but was rescued by the Germans and taken to Lake Como in the north, where he attempted to form a government. In this struggle to occupy Italy the Americans suffered more than 70,000 casualties.

In Asia the Japanese seized Guam, Hong Kong, Singapore, Burma, Thailand, the Malay Peninsula, the Dutch East Indies, New Guinea, and the Philippines within six months of declaring war. General Mac-Arthur managed to escape from the Philippines but promised to return. As a result of these many victories, Japan commanded the western half of the Pacific Ocean and expanded its territorial conquests to more than a thousand miles in southeast Asia.

But then the war in the Pacific took a turn for the better for the Americans with the first major defeat of Japanese naval forces. A large fleet of aircraft carriers and other warships under the command of

Admiral Yamamoto headed for Midway Island, a base of strategic importance because of its location 1,000 miles northwest of the Hawaiian Islands. For the United States, the capture of Midway by the Japanese would have been catastrophic. But American experts had broken the Japanese code, and a fleet under Admiral Chester Nimitz lay in wait. In a titanic battle that lasted from June 3 to June 6, 1942, torpedo bombers from the U.S. aircraft carriers *Yorktown*, *Hornet*, and *Enterprise* decimated the Japanese fleet, sinking four aircraft carriers, a heavy cruiser, and three destroyers, and shooting down or destroying 275 airplanes. Yamamoto retreated with what remained of his fleet. This battle stopped the eastward advance of the Japanese, rescued Hawaii from possible invasion, and restored the balance of naval power in the Pacific to American hands.

Then began a period of successful "island hopping," with the invasion of Guadalcanal in the Solomon Islands in August 1942, Tarawa in the Gilberts in November 1943, Guam and Saipan in 1944, and Iwo Jima in March 1945. The following month—April 1945—marines invaded Okinawa and captured it on June 21. American forces were now poised only 350 miles from Japan itself. The U.S. Pacific fleet consisted of 24 battleships, 26 cruisers, 64 escort carriers, 323 destroyers, and 15,000 combat airplanes.

On October 20, 1944, General MacArthur began an invasion of the Philippines. From October 23 to 25 the naval battle of Leyte Gulf took place. It was the last and greatest naval battle of the war. It extended over hundreds of miles and involved 35 large and small aircraft carriers, 21 battleships, 35 cruisers, hundreds of destroyers, submarines, motor torpedo boats, and more than 1,500 aircraft in four separate engagements. The American forces could have been annihilated because Admiral Halsey and his Third Fleet had been lured away to the north, leaving Admiral Clifton Sprague to protect the invasion of the Philippines, but the Japanese suddenly withdrew from the battle after losing 4 carriers, 2 battleships, 9 cruisers, and 9 destroyers. The American forces then invaded Luzon, the principal island of the Philippines, and captured Manila on February 23, 1945.

In January 1943 Roosevelt met with Winston Churchill in Casablanca and agreed to demand "unconditional surrender" by Germany as the only acceptable terms for ending the war. Achieving that goal began with the invasion of Italy, followed on June 6, 1944, with a massive invasion of France by American and British troops, called Operation Overlord, under the command of General Eisenhower. Some 176,000 Allied troops aboard 4,000 landing craft, supported by 600 warships and an air cover of 10,000 planes, crossed the English Channel; landed along a fifty-nine-mile stretch of the Normandy coastline; and began the recapture of Europe. It was the greatest amphibious landing operation ever undertaken, and it faced stiff opposition by a strong German defense. Weeks of heavy fighting followed before the Allies broke through and occupied Paris on August 25. Six Allied armies, totaling more than 2 million men, slammed their way to the Siegfried Line, smashed it, and crossed the Rhine River on March 7, 1945.

Meanwhile, FDR had won a fourth term as President the previous November when he and his running mate, Senator Harry S. Truman of Missouri, defeated Governor Thomas Dewey of New York and Governor John W. Bricker of Ohio by capturing over 26 million popular and 432 electoral votes, against 22 million popular votes and 99 electoral votes for Dewey. The choice of Truman for Vice President resulted from his superb handling of a Senate committee investigating the National Defense Program. He was a devoted and knowledgeable student of American history who did not wish his committee to be guilty of the blunders committed during the Civil War by the Joint Committee on the Conduct of the War.

On the eastern front, the Soviets had launched a counteroffensive, following a meeting of FDR, Churchill, and Stalin in Tehran, Iran, on November 28, 1943, that reaffirmed Stalin's commitment to enter the war against Japan and establish an international union to keep the peace after the war. The Soviets lifted the siege of Leningrad, recaptured Stalingrad, and drove the Germans out of Russia.

In another action to address possible problems once the war ended, Congress passed the Servicemen's Readjustment Act of 1944, better known as the G.I. Bill of Rights, which authorized the Veterans Administration to assist veterans of World War II in readjusting to civilian life by providing academic training, medical assistance, loans, and employment programs. It was an immediate success. Within ten years more than half of all World War II veterans had taken advantage of one or more of the many benefits provided by the G.I. Bill.

Meanwhile, the Allied forces drove across Europe, and Germany was subjected to constant and devastating air raids. Roosevelt, Churchill, and Stalin met in Yalta on February 4–11, 1945, to plan the shape of Europe and the division of Germany after the war. Two months later, on April 12, 1945, FDR died of a cerebral hemorrhage in Warm Springs, Georgia. The elevation of Harry Truman to the presidency came just as Soviet forces were about to launch an assault on Berlin, something Churchill had pleaded with Eisenhower to prevent. The British Prime Minister wanted the Allied powers to occupy Berlin, but Eisenhower rejected the plea for military reasons. The general felt it was more important to prevent the escape of the German army to mountain strongholds in Bavaria. The capture of Berlin was not worth the loss of American and British lives, he argued. The German capital fell to the Russians on May 2, Hitler committed suicide, and on May 7 his successor, Grand Admiral Karl Doenitz, ordered all German naval and land forces to surrender. The unconditional surrender was signed by German delegates at Eisenhower's headquarters the following day in the city of Rheims.

On July 28, 1945, the Senate ratified the United Nations Charter, which committed the United States to a policy of internationalism, and the United Nations officially began its operations on October 24, 1945. Although isolationism in the United States had not vanished completely, a larger number of Americans now believed the nation could not escape its responsibility in keeping the peace around the world.

Russia finally declared war against Japan on August 8 and invaded Manchuria. When the United States, Britain, and China demanded that Japan surrender unconditionally, the demand was rejected. Whereupon Truman ordered that the first atom bomb be dropped on the military base and city of Hiroshima. The bombing occurred on August 6, killing and injuring over 160,000 people. Three days later a second atomic bomb was dropped on Nagasaki, wiping out the city.

And that did it. On August 14, the Japanese accepted unconditional surrender, but were permitted to retain their emperor, subject to the orders of the supreme commander of Allied forces in the Far East, General Douglas MacArthur.

Thus ended one of the most destructive wars—if not the most destructive war—in world history.

9

The Cold War and Civil Rights

S HORTLY BEFORE THE end of World War II, Harry Truman delivered his first address as President to a joint session of Congress in which he promised to defend the ideals advanced by FDR and bring an end to "Hitler's ghastly threat to dominate the world." Shortly thereafter, Mussolini was captured and hanged by Italian partisans, and Hitler killed himself in his bunker in Berlin. "The armies of liberation," to use Truman's phrase, had defeated fascism, but one danger to world peace still remained: communism. And fear of communism and its possible spread into the free world intensified in the United States for the next several decades. It became the leading issue in shaping both domestic and foreign policy.

The House of Representatives converted the Dies Committee into the Committee on Un-American Activities in 1945, and this committee, under Democratic control during the Seventy-Ninth Congress, avoided controversy. But when the Republicans won a majority in the House following the midterm election of 1946, the chairman of the Un-American Activities Committee, Parnell Thomas of New Jersey, conducted hearings, in October 1947, into the motion picture industry and made almost daily headlines in the newspapers. Movie stars and studio executives appeared before the committee and were asked to name those persons they knew who had joined the Communist Party. Ten accused screenwriters and producers were asked about their affiliation with subversive organizations. The "Hollywood Ten" they were called, and they challenged the right of the committee to inquire into their political beliefs and refused to answer. Convicted of contempt of Congress, they were added to a blacklist, jailed, and denied employment. This blacklist was later expanded to include radio and television performers.

In August 1948, Richard Nixon of California, a freshman member of the committee, launched a celebrated investigation of Whittaker Chambers, an editor of *Time* magazine and a former communist, who accused Alger Hiss, a distinguished former State Department official, of allegedly providing him with secret government documents, documents hidden away in a pumpkin shell. Hiss denied the charge. The committee could not determine which of the two men was lying, but Hiss was later convicted of perjury.

Abroad, the communist menace spread westward. The Soviet Union controlled and dominated Eastern Europe and occupied the German territory surrounding the city of Berlin. Earlier, the city had been divided into four zones, each controlled by one of the four major powers: the Soviet Union, France, England, and the United States. In a speech in Fulton, Missouri, on March 15, 1946, Winston Churchill declared that "from Stettin in the Baltic to Trieste in the Atlantic, an Iron Curtain has descended across the Continent." The Western powers continued to urge the establishment in Eastern Europe of governments elected by the people, but Stalin had no intention of allowing the creation of new, possibly hostile, governments along the Russian border.

He went further. In an effort to drive the West completely out of Berlin he shut off all traffic into the city on July 24, 1948. Truman responded by airlifting supplies of food, fuel, and other necessities into Berlin. From July 1948 to September 1949, with the British and French cooperating, about 2.5 million tons of supplies were flown to the city in an around-the-clock operation.

A Cold War, as distinct from a hot one, now existed between the free world and the Soviet Union. Then, on September 24, 1949, it become known that the Soviets had detonated an atom bomb, largely constructed using secret information stolen from the United States and Great Britain by citizens of both countries who had communist leanings or had indeed joined the Communist Party. The world had suddenly become very dangerous, especially if the antagonists ever began to hurl atomic bombs at each other. In response, Truman announced that the United States would undertake the development and production of an even more terrible weapon, the hydrogen bomb. The annihilation of civilization had now become a real possibility.

In recognition of the new world that had dawned with the arrival of nuclear weaponry, Congress enacted the Atomic Energy Act on August 1, 1946, transferring authority over atomic energy from the War Department, which had developed the bomb, to a civilian committee of five members appointed by the President. Overseeing the activities of this committee was a Joint Commission on Atomic Energy consisting of nine members from the House appointed by the Speaker and nine members from the Senate appointed by the president of the Senate.

The United States also agreed to the twelve-nation North Atlantic Treaty, ratified on July 21, 1949, which declared that an attack on any one member nation would be considered an attack upon all. The twelve nations included Britain, France, Spain, Canada, Belgium, Luxembourg, the Netherlands, Italy, Portugal, Denmark, Norway, and Iceland. In addition, this treaty established the North Atlantic Treaty Organization (NATO), headed by a council to draw up plans for the defense of the member nations. Later, in 1952, Greece and Turkey joined NATO. It was an historic agreement for the United States. This was the first time the country had joined a peacetime European alliance.

ON THE DOMESTIC front the end of the war witnessed an explosion of economic demand. Four years of sacrifice had made Americans hungry for all the goods and services that had been denied them for so long. Individual and corporate savings approached $50 billion. Unfortunately, there were not enough homes, automobiles, appliances, and other commodities to go around. Demand outstripped supply, causing prices to skyrocket. Then, when Congress reduced taxes by some $6 billion, it only provided additional money in the hands of consumers, which added to the pressure.

When the G.I.'s returned home they were eager to resume their civilian lives, but they had trouble finding adequate housing or adequate living conditions. Many of them began or returned to college to complete their education, thanks to the G.I. Bill. Others pursued professional degrees or borrowed money to purchase homes where available.

A housing boom resulted in which new communities, such as Levit-town in New York, sprang up.

Labor demanded increased wages. Unions boasted nearly 15 million members, and their leaders were determined to seek higher wages suffi-cient to maintain the level necessary to meet the rising cost of living. The railroad union began a strike that threatened to paralyze the country, whereupon Truman seized the railroads on May 17, 1946, and offered a compromise settlement that eighteen unions accepted. But the engineers and trainmen did not accept it, so the President asked Congress to grant him the power to declare a state of national emergency whenever a strike in a vital industry under federal control threatened national security. Strikers would be drafted into the army, they would lose their seniority, and the leaders would be fined and jailed. The House of Representatives passed the measure, but the Senate did not follow suit, because by that time the striking workers had returned to their jobs.

To further complicate the labor situation, John L. Lewis led his United Mine Workers out on strike for higher wages and improved working conditions. When negotiations failed, the mines were seized. A new contract was signed granting most of Lewis's demands, but in October 1946 he made new ones. The government refused to budge, supported by a federal judge's injunction. Lewis defied the injunction and called another strike, which resulted in a fine of $10,000 against himself and $3.5 million against the union. Another contract was agreed upon that conceded most of Lewis's demands, and the problem was finally resolved in June 1947.

But the anger toward unions boiled over in Congress after the Re-publicans won control in the midterm election of 1946. In June 1947, the Taft-Hartley Act, considered by some members as "the most vicious, restrictive and destructive anti-labor bill ever brought before the House," was enacted. Truman vetoed it, but Congress overrode his objection. This legislation outlawed the closed shop, in which only union mem-bers could be hired by employers; forbade "unfair" union practices such as secondary boycotts and jurisdictional strikes; permitted employers to sue unions for damages caused by strikes; required cooling-off peri-ods and temporary injunctions to be issued by the President when na-tional health and safety were concerned; and forbade unions from contributing to political parties. The act had a tremendous impact on the voting habits of union members. Those who had voted Republican in the past now switched to the Democratic Party.

THE COLD WAR between the Soviet Union and the West intensified in early 1947, when the Russians lent their support to a communist-led rebellion against the Greek government and demanded territory from Turkey and the right to construct naval bases in the Bosporus. President Truman responded promptly by asking Congress to appropriate $400 million for military and economic aid to Greece and Turkey. "I believe," he declared, in what would be called the Truman Doctrine, "that it must be the foreign policy of the United States to support free peoples who are resisting attempted subjugation by armed minorities or by outside pressures." Through an amendment proposed by Senator Arthur H. Vandenberg to the effect that the United States would withdraw its aid to Greece and Turkey when the Security Council of the United Nations gave evidence that it could act and resolve the matter, the Greek and Turkish Aid measure passed Congress overwhelmingly in May 1947. This bill marked a radical departure from traditional American foreign policy. It was a clear statement that the United States would not stand idly by as Europe attempted to recover from World War II and the Soviet Union sought to expand its power and influence worldwide. Truman's speech defined the communist threat as a global danger and became the future rationale for U.S. military intervention in both Europe and Southeast Asia. The assistance given to both Turkey and Greece helped those countries fight off Russian pressure, and the Greek civil war ended in 1949.

But the near-disasters that had developed in Turkey and Greece could not compare to the problem facing the countries of Western Europe. France, England, Italy, and Germany, among others, faced bankruptcy, and in France and Italy their dire predicament was a clear signal of a possible communist takeover. The United States had already provided some assistance in the form of loans, but it was not enough. The new Secretary of State, George C. Marshall, then devised a plan, which he outlined in a speech at Harvard University on June 5, 1947, by which the United States would assist European nations to rebuild their shattered economies, provided they came up with a comprehensive recovery program. He said that his plan was directed not against any particular country or ideology, but "against hunger, poverty, desperation and chaos." Representatives from sixteen European countries met in Paris and established the Committee for European Economic Cooperation, which worked out a master plan for the reconstruction of Europe's financial base that required between $16.4 billion and $22.4 billion from the United States. Naturally Russia condemned the proposed Marshall Plan as an obvious ploy by the United States to advance its imperialistic ambitions, and it forbade its satellite states from participating.

For ten months Congress debated the European Recovery Program (ERP) but what turned the tide in favor of the bill was the seizure in February 1948 of Czechoslovakia by that country's Communists, and the measure passed overwhelmingly on March 31. Truman signed it on April 3. Between April 1948 and December 1951, the United States contributed a little over $12 billion to Europe through the Economic Cooperation Administration. By 1951 Europe had not only achieved its prewar level of production but its level of industrial production rose to virtually guarantee genuine prosperity for the future. At the same time the communist countries throughout eastern Europe had shriveled economically, due in large measure to the fact that the Soviets carted off to Russia whatever materials would enhance their own economic needs.

Inasmuch as the three Allied zones constituting West Germany were considered the industrial center of Europe and therefore the key to the continent's recovery, and inasmuch as the Soviet Union had refused to settle the German situation, the United States and its allies agreed to consolidate their zones and include it in the ERP. So they went ahead and established a West German Federal Republic in June 1948.

Despite the statesmanlike actions taken by Truman in confronting the Soviet threat during the Berlin airlift, he suffered a steep decline in personal popularity. He was seen as an accidental president who failed to meet the standards set by his predecessor. Even more devastating was the internal disorder of the Democratic Party. The President was battered by both the right and the left, and this situation gave the Republicans great hope that they could capture both Congress and the presidency in the election of 1948. On the right, southern Democrats were angry over the fact that Truman had appointed a Civil Rights

Committee in 1946 and had urged Congress to enact the committee's recommendations to root out racial discrimination. On the left, there were some Democrats who hoped for cooperation with the Soviet Union to ensure global peace. They condemned Truman's Cold War policies as likely to lead to a third world war. These Democrats especially resented his dismissal of Secretary of Commerce Henry A. Wallace in 1946, who was a leader of the Democratic left.

There were a great number of Democratic leaders who hoped that Truman would withdraw from the presidential race in 1948, but he stubbornly determined to seek election as President in his own right. When the party convened in Philadelphia on July 12, it nominated him, along with Alben Barkley, the Senate majority leader, as Vice President, despite the fact that many members believed Truman would be defeated in the general election. Late in the evening Truman finally spoke to the delegates and gave a rousing speech in which he promised to summon Congress into special session to address some of the nation's most pressing problems, especially civil rights.

A bitter floor fight broke out over the civil rights plank of the party platform. This plank called for a permanent civil rights commission and federal legislation outlawing lynching and poll taxes. Despite a prolonged battle that turned ugly toward the end, the plank passed, whereupon thirty-five members of the Alabama and Mississippi delegations walked out of the convention, waving the Confederate battle flag as they departed. Several days later, on July 17, so-called Dixiecrats from thirteen southern states organized the States' Rights Democratic Party and held a convention in Birmingham, where they nominated Governor J. Strom Thurmond of South Carolina for President and Governor Fielding Wright of Mississippi for Vice President. Although they did not expect to win the presidency, they did hope to split the electoral vote so that no candidate would win and the election would go to the House of Representatives, where they could negotiate for their votes and in that way achieve their objectives.

As right-wingers of the Democratic Party had deserted to form a third party, the leftists of the party soon followed their example. On July 22 they held a convention in Philadelphia and formed the Progressive Party with Henry A. Wallace as their presidential candidate, along with Senator Glenn Taylor of Idaho for Vice President. Their platform called for the nationalization of certain basic industries and a commitment of friendship toward the Soviet Union.

With the Democratic Party now split into three segments, it was widely believed that Truman would be defeated by any candidate the Republicans put forward. Meeting in Philadelphia, the GOP hoped to convince General Eisenhower to accept a nomination; others wanted the conservative Senator Robert Taft of Ohio; but on the third ballot the delegates again chose Thomas Dewey, the glamorous former district attorney of New York who had won a conviction against one of the most senior Mafia chieftains. The ticket included Governor Earl Warren of California for Vice President.

Truman was so disliked by the electorate, and his party was so fragmented, that Dewey did not feel compelled to mount an aggressive campaign. In fact his approach was so leisurely that he gave the appearance of someone who felt the presidency was his without having to lift a finger to reach for it. A bad mistake. Truman, on the other hand, knew he was fighting for his political life and went on a whistle-stop rail tour in which he gave 351 hard-hitting speeches to an estimated 12 million people. "Give 'em hell, Harry," some crowds called to him. "Pour it on." And Truman did exactly that. He lambasted the "do-nothing Congress," as he termed the Eightieth Congress, a Republican-dominated legislature. He listed its failings, including its rejection of his program for aid to farmers, and its passage of the Taft-Hartley Act over his veto. Furthermore, Truman called Congress back into a special session on July 26 and demanded that both houses at least fulfill the civil rights promises that the two major parties had adopted at their respective conventions. But Congress failed to do anything noteworthy. Its members convinced the public that they were indeed a "do-nothing Congress."

To the astonishment of the entire nation, Harry S. Truman triumphed over his opposition, winning 303 electoral votes to 189 for Dewey and 39 for Thurmond. In the popular vote the President received 24,105,812 to Dewey's 21,970,065; Thurmond's 1,169,063; and Wallace's 1,157,172. In addition, Truman's Democratic Party won back both houses of Congress, taking a majority of 93 seats in the House and 12 in the Senate.

The reasons for this remarkable reversal of conventional opinion became clear as the tabulation of votes continued through election night. First, in the big cities, the Taft-Hartley Act convinced labor that the Republicans had rejected its support. Next, Truman attracted the farm vote of the Midwest by advocating the retention of price supports at ninety percent of parity, whereas the Republicans mentioned only "flexible" price support. Moreover, the rebellion by leftists against the President convinced Americans that the Truman administration was not soft on communism, as the Republicans tried to insinuate. In addition, the revolt by southerners provided proof to African-Americans that the Democratic Party was not dominated by racist bigots and was their best hope for obtaining much-needed and long-delayed civil rights legislation. More than anything else, the fact that the nation enjoyed peace and prosperity helped the Democratic Party immeasurably. And, finally, the Republicans, starting with Dewey, took the people for granted and acted as though their election were a foregone conclusion, something that is always a mistake in politics.

Truman interpreted his victory as a clear message from the electorate that they wanted a continuation of the domestic reform first initiated by the New Deal. In his inaugural address of January 20, 1949, he described his program as a "Fair Deal," which would raise the minimum wage from to forty to seventy-five cents an hour; expand Social Security beneficiaries to 10 million with big increases in benefits for retirees; extend rent control over 800,000 new housing units for low-income families; enlarge the TVA, irrigation, and other water-control and hydroelectric projects; and enact price supports for farmers. But attempts to repeal the Taft-Hartley Act and obtain legislation for civil rights, national health insurance, and federal aid to education failed. However, by executive decree, Truman did advance civil rights within the armed forces and abolished segregation in the federal civil service.

Unfortunately, another "Red Scare" developed that ended the bipartisan support that Truman had enjoyed in winning passage for many parts of his Fair Deal program. Any number of leading Republicans in Congress, especially Senator Robert Taft, attempted to reap political gain by attacking the patriotism and impugning the loyalty of the Democratic Party generally and the Truman administration specifically. The immediate cause was the Communists' seizure of China in

October 1949. Taking advantage of the widespread corruption in the Nationalist Party of General Chiang Kai-shek, Communist rebels led by Mao Tse-tung drove Chiang and his Nationalist army from the mainland to the island of Taiwan off the coast of China. Truman did not intervene to assist Chiang in the struggle, and he was accused of providing indirect aid to the Communists. In Congress, two Republicans—Walter H. Judd of Minnesota in the House and William Knowland of California in the Senate—accused the Truman administration of virtually handing China over to the Communists. The reason, they claimed, was the fact that the U.S. State Department and Foreign Service were riddled with active members of the Communist Party.

The disaster in China occurred just as new revelations were reported about a widespread Soviet spy network in the United States through which atomic and other scientific secrets were transmitted to the communists. On March 22, 1947, Truman directed the FBI to investigate the loyalty of federal employees, and over the next four years about 200 individuals were dismissed as security risks and another 2,000 resigned. Not only did Alger Hiss, who had held an important position in the State Department, stand trial for allegedly turning over secret government documents to a former Soviet courier and found guilty of perjury, but Julius and Ethel Rosenberg were tried, convicted, and executed for helping the Soviets obtain information about building an atomic bomb.

The panic over the infiltration of communists into the government worsened when Republican Senator Joseph R. McCarthy of Wisconsin gave a speech on February 9, 1950, at a Republican Women's Club in the McClure Hotel in Wheeling, West Virginia, and said that he held in his hand a list of 205 names of card-carrying communists in the State Department. Newspapers around the country picked up the accusation and brought the senator the national attention he craved. When it was subsequently shown that the statement was false, McCarthy increased the virulence of his attacks by accusing a number of political leaders, including General George Marshall, of treason. As chairman of a Senate investigating committee, he falsely and recklessly turned his outrageous attacks against members of his own party as well as Democrats. His investigation of the army finally led the Senate, by a vote of 67 to 22, to condemn him on December 2, 1954, for "conduct that tends to bring the Senate into dishonor and disrepute." Before his death in 1957, he had succeeded in making the term "McCarthyism" synonymous with demagoguery and false accusation.

The Red Scare also inspired Congress to pass the McCarran Internal Security Act of 1950 and the McCarran-Walter Immigration and Nationality Act of 1950, which sought to address the problem of communist infiltration into the United States, both of which were passed over Truman's veto. The security measure required communist organizations to register with the attorney general and provide membership lists and financial statements; the immigration act continued the national origin quota systems and provided for the exclusion and deportation of aliens with unacceptable political opinions, especially those from eastern and southern Europe. However, it did rectify an old injustice by allowing the annual admission of 2,000 Asians on a quota basis.

The Cold War got worse during the latter part of Truman's administration when, on June 25, 1950, communist North Korea attacked the Republic of South Korea. The Japanese had annexed Korea in 1910 but surrendered it to the Allies in 1945, at the conclusion of World War II. Russian troops had penetrated Korea down to the 38th parallel and established a communist government. The Republic of South Korea was created in 1948 and recognized by the UN General Assembly and thirty other member states, including the United States. American troops in the country were then withdrawn.

When North Korea launched its attack against its southern neighbor it had the approval of the Soviet Union, which assumed, wrongly, that the United States would make no effort to protect the South Korean Republic. The UN condemned the invasion—an action the Soviet Union might have vetoed, except that it had walked out of the Security Council six months earlier over the refusal to grant Communist China a seat on that body—and by a vote of nine to zero summoned its members to go to South Korea's rescue. Without asking Congress for a declaration of war, an action that would be repeated by future Presidents during other military crises, Truman authorized the deployment of American troops in Korea and dispatched the Seventh Fleet to protect Taiwan. At the same time the UN placed the troops of fifteen other member nations under U.S. command, headed by General Douglas MacArthur, who was still in Japan as Supreme Allied Commander. These troops repelled the communist invasion and by October 1, 1950, won back the territory up to the 38th parallel.

At this point the Communist People's Republic of China warned that if the UN forces crossed the 38th parallel it would send troops to defend North Korea. Foolishly, no one in the West believed the warning. The UN General Assembly counseled MacArthur to secure all of Korea, and he launched a massive invasion of the north, declaring that he expected to end the war by Christmas. But, as promised, the Chinese sent about 1 million soldiers into the disputed territory and drove the UN troops back to the 38th parallel. MacArthur urged Truman to blockade China's coastline, assist Chiang Kai-shek in an invasion of the Chinese mainland, and drop atom bombs on the country if necessary.

The Joint Chiefs of Staff in Washington counseled an altogether different course of action. An all-out war with China was unthinkable. It might bring the Soviet Union into the war to aid its Communist ally inasmuch as the two nations had reached a mutual defense agreement in 1950. As General Omar N. Bradley, chairman of the Joint Chiefs of Staff, stated, a war with China "would be the wrong war, at the wrong place, at the wrong time, and with the wrong enemy."

So MacArthur was ordered to limit his activity to the defense of the Korean Republic. But the general disagreed with the order and, in an action that directly contradicted the administration's foreign policy, he sent a letter to the Republican minority leader in the House of Representatives, Joseph W. Martin of Massachusetts, that said: "We must win. There is no substitute for victory." Martin read the letter in the House, to the delight of most Republicans. Truman responded by relieving MacArthur of his command. "I could do nothing else and still be the President of the United States," wrote Truman. "Even the Chiefs of Staff came to the conclusion that civilian control of the military was at stake, and I didn't let it stay at stake very long."

The President acted properly, but it triggered wild demands for his impeachment. MacArthur returned home to be greeted with jubilant parades and a triumphant appearance before a joint session of Congress. "Old soldiers never die," he told the assembled members, "they merely fade away." And so he did. He faded away.

With the Korean War continuing, despite the beginning of peace talks in 1951, which wearied and frustrated many Americans, the escalation of wholesale prices, which hurt those living on a fixed income or on Social Security, the repeated assaults by Senator McCarthy on the administration's inability to prevent internal subversion, and the evidence of corruption by some members of the administration, caused Truman's rating in popular opinion polls to plummet to unprecedented lows and gave Republicans renewed hope that they could win the 1952 presidential election.

In an effort to block the nomination of the conservative and anti–New Dealer Senator Robert Taft, who swept the South and Midwest in the early primaries, moderate Republicans such as Senator Henry Cabot Lodge, the grandson of Woodrow Wilson's nemesis of the same name, Thomas Dewey, and Governor Earl Warren of California persuaded General Dwight Eisenhower to run for the presidency. He received the nomination on the first ballot at the Republican National Convention in Chicago on July 7. Senator Richard Nixon of California was chosen for Vice President, having won national attention for his exposure of Alger Hiss and for his attacks on the loyalty of Democrats, attacks that won him the nickname "Tricky Dick."

Truman chose not to run for reelection, knowing that his unpopularity was so widespread it would defeat the ticket. Actually, he had been an outstanding chief executive, and later historians generally rated him a near-great president. The Democratic convention, also meeting in Chicago, passed up Vice President Barkley and Senator Estes Kefauver of Tennessee, and on July 27 drafted Governor Adlai E. Stevenson of Illinois to run for President, along with Senator John Sparkman of Alabama for Vice President.

Stevenson was probably the most gifted public speaker since FDR, and in a series of addresses he promised to advance the programs of the New Deal and Fair Deal and win civil rights for African-Americans. But Eisenhower was a popular and genuine war hero who exuded personal magnetism that captivated his audiences. He promised to clean up the mess in Washington, and he won over both senators Taft and McCarthy, along with their supporters. But Eisenhower remained quiet while McCarthy called General George Marshall a traitor, despite the fact that Marshall was chiefly responsible for raising Eisenhower to high command during World War II. Perhaps Eisenhower's most brilliant stroke was in making a promise in Detroit on October 24 that if elected he would go to Korea and attempt "an early and honorable end" to the Korean War. As a result, he won an overwhelming victory, carrying 39 states for 442 electoral and 33,824,000 popular votes, to 89 electoral votes and 26,584,000 popular votes for Stevenson. He even carried four southern states: Tennessee, Virginia, Florida, and Texas. And the Republicans captured both houses of Congress, though by very narrow margins. The twenty-year control of at least one or more of the executive and legislative branches of the government by the Democrats had come to an end.

There was hope that with such a popular and commanding general in the White House and with Congress in Republican control an energetic, effective, dynamic leadership in national and international affairs would result. No such luck. Eisenhower believed that his predecessors had exercised too much control and therefore he did not attempt to direct Congress in enacting a program that reflected his vision of where the country needed to go. He believed that true leadership consisted of reconciling different opinions on important issues, not constructing programs and guiding the legislature toward their enactment. He much preferred to play golf with successful businessmen. Not surprisingly, therefore, between 1953, when the Republicans gained control of the government, and 1955, when they lost it, the party never established true direction or achieved important accomplishments. And after 1955 the Democrats regained control of both houses of Congress and maintained it for the next forty years, winning increasing majorities with each election.

If the President did little to provide exciting ideas for new programs of reform or improvement, he did exactly what the electorate wanted and needed. They preferred rest and quietude after the long, turbulent years of depression and war. Enough, they seemed to say. Let us rest. And this is precisely what the Eisenhower administration gave them. He steered the government through a series of crises without resorting to war. And he committed himself and his party to many of the social and economic reforms already established during the years of the New Deal and Fair Deal, such as the extension of Social Security, public housing, and aid to education. He followed a policy of economic conservatism and social liberalism. He characterized himself as "liberal on human issues, and conservative on economic ones." He especially opposed governmental intrusion into areas that private utilities could handle, not excluding atomic and power facilities.

As a political realist, Eisenhower understood the importance and value of compromise, and so he cooperated with the Democratic leadership to win passage of more moderate proposals. For example, the Social Security Act of January 14, 1954, added 10.5 million workers to the rolls and increased monthly benefits to all the participants in the program. The Wiley-Dondero bill of May 3, 1954, authorized the construction with Canada of a channel twenty-seven feet deep between Montreal and Lake Erie and established the St. Lawrence Seaway Development Corporation to finance the operation. The seaway was completed in June 1959 and made possible the navigation of ships from Montreal to Lake Superior, except during the winter.

Of particular importance was passage of the Highway Act of 1956, which authorized construction of a 42,000-mile interstate highway system in which the federal government would contribute 90 percent of construction costs. After all, it was an interstate program. New taxes were levied on gasoline to help finance the operation. This elaborate highway system took nearly twenty-five years to complete, and the cost rose to over $75 billion. It was the largest public works project ever attempted, and it effectively changed the way Americans lived and traveled. Congress also passed water conservation measures, school and hospital construction projects, and a health bill that supported medical research.

In achieving his goals, Eisenhower proved to be a very skilled political backroom trader. He realized he had to work with the Democratic majorities in Congress, in particular Sam Rayburn of Texas, Speaker of the House of Representatives, and Lyndon B. Johnson of Texas, majority leader in the Senate, who also recognized that it was in their interest and the interest of the Democratic Party to adopt a policy of accommodation with the administration. The resulting, if limited, success of the Eisenhower administration was attributed to this understanding by both sides.

In keeping with the promise he made during the campaign, Eisenhower went to Korea six months after taking office to lend his authority to assist the working out of a truce. On July 27, 1953, the United States, North and South Korea, and the People's Republic of China signed an armistice agreement that drew a line at the 38th parallel, which would thereafter separate North and South Korea.

Still, the communist threat remained. The Soviet Union continued its ruthless suppression of freedom in eastern Europe, crushing rebellions in East Berlin and Hungary. Acting on Eisenhower's recommendation, Congress raised the defense budget to unprecedented heights, from nearly $13 billion in 1950 to nearly $40 billion in 1960. The rise of what Eisenhower called the military-industrial complex was expected to prepare the nation for any possible threat to its safety. In what was termed the Eisenhower Doctrine, Congress authorized the President to extend military and economic aid to guard the Middle East from communist expansion. Then, when Fidel Castro led an invasion that turned out to be communist in its intent and purposes and captured Cuba, the threat of possible invasion from this island that was only ninety miles from the United States became a frightening possibility. In addition, the development of the hydrogen bomb by both the United States and the Soviet Union worsened fears that the entire planet could be destroyed at any time by an escalation of the Cold War.

Communists in Indochina had been waging a struggle for independence from French rule since 1946. Now, with the conclusion of the Korean War, the People's Republic of China increased its assistance to the Indochinese nationals. An agreement was reached at a foreign ministers conference in Geneva in May 1954 to divide Indochina into two parts, like Korea. Then, on October 11, 1954, the communist-backed Viet Minh captured control of the northern half of what would now be called Vietnam, and a noncommunist government was established in the southern half. In one of his final actions as President, Eisenhower sent 3,500 troops to bolster the noncommunist southern portion of Vietnam.

ONE OF THE most extraordinary developments that appeared in the 1950s was the emergence of a youth culture that found its best expression in music. The expanded number of teenagers in this period dismissed the "swing bands" and melodic music of their parents as old-fashioned and rather tame for their tastes and turned to what was called "rock and roll," a blend of rhythm and blues and southern country music. One of the best and most successful exponents of rock and roll was Elvis Presley, whose hip-swinging style of performing alarmed parents, who feared for their children's moral safety. With the arrival of the British rock group the Beatles, the popularity of rock and roll dominated all other forms of music. What soon evolved was an anti-establishment counterculture in which "hippies," as they were known, wore long hair, engaged in communal living, became sexually promiscuous, experimented with marijuana and other drugs, and foreswore political involvement. This hippie phase of the youth movement faded by the early 1970s. But rock and roll remained a symbol of youthful rebellion.

AMONG THE MOST important domestic issues that arose during the 1950s was civil rights, which Truman had tried to win but failed. As a consequence, he was forced to use executive powers to fight Jim Crow laws. Eisenhower continued this policy, if halfheartedly, but it was up to Congress to initiate legislation that would strengthen existing civil rights laws. Then, on May 17, 1954, in the landmark decision *Brown v. Board of Education of Topeka*, the Supreme Court, under Chief Justice Earl Warren, reversed *Plessy v. Ferguson* (1896), which had allowed segregation in schools provided they were "separate but equal." Now the Court ruled that compulsory racial segregation in public schools was a violation of the Fourteenth Amendment's guarantee of equal rights to all citizens. The following year the Court went farther and instructed all federal district courts to require local authorities to move with "all deliberate speed" toward the desegregation of all public schools. Also in 1955, Rosa Parks refused to give up her seat and move to the back of a public bus in Montgomery, Alabama, and her action touched off a yearlong bus boycott in that city led by the Reverend Dr. Martin Luther King Jr.

Although President Eisenhower suffered a serious heart attack on September 24, 1955, he decided to run for a second term. The Democrats again put forward Adlai Stevenson, who was badly beaten. Eisenhower won all but seven southern states, even though the Democrats retained control of both houses of Congress. He scored 457 electoral and 35,590,472 popular votes to Stevenson's 73 electoral and 26,029,752 popular votes. Eisenhower became the first candidate to win the presidency since the election of 1848 whose political party failed to carry either house of Congress.

Following his election, Eisenhower asked Congress to enact legislation to protect the civil rights of American citizens. But this proved to be exceedingly difficult because of the stiff opposition of southerners in both the House and Senate. The civil rights movement of the 1950s and 1960s, following the lead of Dr. King, was basically nonviolent. Civil disobedience became a very effective strategy for showing the American people, via television, how African-Americans were denied their basic rights as citizens, especially in the South. Passive demonstrators were often assaulted by baton- wielding police and attack dogs as the nation watched these appalling confrontations on television at night.

Congress could no longer disregard the rising indignation of the electorate over its failure to pass civil rights legislation. Finally an effective bill was introduced in the House that was later watered down in the Senate to provide the Civil Rights Act of 1957. This legislation created the Civil Rights Division in the Department of Justice and set up a Commission on Civil Rights. It empowered the attorney general to seek court injunctions against those accused of preventing citizens from exercising their voting rights. Those accused would be tried in federal court by a jury of their peers. Unfortunately, it was a very weak bill and proved to be all but useless. Discriminatory practices continued in the South without letup. Those registrars accused of violating the law were tried by all-white juries and acquitted. And the Civil Rights Act of 1957 did not appreciably increase the number of registered African-American voters over the next several years. Still, Congress had passed the first civil rights bill since Reconstruction. And as Lyndon Johnson said so graphically, "Once you break the virginity, it'll be easier next time."

Five days prior to the President's signing this legislation, the first outright defiance of the Supreme Court's ruling in the *Brown* case occurred on September 3, 1957, when the governor of Arkansas, Orval E. Faubus, called out the National Guard in an attempt to prevent the integration of a high school in Little Rock. Much as Eisenhower personally deplored the *Brown* decision, he could not allow defiance of national authority to go unchecked, so he federalized the National Guard and dispatched regular army troops to reopen the school and keep order. What many southerners had feared had now taken place, namely the executive using his authority as commander in chief to compel obedience to a court order. Now it was obvious to all that the federal government, when necessary, could and would apply military force to protect the rights of African-Americans. Discrimination based on race in whatever guise was now legally over.

In the 1960s the civil rights movement picked up speed when four black college students in Greensboro, North Carolina, entered a whites-only lunch counter, sat down, and refused an order to leave. Many other "sit-ins" followed, especially among young white and black students who protested segregation or took "freedom rides" on interstate buses to force the attention of the public to the discrimination that was still practiced in the South. Violence broke out in Mississippi and Alabama, in which fire hoses and dogs were used, and resulted in the arrests of thousands of black protesters. These atrocities against unarmed citizens helped win passage of a new Civil Rights Act in 1960; it provided criminal penalties for bombings and other actions that attempted to obstruct court orders. It also authorized judges to appoint referees to assist African-Americans to register and vote. Although it was not a major advance against racial discrimination, Lyndon Johnson hoped it would be an expression of "responsible moderation" and "common sense."

At the Democratic nominating convention in Los Angeles in mid-July, a strong civil rights plank was adopted, but southerners did not walk out in protest. On the first ballot the convention chose Senator John Kennedy of Massachusetts along with Lyndon Johnson as his running mate. At the Republican convention Richard M. Nixon was put forward, as well as Henry Cabot Lodge of Massachusetts. The parties also endorsed a strong civil rights bill and the desegregation of public schools.

It was a close race, the closest since 1884, when Grover Cleveland eked out a victory over James G. Blaine. In the 1960 contest, John Kennedy gathered 100,000 more votes than Nixon, out of a record 68.8 million votes cast. Kennedy's total was 34,226,731 popular and 303

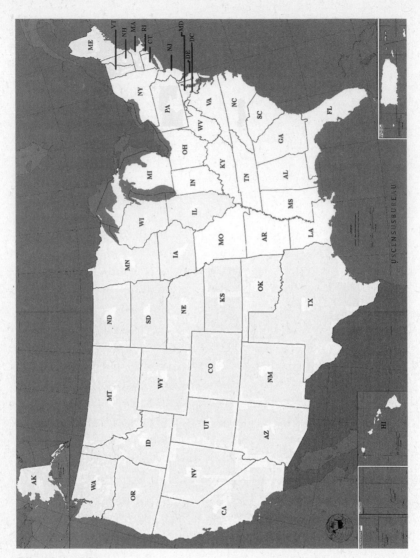

The United States

electoral votes representing twenty-two states to Nixon's 34,108,157 popular and 219 electoral votes from twenty-six states. This was the first election in which fifty states participated. On January 3, 1959, Alaska was admitted as the forty-ninth state, and on August 21, 1959, Hawaii became the fiftieth state in the Union.

The Cold War again troubled the nation's security when the Soviet Union launched its first satellite, Sputnik, into orbit on October 4, 1957. In response, Congress enacted the National Aeronautic and Space Act (NASA) of 1958, which set up a civilian authority to direct the nation's exploration of space. After assuming office, Kennedy asked Congress for an increase of $126 million over the $111 million Eisenhower had requested for NASA. Congress bettered it by adding another $127 million to the President's request.

And not a moment too soon. The Russians won the contest for putting the first man in space when, on April 12, 1961, Yury Gagarin completed a journey into space aboard a rocket-propelled vehicle. Not until May 5, 1961, did Alan Shepard Jr. complete a suborbital 300-mile flight aboard a Redstone rocket. Twenty days later, on May 25, President Kennedy addressed a special joint session of Congress and declared that "this nation should commit itself to achieving the goal, before this decade is out, of landing a man on the moon and returning him safely to earth." Then, on February 2, 1962, John Glenn orbited the earth three times in four hours. But not until July 16, 1969, did astronauts Neil A. Armstrong and Colonel Edwin E. Aldrin Jr. succeed in reaching the moon aboard a gigantic Saturn rocket. Armstrong took his first step on the surface of the moon at 10:56 AM Eastern Standard Time on July 20 as television viewers around the world watched. He and Aldrin planted an American flag on the site and left a plaque that read, "We came in peace for all mankind." After taking rock and soil samples, the two men conducted a number of experiments on the moon. They then successfully rendezvoused with the mother ship, piloted by Lieutenant Colonel Michael Collins, and returned to earth, splashing down about 950 miles from Hawaii on July 24.

It was quite a feat in the space race with the Soviet Union. But this rivalry constituted only one aspect of the Cold War between Russia and the United States. Once Fidel Castro admitted that he was a communist and that Cuba would adopt a communist system of government there was a sense of urgency among Americans to seize the island and restore a liberated administration, especially after American property on the island was seized and Castro became an ally of the Soviet Union. Prior to leaving office, Eisenhower had approved a plan for the invasion of Cuba by anti-Castro Cubans trained and supplied with American arms and money and protected by U.S. aircraft. But it was President Kennedy who gave the executive order to begin the invasion after his military and intelligence officials assured him that Castro did not have sufficient forces to repulse an invasion and that the Cuban people would rise up and join the rebellion. So the invasion began on April 17, 1961, and ended disastrously when the invaders became bogged down in the marshes of the Bay of Pigs. Kennedy refused to allow air support and, as a result, over a thousand anti-Castro Cubans were captured, tried, and sentenced to thirty years in prison. Furthermore, Premier Nikita Khrushchev of the Soviet Union threatened to come to Cuba's aid if the United States did not "call a halt to the aggression against the Republic of Cuba."

Worse, during the summer and autumn of 1962 the Soviets began building missile sites in Cuba capable of launching nuclear bombs against the United States. In a televised speech to the nation on October 22, 1962, President Kennedy, risking a possible war with the Soviet Union, demanded that the bases be dismantled and the missiles removed. Pending compliance, he ordered the U.S. Navy to commence "a strict quarantine on all offensive military equipment under shipment to Cuba." In other words, the United States would stop and search all ships bound for the island, regardless of nationality, and turn back any carrying military weapons. Kennedy said he was requesting an emergency meeting of the UN Security Council to consider a resolution to demand immediate removal of the missiles. "It shall be the policy of this nation," he continued, "to regard any nuclear missile launched from Cuba against any nation in the western hemisphere as an attack by the Soviet Union on the United States requiring a full retaliatory response upon the Soviet Union."

Fortunately, Khrushchev realized he had overplayed his hand, and in an exchange between the two leaders of the communist and free worlds it was agreed that the Soviet Union would remove the missiles and the United States would promise not to invade Cuba. Both sides complied with the agreement, and the likelihood of a nuclear war between the two countries was averted.

Another incident of the Cold War involved the action by the Soviets to seal off East Germany. A year earlier, in August 1961, the communists closed the border crossings in Berlin and built the Berlin Wall, ostensibly to prevent East Germans from escaping into the West. It was an action that would separate East and West Berlin for the next twenty-eight years.

One of the ways that Kennedy hoped to bring about a greater union among free peoples around the world was passage of the Peace Corps Act, on September 22, 1961, in which $40 million for fiscal 1962 was appropriated to prepare thousands of young American men and women for volunteer work providing educational, medical, and other technical services in underdeveloped countries. The overwhelming response by young people in colleges and universities indicated how strongly they believed they could make a difference in helping to improve living conditions throughout the world. The Peace Corps enjoyed great success from the very beginning.

But the need at home in several areas was also great, especially among African-Americans. Still, Kennedy indicated that civil rights were not a top priority for his administration, probably because he needed southern support for other measures he deemed more urgent, such as education and housing. A seemingly vigorous man in his early forties, who successfully concealed his many medical problems from public scrutiny, Kennedy spoke boldly and called for measures in a program labeled the "New Frontier" that would combat tyranny, poverty, disease, and war. But events would occur that would force the young President to change his mind.

Freedom riders who hoped to desegregate the South were attacked in Alabama, and their bus burned by an angry mob. Race riots occurred, forcing the governor to declare martial law to restore order. The violence escalated, and once more the nation witnessed the consequences of racial bigotry. But it had one salutary effect in bringing about passage of the Twenty-fourth Amendment to the Constitution, which outlawed poll taxes as a requirement for voting. At the time when the amendment was ratified—January 23, 1964—Virginia, Texas, Alabama, arkansas, and Mississippi charged a poll tax.

Another clash between state and federal authorities occurred on October 1, 1962, when James Meredith, a twenty-nine-year-old African-American, sought admission to the University of Mississippi. Governor Ross Barnett tried to prevent the enrollment and when rioting resulted President Kennedy dispatched federal troops to restore order and block any effort to prevent Meredith from enrolling.

The Reverend Dr. Martin Luther King Jr. and his Southern Christian Leadership Conference initiated nonviolent demonstrations on April 3, 1963, in Birmingham, Alabama, a city that was determined to maintain its long tradition of segregation. "If we can crack Birmingham," declared King, "I am convinced we can crack the South. Birmingham is a symbol of segregation for the entire South." The police commissioner, T. Eugene "Bull" Connor, was prepared to meet these nonviolent demonstrations with force, using clubs and attack dogs. Approximately 2,000 African-Americans were arrested and jailed.

These continuing disorders in Birmingham prompted Kennedy to demand a strong civil rights bill from Congress. Otherwise, he said, leadership on both sides would pass "to the purveyors of hate and violence." Emanuel Celler, chairman of the House Judiciary Committee, exploded over what was happening in the South. "Police clubs and bludgeons, fire hoses and dogs have been used on defenseless school children who were marching and singing hymns," he raged. The motel where Dr. King was staying and the home of King's brother were bombed, causing the black population of the city to rise up in fury. Rocks were thrown and fire hoses were turned on the rioters. Disorder reigned. But Congress finally responded, and 127 civil rights bills were introduced in the House of Representatives. "The cause of desegregation," wrote Walter Lippmann in the *Washington Post* on May 28, "must cease to be a Negro movement, blessed by white politicians from Northern states. It must become a national movement to enforce national laws, led and directed by the National Government."

Rioting in many northern cities turned streets into bloody encounters between protesters and police. The nation seemed to be descending into turmoil and lawlessness. When Governor George Wallace of Alabama stood at the door of a building to block black students from registering at the University of Alabama on June 11, 1963, Kennedy federalized the Alabama National Guard and forced Wallace to step out of the way. The following day, Medgar Evers, a Mississippi civil rights activist, was shot as he stood at the door of his home. Pressure built quickly to address this troubling issue, and over 200,000 black and white activists marched for "jobs and freedom" from the Washington Monument to the Lincoln Memorial on August 28, 1963, where they heard Martin Luther King Jr. deliver his famous "I have a dream" speech. It was the largest public demonstration ever held in the nation's capital.

Then the violence in the country reached a peak with the assassination of President Kennedy in Dallas, Texas, on Friday, November 22, 1963. It numbed the nation. The temper, mood, and political atmosphere in the country underwent a profound change. Few could believe that a young, handsome, seemingly energetic, well-loved president could be killed in plain sight during a public appearance in the streets of a major city. People wept openly. In a single moment the nation seemed to age and grow morose. Kennedy's body was flown back to Washington, where it lay in state in the White House before being removed to the Rotunda of the Capitol and placed on the catafalque that had supported the remains of President Lincoln. Throughout the night and the next morning, thousands of mourners silently filed past the coffin to pay their respects. Heads of state and foreign dignitaries from around the world arrived to attend the funeral. A brief ceremony in the Rotunda included short eulogies by the Senate majority leader, Mike Mansfield, Speaker of the House John McCormack, and Chief Justice Earl Warren.

Vice President Lyndon B. Johnson had accompanied Kennedy to Texas and was sworn in as chief executive aboard the plane that carried Kennedy's remains back to Washington. Appearing before Congress on November 27, he declared that no eulogy "could more eloquently honor President Kennedy's memory than the earliest possible passage of a civil rights bill for which he fought so long." Then, on January 8, 1964, in his first State of the Union address, Johnson announced the start of a "War on Poverty" in the United States.

In what was interpreted as the wish of the members of Congress to demonstrate forcefully how devastated the entire nation was over Kennedy's assassination, they enacted in quick succession a number of important measures. First, the Clean Air Act of 1963 was passed on December 17, authorizing $95 million for matching grants by state and local agencies to reduce pollution and develop air control programs.

Then came the Civil Rights Act of 1964, which forbade discrimination because of race in most places of public accommodation; authorized the attorney general to institute suits to desegregate public facilities, including schools; banned discrimination on account of race or sex by employers, labor unions, or employment agencies; created the Equal Employment Opportunity Commission; prohibited discrimination in the use of federal funds by states and other local authorities; and created a Community Relations Service to assist individuals and officials in dealing with racial problems at the local level. Southerners in the Senate attempted a filibuster to delay or kill the legislation, which ran on for over two and half months but was finally brought to an end with a cloture vote—a device to shut off debate whereby two-thirds of the senators (at that time) agree to stop the filibuster.

In the presence of members of Congress, cabinet members, foreign ambassadors, and leaders of the civil rights movement, Johnson signed the legislation at 6:45 PM on June 19, in the East Room of the White House, only a few hours after it had been passed. Johnson called on all Americans "to join in this effort to bring justice and hope to all our people."

The Civil Rights Act of 1964 was the most far-reaching civil rights legislation enacted since Reconstruction. It went beyond what President Kennedy had originally proposed and marked a true beginning of the lessening of racial and sex discrimination around the country.

This momentous legislation was achieved because of a mounting awareness around the country of the denial of basic freedoms for African-Americans and the hideous suppression of their attempts to achieve those freedoms. Americans were recognizing, at long last, that conditions for blacks violated everything this country stood for in terms of personal rights. In addition, the assassination of President Kennedy so overwhelmed citizens with grief that they demanded a halt to the civil unrest permeating the entire country. In winning passage of this Civil Rights Act, President Johnson rightly stated: "This has been a year without precedent in the history of relations between the Executive and Legislative Branches of our Government."

And the American people approved of what was happening in Washington. They provided a landslide victory for Johnson and the Democratic Party in the election of 1964. He captured 44 states and the District of Columbia over the 6 states his Republican rival, Senator

Barry Goldwater of Arizona, had won. Johnson had a total of 486 to Goldwater's 52 electoral votes. It was well known that Goldwater had voted against the Civil Rights Act, and that fact helped win him the Deep South: Alabama, Georgia, Mississippi, Louisiana, and South Carolina. This result marked a turning point in the development of the Republican Party in those states. The election also brought five new Republican representatives to the House from Alabama, and one each from Georgia and Mississippi. They were the first southern Republicans elected to Congress since Reconstruction. And more would follow until the South was no longer Democratic but solidly Republican.

Another significant event took place when the Democratic caucus in Congress censured two southern members—John Bell Williams of Mississippi and Albert W. Watson of South Carolina—for publicly supporting Goldwater in the election. That had never happened before. Moreover, they were stripped of their seniority rights as congressmen, whereupon Watson switched parties and later won reelection to the House as the first Republican from South Carolina since Reconstruction. Watson's action was followed by other southerners, most notably Senator Strom Thurmond of South Carolina, who had thrown his support to Goldwater in the election.

WITH A GREATLY increased Democratic majority in Congress, and exercising his extraordinary leadership skills, President Johnson appealed to the members to join in providing the country with a program he called the "Great Society." He wanted to improve the lives of Americans in every section of the country. He urged passage of Medicare legislation for the elderly, to be financed out of the Social Security system. As part of this health care program he called for Medicaid for the needy, both of which were enacted on July 30, 1965. Other parts of the Great Society included an Education Act, passed in April 1965, which provided $1.3 billion in direct aid to public schools as well as parochial schools for a number of "shared services." In addition, the Higher Education Act appropriated $650 million for scholarships for needy students attending colleges and universities. These two education acts were regarded by many as the major successes of Johnson's first year as President following his election.

The Housing and Urban Development Act provided federal assistance for the construction of low-rent public housing and urban renewal that aided cities in removing blight and making their communities more attractive. The Department of Housing and Development was established to speed this initiative. The Food Stamp Act allowed the federal government, in cooperation with state governments, to provide stamps with which the poor could purchase food. And the Economic Opportunity Act created an office to administer ten programs to address the many causes of poverty and hunger in the country, leaving the states free to veto all community action projects that it felt inappropriate. Moreover, the Water and Air Quality Acts required all states to establish and enforce water quality standards for all interstate water routes within their boundaries, and develop air pollution prevention programs, including emission standards for automobiles.

Of particular importance was the enactment of the Immigration Act of 1965, which fundamentally changed the immigration policy of the country by eliminating quotas, placing all nations on an equal footing, and limiting admission to 170,000 annually with a maximum of 20,000 from any one nation.

Much of the credit for this extraordinary program of reform belonged to the President himself. "Lyndon Johnson," wrote the Speaker of the House, Tip O'Neill, "worked closely with the Congress and followed the details of legislation more carefully than any other president I've seen. He left nothing to chance. . . . When it came to politics, that man knew all the tricks. . . . When it came to dealing with Congress, he was the best I've ever seen. . . . And what a talker! That man could talk a bone away from a dog."

But in the area of civil rights much more needed to be done. Voter registration of African-Americans had not improved significantly. So the Reverend Dr. Martin Luther King Jr. launched an offensive in Selma, Alabama, on January 18, 1965. That city claimed a population that was 57.6 percent black, but only 2.1 percent of that number were registered to vote. "We plan to triple the number of registered Negro voters in Alabama for the 1966 Congressional elections," declared King; "then we plan to purge Alabama of all Congressmen who have stood in the way of Negroes. . . . A state that denies people education cannot demand literacy tests as a qualification for voting."

On "Bloody Sunday," March 7, some 600 civil rights activists headed out of Selma, but they got only as far as the Edmund Pettus Bridge, where they were attacked by state and local police and driven back to Selma. The leaders went to court. They demanded the court's protection to hold another march, a fifty-four-mile Freedom March from Selma to the state capital in Montgomery. The court obliged, and on Sunday, March 21, some 3,200 men and women, black and white, set out for Montgomery, walking twelve miles a day and sleeping in the fields along the way. On Thursday, March 25, now numbering approximately 25,000, they reached their destination. Again, rioting occurred, with state troopers and mounted policemen brandishing nightsticks, firearms, and tear gas. A horrified nation watched on television as screaming, bloody marchers fled in panic from their attackers.

Demonstrations multiplied. Sit-ins became commonplace, and the nation was forced once again to confront its history of racial strife and violence. A nation that prided itself on being compassionate and generous toward the less fortunate had to face the fact that bigots and hoodlums regularly sullied this image in the eyes of the world.

A week later President Lyndon B. Johnson, in a televised address to a night session of both houses of Congress, urged passage of stronger voter rights legislation. "It is not just Negroes," he said, "but it is all of us, who must overcome the crippling legacy of bigotry and injustice. And we *shall* overcome." Congress followed through by passing the Voting Rights Act of 1965, which was signed by Johnson on August 5. It was, he said, "a triumph for freedom as huge as any victory that has ever been won on the battlefield." By this act, he declared, "we strike away the last major shackle of those fierce and ancient bonds" that have bound African-Americans to slavery since their arrival on this continent.

The Voting Rights Act suspended literacy and other tests for voting and authorized federal supervision of registration in districts that had used such tests. Registrars were assigned to Alabama, Georgia, Louisiana, Mississippi, North Carolina, South Carolina, and Virginia, and within five months registration of African-Americans in the South increased forty percent. It was a major triumph for an administration that had already achieved many notable successes.

DESPITE THESE MANY successes, the Cold War persisted. And now it resurfaced as a paramount issue and ultimately drove Lyndon Johnson from office. The Vietnam War was another extension of the struggle between the free and communist worlds.

The fighting between the communist North Vietnamese and the noncommunist South Vietnamese intensified, and that intensification made the South Vietnamese more dependent on the United States for economic and military assistance. Consumed with the fear that a victory for the communists in Vietnam would have a domino effect throughout Asia, Johnson committed himself to providing aid at the very beginning of his administration. By the summer of 1964 approximately 21,000 American servicemen were stationed in Vietnam as advisers. But the need for additional troops rose each month

Then, on August 4, 1964, when two U.S. destroyers were attacked in the Gulf of Tonkin, Johnson ordered retaliatory air strikes and asked Congress to approve his action. Three days later Congress passed the Gulf of Tonkin Resolution, one of the most fateful and controversial resolutions in U.S. history. Johnson signed it on August 10. This resolution permitted the President as commander in chief to take all necessary steps to repel an armed attack against U.S. forces and prevent further aggression in Vietnam. The attack on the two destroyers had actually been overblown by the administration and had been used as a pretext for initiating a war with congressional approval.

Despite the massive number of American troops sent to Vietnam and a two-phase plan to bomb North Vietnam, the situation in South Vietnam continued to deteriorate as one civilian government followed another in a series of coups that weakened the effort to bring the war to an end. Johnson increased the number of troops in South Vietnam on July 28, 1965, from 75,000 to 125,000, to serve as fighting personnel, not merely as advisers. The first major ground battle of the war involving American soldiers took place on August 18, 1965, on the Van Tuong Peninsula. Military funds reached almost $2 billion.

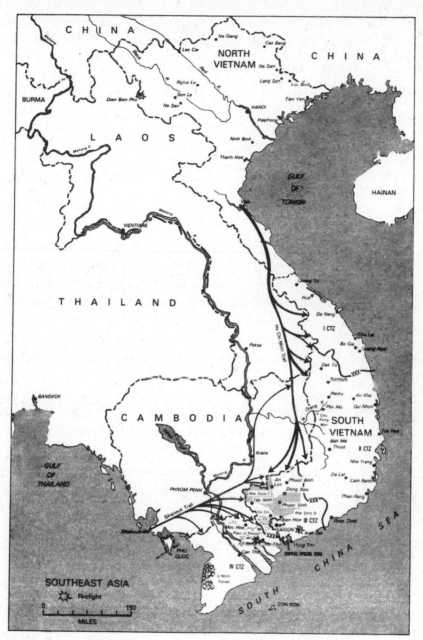

The Vietnam War

By this time opposition to the war had begun to mount. Students in colleges and universities, starting with the University of California at Berkeley, staged demonstrations and sit-ins protesting the war. They burned their draft cards. At the same time the Pentagon informed President Johnson that success in Vietnam was possible only if the troop level was raised from 120,000 to a "minimum essential force" of 500,000.

War spending began to heat up the economy and send inflation soaring. Rioting over civil rights continued in Atlanta, Chicago, Cleveland, and New York. College campuses produced disruptive demonstrations. Worst of all were the increased numbers of Americans killed and wounded in Vietnam that were reported daily. "That broke the back of the Great Society right there," said Speaker Carl Albert. The money necessary to implement the Great Society now went for fighting an unpopular war.

And because the fighting intensified, the cost of the war spiraled upward, to $2 billion a month. Aid was promised to the North Vietnamese by the People's Republic of China in August 1967, and at the same time China shot down American fighter planes that violated its airspace. Johnson increased the forces in Vietnam to 535,000, and each month hundreds of thousands of tons of explosives were dropped on North Vietnam. Higher taxes were demanded as inflation skyrocketed.

The continuing Cold War and the Vietnam War dramatically altered American life and culture. And they divided the nation regarding its goals and aspirations.

Violence, Scandal, and the End of the Cold War

VIOLENCE HAD BECOME a way of life. City streets regularly erupted in violence. Television, which the Radio Corporation of America first tested in 1933 with a signal from the Empire State Building in New York City to Camden, New Jersey, found it an excellent means of attracting viewers, and so more and more television programs appeared in which violence was the central component. And the killing in Vietnam increased. On January 30, 1968, the Vietcong launched a major attack—called the Tet Offensive after the Vietnamese holiday (the lunar new year) on which it occurred—against every important South Vietnamese city and town, and also shelled the American embassy in Saigon. In the fighting U.S. forces suffered heavy casualties, triggering renewed demonstrations and antiwar rallies at home and necessitating the increase in troops in Vietnam to well over 700,000 in order to achieve victory.

Politically, the stepped-up offensive had notable consequences. Senator Eugene McCarthy of Minnesota announced his candidacy for the Democratic presidential nomination on a peace platform, and thousands of young Americans streamed to his side. It was another way of protesting the war. In the New Hampshire primary McCarthy's showing was almost even with Johnson's. The results prompted Robert Kennedy, the brother of the late President and now a senator from New York, to announce his candidacy. He had always opposed the war, but he did it privately. Now he came out publicly and declared that the war could not be won and that the United States should withdraw from Vietnam. "Our enemy," he declared, "has finally shattered the mask of official illusion with which we have concealed our true circumstances, even from ourselves."

Recognizing that his popularity had shriveled to the point where his reelection had become impossible, Johnson announced to a televised audience on March 31 that he was withdrawing his candidacy. He also declared that he would end all U.S. air and naval bombardment of North Vietnam in the hope that peace talks could begin so as to bring about a negotiated settlement. North Vietnam agreed to this condition, the bombing halted, and delegates assembled in Paris on May 10 to initiate preliminary talks. Formal negotiations began on January 16, 1969.

Then, a savage act of violence erupted again when, on April 4, 1968, the Reverend Dr. Martin Luther King Jr. was assassinated by James Earl Ray in Memphis. This killing aroused further violence in more than 100 cities, including Washington, D.C. The country was faced with the fact that its streets at home and the streets in Vietnam were soaked with blood because of Americans intent on killing to settle opposing social and political problems.

Indeed, 1968 proved to be a very bloody year. Two months later, on June 5, Robert Kennedy, while campaigning in California, was assassinated by a deranged Jordanian immigrant, Sirhan Sirhan. Again the nation wept. Many people wondered aloud if this country had begun to descend into unrecognizable chaos. Later, a study showed—to no one's surprise—that the United States sold more firearms than any other country on the globe, and its citizens owned more firearms than any other people. Worse, more Americans died from firearms than was true in any other industrial nation. It was an unenviable record, but since the Second Amendment to the Constitution guaranteed the right to bear arms, the government made no serious attempt to control the distribution of guns, since so many citizens owned weapons and did not wish their right infringed in any way. Politically, it guaranteed defeat at the polls for any official to attempt to enact controlling legislation.

To make matters even more alarming, the Democratic Nominating Convention, meeting in Chicago between August 26 and 29, became a battleground between the city's police and angry antiwar protesters.

Security forces, a barbed-wire fence, and checkpoints ringed the International Amphitheater, where the convention was held. Radicalized students taunted the police and sang "We Shall Overcome," the civil rights anthem, and were peppered with tear gas by the infuriated police. Television cameras recorded the mayhem, to the shock and amazement of the national viewing public. Police used clubs indiscriminately, and cameramen, journalists, and bystanders were assaulted. According to a later investigation, what happened was a "police riot." Despite the mayhem in the streets, the delegates inside the convention hall nominated Hubert Humphrey, the Vice President under Johnson, once Senator Edward M. Kennedy of Massachusetts, the brother of John F. and Robert F. Kennedy, chose not to run. Senator Edmund S. Muskie of Maine was named to complete the ticket. The Republicans, meeting in Miami, had an easier time of it, and on August 8 chose Richard M. Nixon and Spiro Agnew, the governor of Maryland, to stand as their nominees.

More than likely, the "police riot" in Chicago helped win the election for Nixon in a very close contest. Nixon garnered 31,004,304 popular votes to Humphrey's 30,691,699. The margin of difference was 0.01 percent. George C. Wallace, the former governor of Alabama, who was the candidate of the American Independent Party, a southern conservative organization, won 9,787,691 popular votes. All told, Nixon captured 32 states for an electoral vote of 301 to Humphrey's 14 states and 191 electoral votes. Wallace had 46 electoral votes from five southern states.

EARLY IN FEBRUARY 1969, the Vietcong launched a new, ferocious offensive and inflicted heavy losses on U.S. forces. To impede communist operations in Vietnam, Nixon secretly ordered an intense bombing of Cambodia. Demonstrations around the country mounted in number and even Congress became more vocal in demanding the withdrawal of U.S. troops. "The Americans who have died in Vietnam will not have died in vain," declared one Congressman, "if their deaths have taught the United States to mind its own business and to lead the world by its example." Finally, Nixon announced that 25,000 troops would be withdrawn by August and a timetable would be devised to bring the war to a speedy end. He also expressed the need to make progress at the negotiations in Paris. By this time it was estimated that millions had taken part in massive antiwar demonstrations.

Then, on November 17, 1969, Seymour Hersh reported in the *New York Times* that American troops had been responsible for the massacre of more than 100 South Vietnamese civilians—women, children, and the elderly—in the village of My Lai in Quang Ngai province in March 1968. A horrified nation demanded an accounting. Several soldiers, among them Lieutenant William Calley, were court-martialed. In March 1971 Calley was convicted of premeditated murder of at least twenty-two Vietnamese citizens and sentenced to life imprisonment. But his sentence was later reduced, and he was released after serving only three and a half years. His commanding officer, Captain Ernest Medina, whom Calley accused of ordering him to kill the civilians, was also tried but found not guilty.

In an effort to clear out communist sanctuaries along the Cambodian border with South Vietnam, Nixon authorized American troops to invade and destroy these sanctuaries on April 30, 1970. Then, in late December 1970, Congress repealed the Gulf of Tonkin Resolution, and the President signed it on January 31, 1971.

This incursion into Cambodia, along with the expansion of American involvement in a war in Laos, the country that bordered Cambodia on the north, produced further demonstrations on college campuses. One such demonstration, at Kent State in Ohio, resulted in the killing of four students who were shot to death by National Guardsmen on May 4, 1970. The picture of a terrified, screaming young woman leaning over the body of one of these students and pleading for an answer deeply affected the nation. Two more students were killed by state police at Jackson State College in Mississippi on May 14. Then, on July 1, 1970, the *New York Times* published the Pentagon Papers. These were classified documents that detailed decisions leading to the United States' involvement in Vietnam. The *Times* had obtained them from Daniel Ellsberg, a former Defense Department employee, and their publication further eroded confidence in the war and the administration's handling of it. In addition, the Pentagon Papers made the administration extremely paranoid about information being leaked to the media. The administration became more secretive and more determined to spy on the activities of citizens where leaks were suspected.

But the President scored an important breakthrough in foreign affairs when, in February 1972, he visited Communist China and agreed to a joint communiqué on the need for greater interaction between China and the United States. Only a well-known anticommunist like Nixon could have executed such a historic diplomatic coup. Then, after extended negotiations in Paris, an agreement between North Vietnam and South Vietnam and between the United States and the Vietcong's Provisional Revolutionary Government of North Vietnam was reached on January 27, 1973, to end the Vietnam War. Not surprisingly, the fragile South Vietnamese government soon collapsed, the country was overrun by the Vietcong, and the remaining Americans in Saigon had to be hurriedly evacuated by helicopter. It was a soul-searing defeat for the American nation, and the domino effect so feared by Johnson did not occur. It should have been a lesson that would not need to be relearned. Unfortunately, that did not happen. Too many officials in authority knew little about American history.

After the United States ceased its bombing of Cambodia, the communist-led Khmer Rouge seized control of the country. Again, American citizens and the embassy staff had to be rescued by helicopter. A bloody purge ensued, ending on April 17, 1975, when the pro-West forces in Cambodia surrendered to the forces of the Khmer Rouge.

AS THE PRESIDENTIAL election of 1972 approached, the administration became involved in an operation so stupid and criminal that it would destroy the reputations of many of the participants. It was one of the worst scandals in American history, and it began to unfold on the night of June 17, 1972, when five men were caught at 2:30 AM in a burglary attempt at the office of the Democratic National Committee in the Watergate, an apartment-hotel complex in Washington adjacent to the Potomac River. As was quickly learned, these men had connections to the White House and the Republican National Committee to Reelect the President (CREEP), and they were attempting to gain information that could be used in the forthcoming election. Ironically, Nixon and his running mate, Spiro Agnew, overwhelmingly defeated the Democratic ticket: Senator George McGovern and R. Sargent Shriver, a brother-in-law of the Kennedys. Nixon and Agnew won every state but Massachusetts and the District of Columbia, for a total of 520 electoral and 47,169,911 popular votes to 17 electoral and 29,170,383 popular votes for McGovern and Shriver. Nixon garnered over 60 percent of the popular vote, to 37.5 percent for McGovern. It was a sizable victory for the Republican ticket—the third-highest electoral total in the history of presidential elections—but would soon end in one of the most notable defeats any president had ever sustained.

In Congress there was mounting opposition to the President's habit of impounding funds for programs enacted by the legislature that he did not approve. Earlier, Nixon had tried and failed to get Congress to give him authority to decide where spending cuts should be made. So he bypassed Congress and simply blocked execution of the appropriations where he disapproved. Several leaders of the Democratic majority protested. They pointed out that the constitutional balance between the executive and legislative branches was being eroded, that Nixon was involved in an outright and improper encroachment of congressional authority, that he was violating the fundamental law of the land.

Congress also resented the President's exercise of his authority as commander in chief to involve the nation in foreign wars without the approval of the legislature. It finally decided to act, despite threats of a presidential veto. In 1973 it passed the War Powers Resolution, which required the chief executive to consult with Congress before committing troops in any hostilities. It further required the termination of any military engagement within sixty days unless Congress declared war or authorized a continuation of the engagement. Nixon vetoed the resolution, arguing that it violated his constitutional obligations, but on November 7, 1973, Congress overrode the veto. The War Powers Act became law without the President's signature and has been regularly ignored or bypassed by subsequent chief executives.

The increasing awareness of Nixon's disregard of constitutional limitations on the presidency was suddenly overshadowed by the problems besetting the Vice President. Spiro Agnew was indicted on the charge of accepting payoffs from construction company executives while governor of Maryland and while Vice President. The case was settled when Agnew pleaded no contest to a single charge of income tax evasion on October 10, 1973. It was part of a plea bargain, and he resigned his office as Vice President of the United States.

Since the Twenty-fifth Amendment to the Constitution provided that the President nominate a replacement for the Vice President when the position became vacant, Nixon chose Gerald R. Ford, the minority leader of the House of Representatives. Both the Senate and the House confirmed the appointment, and Ford assumed the office of Vice President.

OF PARTICULAR IMPORTANCE in 1973 was the decision of the Supreme Court in *Roe v. Wade*. The Court struck down state anti-abortion laws as a violation of the right of privacy guaranteed under the Fourteenth Amendment to the Constitution. The court affirmed a woman's right to decide whether or not to terminate her pregnancy. The ruling stated that during the first three months of pregnancy any government interference with a woman's decision to abort the child was unconstitutional. During the next three months a state may legislate to protect a woman's health, and during the final three months the state could forbid abortion. As a result of this decision the number of legal abortions quickly multiplied, setting off a national debate between those who opposed abortion and called themselves pro-life and those who favored a choice. Organizations were formed by both sides, and every future appointment to the Supreme Court brought concern as to a candidate's position on the *Roe* decision.

NATIONAL POLITICS SOON overshadowed all other issues. The attempted burglary at the Watergate quickly assumed momentous proportions. Nixon repeatedly denied any involvement in the break-in, even though there was an extensive cover-up, orchestrated by the White House, to protect the would-be burglars. Perjury, obstruction of justice, and bribery were just a few of the crimes the White House allegedly committed. The burglars came before John J. Sirica, the chief judge of the U.S. District Court of the District of Columbia. Five of them pleaded guilty, and a jury found two others guilty. During the trial, it became evident that two of the President's closest advisers, H. R. Haldeman and John R. Ehrlichman, were involved in a cover-up, and on April 30, 1973, Nixon announced their resignation, along with that of John Dean, his legal counsel, and Attorney General Richard Kleindienst, who was replaced by the secretary of defense, Elliot Richardson.

Early in 1973 the Senate had voted to create a committee to investigate activities during the presidential campaign of 1972. Senator Sam J. Ervin Jr. of North Carolina headed the committee. This Senate Watergate Committee commenced public hearings on May 17, and its televised proceedings attracted national attention. During the hearings, from June 25 to June 29, John Dean, recently fired, revealed that Nixon had been party to the cover-up. In addition, Alexander Butterfield, a former presidential aide, informed the committee on July 16 that since 1971 the President had tape-recorded all his conversations in the White House and the Executive Office Building. Although Nixon vowed publicly, "I am not a crook," he knew that the tapes would prove otherwise. Among other things, the committee learned that the White House kept an "Enemies List" of politicians, journalists, and other public figures to be used for possible investigation by the Internal Revenue Service, and a "Plumbers" unit which involved wiretaps of suspects in order to stop press leaks.

Both the Senate committee and Judge Sirica subpoenaed the tapes. They were to be turned over to the special prosecutor, Archibald Cox, a professor at Harvard Law School and former Solicitor General in the Kennedy and Johnson administrations, who had been appointed by Attorney General Richardson in May. On July 23, knowing what the tapes contained, Nixon refused to surrender them, citing executive privilege. These subpoenas, he insisted, constituted "such a massive invasion of presidential conversations that the institution of the presidency itself would be fatally compromised" if he complied. But, on August 29, Judge Sirica ordered nine tapes to be delivered to him for private review. Instead, Nixon offered transcripts, which he himself would edit and Senator John C. Stennis of Mississippi would verify. Cox refused the offer, whereupon the President ordered Richardson to fire Cox. Rather than obey the order, Richardson resigned on Saturday, October 20. The recently appointed Deputy Attorney General, William Ruckelshaus, also declined to discharge Cox, and Nixon fired him. Finally Nixon got the Solicitor General, Robert H. Bork, next in line to become acting attorney general, to do his dirty work. Bork dismissed Cox during this so-called "Saturday night massacre" of October

20, 1973. A Texan trial lawyer, Leon Jaworski, was then appointed special prosecutor, replacing Cox.

There were now calls for Nixon's impeachment, and the House Judiciary Committee initiated an inquiry. Although a number of House members objected to any consideration of impeachment, sixteen such resolutions were submitted by eighty-four members for consideration by the Judiciary Committee. With mounting public demand and the threat of impeachment increasing, Nixon finally agreed to comply with the subpoena and he released some of the tapes. One of them revealed a gap of eighteen and a half minutes, which experts later decided was caused by multiple erasures. This gap involved a conversation between Nixon and Haldeman on June 20, 1972.

The House Judiciary Committee of thirty-eight members, chaired by Peter Rodino of New Jersey, began its hearings on October 30, 1973. Five months later a Watergate grand jury indicted seven of Nixon's former advisers and aides, and Judge Sirica subsequently directed that the evidence be turned over to the Judiciary Committee. It included a sealed report that apparently cited Nixon as a co-conspirator in the Watergate cover-up.

On April 11, the impeachment committee voted 33 to 3 to subpoena the tapes of conversations held in February, March, and April 1973. Five days later Special Prosecutor Jaworski issued a subpoena for sixty-four tapes to be used in the trials of the indicted advisers and aides. Nixon refused, but on April 30 he released over 1,000 pages of edited conversations. The committee rejected his edited version of what it had asked for and demanded the tapes. In a letter to Rodino, Nixon said he was "determined to do nothing which . . . would render the executive branch henceforth and forever more subservient to the legislative branch, and would thereby destroy the constitutional balance."

The President was certain that the Supreme Court would uphold his opinion when Jaworski appealed to it for a decision, since he, Nixon, had appointed nearly a majority of the justices. But on July 24, 1974, the Court unanimously (with William Rehnquist abstaining) agreed in an opinion written by Chief Justice Warren E. Burger that the President must surrender evidence in what was obviously a criminal proceeding.

Three days later, on July 27, 1974, the Judiciary Committee's articles of impeachment were approved. Nixon was charged with having "engaged personally and through his subordinates . . . to delay, impede, and obstruct" the Watergate investigation, conceal evidence, and protect individuals engaged in criminal activity. He was also accused of "violating the constitutional rights of citizens, impairing the due and proper administration of justice in the conduct of lawful inquiries, and of contravening the law governing agencies of the executive branch, and the purposes of these agencies." Furthermore, he was charged with defiance of committee subpoenas, thus impeding the impeachment process.

On August 5, Nixon released the transcripts of three conversations with Haldeman recorded on June 22, 1972, conversations that had occurred six days after the break-in and proved to be what was called the "smoking gun." The "smoking gun" revealed that Nixon had been aware of the cover-up and had personally ordered a halt to the FBI investigation into the Watergate burglary. In addition, the vulgarity of the language used by the President on these tapes shocked the nation. They revealed a foulmouthed bigot who had disgraced his office. The general public now realized the extent of Nixon's betrayal of his oath to preserve, protect, and defend the Constitution of the United States.

The impeachment process now moved to the full House, and on August 7, 1974, the members voted to allow live radio and television coverage of the impeachment debate. But Nixon was frankly told by several leaders of the Republican Party that he could expect no more than ten votes against impeachment in the House and no more than fifteen in the Senate against his removal.

The next day, having little choice, Nixon announced his resignation on television, declaring that he "no longer had a strong enough political base" to continue in office. The resignation took effect the following day, August 9, at which time Gerald Ford took the oath of office. One of the first things President Ford did was nominate Nelson Rockefeller of New York to serve as Vice President. The nomination was approved by both houses of Congress in accordance with the procedure outlined in the Twenty-fifth Amendment to the Constitution. "Our long national nightmare is over," Ford declared. "Our great republic is a government of laws and not of men."

This was the first time in American history that both the President and Vice President advanced to the highest level of the executive branch of the government without being elected by the people.

A month later, on September 8, 1974, to the shock and anger of many, Ford gave Nixon a full and unconditional presidential pardon. He denied that a "deal" had been struck at the time of his elevation in testimony given to the House Judiciary Subcommittee on Criminal Justice on October 17. Rather, he insisted, it was his wish to end the controversy over Watergate and restore peace to the country. But a great many of the electorate found it difficult to accept the fact of the pardon, and they noted that the speed with which it was given and the failure to prepare the public for it beforehand gave credence to the accusation of another "corrupt bargain." Ford would pay the price for his action at the next presidential election in 1976, but by the time of his death in 2006 many Americans had come to believe that what he had said was true, that there had been no "deal," and that the nation needed to heal and be done with the Watergate scandal.

Two attempts on the life of Gerald Ford were made in September 1975. Fortunately, both failed. On September 5, Lynette Fromme pointed a Colt .45-caliber handgun loaded with four bullets at Ford but was apprehended before she could shoot. Then, on September 22, Sara Jane Moore fired a single shot at Ford as he was leaving the St. Francis Hotel in San Francisco. A bystander, Oliver Simple, grabbed her arm as she pulled the trigger and deflected the bullet. Ford again escaped possible injury or death. Although given a life sentence, Moore was pardoned on December 31, 2007, after thirty-two years in prison.

It is not clear whether either attempt was motivated in part by the pardon or by the fact that Nixon never confessed his guilt, although he did admit making mistakes. Actually, his acceptance of the pardon was interpreted by many as an admission of guilt. Although he himself escaped trial and possible imprisonment for his crimes, his aides were accused, tried, and convicted of conspiracy, obstruction of justice, perjury, and violating federal campaign laws. They received varying prison sentences. Later, in 1975, investigations by congressional committees revealed that the CIA had conducted extensive and illegal intelligence operations during the Nixon administration.

There were two important results from the Watergate debacle. The first was passage of the Campaign Finance Act in 1974, which established spending limits and required full disclosure of campaign contributions and expenses. The second was the overwhelming defeat of

Republicans in both the midterm election of 1974 and the presidential election of 1976.

The year 1976 brought not only a presidential election but also the bicentennial of the signing of the Declaration of Independence on July 4, 1776. The nation celebrated the event with many festive events and parades, including an impressive display of sailing ships in New York Harbor. It proved to be a welcome relief from all the scandals and violence that had taken place during the past several years.

Democrats not only celebrated July 4 but keenly looked forward to the approaching presidential election. There were numerous candidates, but Governor Jimmy Carter, a peanut farmer from Plains, Georgia, won a series of primaries early in the campaign and went on to take the nomination at the Democratic National Convention in New York City on July 15. The fact that Hubert Humphrey had withdrawn as a candidate eliminated the best-known possible rival. Carter then chose Senator Walter F. Mondale of Minnesota as his running mate.

The Republicans chose Ford, despite a strong bid to replace him by Ronald Reagan, the governor of California. In place of Rockefeller, who withdrew, the convention named Senator Robert Dole of Kansas to run for Vice President. Even though Carter enjoyed many advantages during the contest—especially the soaring inflation, the Watergate scandal, and the pardon of Nixon—he barely won the election. He received 40,829,056 popular and 297 electoral votes to Ford's 39,146,006 popular and 240 electoral votes—a 2.1 percent difference. The Democratic Party also retained control of both houses of Congress, electing 292 House members, to 143 Republicans. In the Senate the Democrats held a 62 to 38 advantage.

The Speaker of the House, Thomas P. (Tip) O'Neill of Massachusetts, met Jimmy Carter in Georgia after the election to discuss policy. The President-elect explained his wish to conserve energy and his desire to see conservation enacted by Congress. The Speaker wisely recommended that he consult with committee chairmen about any of his projects. But Carter foolishly dismissed the suggestion, claiming there was no need. If necessary, he said, he would appeal over the heads of the chairmen to the people. At that moment, Tip knew they were in trouble.

During the inauguration on January 20, 1977, Carter broke with tradition and, after the swearing-in ceremony, he and his wife walked down Pennsylvania Avenue from the Capitol to the White House, rather than being driven. Apparently he wanted to convey a more populist image, one that eschewed formality.

But the new president did not have a strong staff; nor was he able to build popular approval. Worse, he failed to win support among Democrats in Congress. None of his proposals on welfare, energy, and taxes were enacted in the form he set forth. Thus, despite large majorities in both houses of Congress, little of note was accomplished during the Carter administration. Even Republican lawmakers were mystified. The President would inform the members about what he wanted, declared one Republican, "and that was the end of it." There was no follow-through, no active participation in the lawmaking process. Carter was good at detail, trying to micromanage the process, "but he didn't have a clear vision for the country, and he wound up judging the Congress and not leading it." One Democrat said that Carter knew "more about more things than any President in the history of the United States. . . . And yet . . . he . . . didn't pat you on the back, he just didn't get along with people."

In attempting to micromanage his administration, Carter found it an impossible task, and only produced a lack of confidence in his leadership by the public. Tip O'Neill claimed that Carter's leadership style also resulted in the loss of twelve House seats and three Senate seats in the midterm election of 1978.

Carter also held a particularly unfortunate ten-day domestic economic summit at Camp David, a presidential retreat in Maryland, to deal with mounting inflation and what he regarded as an energy crisis. Over a hundred participants of different backgrounds attended. In a televised speech on July 15, 1979, he described what others called a national malaise, although he termed it a "crisis of confidence" because of economic conditions in the country. It set a tone that profoundly discouraged the nation. He also reshuffled his cabinet and forced the resignations of several members.

Inflation remained a problem, and when oil prices rose sharply in 1979 the Consumer Price Index registered an annual price rise of almost 18 percent. Gasoline prices climbed over the $1-per-gallon mark. The Federal Reserve Board raised the prime interest rate to a high of twenty percent in order to reduce the amount of money available for loans. And installment buying was discouraged by additional restrictions on consumer credit.

To make matters worse for the Carter administration, a "sting" operation conducted by the FBI revealed that a number of congressmen took bribes in return for official favors. A front organization, called Abdul Enterprises Ltd. (Abscam was the name of the sting), solicited business by claiming that its agents represented Arab businessmen who were prepared to offer bribes for legislative favors. FBI agents dressed as Arab sheikhs videotaped their meetings with congressmen. A number of members were indicted and found guilty in 1980 and 1981. Several resigned and others were defeated for reelection. Michael Myers, a Democratic representative from Pennsylvania, was the first to be convicted of bribery, conspiracy, and interstate travel to aid racketeering; and on October 2, 1980, he had the dubious distinction of being the first member to be expelled from the House since 1861. Even Carter himself and his brother Billy were investigated but cleared by a federal special prosecutor of possible loan violations in connection with their peanut business.

Although things went steadily downhill for the Carter administration, in foreign affairs there were several successes. The President signed a Panama Canal treaty in Washington with the head of the Panamanian government which provided for the repeal of the Hay-Bunau-Varilla Treaty of 1903, the turning over of ownership and control of the canal to Panama in 2000, and guaranteeing the neutrality of the canal in war and peace. The treaty was ratified by two-thirds of the electorate in Panama in a referendum on October 23, 1977, but just barely by the U.S. Senate on March 16, 1978. The Senate vote was 68 to 32, winning passage by one vote, and only after adding an amendment and reservation that safeguarded the right of the United States to protect the canal by force if necessary.

Regarding the People's Republic of China, the U.S. entered into formal diplomatic relations in 1979, with an exchange of ambassadors, and Carter withdrew recognition of the Republic of China in Taiwan and renounced the mutual defense treaty between it and the United States.

Carter's most notable achievement in foreign affairs was his management of a peace treaty between Israel and Egypt. Those two nations had been at war since 1973, when Egypt and other Arab states launched a surprise attack on Israel. Under pressure from Washington, President Anwar el-Sadat of Egypt and Prime Minister Menachem Begin of Israel exchanged visits in 1977 but failed to reach an agreement. Then

Carter invited Sadat and Begin to Camp David in September 1978 and worked out the Camp David Accords, in which the two belligerents agreed to sign a peace treaty within three months. On March 26, 1979, in the Rose Garden at the White House, Begin and Sadat, despite the opposition of other Arab states, signed a treaty of peace. It provided for the gradual evacuation of the Sinai Peninsula by Israel and the establishment of normal diplomatic and trade relations. However, it did not settle the Palestinian situation in the Gaza Strip or the West Bank of the Jordan River.

Then Carter suffered a particularly devastating blow in Iran. The trouble began when the Shah of Iran fled the country after a successful revolt by Islamic fundamentalists. When he was admitted to the United States on October 22, 1979, to obtain medical treatment, Ayatollah Khomeini, the Muslim cleric directing the revolt, urged his followers to demonstrate. On November 4, 1979, hundreds of Iranian students stormed the U.S. Embassy in Tehran and demanded the return of the Shah for trial. They seized and held about 100 hostages, most of whom were members of the American diplomatic mission. Carter refused to extradite the Shah and froze all Iranian assets in the United States. Two weeks after the hostages were taken the students released thirteen American women and black men but continued to hold the others. Neither the Shah's exit from the United States to Panama, nor his subsequent death eight months later, nor the requests of the United Nations persuaded the Iranians to release the hostages.

Carter's pursuit of diplomatic options and his call for worldwide economic sanctions against Iran had no effect. So he quietly authorized a military operation in the hope of ending the crisis. On April 24, 1980, a commando raid ended in failure and the loss of eight lives before the would-be rescuers could even reach Tehran. To the country at large, it now seemed that the United States government was utterly helpless.

Earlier, another crisis had developed when the Soviet Union invaded Afghanistan in December 1979, to prop up a faltering and unpopular communist regime. Carter responded by placing an embargo on grain shipments to Russia and discouraging American athletes from participating in the Olympic games scheduled to take place in Moscow during the summer of 1980. It seemed that the Cold War was still in full force.

These developments severely damaged Carter's drive for a second term as President. He was challenged by Senator Edward M. (Ted) Kennedy of Massachusetts, the younger brother of John and Robert, although this challenge faded after initial successes in the primaries in Massachusetts, Connecticut, and New York when, in a national television program, Kennedy failed to explain why he wished to be President. Carter won renomination at the Democratic National Convention on August 14 in New York City. But he and his running mate, Walter F. Mondale, faced a hard-driving Republican in Ronald Reagan, a former movie actor and governor of California, who had attracted widespread support from conservatives with his call for lower taxes and a less active government. Reagan attacked Carter's economic and foreign policies and advocated what he called "supply-side" economics, that is, the process of lowering taxes as a way of achieving prosperity. Reagan's most important challenger for the Republican nomination, George Herbert Walker Bush, called "supply-side" economics "voodoo economics."

But Reagan's charm, relaxed demeanor, and attractive television manner proved unbeatable and he swept to repeated primary victories, winning nomination on the first ballot at the Republican National Convention in Detroit on July 16. After an initial but failed attempt to entice Gerald Ford to accept the vice presidential nomination, Reagan chose Bush to complete the ticket. It seemed at first as though the campaign might develop into a close race, but Reagan quickly pulled ahead, attracting blue-collar workers who had traditionally voted Democratic to join him in his conservative crusade to improve economic conditions throughout the country.

The election itself provided an unexpected landslide for Reagan. In fact, so complete was the victory from the outset of the counting that Carter conceded the election before the polls closed on the West Coast. Many candidates running for lesser offices in the west felt that they lost as a result of Carter's early concession because Democrats, knowing the election was lost, failed to appear at the polls. Reagan took forty-three states, including every southern state except Georgia, for a total of 489 electoral and 43,901,812 popular votes to Carter's 6 states and the District of Columbia for a total 49 electoral and 35,483,820 popular votes.

The Republican Party also won control of the Senate, although Democrats retained their majority in the House. Still, Republicans had won thirty-three House seats, and because of the Dixie-Republican alliance, especially on issues like taxation and big government, the tone and style of the lower chamber became increasingly conservative. Many of the leading and most influential liberals were defeated in the House. The Speaker, Tip O'Neill, blamed the resulting defeat directly on Carter. "Ronald Reagan didn't win the 1980 election as much as Jimmy Carter lost it. . . . The fact is that by election day a great many Americans couldn't wait to get rid of him." Against a really strong candidate in a robust economy, he insisted, "Ronald Reagan would have had no more chance of being elected president of the United States than the man in the moon." Perhaps.

Many Democrats in Congress were demoralized following this election, and they did not look forward to a contest with the popular President over his announced intention of cutting domestic spending in order to increase the military budget. But according to those in California who knew Reagan fairly well, the President-elect was "all bark and no bite." As governor of California he had actually increased spending and raised taxes.

As it turned out, Reagan never had much interest in the details of legislation, but he was a born political infighter. He pleaded with members of Congress over the telephone; he buttonholed them on their visits to the White House; he worked through his staff and a "savvy team of congressional liaison men"; and he frequently addressed the American people on television, which he employed with consummate skill to support his program. "All in all," commented Tip O'Neill, "the Reagan team in 1981 was probably the best run political operating unit I've ever seen."

For the first time in American history the inauguration of the President took place on the West Lawn of the Capitol building. In his inaugural address, Reagan, the oldest person to be elected chief executive—he was less than a month shy of turning seventy—declared that "government is not the solution to our problem; government is the problem." Furthermore, he went on, it was time "to get government back within its means, and to lighten our punitive tax burden." Conservatives listening to him screamed their approval, and from that moment on he became their enduring hero.

Minutes after Reagan finished his inaugural address, the fifty-two American hostages in Tehran were released by the Iranian government in what appeared to be a final rebuke to Jimmy Carter.

It did not take long for the Democratic leadership to be overwhelmed by the deft political maneuvering of Reagan and his incomparable staff. The President inherited an economy crippled by high inflation and high interest rates. Indeed, the prime lending rate in 1981 fluctuated between 20 and 20.5 percent. For one thing, Reagan insisted on strict party discipline. Coupled with the support of southern conservative Democrats, the huge majority "we enjoyed during the Carter years," said Speaker O'Neill, "disappeared. . . . The new president jumped in with both feet." A masterful politician and manipulator, Reagan provided extraordinary leadership of Congress. Some House members claimed that they saw Reagan more during the first few months of his administration than they could recall seeing Carter during his entire four years in office.

Democrats soon discovered they could work with the President. They had many arguments, some of which grew very heated, but they learned, as Tip O'Neill said, "to disagree without being disagreeable." That sentiment infiltrated Congress. "Speaker Tip O'Neill and President Reagan would be competitive and partisan in their business dealings and cordial after hours," reported Donald Sundquist, a Republican from Tennessee. And indeed Tip and Reagan regularly met after six PM to have a drink together. "And the same was true for most of the rest of us. After the House adjourned, everybody was decent to each other and could share a laugh."

As a result, Reagan got his Economic Recovery Act passed in 1981, providing a tax cut designed to reduce the size of government and stimulate business expansion. It was supply-side economics writ large. An unbelievable total of forty-eight Democrats, most of them southern conservatives who called themselves "Boll Weevils," broke ranks with their party and voted for the measure, while only one Republican defected. "We saved Ronald Reagan's programs his first four years," boasted one Boll Weevil. Because there were enough Democratic defectors, Republicans "controlled the agenda on economic issues." Consequently, Medicare benefits and student loans were lowered, nutrition programs for children were cut, and unemployment compensation was reduced. Passage of the tax bill and the Budget Reconciliation Act, which projected reduced spending by the government for the next three years, prompted Reagan to declare that his proposals represented "an end to the excessive growth in government bureaucracy and government spending and government taxing." But the huge loss of revenue that resulted forced the administration to ask Congress to raise the debt ceiling above the trillion-dollar mark. And it was done, lifting the ceiling to $1.080 trillion through September 30, 1982. By the end of 1981, the federal deficit was headed beyond $100 billion and the economy was in decline.

Shortly after taking office, Ronald Reagan was shot in the chest on March 30, 1981, at 2:30 PM, by twenty-five-year-old John W. Hinckley Jr., while emerging from the Washington Hilton Hotel. Also wounded in the attack were the Presidential Press Secretary, James S. Brady, a Secret Service officer, and a police officer. Rushed to the George Washington University Hospital, Reagan jokingly expressed the hope that the surgeon who would perform the operation to extract the bullet was a Republican. Fortunately he recovered from the operation and was released from the hospital on April 11. Hinckley was later found not guilty of any crime by reason of insanity and he was duly incarcerated.

Reagan had no intention of slowing his efforts to increase defense spending and reduce taxes and the cost of many domestic programs. Indeed, he succeeded in providing the greatest increase in military appropriations in American history, along with the largest tax cuts this country ever experienced. Of course these sent the deficit soaring; and the national debt rocketed into the trillions. Richard Cheney, Republican from Wyoming, later commented that Ronald Reagan proved that "deficits don't matter." Some Americans worried that if "deficits don't matter," in time the country could face bankruptcy.

One thing Democrats learned about Reagan after several skirmishes was the fact that he "would compromise at the right time." He was not perpetually "hard-nosed," declared John Murtha, Democrat from Pennsylvania. On a proposed $15 billion slash of defense funds, for example, "we knew that he was willing to compromise, but he didn't compromise until the end. I mean he fought it right through to the end and then he would compromise."

But Reagan did succeed in obtaining budget and tax cuts sufficient to alter government policy significantly. Personal income taxes were reduced twenty-five percent across the board over thirty-three months. Beginning in 1985, tax rates, personal exemptions, and regular deductions were to be indexed to reflect cost of living increases. In addition, the capital gains tax was reduced from 28 to 20 percent, and the amounts to be excluded from estate and gift taxes were increased. As for the budget, such areas as education, health, housing, environment, food stamps, school meals, the National Endowment for the Arts and Humanities, and urban aid programs were slashed. On the other hand, Reagan won huge appropriations for the military. The defense budget was increased from $180 billion to $279 billion. Funds were provided to rebuild the navy, purchase bombers and missiles, and construct a space-based strategic defense system, popularly known as "Star Wars." Consequently the deficit soared from $79 billion in 1981 to $185 billion in 1986, obliging Reagan to abandon one of his most important principles and ask Congress to raise taxes. Even with this increase, the deficit rose to a high of $290 billion, and the national debt tripled.

MODERN METHODS OF accomplishing goals changed many of the ways Americans lived and how their government functioned. For example, television provided Americans with entertainment, information, and access to places they never knew existed and events that they never expected to witness. For one thing, the public for the first time could literally watch laws enacted in Congress. The beginning of public television came when the Cable Satellite Public Affairs Network (C-Span) introduced continuous coverage of Congress, both House and Senate. Speaker O'Neill said that permitting live, televised coverage of the debates in the House of Representatives was "one of the best decisions I ever made." The electorate came to realize that many of their representatives were hardworking and intelligent men and women. This medium also provided members with a means of communicating directly with their constituents back home. But one obvious disadvantage was the fact that members who in the past spent a good part of the day on the chamber floor listening to the arguments put forward by their colleagues now watched them intermittently on television from their offices. Gone were the great days of congressional debate when a Daniel Webster, a Henry Clay, a John C. Calhoun, a Thaddeus Stevens, a William Jennings Bryan could mesmerize an audience, influence voting, and demonstrate the qualities of statesmanship.

It did not take much imagination for some members to recognize that television provided an excellent means of attacking the opposition. Representative Newt Gingrich of Georgia was particularly astute in recognizing how television could assist him and his Republican colleagues to wrest control of the House of Representatives from the Democrats. "I figured out [that] if I could start making speeches on C-Span, then I would reach a dramatically bigger audience than people who flew five hundred miles to speak to a Kiwanis club." He and a small band of followers began delivering short one-minute jabs at the Democrats in the morning and longer "Special Order" jabs in the evening. Special Orders entitle a member to take the floor after the House has finished its business and speak for an hour on any subject he or she desired. The House is usually empty by that time, and the speeches were normally intended for home consumption. But Gingrich used them to charge that the House had been corrupted under Democratic rule. He said the opposition was "ruthlessly partisan in changing the rules of the House, stacking committees . . . and questioning the [Reagan] administration."

The number of one-minute speeches by members in the morning increased from 110 in March 1977 to 344 by March 1981. Unfortunately, this type of activity only generated incivility within the chamber and drove members apart. It "will poison the national dialogue and cripple domestic debate," predicted David Obey, Democrat from Wisconsin.

And indeed it did. Gradually the poison of confrontation and personal attack, rather than compromise and bipartisanship, worked its way through the legislature and within a short period of time destroyed all vestiges of courtesy and civility among the members of Congress. A new era had begun, an era of partisanship that would dominate debates for the remainder of the twentieth century and would continue into the twenty-first century.

TENSION BETWEEN THE United States and the Soviet Union escalated during the Reagan administration. Referring to communist Russia as an "evil empire," the President initiated restrictions that suspended trade between the two countries involving electronic equipment, computers, and other advanced technology. On a trip to Europe in June 1982, Reagan spoke to a joint session of the two houses of the British Parliament—the first such speech a U.S. president had ever given to that body—and then visited the Berlin Wall, calling on the communists to "tear down this wall."

So anxious were Reagan and his colleagues in the White House to block Soviet aggression that he allowed his aides to become involved in an attempt to overthrow the Marxist Sandinista regime in Nicaragua. They cooked up a scheme to provide military assistance and funds to the counterrevolutionary anti-Sandinista, or Contra, forces. Twice, in 1982 and 1983, Congress barred assistance to the Contras, and in an amendment (the Boland Amendment) to a spending bill, passed on October 12, 1984, it forbade the Pentagon, the CIA, and other intelligence agencies from furnishing "miliary equipment, military training or advice, or other support for military activities, to any group or individual . . . for the purpose of overthrowing the government of Nicaragua." This amendment was renewed in 1985 and extended through the 1986 fiscal year.

To circumvent this restriction, the administration used funds from secret arms sales to Iran, along with other financial assistance provided by foreign governments and private individuals, to support the Contra effort to overthrow the Sandinistas. This ploy began in the spring of 1985, when Israeli intelligence informed the American government that Shiite Muslims were willing to assist the release of foreign hostages held in Lebanon in exchange for arms to be sold to Iran. On January 17, 1986, Reagan approved covert arms sales to Iran through the CIA. He ordered the CIA Director, William J. Casey, not to tell Congress about it, thus initiating a systematic conspiracy to deceive Congress and cover up the activities of members of the National Security Council, an agency first established in 1947, who were funneling the funds to the Contras.

What was happening was clearly a violation of the law, and an impeachable offense for those involved. When some of the details of this scandal leaked out, the President, on November 2, appointed a three-man commission, headed by a former Texas Senator, John Tower, a Republican, to look into the matter. The commission later identified Robert MacFarlane, former director of the National Security Council; his successor, Rear Admiral John M. Poindexter; and his aide, Lieutenant Colonel Oliver North, along with Casey, as the men responsible for arranging the sale to Iran and diverting the profits from the sale to the rebels fighting the Sandinista government in Nicaragua. The commission also criticized Reagan for failing to keep abreast and in control of what was happening in his administration. A joint House and Senate report also accused the President of permitting a "cabal of zealots" to engage in activities that defied the law. Once the scandal became public, Oliver North systematically shredded all written evidence before Congress could subpoena the documents.

So flagrant were these violations that a number of Democratic congressmen demanded the impeachment of the President. But calmer heads opposed the move. "I have lived through the impeachment of Nixon," said Jim Wright, the majority leader in the House of Representatives, "and I didn't want to see that revived in our country again."

The investigations by Congress produced convincing evidence that the Reagan administration had "lied to and deceived Congress and the public, scorned the constitutional rights and responsibilities of Congress in the conduct of foreign policy; [and] abdicated the conduct of that policy to private, profit-seeking persons." But, said Speaker Tip O'Neill, "we're not going to go through another impeachment. It's too hard on the country. We're not going to do it."

Reagan accepted full responsibility for the Iran-Contra affair, declaring that he had sent aid to Iran in the hope of improving relations, not to free hostages in Lebanon. Aides swore that he had not been informed of the secret arrangements for funneling funds to the Contras. Meanwhile, the U.S. Court of Appeals for the District of Columbia appointed Lawrence E. Walsh as independent counsel, and his investigations led to the indictment of fourteen individuals, all of whom were convicted. Poindexter resigned, North was fired, and both men were indicted. On May 4, 1989, North was convicted of three felonies, including destroying and falsifying official documents, though he was acquitted of nine other charges. He was fined and put on probation for two years, but a federal judge overturned the findings and dismissed the charges. A federal appeals court also threw out the felony convictions of Poindexter. MacFarlane pleaded guilty to four counts of illegally withholding evidence from Congress and was sentenced to two years' probation and a $20,000 fine. President George

Herbert Walker Bush pardoned two others in 1992. Caspar Weinberger, the secretary of defense, was charged with four counts of perjury and making false statements, but President Bush pardoned him as
well.

In his final report Lawrence Walsh stated that there was no credible
evidence that Reagan himself had violated any criminal statute. "Nevertheless, he set the stage for the illegal activities of others by encouraging and, in general terms, ordering support of the Contras ... when
funds for the Contras were cut off by the Boland amendment." Most
probably, Jim Wright later said, Reagan "was not really focused on
what he was saying" to his aides or agreeing to, "and had no memory
of it."

IN FOREIGN RELATIONS Reagan felt obliged to send troops to
Lebanon in 1983 as part of an international peacekeeping force to help
quell a raging civil war that had brought the country to near-ruin. But
his efforts failed. On October 23, 1983, a suicide bomber crashed his
truck, laden with explosives, into the U.S. Marines barracks and killed
241 American servicemen. The President promptly withdrew the remaining troops from the country. Despite this tragic disaster, Reagan
himself suffered no political ill effects. He remained as popular as ever.
Thereafter he was known as the Teflon President, because nothing politically unfavorable could stick to him.

He enjoyed one final success in foreign affairs when he agreed with
the new Soviet leader, Mikhail Gorbachev, to end the deployment of
intermediate-range nuclear forces (INFs) in Europe. On assuming
power as chairman of the Soviet Communist Party in 1985 Gorbachev
inherited severe economic problems that required a different direction
for Russia. He announced a new policy of "openness," or glasnost, to
rid the country of Soviet-style secretiveness and repression. He advocated a form of free speech and a certain degree of political freedom. In
addition, he proposed a policy of "restructuring," or perestroika, by
which the failing Soviet economy could be improved by adopting
free-market policies of western capitalistic societies.

To achieve the goals of glasnost and perestroika, Gorbachev had to
cut the size of the Soviet military apparatus and redirect Russia's eco-

nomic activities. That meant lessening the tension and bitterness between the Soviet Union and the free world—in short, to end the Cold War. Moreover, the arms buildup of the United States under Reagan placed a heavy strain on the Soviet economy and the ability of the Russians to maintain an equal balance of military power. So Gorbachev extended a welcoming hand to Reagan by offering to cease the deployment of intermediate-range nuclear forces aimed at Europe. The President responded favorably, and after several meetings the two leaders agreed in Washington in December 1987 to the INF Treaty banning all intermediate-range missiles targeted on western Europe. In effect, this treaty marked the end of the Cold War and the beginning of friendlier relations between the Soviet Union and the West.

NOT ONLY DID the Iran-Contra scandal mar the Reagan legacy, but the allegedly improper behavior of many of his administrative aides also brought a degree of shame. The Environmental Protection Agency lost several of its most important chiefs, who resigned in disgrace because of their mishandling of funds. A presidential aide was convicted of perjury, and the secretary of labor was indicted on charges of fraud and was obliged to resign, although he was later acquitted. Moreover, the attorney general was investigated for influence-peddling; and the secretary of housing and urban development was also investigated for improper behavior in the awarding of housing grants.

Democrats made good use of these scandals to win back control of the Senate whereby they defeated the nomination of Robert Bork, a highly conservative Reagan appointee, to the Supreme Court. And the ever-mounting deficit and trade imbalance, the decline of the real estate market, and the resulting damage to savings and loan institutions appeared to indicate a general nationwide economic collapse. In fact the savings and loan disaster was so extensive that it required federal assistance, to the tune of more than $500 billion. There had never been so many banks and savings and loan operations go bankrupt since the Great Depression. Then, on October 19, 1987, the stock market plunged 508 points, the largest one-day decline in its history.

So sure were Democrats of victory in the presidential contest of 1988 that a great many candidates threw their hats into the ring. The front-runner, Gary Hart, a former senator from Colorado, was obliged to withdraw when newspapers reported alleged sexual misconduct. Another candidate, Jesse Jackson, an African-American civil rights leader, also campaigned for the nomination with the support of what he called a "rainbow coalition" of minorities and the disadvantaged. Senator Albert Gore was another contender. But Governor Michael Dukakis of Massachusetts won enough primaries to bring him the nomination on July 20 when the Democratic National Convention met in Atlanta. He chose Senator Lloyd Bentsen of Texas as his running mate.

The Republicans, meeting in New Orleans, chose Vice President George Herbert Walker Bush to head their ticket on August 17, and picked Senator J. Danforth Quayle of Indiana to complete the ticket. In a particularly nasty but effective negative campaign by the Republicans—in which Dukakis was accused of coddling criminals in his state and laughed at when shown riding on a tank wearing a helmet—Bush wiped out Dukakis's early lead and went on to win 48,886,097 popular and 426 electoral votes from 40 states, as opposed to Dukakis's 41,809,074 popular and 111 electoral votes from 10 states. But the Democrats continued to control Congress.

Prior to Reagan's departure from office several notable measures were enacted. A tax reform bill exempted a large number of low-income Americans from paying federal income taxes, eliminated a number of previously allowed deductions and tax shelters, designated capital gains as income, reduced the corporate tax rate from 46 percent to 34 percent, and combined a number of personal income brackets. In addition, the Japanese-American Reparations Act of August 10, 1988, provided $20,000 to each surviving Japanese-American who had been interned in a relocation camp during World War II. And welfare reform required states to provide education and training programs for adult welfare recipients.

BUSH'S ELECTION IN 1988 marked the first time that a sitting Vice President moved to the White House, other than by the death or resignation of the President, since Martin Van Buren in the election of 1836. In his inaugural address Bush said he would attempt to bring about a "kinder" and "gentler"America in place of the raucous, violent country it had become in the past few years. But in one of his first actions in foreign affairs, he dispatched troops by air to Panama in December 1989 to capture its dictator, Manuel Noriega, who had been indicted in the United States for drug trafficking and money laundering. A democratic government, chosen in free elections, replaced the Noriega regime.

In his inaugural address Bush also stated that "a new breeze is blowing and a world refreshed by freedom seems reborn." Indeed, the internal weakness of the Soviet Union began to manifest itself in political upheavals that erupted throughout eastern Europe. The Solidarity Movement in Poland produced a noncommunist government in 1990; in Lithuania, Latvia, and Estonia the populace demanded freedom from the Soviet Union; Hungary declared itself a free republic, as did Czechoslovakia, Romania, Uzbekistan, Ukraine, Georgia, Azerbaijan, and Armenia. In East Germany thousands of people fled to West Germany through the open borders of Czechoslovakia, Hungary, and Poland. People danced on the Berlin Wall and on December 22, 1989, the Brandenburg Gate was reopened and the wall itself was demolished, symbolically ending the Cold War that had been going on for the last forty-five years.

Communism seemed in full decline. In Russia the policies of glasnost and perestroika helped bring about the downfall of Soviet leader Mikhail Gorbachev, who resigned in December 1991. Boris Yeltsin took over as president of Russia. In Nicaragua free elections took place in February 1990, driving the Sandinistas from power. Even in Communist China there were indications that the country was veering toward a more democratic state. Thousands of students demonstrated in the streets of Beijing and in Tiananmen Square in the spring of 1989, they paraded a thirty-foot-high "Goddess of Freedom" modeled on the Statute of Liberty. But the repressive communist leaders of China brutally crushed this rebellion. Tanks and machine guns mowed down hundreds of protesters, and many more were imprisoned or executed after show trials were staged. Eastern Europe had been liberated but in Asia, and the Middle East, the forces of repression still reigned.

A new threat to world peace arose on August 2, 1990, when the dictator of Iraq, Saddam Hussein, seized the border country of Kuwait, which sits on a valuable oil pool. Anxious to protect this nation's access to the oil in the Middle East, Bush succeeded in urging the United Nations to take action against Iraq. The UN ordered Hussein to withdraw his troops and set a deadline for compliance. At the same time, the United States rushed troops to Saudi Arabia and Bush worked diligently to create an international coalition to check this unprovoked aggression. Congress authorized the President to employ military force to carry out the UN sanctions. By the end of 1990 an army of 500,000 had been deployed to the area, directed by General Colin Powell, chairman of the Joint Chiefs of Staff, and executed by General Norman Schwarzkopf, field commander of Operation Desert Storm. This Gulf War, as it was called, began on January 16, 1991, when a military attack force crushed the Iraqi army. The war ended quickly with a remarkably low number of U.S. casualties—147 Americans were killed in the operation. On February 25, Saddam agreed to withdraw his troops from Kuwait and accepted the terms of a cease-fire. He also accepted a UN resolution calling for the destruction or removal of all Iraq's chemical and biological weapons. The independence of Kuwait was reaffirmed, and Hussein was permitted to remain in power.

Bush also dispatched troops to Somalia in August 1992, to protect food supplies being shipped into the country because of a severe famine made worse by warfare between competing factions. Then, after the killing of eighteen U.S. troops in Somalia on October 3 and 4, Bush ordered 15,000 additional troops to that country but announced that they would be withdrawn in March 1994 to allow the UN to find a political solution to the problem.

Because of the failure by Congress to safeguard its constitutional jurisdiction in declaring war, three Presidents—Reagan, Bush, and later Clinton—took advantage of it by sending troops to Lebanon, Grenada, Libya, Kuwait, Somalia, Bosnia, Kosovo, Serbia, and Yugoslavia without any legislative authorization. In taking these actions they cited resolutions by the UN or NATO. The War Powers Resolution was simply ignored.

The coalition Bush had built to drive Hussein from Kuwait decided against invading Iraq proper to oust the dictator from power. It was judged to be a dicey operation and not worth the risk or the possible consequences of such an action. It was a wise decision, one that unfortunately went unheeded a decade later.

The Conservative Revolution

ONE OF THE ways in which a kinder and gentler country started to emerge was the passage, on July 26, 1990, of the Americans with Disabilities Act. This law prohibited discrimination against individuals with physical or mental disabilities in employment and in the use of public facilities. Bush also appointed Clarence Thomas, an African-American, to the Supreme Court. Thomas replaced Thurgood Marshall, the first African-American to serve on the high court, who had been appointed by President Johnson in 1967 and retired in 1991. In televised hearings, Thomas faced questions about his alleged sexual harassment of Anita Hill, who had worked in his office, his ability, and his highly conservative views. Nevertheless, the Senate confirmed his nomination by a vote of 52 to 48.

The appointment of what seemed like an inferior candidate for the Supreme Court in order to improve his standing with black and conservative voters, and the grilling of a woman by an all-male committee over sexual harassment, damaged Bush's reputation among many Americans. Even worse, the economy throughout his administration appeared to be in a worrisome decline. Unemployment escalated, approaching ten percent in some states, and the deficit kept getting worse. In an effort to control the deficit, Bush made one of his most serious mistakes when he agreed, in 1990, to a budget deal with the Democrats to raise $134 billion in new taxes over five years. This was a reversal of a promise he made before his election that he would not raise taxes: "Read my lips, no new taxes," he had said. His subsequent action horrified his conservative base. It was such a flagrant disregard of a campaign promise that it cost him dearly when he stood for reelection.

Bush's success in building a coalition that drove Saddam Hussein from Kuwait was the high point of his administration. Unquestionably, this successful war discouraged many of the leading Democratic candidates from challenging his bid for a second term. But a relative unknown, Governor William Jefferson Clinton of Arkansas, decided to go for it; and after a series of hard-fought primaries in which his sexual affairs and draft evasion received widespread attention, he managed to win the nomination at the convention held in New York from July 13 to 16, 1992. He chose Senator Albert Gore Jr. of Tennessee to run with him.

Bush and Quayle again headed the Republican ticket, chosen in Houston on August 20; but they ran a dispirited race against an opponent whose several bus trips around the country displayed an energy and youthfulness that offered the electorate a sharp and favorable contrast in style and manner. But the faltering economy more than anything else played the decisive role in this election. At Clinton's headquarters a brief but effective sign emphasized this issue. It read, "It's the economy, stupid."

Concern over the economy produced a third candidate, H. Ross Perot, a Texan billionaire. He was particularly concerned about the size of the federal budget. At one point he withdrew from the campaign but then turned around and reentered it. The three men held three televised debates—a practice that had begun with Kennedy and Nixon in 1960—and in one of them Bush was seen looking at his watch, obviously concerned about ending what was to him an endurance contest. Perot did well in the debates, boasting that he had never held public office and that he could not be blamed for running up a huge government deficit.

The final result came as a surprise to Bush. He, a family man and a wartime hero, had been defeated by a womanizer and draft dodger. It was a shock. And this election attracted 55 percent of the voting population, the largest in over twenty years. Clinton garnered 44,908,254 popular and 370 electoral votes to Bush's 39,102,343 popular and 168 electoral votes. Perot received no electoral votes, but he did attract 19,741,065 popular votes. Not since Theodore Roosevelt's Bull Moose candidacy in 1912 had a third-party candidate done as well as Perot.

Clinton's 370 electoral votes came from 32 states; Bush's 168 came from 18 states.

And Congress continued under Democratic control. Not only was Bush dismissed from office, but a great many Congressmen as well. The largest number of turnovers in the House of Representatives in forty years occurred. Forty-four members of the lower chamber were defeated in primaries or the general election, and over 100 new members were elected. These new members included 39 African-Americans, 19 Hispanic-Americans, 7 Asian-Americans, 1 Native American, and 48 women. Carol Moseley Braun of Illinois was elected to the Senate, the first African-American female to achieve that honor. She and 5 other women now comprised the entire female representation in the upper house. The number of women in the lower chamber rose from 28 to 48.

The reason for this massive turnover was most probably due, in large part, to a scandal in which it was revealed in early 1991 that 325 sitting and former members of the House overdrew their accounts in the House Bank and paid no penalty. The House Bank was a kind of checking service in which members deposited their salaries and drew against them. When overdrafts occurred, they were covered from the general pool and the individuals were not charged for issuing bad checks.

Republicans demanded an investigation by the House Ethics Committee, but Democrats countered that no federal money was involved and no crime had been committed. James Nussle of Iowa appeared on the floor of the House with a paper bag over his head and demanded to know who had issued the overdrafts. The partisan rancor that resulted only further poisoned the atmosphere in Congress, and the turnout at the election reflected popular disgust with the antics of the members. One happy result was the creation, in 1992, of a house administrator to oversee financial (mostly payrolls) and other nonlegislative matters such as internal mail. The House Bank was also abolished.

Not surprisingly, the Twenty-Seventh Amendment to the Constitution was ratified in 1992. This amendment prohibited Congress from increasing the salary of its members until a new election had taken place and a new Congress had been sworn in. James Madison had first proposed this amendment when he submitted his Bill of Rights in

1789, but it was one of two amendments proposed that was not ratified when the first ten amendments were adopted.

As President, Clinton got off to a bad start, foolishly assuming that the electorate wanted a program of liberal reform. On taking office he announced his opposition to the ban on gay and lesbian personnel in the armed services. A firestorm of protest resulted, and he was forced to accept a policy of "Don't ask, don't tell," namely that gays and lesbians could enter the military if they remained quiet about their sexual preferences.

Clinton followed that mistake with a major blunder. He appointed his wife, Hillary Rodham Clinton, to head a task force to plan a comprehensive health-care system for the country. That plan was announced by the President in a nationally televised speech before a joint session of Congress. It proved to be unbelievably complicated. The bill itself ran to over thirteen hundred pages and was assigned to three committees of the House. Not one of these committees could come up with an acceptable measure, while Republicans took pleasure in condemning this needlessly complex plan. By the end of the year the health-care bill was beyond resuscitation, and declared dead.

President Clinton had better luck in persuading Congress to enact the Brady Bill, a gun control law, named for James Brady, an aide who had been severely wounded in the attempted assassination of President Reagan in 1981. This measure imposed a five-day waiting period for handgun purchases and was later augmented to prevent the sale of guns to convicted felons. And in July 1994 Congress passed an anticrime bill that outlawed several kinds of assault weapons.

These anticrime measures reflected the genuine concern of many Americans about the level of violence that had enveloped the country over the past decade, a level that matched that of the 1960s. In 1993 a radical Muslim group bombed the World Trade Center in New York City, killing half a dozen people and wounding many others. That same year in Waco, Texas, a fundamentalist religious group known as the Branch Davidians held off federal officers from searching their compound in a gun battle that resulted in the deaths of many of the residents. Presumably in retribution for this killing, a terrorist attack in

1995 destroyed the federal office building in Oklahoma City, and 169 men, women, and children lost their lives. That such an outrage by American citizens could take place in this country seemed unbelievable. But it clearly demonstrated that there were angry, armed individuals who felt contempt toward the government and did not hesitate to take the law into their own hands. The perpetrators of this tragedy were apprehended, tried, and punished.

Violence and corruption. They dominated the news during the 1990s. The health-care fiasco provided Republicans with additional arguments about how the government had been corrupted by continued Democratic control over the past forty years. There were additional scandals, too. One of them forced the resignation of Robert Packwood from the Senate when several women charged him with sexual harassment. Another involved the Congressional Post Office in which a grand jury found evidence that funds had been embezzled and stamps provided to members had been exchanged for cash.

These scandals increased public anger over the behavior of their federal officials, and Newt Gingrich, a House leader of Republicans, kept reminding the electorate that it was time for a change. Forty years of uninterrupted Democratic control of the House proved it. He recruited young, energetic Republicans to run for office, raised money to help them in their campaigns, and sent them training tapes to educate them further in the ways of winning office. On September 27, 1994, some 300 Republican congressional incumbents and challengers to Democratic incumbents gathered on the steps of the Capitol and unveiled Gingrich's "Contract with America," by which they promised to cleanse the House of its corruption in the first 100 days of the next Congress if the public elected at least forty new Republicans.

And change did come—with devastating force. In the midterm election of 1994 the Democrats hardly knew what hit them. They lost 52 seats in the House of Representatives, whereas not a single incumbent Republican failed to win reelection. Even the Democratic Speaker, Thomas Foley, lost his election. The Republicans captured control of the House, 230 to 204, and a conservative revolution began in earnest.

Foley was the first sitting Speaker to lose since 1862, when Galusha A. Grow of Pennsylvania was defeated. Newt Gingrich was credited with this unexpected triumph and was elected the new Speaker. Republicans now ruled the lower chamber after forty years in the wilderness, and they also won control of the Senate, 53 to 47, which they had not done since 1986. Furthermore, they picked up a dozen new governorships.

Most of the items listed in the "Contract with America" were passed in the House of Representatives, except the one calling for a constitutional amendment to limit members' terms to twelve years, and a missile defense system in space. But few got past the Senate. Gingrich was particularly anxious to obtain a balanced budget. He would have preferred a constitutional amendment, but failing that objective he warned the administration that a balance between income and expenditures had to be reached by 2002. The House Budget Committee reported out a bill that trimmed $1 trillion in spending cuts over the next seven years. Hundreds of programs and several cabinet departments (Education and Commerce and Energy) were eliminated in this proposal. Leon Panetta, a California Democrat, accused Gingrich of attempting to hold a gun to President Clinton's head by threatening to "shut down the government" if the Republicans "did not get their tax cuts to help the rich and cut spending that would help the young, the old, the poor and the needy." Clinton encouraged Democrats in the House to lambaste the Republicans for their efforts to slash the budget that helped those dependent on the government's social programs. And whereas the GOP appeared rigid and unreasonable about fiscal matters, the President seemed more open to compromise as he slowly nudged his party away from its extreme liberalism to a more moderate centrist position. He even agreed to a welfare reform bill that, among other things, cut welfare grants and required able-bodied welfare recipients to find work. Later Clinton would say that "the era of big government is over."

When Clinton vetoed a stopgap spending bill, funding for most government offices ran out on November 13, 1995. As a result almost 800,000 federal employees were ordered home. Vital services like law enforcement remained operative, but a wide range of government operations—from tourist attractions like the National Gallery of Art in Washington and the Yosemite, Yellowstone, Smoky Mountains, and Grand Canyon national parks to the processing of Social Security applications—were shut down. If, said Gingrich, the only way we could demonstrate "that we were really going to balance the budget" was by closing the government, then so be it. Otherwise, "you never would have gotten Clinton and his staff to realize how deadly serious we were."

The public reacted to the shutdown with anger and disbelief. It was probably more the idea of a government shutdown to prove a point than the closing of tourist sites that offended them. What kind of government is this? asked many outraged citizens. A banana republic?

Then Speaker Gingrich made a colossal mistake. At a breakfast meeting with reporters he revealed that he had imposed the shutdown in part because he and other Republicans had been snubbed by Clinton on an overseas diplomatic trip to attend the funeral of the assassinated prime minister of Israel, Yitzhak Rabin, by making him and the Senate majority leader Robert Dole exit the plane from the rear door.

The reporters guffawed. Newspapers around the country highlighted the story. On November 16, 1995, a cartoon appeared on the front page of the New York *Daily News* showing Gingrich as a screaming baby in a diaper under a boldface headline: "CRY BABY." The caption read: "Newt's Tantrum. He closed down the government because Clinton made him sit at the back of the plane." Suddenly Gingrich had become the villain of the shutdown drama.

After a weekend of talks between the opposing sides a truce was announced on Sunday evening, November 19, sending federal employees back to work on Monday. A continuing resolution was passed to cover government expenses through December 15, as the House leadership labored for the next four weeks to reach a budget deal with the White House. But disagreements and recriminations brought the negotiations to a halt, and at midnight on December 15, the government shut down again—just in time for Christmas. This time the shutdown lasted twenty-one days.

With 250,000 federal employees locked out, Congress adjourned for the Christmas holiday and members went home to face very angry constituencies. By the time they returned to Washington in January, they knew that the so-called Republican revolution was in trouble. "Enough is enough," cried Senator Robert Dole. Even Gingrich capitulated. He told the Republicans assembled in the House on January 5, 1996, that it was time to end the shutdown. Later that day both the House and Senate passed a series of appropriation bills that reopened the government and terminated the battle between Congress and the

White House, a battle Clinton had clearly won. But many conservatives did not forgive Gingrich for failing to stand his ground and for not refusing to concede.

With a booming economy, falling deficits, and his wise move toward a more centrist political position, Clinton was reelected to a second term in 1996 over Senator Dole, a wounded veteran of World War II who ran a lackluster campaign. Ross Perot was nominated by a much shriveled Reform Party and mustered only half the support he had enjoyed four years earlier. Clinton polled 45,628,667 popular and 379 electoral votes to Dole's 37,869,435 popular and 159 electoral votes. Almost all the electoral votes for Dole came from the South and mountain states of the West.

In foreign affairs, Clinton showed an unsteady hand. Like his predecessor, he both dispatched troops to Somalia as part of a peacekeeping operation, and then abruptly withdrew them when a dozen or more American soldiers were killed. He did help broker an agreement between the Israelis and Palestinians to allow Palestinian self-rule in the Gaza Strip and the West Bank, but these efforts failed to achieve peace when extremists on both sides kept up their shooting and killing on a regular basis.

When communist-controlled Yugoslavia split into five independent nations, Bosnia, one of the five, and ethnically and culturally divided between Christian and Muslim, erupted in a bloody civil war. Pursuing a program called "ethnic cleansing," the Christian faction in Bosnia massacred or deported Muslims. To help bring an end to this bloodletting and stop the fighting, Clinton committed U.S. troops to a NATO peacekeeping force in Bosnia in 1995.

What remained of Yugoslavia sought to put down a rebellion of ethnic Albanians in Kosovo who were seeking independence. Slobodan Milosevic, the president of Yugoslavia, responded with brutal force, whereupon in 1999 an expanded NATO that now included Poland, Hungary, and Czechoslovakia, began a massive bombing campaign against Yugoslavia's military bases and brought the fighting to an end. Milosevic was later tried by an international tribunal for his crimes, but he died in prison before the final verdict could be rendered by the court.

Clinton did display a degree of determination and courage in foreign affairs when he threw his support behind a North American Free

Trade Agreement (NAFTA) in November, 1993, which set up a free trade zone or common market consisting of Canada, Mexico, and the United States. Despite congressional objections, he also provided billions of dollars in aid to Mexico to help its troubled economy. Many labor unions objected to NAFTA for fear of losing jobs to the poorer paid workers in Mexico.

THE LATTER HALF of the twentieth century witnessed additional and profound changes in American life and activity. Because of wars and the attraction of cheap labor in the southern and western states of the nation, a shift in population to those areas resulted, creating what was called the Sun Belt. A great number of people along with a good deal of economic activity moved southward from what was called the Rust Belt of the North and thereby shifted the balance of political and economic power away from the Northeast, where it had been lodged for decades. For the most part these migrants were conservative in their political views, and they helped establish a Republican majority in many of these states.

They also tended to join Evangelical churches, which emphasized the importance of a personal encounter with the Almighty as a means of salvation. By the end of the century, Evangelical church membership outnumbered the more traditional Protestant denominations. And they increasingly played a pivotal role in politics, both on the national and state levels. The Roman Catholic church in the United States also changed because of the recommendations of the Second Vatican Council in 1965 in which services were conducted in English rather than Latin, and communicants were urged to follow their own properly formed consciences in conducting their lives. But the church faced a serious scandal when it was revealed that a great number of priests had sexually abused young boys and that bishops had participated in an extensive cover-up when informed of these crimes by moving the accused priests to different perishes. Many dioceses were later sued and ordered to pay millions of dollars in damages, necessitating a few dioceses to seek protection in bankruptcy courts.

Much of this new direction in American life may have been the result of the so-called sexual liberation of the 1970s, when the young in society engaged in more frequent sexual activities. These encounters became so prevalent that they produced a large number of teenage pregnancies and many one-parent families. Among homosexuals a dreadful epidemic broke out in the 1980s, when a virus known as acquired immune deficiency syndrome, or AIDS, caused the deaths of countless individuals, many of whom contracted the infection by injecting themselves with illegal drugs.

In 1979 the Reverend Jerry Falwell, pastor of a Baptist church in Virginia, had founded an organization he called the Moral Majority, a conservative religious group that became politically active. Among other things, it lobbied Congress and party leaders to enact legislation that would halt the "immoral behavior" which was "corrupting the nation" and would restore "traditional family values" and the "free enterprise system" which had been the bedrock of American life for the past 200 years. This extreme right-wing movement proved to have enormous political power in local and national elections and increasingly edged the Republican party toward a greater commitment to religious values.

Other important changes to American society included the fact that men and women lived longer than previous generations, thanks in large part to the advances in medical science, such as the discovery of drugs to cure or prevent numerous diseases. In the last half of the twentieth century the number of Americans who lived to retirement age doubled. Many lived into their seventies and eighties, and by the twenty-first century it was not uncommon for men and women to live to be 100. This caused a surprising turnaround in the early twenty-first century. More people left the South than arrived in the Sun Belt. Census reports showed that from 2000 to 2005, approximately 120,000 people left and only 87,000 arrived in the South. A decade earlier, something like 57,000 had left and 92,000 had arrived. Evidently men and women who reached their seventies or eighties, especially if their spouses had died, moved back north to be with their children and grandchildren. Still, of the ten cities in the country with the highest number of residents by the middle of 2007, four of them were located in the south: Houston with 2,144,491, Phoenix with 1,512,986, San Antonio with 1,296,682, and Dallas with 1,232,940. Only New York, Los Angeles, and Chicago had higher numbers of populations.

The decision of the Supreme Court in *Roe v. Wade* allowed women to undergo abortions legally, and this right became a rallying cry in the women's liberation movement, which really picked up steam in the 1980s. There had been a women's rights movement as early as the Jacksonian era, if not earlier, and with slow progress many notable achievements had been won after a long, hard fight. But the movement now went beyond such matters as women's suffrage and legal recognition of their rights as citizens. Women wanted equality with men in employment, in educational, cultural, and athletic activities, and in many other areas of activity and opportunity. In March 1972, Congress passed and sent to the states for ratification an equal rights amendment (ERA) to the Constitution which said that the "equality of rights" shall not be denied or abridged on the basis of sex. In the House of Representatives, Martha Griffiths, a Democrat from Michigan, led the fight for the amendment and insisted that women were discriminated against in employment, property rights, divorce proceedings, pensions, and inheritance. Although some twenty states ratified the ERA in the early months, an opposing and more conservative group protested against it, insisting that traditional family values would be undermined if the amendment was ratified. And that ended the ERA. The amendment went down to defeat when the time limit for ratification expired in 1982.

But women did make headway in many fields, not just as nurses, secretaries, clerks, and grade school teachers. They broke through the glass ceiling, as it was called, and became business executives, police officers, lawyers, governors of states, members of Congress, and leaders in many other important fields of endeavor. In 2007, Nancy Pelosi, a Democrat from California, was elected Speaker of the House of Representatives, the first female Speaker in the history of the House. As such she became one of the most powerful politicians in the country, after the President. By her election she had crashed through a "marble ceiling," as she labeled it.

Of monumental importance in changing the way Americans conducted their lives was the introduction of the personal computer by International Business Machines (IBM) in the 1960s. Computers of gargantuan size had been in use decades earlier, but the invention of the microchip in 1971 made it possible to create, find, organize, and store information on much smaller machines operated in the home and in businesses. Data and word processing became possible when the

Microsoft Company, headed by Bill Gates, provided the necessary programming software. Suddenly, an electronic industry emerged, especially in a part of California between San Jose and San Francisco, known as Silicon Valley, which supplied the country with the hardware that opened up a new world of communicating. The speed and capacity of microchips improved almost every other month, so that computers became more portable and essential in conducting one's business and private affairs. In time computers became so vital to business, government, and individual activity that any breakdown of the computer system could paralyze the normal functions of daily life.

The Internet made it possible to access information in a matter of minutes, both at home and at work. Instant communication between individuals and between companies was provided via e-mail. And the World Wide Web, created in 1991, made it possible to access information on every imaginable subject or activity with just a few clicks on the mouse on the computer. Web sites grew in number and importance each year. The nation entered an Information Age that demanded high-speed transmission among and between individuals and corporations. Personal computers became an essential part of everyday life. This technological age both created new jobs and destroyed old ones. Computers frequently took the place of the go-between, that is, those who play the role of an intermediary between a client and a product.

The invention of wireless telephones or cell phones and BlackBerrys added to the speed with which Americans could communicate with one another. The United States became a nation that supplied services of many kinds as well as a producer of physical products that could be packaged and sold around the world. And the invention of the transistor in 1947 ushered in the digital age.

The scientific advances in the last half of the twentieth century were spectacular not only in producing improved machines and the ways of operating them, but in such fields as medicine, biology, and chemistry. The secrets of the molecular structure of humans were unlocked in the 1950s, by which it became possible to clone living animals. Organ transplants, including heart transplants, proved possible. Stem-cell research offered the possibility of curing hereditary and life-threatening diseases, but this research raised moral and ethical questions that were not easily answered.

Of particular concern to an older generation was the fact that the family in which children were raised by two parents of the opposite sex, one of whom (usually the male) worked and the other (usually the female) stayed home and raised the children, was disintegrating at an alarming rate. Marriage was often put off until the male had reached his mid-thirties and the female her late twenties. Worse, divorce became commonplace. Every other marriage seemed to end in divorce, which was easier to obtain than had been the case a generation earlier. More and more children were born to single mothers. Indeed, every fourth child arrived in a home in which the father was missing. Too often such a family lived at or near the poverty level. The resulting emotional and psychological scars resulting from this situation were and remain incalculable. Crime rates among the young increased substantially, most especially in urban areas.

Another concern was the growing number of Latinos coming into this country. Thousands illegally crossed the Mexican border into the United States, where they accepted low-paying farmwork. Not all were Mexicans. Many came from other Latin American countries and poured across the Mexican–U.S. border in their search for a better life. They settled, for the most part, in the Southwest, from Texas to California. By the beginning of the twenty-first century Latinos constituted over a third of the populations in California, Arizona, and Texas, and nearly half the population in New Mexico. In the East there was a steady stream of Puerto Ricans into the continental United States, and Cuban refugees settled in Miami and surrounding communities, making English a second language in this area. As a matter of fact, many cities to the north followed a general trend in making signs, directions, and information available in both English and Spanish. A great deal of anti-immigration sentiment was generated, especially since so many of these immigrants were in the United States illegally. Congress attempted to deal with the problem by passing the Immigration Reform and Control Act of 1986, which penalized employers of illegal immigrants and granted amnesty to those immigrants who had already arrived. But the problem kept getting worse because the border with Mexico was not adequately policed. Building fences was impractical along a 1,000-mile line (to say nothing of the cost), and as one Mexican consul in Chicago stated, "For every foot of fence built above the ground an equal amount would have to be constructed under it."

Immigration from Asia also gained momentum in the 1980s, and Asians became not only a fast-growing minority but a prosperous one as well. No longer satisfied with menial employment, they sought and achieved better jobs through their reliance on education. Asian children in school were among the brightest and most dedicated. As graduates they entered the fields of science, medicine, business, and industry.

The fact that the population of the United States in the census of 2000 reached nearly 300 million and that it had grown by more than 30 million over the past ten years said something that was very significant, in that the 30 million represented the largest population increase for a ten-year period in the history of the United States.

SINCE THE BEGINNING of his administration, Clinton had endured any number of investigations by Republicans into the operations of the White House, including the travel office and the involvement of the Clintons in the Whitewater land scheme in Arkansas. The obvious purpose of these investigations was to find sufficient cause to initiate impeachment proceedings. Clinton's sexual activities also came in for a renewal of charges that began when he was governor of Arkansas. In particular, Paula Jones, a former employee, claimed that she had suffered sexual harassment. Worse, he was accused of inappropriate behavior toward a White House intern, Monica Lewinsky, that had allegedly occurred in the Oval Office, no less. The Attorney General, Janet Reno, appointed Kenneth Starr to investigate the allegations, and in testimony before a grand jury in January 1998, the President swore he had had no improper relations with Lewinsky, a denial he repeated several more times to members of Congress, his cabinet, and others.

Nevertheless, the truth finally emerged. Continued revelations of incriminating evidence eventually forced Clinton to admit before a television audience on August 15, 1998, that he had indeed carried on an "inappropriate" affair with Lewinsky. But he went on to insist that he had done nothing illegal. Certainly nothing impeachable. And a good many people believed him. "I think the American people," declared Republican Senator Robert E. Bennett of Utah, "have come to the conclusion that they do not want to drive the president out of office just because he's not faithful to his wife, and they turned off all the rest of it."

Kenneth Starr submitted his evidence of Clinton's improper behavior to Congress in thirty-six boxes of documents in September, shortly after it had returned from recess. Starr declared that the President's actions may indeed "constitute grounds for impeachment." After all, he had lied to a grand jury under oath. A good bit of this evidence was placed on the Internet at the direction of Newt Gingrich, and, said Bob Livingston, a Republican leader in the House of Representatives, "I'm convinced, with the wisdom of the American people that they sensed a degree of unfairness there. Public attitude switched from being totally against Clinton to against the Republicans." On October 8, 1998, the House adopted a resolution, 258 to 176, instructing the Judiciary Committee, chaired by Henry Hyde of Illinois, to examine the evidence and decide whether the president had committed impeachable offenses "or whether it was just something personal and not a matter of national concern."

Hearings by the thirty-seven-member committee were quite heated, and as far as the Republicans were concerned, insisted Henry Hyde, the charges "had nothing to do with sex and everything to do with perjury and swearing under oath." But the Democrats on the committee and in Congress "were successful in defining the issue as a very personal one that lying about is not uncommon," that sexual misbehavior was not a high crime or misdemeanor. They further warned the Republicans of a backlash. "As you judge the president of the United States," cautioned Representative Charles Rangel of New York, "the voters will be judging you on November 3rd."

And indeed the electorate demonstrated its displeasure by reducing the number of Republicans in the House by five members. "Instead of gaining seats" as they expected, said Livingston, who served as chairman of the Appropriations Committee, "we lost five. I was furious. That's because I'd worked my butt off all year to campaign and raised a ton of money. And they were all turned into anti-Clinton ads and that's not what I'd raised them for. I said that I'd raised the money to spend on pro-Republican ads. We didn't talk about what we had done right. We talked about what he [Clinton] had done wrong. And we blew it."

Livingston then decided to challenge Gingrich for the speakership, but Gingrich, knowing he was sure to lose (there had been a previous failed effort to unseat him as Speaker) resigned both his seat and as Speaker. The Republicans then chose Livingston as Speaker-designate. The irony is that both Gingrich and Livingston were involved in adulterous affairs themselves, as they later admitted.

At the urging of the leadership, the Judiciary Committee agreed on December 11–12 that Clinton had in fact "committed perjury and obstructed justice." Furthermore, the committee declared that "it would be a dereliction of duty if we didn't proceed . . . with impeachment with a view towards removing him from office." The vote was 21 to 16 for impeachment, but the committee members realized that a successful prosecution of their charges would be a long shot at best, since removal by the Senate required a two-thirds vote.

The committee presented its report to the full House of Representatives, and for thirteen and a half hours over two days, December 18 and 19, the members heatedly debated the merits of the findings. The Democrats insisted that censure was the appropriate action to take, but on a procedural vote that suggestion was defeated. Then, it was revealed that the Speaker-designate, Bob Livingston, had also committed adultery, whereupon he announced his resignation. In his place the Deputy Whip, J. Dennis Hastert of Illinois, was elected Speaker by the full House on January 6, 1999, thanks in large part to the efforts of the Republican Whip, Tom DeLay of Texas.

The House then proceeded to vote on the impeachment issue, but the outcome was predictable, given the size of the Republican majority. The vote was 228 to 206 on the perjury charge and 221 to 212 on the obstruction of justice charge. A thirteen-member committee, chaired by Henry Hyde, was approved to serve as managers of the impeachment trial in the Senate. To their surprise and dismay, these members found the Senate unsympathetic to their efforts. We were "the proverbial skunk at the garden party," declared Hyde. "Nobody wanted us. The senators wanted to get it over with in a hurry and following the polls and finding that this impeachment was not the most popular move in the world," they wanted to get rid of it as quickly as possible. "There was nobody really enthusiastic for what we were doing, including our own [Senate Republican] leadership."

The trial in the Senate began on January 7, 1999, with Chief Justice

William Rehnquist presiding. To begin the proceedings, Hyde reminded the senators of their duty as impartial jurors. Other members of the prosecuting committee argued that Clinton had lied under oath to a federal judge, had disgraced his office, and deserved punishment like any other citizen. The defense was a high-powered group of eight lawyers, headed by Charles Ruff, the White House counsel. Ruff insisted that the vision of the managers was far too dark. "I believe it to be a vision more focused on retribution," he said, "more designed to achieve partisan ends." The vision of the defense is far different, he continued. "We know the pain the president has caused our society and his family and his friends, but we know, too, how much the president has done for this country."

Any comparison of the presentations by the prosecution and defense left little doubt that the House prosecutors failed to convince the senators to vote to remove Clinton from office. To the public at large it appeared to be a matter of partisan hatred for a morally flawed President and a desire to exact retribution. On February 9, 1999, after nearly five weeks of testimony and deliberation, the senators voted against removal and acquitted Clinton. Ten Republicans and all forty-five Democrats voted not guilty to the charge of perjury; fifty senators voted not guilty to the charge of obstruction of justice, but another fifty voted guilty. Later Clinton expressed his "profound" regret for what he had imposed on Congress and the American people.

The intense bitterness and partisanship of the scandal and trial carried over into the presidential election of 2000. The Democrats nominated Al Gore of Tennessee, the sitting Vice President, to head their ticket, along with Senator Joseph Lieberman of Connecticut, the first Jewish vice presidential candidate. The Republicans chose Governor George W. Bush of Texas, son of the former President; and Richard Cheney of Wyoming, who had been Secretary of Defense under President George H. W. Bush. A third party, the Green Party, emerged and put forward the consumer advocate Ralph Nader for the top position.

In the campaign Bush presented himself as an outsider who would restore "honor and dignity" to the White House after Clinton had sullied it. He insisted that he was a "uniter," not a "divider," a "compassionate conservative." Gore made the mistake of distancing himself from Clinton and thereby losing the ability to claim credit for the administration—of which he had been an important part—for the prosperous years in which surpluses in running the government helped reduce the national debt. Even so, he won a majority of the popular vote, garnering several hundred thousand more votes than Bush. But the electoral vote was so close that a battle resulted over the Florida returns. It seems that voting irregularities and malfunctioning voting machines produced punch-card ballots that occasionally carried what was called a "hanging chad," which confused both machine and human counters. Gore supporters demanded a recount in selected counties where the outcome was in dispute. But the Republican secretary of state halted the recount and declared Bush the winner of Florida's votes. Gore's lawyers asked the Florida supreme court for a ruling, and this court ordered the recount to resume. Whereupon the Bush lawyers appealed to the U.S. Supreme Court, which ruled, by a partisan vote of 5 to 4 on December 12, that the recount be halted. With Florida now in the Bush column he had 271 electoral votes to 267 for Gore. It is also likely that the candidacy of Ralph Nader drew many votes away from Gore, votes that might have reversed the final result and put the Vice President in the White House. Nationwide, Nader polled two and a half million votes. In Florida he captured over 95,000 votes, just enough to throw the state to Bush.

BECAUSE OF HIS own several disappointments in business and limited experience in government, Bush chose Dick Cheney as his running mate, a staunch conservative who enjoyed a successful career as a member of the House of Representatives and had joined the Republican leadership team in the lower chamber where he was elected minority whip. He might have gone on to win the office of Speaker had he not accepted the post of secretary of defense in the first Bush administration. No doubt with the younger Bush's encouragement, Cheney soon became a potent force within the new administration in deciding national policy. One of the most influential Vice Presidents in American history, he exercised almost as much power in foreign and domestic affairs as did the President. Together, these two men helped solidify executive authority and privilege. Bush also brought to the White House as an adviser Karl Rove, the man he called the "architect," who planned the strategy by which Bush was elected both governor of Texas and President of the United States.

Equally important to an extent was the minority whip in the House, Tom DeLay of Texas. He was another staunchly conservative Republican who played political hardball and virtually cut the Democrats out of any involvement in the business of the House. He masterminded what was called the K Street Project, named after the street in Washington where many lobbying firms are located. The word soon went out that if lobbyists wished to have any influence on legislation, their financial contributions had to be Republican. Supporting Democrats would ensure defeat for any project the lobbyists might advance. Because many former members of Congress remained in Washington after they retired (or were retired by the electorate), they joined various lobbying companies and had easy access to the power brokers in Congress. Therefore, a great deal of lobbyists' money flowed into Republicans' campaigns, and with this advantage Tom DeLay exercised strict discipline on Republican House members. The Texas legislature solidified his leadership by gerrymandering five additional Republican districts, which increased that party's majority in the U.S. House of Representatives. After the midterm election of 2002 the Republicans also controlled the Senate. Now the two branches of the federal government—the White House and Congress—were under one party, which meant that the President could and did dictate national policy. Throughout his first term Bush did not veto a single piece of legislation.

After a rather turbulent life as a young man, Bush became a born-again Christian, thanks to the efforts of his wife, Laura, and the Reverend Billy Graham. As President, he therefore inaugurated what he called a "faith-based initiative" to provide federal support for church-related programs that would include such services as helping teenagers avoid pregnancy. He also forbade federal support of stem-cell research, one of the most modern techniques for exploring new ways to combat disease and advance health care. Clearly affiliated with the Religious Right, something Karl Rove believed would solidify the President's conservative base and provide Republicans domination of national politics for years to come, Bush expected his administration to be morally above reproach, thereby restoring virtue to the operation of government.

One of his most important actions, taken soon after his inauguration, was the proposed No Child Left Behind Act that aimed to improve primary and secondary schools by directing federal money toward those institutions that raised the level of students' performance in math, science, and English. By establishing federal standards in these academic areas—historians were particularly distressed because history was omitted from the list—this legislation undercut the authority of local and state school boards. Critics argued that the program emphasized testing and not teaching.

It soon became clear that the Bush administration supported and wished to advance the interests of American business. That fact was emphasized by a secret meeting Vice President Cheney, a former CEO of Halliburton, a leading oil equipment company, held with executives from the oil-producing companies. The participants agreed to an energy policy that approved the drilling of oil in Alaska's National Wildlife Refuge and provided subsidies for extracting oil from the Gulf of Mexico. The administration also interpreted the Clean Air Act so as to benefit the electric utilities, and put the Environmental Protection Agency under the direction of men and women who understood the value of corporate participation.

Inevitably, business leaders took advantage of the situation, and a number of corporate scandals resulted, the most prominent involving Enron, the Houston-based energy enterprise. Price rigging, fraudulent accounting practices, and insider trading all contributed to Enron's collapse. Thousands of employees lost their jobs and pensions. Officers of the company were indicted, found guilty, and imprisoned. Enron's accounting firm, the venerable Arthur Andersen Company, closed its doors as a result of its actions in attempting to cover up the scandal.

Business especially benefited from Bush's insistence on cutting taxes. Like Reagan before him, Bush argued that the economy would grow as a result of tax cuts and that all citizens would share in the anticipated prosperity. The young President quickly implemented his plans. The Economic Growth and Tax Relief Act of 2001 cut income taxes, phased out the estate tax by 2010 unless Congress intervened, and extended the earned income credit for low-income families and individuals. Two years later further tax cuts were enacted. The taxes on dividends and capital gains were reduced. And although middle-class and low-income families benefited by these cuts, the wealthy benefited the most.

This reduction in the amount of money obtained from taxpayers caused the national debt to rise to record levels. Unlike Reagan, who advocated tax reduction as a means of shrinking the government, Bush increased expenditures during his administration. The surpluses left by the Clinton administration quickly disappeared, and the national debt swelled to $9 trillion. Much of this debt was owed to foreign investors, such as China, which also sold goods to the United States at cheaper prices than domestic products and thereby increased the nation's huge trade imbalance.

What made the debt situation worse was the ballooning Social Security and Medicare obligations resulting from those born immediately after World War II and known as the baby boomer generation who were nearing retirement. Sooner or later both Social Security and Medicare programs would need attention, but neither Congress nor the administration had any genuine solutions to potential shortfalls in these programs.

The Bush administration also acted unilaterally in addressing foreign affairs. It abandoned the Kyoto Protocols, which set mandatory limits regarding atmospheric pollution, as well as UN conventions that banned biological weapons and nuclear tests. It behaved as though it could do as it pleased in foreign affairs and not be guided by the needs or wishes of other nations.

And then came the blow. On September 11, 2001, terrorists, armed with box cutters, commandeered four airplanes and rammed two of them into the World Trade Center in New York City, killing nearly 3,000 people. Another plane slammed into the Pentagon and killed almost 200. A fourth plane, headed for the Capitol or the White House in Washington, crashed in Pennsylvania when courageous passengers rebelled against the seizure of the plane and fought the terrorists. Passengers, crew members, and terrorists, numbering 246, died in the crash. These well-planned and -executed operations were the work of a radical Muslim organization known as Al Qaeda, led and financed by Osama bin Laden, and supported by Taliban leaders in Afghanistan who had seized control of the country in 1996, after first overthrowing a government supported by the Soviet Union. The United States had assisted the Taliban in its struggle for independence since this happened during the Cold War. The Muslim radicals regarded the United

States as the "great Satan" who with the arrogance of power sought to dictate policy in the Middle East, especially in its support of Israel.

At first Bush seemed dazed by what had happened on 9/11, as it came to be known, but he soon rallied and called on the nation to end terrorism in the world, promising to vanquish Al Qaeda and capture Osama bin Laden "dead or alive." Congress promptly passed a resolution by which the President was given sweeping powers to "use all necessary and appropriate force against those nations, organizations, or persons he determines planned, authorized, committed, or aided the terrorist attacks that occurred on September 11, 2001." With the cooperation of Britain and other nations, he immediately attacked Afghanistan, and, after extensive bombing raids and advances by ground forces, toppled the Taliban regime within six months and knocked out Al Qaeda's operations in that country. But both bin Laden and many of the Al Qaeda leaders escaped, probably into remote areas of northern Afghanistan and southern and eastern Pakistan. As late as 2008 bin Laden remained at large, although by that time he was more a symbol of Muslim terror than a strategic operator, and the Al Qaeda network was back in full operation.

An interim government was established in Afghanistan and democratically elected a president, Hamid Karzai. But his authority was limited to an area around the capital city of Kabul while various warlords controlled the countryside. The Taliban also remained a power within Afghanistan and by the spring of 2007 had begun a renewed fight to regain control. Unfortunately, Bush made no effort to see the intervention in Afghanistan to a successful conclusion. Instead he directed his attention toward another Middle Eastern target, Iraq.

It has been suggested that Bush most likely aimed to overthrow Saddam Hussein on becoming President, and he had the active support of his Vice President, Richard Cheney, and his Secretary of Defense, Donald Rumsfeld. The refusal of his father to pursue Hussein following the Gulf War may have played an essential part of his thinking, that is, he would finish what his father had left undone. In a public announcement he denounced the regimes of Iran, Iraq, and North Korea as an "axis of evil, aiming to threaten the peace of the world." These nations, he believed, were seeking to develop or in fact had developed chemical, biological, or nuclear weapons of mass destruction (WMD).

Bush also insisted that the war on terrorism necessitated the United States to "deter and defend against the threat before it is unleashed." In other words, this novel and dangerous policy meant that the United States could and would act preemptively and alone, if necessary. This was a major alteration of American foreign policy and would lead to an undermining of its influence and authority in western Europe and other parts of the world. The United States was seen as the "bully" of the globe, intent on imposing its will, policies, and goals on other nations.

This war on terror and the need to protect national security drove the Bush administration farther into pursuing actions that increased presidential prerogatives so that oversight of its activities, whether by Congress or the courts, could be sidestepped. In the fall of 2001 the Patriot Act (Uniting and Strengthening America by Providing Appropriate Tools Required to Intercept and Obstruct Terrorism) was passed by which the federal government assumed unparalleled authority to obtain information about the activities of citizens and apprehend likely terrorists. A second Patriot Act, passed in 2003, expanded the government's surveillance and secret arrest powers. What troubled many Americans was the fact that the administration had the unlimited authority to wiretap citizens without first obtaining a court order. In exercising its increased powers, the government rounded up over 1,000 suspects, some of them American citizens, and locked them up in a camp in Guantanamo, Cuba. Few were brought to trial. The administration felt it had the right to bypass the courts in the name of national security.

The Homeland Security Department was established in 2002; twenty-two different agencies, including immigration, naturalization, customs, Secret Service, coast guard, and airport operators were incorporated into this one department. FEMA (Federal Emergency Management Agency) was mistakenly added to Homeland Security, as was demonstrated shortly thereafter when Hurricane Katrina struck the Gulf coast on August 29, 2005, and it failed to adequately assist the victims of this storm. After the Defense Department, Homeland Security had more employees than any other federal agency. Many citizens rightly worried that civil liberties and privacy rights would be violated.

Emboldened by the opportunity to assume even greater power in running the government, the Bush administration decided to launch a preemptive attack against Iraq. Encouraged by his close associate Vice President Cheney; the Secretary of Defense, Donald Rumsfeld; and the deputy secretary, Paul Wolfowitz, with the active support of the National Security Adviser, Condoleezza Rice, and the reluctant agreement of the Secretary of State, Colin Powell, President Bush decided to ask Congress for authority to overthrow the Hussein dictatorship. These advisers expected the Iraqi people to welcome an American invasion and bring a measure of democracy to the country. More troubling was the fear that Hussein had obtained biological and chemical weapons and was attempting to obtain uranium deposits from Niger in Africa in order to build weapons of mass destruction, even though UN weapons inspectors had failed to discover any trace of WMD within Iraq. The Bush advisers also believed that Hussein had connections with Al Qaeda operatives stationed around the world. In all, the evidence seemed overwhelming to support a military strike to spare humanity a catastrophic blow.

The trouble with this evidence was that none of it was true. There were no WMD in Iraq; nor were there connections to Al Qaeda. Intelligence agencies in the government tried to alert the administration to these errors, but they were ignored. Brent Scowcroft, the former National Security Adviser to George H. W. Bush, warned that an invasion of Iraq "could turn the whole region," not simply Iraq itself, "into a cauldron, and thus destroy the war on terrorism."

On October 10, 2002, Congress, including many Democrats in both houses who voted with the Republican majority, some of whom later repudiated their action, agreed to permit a preemptive strike against Iraq. Still the Bush administration held back for the moment, when foreign nations disapproved. On November 8, the UN unanimously passed a resolution giving Iraq three and a half months to permit weapons inspectors to determine whether WMD actually existed within the country. Hussein had expelled the inspectors in 1998, but now he agreed to their return, and although he had no WMD he regularly, and foolishly, created problems for the inspectors in carrying out their assignment. He was also required to produce a full statement of his country's weaponry.

The Bush administration, itching to start a war with Iraq, chose to believe that the action of the Iraqi dictator proved he had hidden WMD and therefore had violated the UN resolution. In February 2003, Secretary of State Powell spoke before the UN and argued the case for war. But France, Russia, and Germany opposed any such action and the UN refused to sanction the U.S. demand. Frustrated but still determined to take action, Bush went ahead and signaled the start of a U.S/British assault on March 19 to topple Hussein. He asserted the claim that the United States "has the sovereign authority to use force in assuring its own national security." He argued that the invasion was linked to the continuing war against terrorism.

The invasion of Iraq proved to be one of the most disastrous foreign policy mistakes ever committed by the United States. A relatively small, high-tech force was employed; no plans had been devised about occupying the country; and no plans had been worked out as to how and when American forces would be withdrawn.

The actual war proceeded rapidly. A coalition of armed forces from a number of European countries, including Spain, Italy, Poland, and several other nations, was formed. About 150,000 American troops based in Kuwait, along with a smaller British force, swept northward and overwhelmed the Iraqi army, which melted away. Hussein disappeared, the major cities were captured, and looting by the native population began immediately. A nearly total breakdown of essential services like water and electricity resulted, and Iraq headed toward civil war between Sunni Muslims who had ruled the country with Hussein and Shiite Muslims who represented the majority of the people in Iraq. On May 1, 2003, Bush flew to the aircraft carrier *Abraham Lincoln*, and standing under a banner that read "Mission Accomplished," he announced to cheering sailors and a live television audience of millions that the war against Iraq had been successfully ended.

Nothing could have been farther from the truth. To be sure, it was not a war that the United States had fought before against enemy armies. This was a war of random car bombings, kidnappings, mortar attacks, and guerrilla opposition to what was seen by many Iraqis as an occupation army, not a liberating force. The Bush administration had been warned that it would take a much larger army than the one provided to subdue the country and restore law and order. But under the mistaken belief of Secretary Rumsfeld that his so-called high-tech army could do the job just as well, the country quickly became chaotic.

In the summer of 2003, a Coalition Provisional Authority headed by Ambassador Paul Bremer established a Governing Council to run Iraq. A heavily fortified "Green Zone" was set up to protect the officials of this government against the rising number of terrorist militiamen, who singled out American soldiers, workers, officials, and their allies for assassination. By the spring of 2008 over 4,000 American soldiers had been killed in Iraq and thousands more severely wounded. Millions of Iraqis fled the country, fearing for their lives. And the United States suspected and later offered proof that Iran, an overwhelming Shiite nation, was supplying the insurgents with weapons.

The unexpected but dramatic capture of Saddam Hussein, found hiding underground in December 2003, provided at least a semblance of success in fighting this war, but it did not deter terrorists from their almost daily assault on both the Americans and native Iraqis. Hussein himself was later tried, found guilty, and hanged. The reputation of the United States was further damaged when cameras graphically revealed the barbaric use of torture by Americans of prisoners held in Baghdad's Abu Ghraib prison in April 2004. In violation of the Geneva Conventions, U.S. military personnel posed for pictures that showed naked prisoners in grotesque positions or being threatened by vicious dogs. Several of these U.S. guards were later tried by a military court and convicted. Further embarrassment ensued when weapons inspectors concluded that whatever biological and chemical weapons Hussein might have had were most likely destroyed before the country was invaded. Slowly Americans began to realize that the war should never have been waged.

And the war raged on. Terrorists broadened their attacks to include the British consulate in Istanbul in November 2003 that resulted in scores of deaths. In March 2004, a well-coordinated bombing of Madrid's subways resulted in the killing of over 200 people. The newly elected Spanish government immediately withdrew its troops from the coalition in Iraq.

Another reason for the intense hatred of the United States by Muslim terrorists was the continuing support America had provided Israel, a hatred that intensified because of Israeli settlements in the West

Bank and the Gaza Strip, and Israel's resistance to Palestinians' demands for a separate and independent state. The killing of both Israelis and Palestinians grew worse. Hamas, a militant terrorist group in Palestine, sworn to Israel's destruction, organized car bombings in crowded Jewish communities. Ariel Sharon, the Israeli prime minister, ordered a massive strike to kill off the Hamas leadership. At first the Bush administration tried to duck from any involvement in the dispute, but it later reversed itself and joined with the UN in attempting to work out a peace agreement by which a Palestinian nation would be formed and Israel recognized by Arabs as an independent state in the Middle East. Negotiations at times seemed to go forward, but at other times they verged on collapse. When Ariel Sharon suffered a severe stroke, he was replaced by Ehud Olmert. And the killing just went on and on.

As THE PRESIDENTIAL election of 2004 approached, Democrats found themselves in a difficult situation. They could not oppose the war without appearing unpatriotic but they also knew that the war was poorly planned and executed. Furthermore, they feared being seen as lacking support for the troops in the field. And in finding a candidate, they needed someone who could provide the kind of leadership expected in a President, especially during wartime. As the primary season got under way, Vermont's governor, Dr. Howard Dean, took the lead among several possible Democratic candidates by opposing the war and attracting large financial contributions via the Internet. But after a slow and shaky start, Senator John Kerry of Massachusetts pulled ahead because of his heroic exploits during the Vietnam War. Indeed, he had been wounded twice in that war and decorated for bravery. To many Democrats he appeared to be the leader they needed to bring the Iraqi war to a swift conclusion. Kerry was nominated for the presidency, along with Senator John Edwards of North Carolina as Vice President.

During the campaign Kerry and Edwards insisted that Bush's tax cuts had benefited the wealthy at the expense of the middle and poorer classes of Americans. They also offered a program to protect Social Security, prevent outsourcing of American jobs overseas, improve funding for education, and insure better health care for all citizens. But the only real issue Americans responded to was who could best provide the leadership necessary in this on-going war against terrorism. Democrats praised Kerry's heroic war record and questioned Bush's failure to serve in the Vietnam War, arguing that his enlistment in the Air National Guard was just a convenient escape from the more dangerous task of fighting in the jungles of Vietnam. Republicans struck back by suggesting that Kerry's record in the war was fake. A group called Swift Boat Veterans for Truth claimed that his supposed heroism was a lie, a falsehood that Kerry did not immediately dispute. Even worse was his voting record in the Senate where he "voted against before voting for" a particular bill. He was dubbed a "flip-flopper," one who could not make up his mind about anything and tried to have it both ways. As for the war in Iraq, Bush insisted during the campaign that the country must "stay the course." To pull out would spell victory for terrorism and sink Iraq into a worse chaotic state than it already suffered.

Another issue that figured prominently in this election was same-sex marriage. The Massachusetts supreme court ruled that marriage of gay couples could not be denied, an argument repeated by some politicians in Oregon and California. Bush himself said he favored a constitutional amendment banning same-sex marriage. This issue triggered a strong reaction among evangelical groups, who came out in record numbers to vote for the "born again" Christian, George W. Bush. Their appearance at the polls seemed to vindicate the contention of Bush's close political adviser, Karl Rove, that capturing the evangelical base was essential to success. Not surprisingly, eleven states passed measures outlawing same-sex marriages.

Bush triumphed, capturing 51 percent of the popular vote to Kerry's 48 percent. But it was a closer election in the electoral college, where Bush received 279 votes to Kerry's 252. Had Ohio gone to Kerry, its 20 electoral votes would have reversed the outcome. And that state also passed a ban on gay marriage by 62 percent, the issue that undoubtedly brought many conservatives to the polls in Ohio and gave Bush the victory by a narrow margin.

Bush chose to interpret his success as a mandate to continue the war until the terrorists had been subdued and a democracy established in Iraq. He claimed he had acquired considerable political capital from this election, which he planned to use to further his plans for reducing taxes, reforming Medicare, and reorganizing other social insurance projects by encouraging the participation of private business entities.

So the war in Iraq continued unabated, and with each passing month public approval for Bush lessened as the killing, especially of Iraqi civilians, mounted. Furthermore, the cost of the war each month soared into the billions of dollars. At the same time both Bush and Vice President Cheney assured the nation that great progress was being made and victory was imminent. In the summer of 2004, the Coalition Provisional Authority transferred its authority to an interim Iraqi government, and Paul Bremer returned home. He was replaced by U.S. Ambassador Zalmay Khalilzad. Then, in January 2005, a national election was held to elect an assembly that would write a new constitution for Iraq. Kurds from the north and Shiites from the south responded heartily to this opportunity—the Sunnis in the central section less so—and together they formed a coalition government. In October, a new constitution was approved and Nuri al-Maliki was chosen as prime minister. Ambassador Khalilzad worked out an agreement to amend the constitution so that Sunnis could participate in this government, but nothing came of it. Khalilzad was replaced in March 2007 by the veteran diplomat Ryan Crocker.

Then, on February 22, 2006, the war took a turn for the worse when terrorists—presumably Sunnis—destroyed one of the holiest of Shiite shrines, the gold-domed Askariya Mosque in Samarra, and Iraq descended into full-scale civil war. Hundreds of corpses, many with visible signs of torture, were discovered in alleys and vacant lots. It has been estimated that at least 10,000 civilians died in the final months of 2006.

The situation had become so bad that the American people began having doubts about prolonging the war. And an increasing majority felt the invasion had been a mistake. Bush's popularity went into a steep decline and fell into the 30 percent approval range. Secretary of Defense Rumsfeld also faced mounting criticism, even from the military, and he later resigned from office. A number of retired generals voiced their complaints about how the war had been initiated, how it had been planned and executed, and how unacceptable was the cost in lives and money. By 2006 over $300 billion had been spent in prosecuting the war. And Bush kept asking for additional supplements.

Further mistakes by the Bush administration followed. A contract, approved for a company in Dubai owned by the United Arab Emirates to operate American seaports, set off a popular protest. Even Republican members of Congress expressed outrage. Bush had no choice but to quash the arrangement—and he did so on March 10, 2006. An even worse disaster for the administration developed on August 29, 2005, when Hurricane Katrina slammed into the Gulf Coast and devastated the region. New Orleans was especially hard-hit because the storm breached the levees holding back the Mississippi River and water poured through the city, destroying homes and drowning thousands of people. The low-lying districts where poor blacks lived took the heaviest blow. For days stranded people stood on the roofs of their devastated homes and held up signs that read "Help." Thousands fled the city. Many of the poorest inhabitants who had no way of escaping were crowded into the Superdome, where the facilities could not keep up with demand. The administration failed to respond adequately: FEMA was especially criticized for its failure to appreciate how serious the problem had become and how inadequate its attempts to deal with the situation.

Other scandals surfaced. Jack Abramoff, a well-heeled lobbyist who had close ties to the Republican leadership, was indicted and pleaded guilty to conspiracy to corrupt public officials, mail fraud, and tax evasion. He named congressmen who had aided him in his schemes and accepted bribes, free golf trips to Scotland, and other gratuities. Tom DeLay, the House majority leader from Texas, was indicted for his involvement in the Texas gerrymandering scheme, which netted the Republicans additional seats in the U.S. House of Representatives. He was forced to give up his leadership position, and he subsequently resigned from the House. Representative Randy "Duke" Cunningham, a Republican from California, went to prison for accepting millions in bribes; and Mark Foley, a Republican representative from Florida, was forced to resign because of improper messages he sent to former male pages in the House. The Vice President's chief of staff, I. Lewis (Scooter) Libby, was indicted on charges of perjury and obstruction of justice in a case growing out of the unlawful disclosure of a CIA agent in order to penalize critics of the Iraq war. He was found guilty of four counts of felony in March 2007. Democrats charged Republicans with a "culture of corruption" that permeated Congress because of their twelve-year control.

In the midterm election on November 7, 2006, the Democrats scored a victory that no one anticipated. It had been expected that the House would go Democratic, but not the Senate. To everyone's surprise the Democrats did indeed capture the upper house, by a single vote. Unquestionably, the war in Iraq was the crucial issue that decided the outcome of this election. The American people wanted a quick resolution to the problem and the return of U.S. troops. The Iraq Study Group—a bipartisan panel cochaired by a Republican, James A. Baker, former secretary of state under George H. W. Bush; and a Democrat, Lee H. Hamilton, former member of the House of Representatives from Indiana, that the Bush administration initially opposed but then changed its mind and gave grudging support—recommended a complete change of direction by the government. It advised that the administration initiate a diplomatic offensive and cease making "an open-ended commitment to keep large numbers of American troops deployed in Iraq." But the President chose to pursue a different course and decided to increase the number of American soldiers in the combat zone. He called it a "surge" that would bring ultimate victory. No longer aiming to make Iraq a democracy, Bush now settled for an end of violence and the establishment of a government that could provide stability.

For the past six years there had been relatively no oversight by Congress on the intrusion of the executive into areas beyond what the Constitution allowed. Wiretapping of citizens without judicial authorization, signing legislation and directing exceptions to the law, and advancing presidential authority at the expense of Congress now came to a screeching halt when the Democrats assumed majority status of the legislature in January 2007. One of the first remarkable things they did was elect Nancy Pelosi of California as Speaker of the House of Representatives. She was the first woman to hold that office, having served previously as minority leader. She promised a long list of legislative action by the House: increase the minimum wage, support the recommendations of the Iraq Study Group, allow Medicare to negotiate for better drug prices, call a halt to sending more troops to Iraq, reduce interest rates on college loans, and other reforms in the first 100 hours (not days) of

Democratic control. Committee chairmanships were assumed and a series of investigations begun that uncovered activities in the White House that demonstrated how far and how aggressive had been the efforts of the administration to expand and protect presidential powers.

Most important of all, both the Senate and the House in March 2007 passed supplemental spending bills for the war that included a provision calling for the withdrawal of American troops from Iraq by 2008. Bush vetoed it, and the Democrats were unable to override it. He also threatened to veto any bill that came before him if it contained a benchmark giving a date for withdrawal. Democrats insisted that their action was in accordance with what the electorate had demanded just six months earlier. Critics now declared that the war was unwinnable and might lead to sectarian violence not only in the Middle East but throughout the Muslim world. By the end of 2007 the Democrats completely failed in their efforts to end the war. They lacked the necessary votes in the Senate to block filibusters, and the Republicans in the House stood united behind the President in preventing the override of his vetoes. By the beginning of 2008 the Democrats had little to show for their astounding victory in 2006 in ending the war.

In the meantime Iran continued to develop a nuclear program in defiance of UN resolutions demanding a halt to such activities. The likelihood of atomic weapons reaching radical terrorists became frighteningly possible. The United States, the only superpower in the world, had lost the respect of most nations and its ability to enforce peaceful solutions to international problems. Some Americans even wondered if their Great Republic was now in full decline, its place as the world leader to be taken by the rising powers of China or India. They were shocked at finding themselves disliked and criticized by the people of many countries around the world. And because of mounting foreclosures on homes resulting from subprime lending practices, the increase of unemployment, the weakness of the dollar overseas, an erratic stock market, and climbing gasoline and food prices, it appeared at the beginning of 2008 that the nation was headed toward a recession.

Still, America's large consumer society, technological superiority, and creative genius remained viable and gave hope that its people could find the leadership that would bring the country safely through this trying period of their history.

Reading List

CHAPTER I: Discovery and Settlement of the New World

Brian M. Fagan, *The Great Journey: The People of Ancient America* (1987).

William D. Phillips, *The Worlds of Christopher Columbus* (1992).

David Weber, *The Spanish Frontier in North America* (1992).

Samuel Eliot Morison, *The European Discovery of America* (1971, 1975).

William T. Hagen, *American Indians* (1961).

Bernard Bailyn, *The Peopling of British North America* (1986).

W. J. Eccles, *France in America* (1972).

John E. Pomfret and Floyd M. Shumway, *Founding the American Colonies, 1583–1660* (1970).

Edmund Morgan, *American Slavery, American Freedom: The Ordeal of Colonial Virginia* (1975).

Colin Calloway, *New Worlds for All: Indians, Europeans, and the Remaking of Early America* (1997).

Michael Kammen, *Empire and Interest: The American Colonies and the Politics of Mercantilism* (1970).

Winthrop Jordan, *White over Black* (1968).

Ira Berlin, *Many Thousands Gone: The First Two Centuries of Slavery in North America* (1999).

Laurel Thatcher Ulrich, *Good Wives: Image and Reality in the Lives of Women in Northern New England, 1650–1750* (1982).

Edmund Morgan, *The Puritan Dilemma: The Story of John Winthrop* (1958).

Jon Butler, *Awash in a Sea of Faith: Christianizing the American People* (1990).

CHAPTER 2: Independence and Nation Building

Gary B. Nash, *The Unknown American Revolution: The Unruly Birth of Democracy* (2005).

Edmund Morgan and Helen Morgan, *The Stamp Act Crisis* (1953).

Bernard Bailyn, *The Ideological Origins of the American Revolution* (1967).

David Hackett Fischer, *Paul Revere's Ride* (1994).

John Ferling, *Almost a Miracle: The American Victory in the War of Independence* (2007).

Gordon Wood, *The Creation of the American Republic* (1969).

Garry Wills, *Inventing America* (1978).

Jack Rakove, *Original Meanings: Politics and Ideas in the Making of the Constitution* (1996).

James Roger Sharp, *American Politics in the Early Republic* (1993).

Joseph Ellis, *Founding Brothers: The Revolutionary Generation* (2000).

Ralph Ketchum, *Presidents above Party: The First American Presidency, 1789–1829* (1984).

R. Kent Newmyer, *The Supreme Court under Marshall and Taney* (1968).

CHAPTER 3: An Emerging Identity

Rowland Berthoff, *An Unsettled People: Social Order and Disorder in American History* (1971).

George R. Taylor, *The Transportation Revolution* (1951).

Douglas C. North, *The Economic Growth of the United States* (1961).

Stuart Bruchey, *Enterprise: The Dynamic Economy of a Free People* (1990).

Russell B. Nye, *The Cultural Life of the New Nation* (1976).

Marcus Cunliffe, *The Nation Takes Shape, 1789–1837* (1959).

Ray Billington, *Westward Expansion* (1967).

Ron Chernow, *Alexander Hamilton* (2004).

George Dangerfield, *The Awakening of American Nationalism* (1965).

Robert V. Remini, *Andrew Jackson and the Course of American Empire, 1767–1821* (1977).

John R. Howe, *From the Revolution through the Age of Jackson* (1973).

CHAPTER 4: The Jacksonian Era

Alexis de Tocqueville, *Democracy in America* (1835).

Arthur M. Schlesinger Jr., *The Age of Jackson* (1945).

Richard Hofstadter, *The American Political Tradition and the Men Who Made It* (1948).

Sean Wilentz, *The Rise of American Democracy: Jefferson to Lincoln* (2005).

Harry L. Watson, *Liberty and Power: The Politics of Jacksonian America* (1990).

Merrill Peterson, *The Great Triumvirate: Webster, Clay, and Calhoun* (1987).

Ronald Walters, *American Reformers, 1815–1860* (1978).

William G. McLoughlin, *Revivals, Awakenings, and Reform* (1978).

Nathan Hatch, *The Democratization of American Christianity* (1987).

Merle Curti, *The Growth of American Thought* (1951).

Peter S. Field, *Ralph Waldo Emerson* (2003).

CHAPTER 5: The Dispute over Slavery, Secession, and the Civil War

Frederick Merk, *Manifest Destiny and Mission in American History* (1963).

Holman Hamilton, *Prologue to Conflict: The Crisis and Compromise of 1850* (1964).

David Potter, *The Impending Crisis, 1848–1861* (1976).

Alfred D. Chandler Jr., *Strategy and Structure: Chapters in the History of American Industrial Enterprise* (1962).

Nancy Cott, *The Bonds of Womanhood* (1977).

Robert Fogel and Stanley Engerman, *Time on the Cross: The Economics of American Negro Slavery* (1974).

Kenneth Stampp, *The Peculiar Institution* (1955).

Eugene Genovese, *Roll Jordan Roll: The World the Slaves Made* (1974).

Charles P. Roland, *The Story of the Civil War* (1991).
James M. McPherson, *The Battle Cry of Freedom* (1988).

CHAPTER 6: Reconstruction and the Gilded Age

Eric Foner, *Reconstruction: America's Unfinished Revolution, 1863–1877*
(1988).
C. Vann Woodward, *Reunion and Reaction* (1956).
Richard Hofstadter, *The Age of Reform* (1955).
Alan Trachtenberg, *The Incorporation of America: Culture and Society in
the Gilded Age* (1982).
Edward Kirkland, *Industry Comes of Age: Business, Labor, and Public
Policy, 1860–1897* (1961).
Morton Keller, *Affairs of State: Public Life in the Late Nineteenth Century*
(1977).
H. Wayne Morgan, *From Hayes to McKinley, 1877–1890* (1967).
Michael Kazin, *The Populist Persuasion* (1998).

CHAPTER 7: Manifest Destiny, Progressivism, War,
and the Roaring Twenties

Walter LaFeber, *The New Empire: An Interpretation of American Ex-
pansion, 1860–1898* (1998).
Alfred Chandler Jr., *The Visible Hand: The Managerial Revolution in
American Business* (1977).
Michael McGerr, *A Fierce Discontent: The Rise and Fall of the Progres-
sive Movement in America, 1870–1920* (2003).
Robert H. Wiebe, *The Search for Order, 1887–1920* (1967).
Oliver W. Larkin, *Art and Life in America* (1949).
George E. Mowry, *The Era of Theodore Roosevelt* (1958).
Arthur Link, *Woodrow Wilson and the Progressive Era* (1954).
David J. Goldberg, *Discontented America: The United States in the 1920s*
(1999).
William Leuchtenburg, *The Perils of Prosperity, 1914–1932* (1958).
Arthur M. Schlesinger Jr., *The Crisis of the Old Order* (1957).

CHAPTER 8: The Great Depression, the New Deal, and World War II

David Kennedy, *Freedom from Fear: The American People in Depression and War* (1999).

Robert S. McElvaine, *The Great Depression: America, 1929–1940* (1984).

Herbert Feis, *Churchill, Roosevelt, Stalin* (1957).

Henry Steele Commager, *The Story of World War II* (1945).

Chester Wilmot, *The Struggle for Europe* (1952).

Robert Jungk, *Brighter Than a Thousand Suns* (1958).

Martin Sherwin, *A World Destroyed: The Atom Bomb and the Grand Alliance* (1975).

CHAPTER 9: The Cold War and Civil Rights

John Lewis Gaddis, *The Cold War* (2005).

James Patterson, *Great Expectations: The United States, 1945–1974* (1996).

Walter LaFeber, *America, Russia, and the Cold War, 1945–1966* (1967).

Ellen Schrecker, *The Age of McCarthyism* (2002).

David McCullough, *Truman* (1992).

Arthur M. Schlesinger Jr., *A Thousand Days* (1965).

Robert Dallek, *Lyndon Johnson* (2005).

David Halberstam, *The Best and the Brightest* (1972).

CHAPTER 10: Violence, Scandal, and the End of the Cold War

Carl Bernstein and Bob Woodward, *All the President's Men* (1974).

Stanley Kutler, *The Wars of Watergate* (1990).

Jonathan Schell, *The Time of Illusion* (1976).

Arthur Link and William Catton, *American Epoch, 1938–1980* (1980).

Kevin Phillips, *The Emerging Republican Majority* (1969).

Bruce Schulman, *The Seventies: The Great Shift in American Culture, Society, and Politics* (2001).

John Karaagac, *Between Promise and Policy: Ronald Reagan and Conservative Reformism* (2000).

Haynes Johnson, *Sleepwalking through History: America in the Reagan Years* (1992).

CHAPTER 11: The Conservative Revolution

Lee Edwards, *The Conservative Revolution: The Movement That Remade America* (1999).

William Berman, *From the Center to the Edge: The Politics and Policies of the Clinton Administration* (2001).

Sam Roberts, *Who Are We Now: The Changing Face of America in the Twenty-First Century* (2004).

James Hunter, *Culture Wars: The Struggle to Define America* (1991).

Seymour Hersh, *Chain of Command: The Road from 9/11 to Abu Ghraib* (2004).

Michael Gordon and Bernard Trainor, *Cobra II: The Inside Story of the Invasion and Occupation of Iraq* (2006).

Index

Page numbers in *italics* refer to maps and illustrations.

abolitionists, 112, 115, 119–22, 128,
    134–35, 137, 140, 144, 151
abortion, 283, 314–15
Abramoff, Jack, 334–35
Abscam scandal, 290
Abu Ghraib, 330
Adams, Charles Francis, 128, 148,
    177
Adams, Henry, 166
Adams, John, 34–35, 37, 39–40, 45, 52,
    62–66, 70, 116, 198
Adams, John Quincy, 79–82, 81,
    84–86, 88–94, 121, 128, 190
Adams, Sam, 34, 35, 37
Adams-Onís Treaty (1819), 81, 82
Afghanistan, 291, 325–26
African-Americans, 133, 164–66, 177,
    181, 198, 206, 208–9, 213, 253, 257,
    262–63, 267–70, 272–74, 302, 305,
    307; male suffrage, 161–62; in Union
    Army, 148–49. *See also* civil rights;
    racial discrimination; segregation;
    slavery
Africans, 7–8, 22, 133
Agnew, Spiro, 279, 281–83

Agricultural Adjustment Act (AAA,
    1933), 222, 226, 229
Agricultural Market Act (1929), 214
agriculture, 20–22, 76–77, 116, 132–34,
    172, 183–84, 187, 206, 211, 213–14. *See
    also* farmers and farm relief
Aguinaldo, Emilio, 192
AIDS, 314
air pollution, 272
Alabama, 8, 72–73, 80, 82, 134, 141,
    162, 218, 251, 263, 267–68, 271–73;
    University of, desegregated,
    268–69
Alabama (Confederate ship), 147
Alaska National Wildlife Refuge,
    oil-drilling issue, 324
Alamogordo atomic test (1945), 240
Alaska, 84, 123, 189, 265
Albania, WW II and, 231
Albany, 9
Albany Plan of Union (1754), 28–30, 37
Albert, Carl, 276
Alcott, Bronson, 112
Aldrin, Col. Edwin E., Jr., 265
Algiers, 67

Algonquin tribes, 9, 11, 27

Alien and Alien Enemies Acts
(1798–1800), 64

Alien and Sedition Acts (1798),
63–64

Allies: WW I, 202–3; WW II, 233,
241, 243–44

Allison, William B., 172

Al Qaeda, 325–26, 328

Ambrister, Robert, 80

America, origin of name, 6

America First, 205

American, 196

American Antislavery Society, 120

American character, 75–78, 87

American colonies, 12, 10–36;
legislatures of, 22–23; map of,
in 1652, 21; royal, proprietary, or
corporate, 17–20, 22. *See also* specific
colonies and states

American Colonization Society, 134

American Federation of Labor (AFL),
183, 229–30

American flag, 40

American Independent Party, 279

American Revolution, 32–45

Americans with Disabilities Act
(1990), 305

American System, 79, 89–90

American Woman Suffrage
Association, 159

Ames, Oakes, 169–70

Anderson, Sherwood, 209

André, Maj. John, 44–45

Andros, Sir Edmund, 23

Anglican Church, 13, 16, 19

Annapolis Convention (1786), 47

Anthony, Susan B., 115, 159

anti-communism, 230–31, 245–46,
253–55

Antietam, Battle of, 147

anti-immigration movement, 137,
317–18

anti-imperialism, 189, 191, 193

antitrust, 182, 193–94, 197

antiwar demonstrations, 276, 278–79

Anzio, Battle of, 241

Appomattox, surrender at, 152–53

Arbuthnot, Alexander, 80

Argentina, 84

Arizona, 126, 189, 317

Arkansas, 8, 134, 143, 155, 162, 267

Armada, 9–10

Armenia, 303

Armstrong, Neil A., 265

Army Appropriations Act (1867), 161

Arnold, Benedict, 44–45

art and architecture, 118, 209

Arthur, Chester A., 176–77

Arthur Andersen Company, 324

Articles of Confederation, 40–41,
45–49, 51

Asian-Americans, 307, 318

Askariya Mosque bombing, 333

Astor, John Jacob, 187

Atahuallpa, emperor of Incas, 7

Atlanta, 150–51

Atlantic Charter, 235

atomic bomb, 240, 244, 246–47, 254,
256

Atomic Energy Act (1946), 247

Audubon, John James, 118

Auschwitz, 241

Austria, 84, 231

Austrian-Hungarian empire, 203

automobiles, 206, 229; emission
standards, 272

aviation, 207

Axis powers, 235–36, 240

Azerbaijan, 303

Aztecs, 2, 6–7

Babcock, Gen. Orville E., 170

Baker, James A., 335

Balboa, Vasco de, 8

Baldwin, Joseph, 118

Ball's Bluff, Battle of, 144

Baltimore, Lord, 16

Baltimore and Ohio Railroad, 132

Bank Bill, 106

Bankhead, William, 227

Banking Act: (1933), 222; (1935), 225

Bank of the United States: First, 57–59, 75, 79; Second, 79, 99–100, 105–10, 122

banks and banking, 76, 110–11, 167, 171, 178, 184, 198–99, 215–17, 220–21, 223, 225, 301

Barbary states, 67–68

Baring Brothers, 184

Barkley, Alben, 251, 257

Barksdale, William, 139

Barnett, Ross, 268

Baruch, Bernard, 202

Bay of Pigs invasion, 266

Beatles, 261

Beauregard, Pierre G. T., 142, 144

beef industry, 182, 196

Begin, Menachem, 290–91

Belgium, 202–3, 232, 247

Belgium Relief Commission, 202

Belknap, William, 170

Bell, John, 141

Belmont, August, 185

Bennett, Robert E., 318

Bentsen, Lloyd, 302

Berger, Victor, 211

Berkeley, Lord John, 19

Berle, Adolph A., 219

Berlin, 244, 260; airlift, 246, 250; Wall, 267, 298, 303

Berlin, Irving, 208

Berlin and Milan decrees, 70–71

Bessarabia, 231

Biddle, Nicholas, 105, 107–9

big business and corporations, 166–73, 176–78, 183, 186–88, 194–96, 198–99, 202, 217, 302, 324. *See also* monopolies and trusts

Bill of Rights (1789–91), 51–54, 307–8

bills of attainder, 50

Bingham, John A., 163, 169

Bin Laden, Osama, 325, 326

Birds of America (Audubon), 118

Birmingham demonstrations, 268

Birney, James G., 112

Birth of a Nation, The (movie), 207

bituminous coal case, 226

Black, James, 169

Black Codes, 157–58

blacklist, 246

Blaine, James G., 164, 167, 171, 173, 177, 179, 263

Blair, Francis P., 164

Bland, Richard P. "Silver Dick," 172

Bland-Allison Act, 181

Bloody Sunday (Selma, 1965), 273

Boland Amendment (1984), 298, 300

Bolivar, Simon, 93

Boll Weevil Democrats, 294

Bonus March, 216–17

boom: post–Civil War, 187–88; post–WW I, 206–7, 209, 213; post–WW II, 247–48; of 1990s, 312

Booth, John Wilkes, 153

bootlegging, 207–208

Borah, William E., 211

Bork, Robert H., 284, 301

Bosnia, 304, 312

Boston, 14, 24, 35–36, 131; Massacre, 35; Tea Party, 36

Boston Whig, 128

Boutwell, George, 163, 167

Bowdoin, James, 46

boycotts, 248

Bradley, Joseph P., 174

Bradley, Gen. Omar N., 256

Brady, James S., 295, 308

Brady Bill, 308

Brandywine Creek, Battle of, 43

Braun, Carol Moseley, 307

Brazil, 84

Breckinridge, John, 69, 141

Bremer, Paul, 330, 333

Bricker, John W., 243

Brisbane, Albert, 113

Brook Farm, 113

Brooks, Preston S. "Bully," 138, 157

Brown, B. Gratz, 169

Brown, John, 140

Brownson, Orestes, 112

Brown v. Board of Education of Topeka, 261, 262–63

Bryan, William Jennings, 185–86, 193, 197, 296
Buchanan, James, 138–39, 179
Budget Bureau, 211
Budget Reconciliation Act (1981), 294
Buena Vista, Battle of, 124
building and loan associations, 217
Bulgaria, 233
Bull Moose Party, 197–98, 306
Bull Run, Battle of: First, 144; Second, 147
Bunker Hill, Battle of, 38
Bunyan, John, 196
Burchard, Samuel D., 179
Bureau of Corporations, 194
Bureau of Internal Revenue, 146
Burger, Warren E., 285
Burgoyne, Gen. John, 38, 43–44
Burma, 241
Burnside, Gen. Ambrose, 148
Burr, Aaron, 65–66
Bush, George Herbert Walker (elder), 292, 299, 302–7, 321, 328, 335
Bush, George W. (younger), 321–29, 332–36
Bush, Laura, 323
Butler, Andrew Pickens, 137–38
Butler, Ben "Beast," 163
Butler, Dr. Elizur, 102
Butler, William O., 128
Butterfield, Alexander, 284

Cabot, John, 9
Cabrillo, Juan, 8
Calhoun, John C., 78, 80, 88, 91, 93, 102–4, 130, 296
California, 8, 123–26, 128–30, 238, 317, 332; University of, at Berkeley, demonstrations, 276
Calley, Lt. William, 280
Calvert, Cecil, second Lord Baltimore, 16–17
Calvert, George, first Lord Baltimore, 16
Cambodia, 279–81
Camden, Battle of, 44

Campaign Finance Act (1974), 287
Camp David Accords, 291
Canada, 8, 27–28, 36, 45, 55, 72, 73, 123, 247, 259, 313
Canning, George, 85
Cannon, Joseph, 197
Capitol: construction of, 65; burned 73
Carnegie, Andrew, 188
Carnegie steel company, 183
Carolina colony, 5, 17–19
Caroline, queen of England, 17
carpetbaggers, 162, 175
Carter, Billy, 290
Carter, Jimmy, 195, 288–93
Carteret, Sir George, 19
Cartier, Jacques, 8
Casablanca Conference, 242–43
Casey, William J., 298–99
Cass, Lewis, 128
Cassiday, George L., 208
Castlereagh, Lord, 72
Castro, Fidel, 260, 265–66
Catawba tribe, 18
Cayuga tribe, 9
Celler, Emanuel, 268
Central American States, Federation of, 84
Central Intelligence Agency (CIA), 287, 298, 334–35
Chamberlain, Neville, 231–33
Chambers, B. J., 176
Chambers, Whittaker, 246
Champlain, Samuel de, 8
Chancellorsville, Battle of, 149
Chandler, Alfred D., Jr., 187
Chandler, Zachariah, 144
Charles I, king of England, 14, 17
Charles II, king of England, 17–20, 23
Charleston, 17, 44; slave revolt, 119
Charles V, king of Spain, 7
Chase, Salmon P., 152, 163
Chase, Samuel, 70
Château-Thierry, Battle of, 202
Chattanooga, Battle of, 150
Cheney, Richard, 295, 321–24, 326, 328, 333

Cherokee Nation, 18, 100–102, 101
Cherokee Nation v. Georgia, 102
Cheves, Langdon, 83–84
Chiang Kai-shek, 236, 254, 256
Chicago, 76, 132, 183, 196, 314; riot of
  1968, 278–79
Chickasaw tribe, 100, 101
child-labor laws, 193, 195, 199, 211,
  229
Chile, 84
China: People's Republic of, 253–56,
  260, 276, 281, 290, 303, 336; WW II
  and, 235–36, 244
Chinese Nationalist Party, 254
Chisholm v. Georgia, 60
Choctaw tribe, 100, 101
Choiseul, Étienne-François de, 28
Churchill, Winston, 233–35, 242–44,
  246
Cigar Makers' International Union,
  229
citizenship rights, 158–59, 210–11, 238
civil disobedience, 262
"Civil Disobedience" (Thoreau), 117
Civilian Conservation Corps (CCC),
  222
civil liberties, 327
civil rights, 251–53, 257, 261–65,
  267–69, 272–74, 276, 302
Civil Rights, Commission on, 262
Civil Rights Act: (1866), 158–59;
  (1875), 166; (1957), 262; (1960), 263;
  (1964), 268–71
Civil Rights Committee, 250–51
Civil Rights Division, 262
civil service, 175, 179, 253–54
Civil Service Commission, 177
Civil Service Reform Act (1883), 177
Civil War, 84, 119, 126, 131, 135, 142–53,
  164, 184, 243
Clark, Beauchamp "Champ," 198, 200
Clark, William, 69
Clay, Henry, 71–72, 78–84, 88–90, 94,
  104–8, 110, 123, 126, 129–30, 296
Clayton Antitrust Act (1914), 199
Clean Air Act (1963), 269, 324

Clemenceau, Georges, 203
Cleveland, Grover, 179–81, 184–85, 263
Clinton, George, 60
Clinton, Gen. Henry, 38, 42, 44–45, 49
Clinton, Hillary Rodham, 308
Clinton, William Jefferson "Bill," 304,
  306–8, 310–13; impeachment of,
  318–21
Coal Conservation Act, 226
coal industry, 132, 199
Coalition Provisional Authority, 330,
  333
Cobb, Thomas W., 82
Coinage Act (1873), 171
Cold Harbor, Battle of, 150
Cold War, 246–47, 249–51, 255–56,
  260, 265–67, 274–76, 291, 301, 325;
  end of, 303
Colfax, Schuyler, 164, 167, 170
Collins, Col. Michael, 265
Colombia, 84, 194–95
Colorado, 126
Colt, Samuel, 118
Columbia, South Carolina, capture
  of, 152
Columbus, Christopher, 5
Committee for European Economic
  Cooperation, 250
Committee for Industrial
  Organization (CIO), 229–30
committees of correspondence, 34
Common Sense (Paine), 38–39
Commonwealth v. Hunt, 87
communism, 202, 204, 209, 216,
  230–31, 245, 249–51, 253–56, 260,
  280. *See also* anti-communism; Cold
  War; Red Scare
Communist Party (U.S.), 219–20, 245,
  254
communitarianism, 113–14
Community Relations Service, 270
Compromise of 1790, 56
Compromise of 1850, 130–31, 135–36
Compromise Tariff of 1833, 104
computers, 315–16
Concord, Battle of, 37, 41

Confederate Army, 143–44, 147–50, 152–53

Confederate States of America, 142–44, 147–56, 161–62

Congaree tribe, 18

Congress of Verona (1822), 84

Conkling, Roscoe, 175–76

Connecticut, 16, 23, 27–28, 36, 46

Connecticut Compromise, 50

Connor, T. Eugene "Bull," 268

Conscription Act (1863), 149

conservation, 193–94, 197, 288, 315

conservative(s), 225–27, 279, 293–94; revolution, 309–12, 314, 322–24

Constitutional Convention, 47–51, 53, 57

Constitutional Union Party, 141

Continental Association, 37

Continental Congress: First (1774), 37; Second (1775–83), 38–40, 42, 44–45; under Articles of Confederation (1783–87), 45–48, 51–52

Contract with America, 309–10

Cooke, Jay, 167, 171

Coolidge, Calvin, 205, 210–12, 216

Cooper, Anthony Ashley, earl of Shaftesbury, 17

Cooper, James Fenimore, 76

Copperheads, 148, 151

Cornell, Alonzo B., 176

Cornwallis, Lord, 42, 44–45

Coronado, Francisco de, 8

Corporate Bankruptcy Act (1934), 224

corruption, 97, 99, 166–72, 174–75, 178–80, 196, 209–10, 290, 297, 301, 309, 324, 334

Cortés, Hernán, 6–7

Cosmopolitan, 196

cotton, 22, 24, 50, 76, 79, 92, 132–34, 214

Cotton, John, 15–16

cotton gin, 77, 133–34

Coughlin, Father Charles E., 224

Council of Foreign Plantations, 23

Council of the Indies, 7

Council of Trade, 23

counterculture (hippies), 261

Covode, John, 144, 162

Cox, Archibald, 284

Cox, James M., 205

Coxey, Jacob S., 185

Crawford, William H., 88–89

credit, 76, 78–79, 199, 289

Credit Mobilier scandal, 167–70

Creek tribe, 100, 101

Creek War of 1812, 72–73, 100

crime and violence, 308–9

Crisis, The (Paine), 42

Crocker, Ryan, 333

Cromwell, Oliver, 17

Crusades (1095), 4

C-Span, 296–97

Cuba, 6, 190–92, 260; Bay of Pigs and missile crisis, 265–67

Cuban refugees, 317

cummings, e. e., 209

Cunningham, Randy "Duke," 334

currency, 38, 46, 76, 78, 79, 99, 110, 198; greenbacks, 145, 171–72; hard vs. soft money, 178–79; paper, 50, 105, 110. *See also* gold; silver

Currency or Gold Standard Act (1900), 193

Curtis, Charles, 213, 219

Czechoslovakia, 231–32, 250, 303, 312

Czolgosz, Leon, 193

Daladier, Edouard, 231

Dale, Thomas, 11

Dana, Charles A., 167

Dartmouth College case, 75

Daughters of Liberty, 33

Davis, David, 173–74

Davis, Jefferson, 142–43

Davis, John, 212

Dawes, Henry L., 167

Dean, Dr. Howard, 331

Dean, John, 283–84

Debs, Eugene V., 193, 195

debtors' prison, 86–87, 105

Declaration of Continental Congress (1774), 37

Declaration of Independence
(1776), 40, 46; bicentennial, 288;
centennial, 173
"Declaration of Rights and
Grievances" (1765), 32
Declaratory Act (British, 1766), 33
Defense Department, 280, 327
De Large, Robert C., 164
Delaware, 20, 42, 47, 51, 143
Delaware tribe, 100
DeLay, Tom, 320, 323, 334
democracy: expansion of, 86–87, 94,
96–97, 99, 116, 166, 196–97; global
mission and, 189–90, 192. *See also*
voting rights
Democracy in America (Tocqueville),
90–91, 97–98
Democratic National Committee,
Watergate burglary, 281–82
Democratic Party: Bush II
administration and, 323, 328,
335; Carter administration and,
289; changes in, with Kansas-
Nebraska Act, 136–37; Chicago
Convention of 1968 and, 278–79;
Clinton administration and, 310;
Clinton impeachment and, 319;
development of, under Jackson, 91,
93; early-20th-century reforms and,
197; Eisenhower administration
and, 259; elections of 1864, 151;
elections of 1866, 160; elections of
1870, 164; elections of 1872, 169;
elections of 1876, 173, 174; elections
of 1880, 176; elections of 1884 and
first presidency since Civil War,
179–80; elections of 1890, 183;
elections of 1892 and control of
Congress and presidency, 184–85;
elections of 1896, 185–86; elections
of 1900, 193; elections of 1912, 198;
elections of 1916, 200; elections of
1918, 203; elections of 1920, 205;
elections of 1924, 212; elections of
1928, 213; elections of 1932, 218–20;
elections of 1934, 224; elections of
1936, 226–27; elections of 1940, 234;
elections of 1948, 250–53; elections
of 1952, 257; elections of 1954, 258;
elections of 1956, 261–62; elections
of 1960, 263–65; elections of 1964,
270–71; elections of 1968, 277–79;
elections of 1972, 281–82; elections
of 1976, 288; elections of 1980,
292–93; elections of 1988, 301–2;
elections of 1992, 306–7; elections
of 1994, 309–310; elections of 2000,
321–22; elections of 2004, 331–32;
elections of 2006, 335–36; Hoover
administration and, 217; labor and,
249; Peace or Copperheads, 148;
Reagan administration and, 293–95,
299; slavery and, 121; split in, and
Civil Rights Act of 1964, 271; split
in, and coalition of southern, with
Republicans, under FDR, 227; split
in, and elections of 1848, 128; split
in, and elections of 1860, 140–41;
tariff reform and, 179, 181; Truman
and division in, 250–52; Tyler
administration and, 122; Versailles
Treaty and League of Nations and,
204; WW II and, 233, 234. *See also*
Dixiecrats; southern Democrats
Democratic-Republican Party
(Jacksonian, *later* Democratic
Party), 91, 93
Democratic-Republican Party
(Jeffersonian Republican Party),
59–60, 63–65, 74, 87
Democratic Review, The, 122, 189–90
Denmark, 232, 247
Depression, 211, 214–30
desegregation, 261, 263, 268–70
Desert Storm, Operation, 304
Detroit, 72, 76
Dewey, Comm. George, 191
Dewey, John, 219
Dewey, Thomas, 243, 252–53, 257
Dickinson, John, 32, 34, 40
Dies, Martin, Jr., 230
Dinwiddie, Robert, 28

Dix, Dorothea, 115
Dixiecrats, 251
Dixie-Republican alliance, 292–94
Dodge, Grenville, 167
Doenitz, Adm. Karl, 244
Dole, Robert, 288, 311, 312
Dominion of New England, 23
Donnelly, Ignatius, 178, 183
Dos Passos, John, 209
Douglas, Stephen A., 130, 136–37, 140
Dow, Neal, 115, 176
draft, 201, 233, 234; riots, 149; Vietnam
    War and, 276
Drake, Francis, 9–12
Dred Scott decision, 139, 140
Dreiser, Theodore, 209
Dubinsky, David, 229
DuBois, W. E. B., 198, 209
dueling, 90–91
due process, 139, 159
Dukakis, Michael, 302
Dunkirk evacuation, 233
Duquesne, Fort, 28
Dutch colonies, 9, 18, 20, 22
Dutch East Indies, 241
Dutch West India Company, 9, 18

Eastern Europe, 246, 303
East India Tea Company, 35
Eaton, John H., 100
Eaton, Peggy O'Neale, 100
Eclectic Reader (McGuffey), 116
Economic Cooperation
    Administration, 250
Economic Growth and Tax Relief Act
    (2001), 324
Economic Opportunity Act (1965), 272
Economic Recovery Act (1981), 294
Edison, Thomas, 172, 207
education, 47, 87, 116, 253, 258, 271, 296,
    324; desegregation and, 261, 263;
    student loans and, 294, 335
Education Act (1965), 271
Edwards, John, 331
Edwards, Jonathan, 25–26
Egypt, 241, 290

Ehrlichman, John R., 283
Eighteenth Amendment (1919), 207,
    212; repeal of, 218–19, 221
Eisenhower, Dwight D., 241, 243–44,
    252, 257–63, 265–66
Eisenhower Doctrine, 260
El Alamein, Battle of, 241
election, direct: nominating
    conventions and, 197; primary,
    196–97; senators, 184, 197–98
elections: (1789), 52–53; (1796), 62;
    (1800), 65–66; (1804), 70; (1824),
    87–90, 99; (1828), 91, 94; (1832),
    105–6, 107; (1836), 111, 302; (1840),
    111–12, 122; (1844), 123; (1848),
    128; (1854), 137; (1856), 138; (1860),
    140–41; (1864), 151; (1866), 159–60;
    (1870), 163–64; (1872), 167, 169;
    (1876), disputed, 173–75; (1880),
    176–77; (1884), 179–80; (1888), 180;
    (1890), 183; (1892), 183–85; (1896),
    185–86; (1900), 193; (1904), 195;
    (1908), 197; (1912), 197–98; (1916),
    200; (1918), 203; (1920), 204–5;
    (1924), 211–12; (1928), 213–14; (1932),
    218–20; (1934), 224; (1936), 226–27;
    (1940), 233, 234; (1944), 243; (1946),
    245, 248; (1948), 250–53; (1952),
    257–58; (1956), 261–62; (1960),
    263–65; (1964), 270–71; (1968),
    277–79; (1972), 281–82; (1974), 288;
    (1976), 287–88; (1978), 289; (1980),
    292–93; (1988), 301–2; (1992),
    306–7; (1994), 309–10; (1996),
    312; (1998), 319; (2000), disputed,
    321–22; (2002), 323; (2004), 331–32;
    (2006), 335–36
Electoral College, 50, 65, 98–99
Electoral Commission (1877), 173–74
electricity, 172, 187, 206–7, 212, 225,
    324; rural, 218, 222
Eleventh Amendment (1798), 60
Eliot, T. S., 209
Elizabeth I, queen of England, 9–10
Elkins Act (1903), 194
Elliott, Robert B., 164

Ellsberg, Daniel, 280
emancipation, 145
Embargo Act (1807), 70–71
Emergency Banking Relief Act (1933), 221
Emergency Railroad Transportation Act (1933), 222
Emergency Relief and Construction Act (1932), 217
Emergency Relief Appropriation Act (1935), 224–25
Emerson, Ralph Waldo, 112, 113
employment, 222–24. *See also* unemployment
energy crisis, 288–89
Enforcement Acts (1870–71), 165
English, William H., 176
Enron, 324
Environmental Protection Agency (EPA), 301, 324
Equal Employment Opportunity Commission, 270
Equal Rights Amendment (ERA), 315
Erie Canal, 76
Erie Railroad, 132
Eriksson, Leif, 2–3
Ervin, Sam J., Jr., 284
Espionage Act (1917), 201
Estaing, Count Charles d', 43–44
Estonia, 231, 303
European Recovery Program (ERP, 1948), 250
Evangelical Protestantism, 115, 133, 313, 332
Everett, Edward, 141, 149
Evers, Medgar, 269
ex-Confederates: amnesty and, 155–57; in Congress, 165–66
executive branch. *See* president
Ex parte Milligan, 164
Expedition Act (1903), 194
"Exposition and Protest" (Calhoun), 93

Fair Deal, 253, 257, 258
faith-based initiative, 323
Fall, Albert B., 210

Falwell, Rev. Jerry, 314
Farm Credit Act (1933), 222
farmers' alliances, 178–80, 183–84
farmers and farm relief, 177–78, 183–84, 199, 211, 213–14, 217, 222–24, 253. *See also* agriculture
Farm Loan banks, 199
Farragut, Adm. David G., 147, 160
fascism, 216, 230–31, 238
Faubus, Orval E., 262
federal budget: deficits, 294–96, 301, 305, 312, 325; defense spending, 230, 233, 239–40, 260, 295–96; Depression and, 217–19; domestic spending cuts, 295–96, 310; government shutdown and, 310–12; surpluses, 325
Federal Bureau of Investigation (FBI), 254, 286, 290
Federal Communications Commission (FCC), 212
federal courts, 50, 53–54, 69
Federal Deposit Insurance Corporation (FDIC), 223
Federal Election (Force) Bill (1890), 181
Federal Emergency Management Agency (FEMA), 327, 334
Federal Emergency Relief Act (FERA, 1933), 222
Federal Farm Board, 214
Federal Farm Loan Act (1916), 199
Federal Farm Mortgage Foreclosure Act (1934), 224
federal government: checks and balances, 48–49, 102; powers, vs. state, 59–60, 64; relief programs, 215, 217–18, 221; structure of, 48–51. *See also* federal budget; *and specific branches*
Federal Home Loan Bank Act (1932), 217
Federalist Party, 59, 63, 65–66, 69, 74, 78, 108
Federal Reserve Act (1913), 199, 225
Federal Reserve Bank, 217, 225

Federal Reserve Board, 199, 289
Federal Reserve System, 110, 215
Federal Securities Act (1933), 222
Federal Trade Commission Act (1914),
  199
Ferdinand and Isabella, of Spain, 5
Ferdinand VII, king of Spain, 84
Fessenden, William P., 157–58
Field, James G., 184
Fifteenth Amendment (1870), 164–66,
  177
Fifth Amendment, 139
Fillmore, Millard, 128, 130, 138
Finland, 232
Finney, Charles Grandison, 115
First Immigration Quota Act (1921),
  210
Fitzgerald, F. Scott, 209
Five Civilized Nations, 100–102, 101
Fletcher v. Peck (1810), 75
Florida, 8, 28, 44, 79–82, 81, 84, 89,
  141, 162, 178, 189; election of 2000
  and, 322
*Flush Times of Alabama and Mississippi,
  The* (Baldwin), 118
Foley, Mark, 334
Foley, Thomas, 309
Food, Drug, and Cosmetic Act (1938),
  229
Food Administration program, 202
food and drug regulation, 193
Food Stamp Act (1965), 272
food stamps, 296
food tariffs, 199
Force Bill (1833), 104
Ford, Gerald R., 283, 286–88, 292
Ford, Henry, 206
Ford, James W., 219
Foreign Service, 254
Forrest, Nathan Bedford, 165
Foster, William Z., 219–20
Four Freedoms, 235
Fourier, Charles, 113
Fourteen Points, 202–3
Fourteenth Amendment (1868),
  159–62, 166, 261, 283

Frame of Government, 20
France, 8–9, 26–28, 43–45, 56, 59–60,
  63, 65, 68–71, 84–85, 147–48, 202–4,
  246, 247, 249, 329; Revolution,
  59–60; WW II and, 231–33, 236, 243
Franklin, Benjamin, 28–30, 32, 39–40,
  43, 45, 116
Fredericksburg, Battle of, 148
Frederick the Great, king of Prussia,
  28
freedmen, 157–58, 160
Freedmen's Bureau, 157–58, 170
freedom riders, 263, 267
Free Soil Party, 128, 136
Frelinghuysen, Theodorus, 25
Frémont, John C., 125, 138
French-Huron alliance, 9
Fromme, Lynette, 287
Frost, Robert, 209
Fugitive Slave Act (1850), 135–36
fugitive slaves, 120–21, 130
Fuller, Margaret, 112
Fulton, Robert, 75
Fundamental Constitutions of
  Carolina (1663), 17
"Fundamental Orders of Connecticut,
  The," 16
fur trade, 8, 9, 21, 24, 28, 77, 187

Gadsden Purchase, 189
Gagarin, Yury, 265
Gage, Gen. Thomas, 37, 38
Galloway, Joseph, 37
Gama, Vasco da, 5
Gandhi, Mahatma, 117
Garfield, James A., 160–61, 167, 175–77
Garner, John Nance, 218
Garrison, William Lloyd, 134–35
Gates, Bill, 316
Gates, Gen. Horatio, 43, 44
Gaza Strip, 312, 331
Genet, Edmond-Charles-Édouard, 60
Geneva Conventions, 330
George III, king of England, 37, 38, 43
Georgia, 8, 51, 73, 80, 100–102, 134,
  141, 162, 271, 273; founding of, 20

Georgia Scenes (Longstreet), 118

German Afrika Corps, 241

German-Americans, 22, 131–32, 136

Germantown, Battle of (1778), 43

Germany, 131, 199–205, 329; East, 246, 267, 303; Nazi and WW II, 220, 230–38, 240–44; West, 249–50, 303

Gerry, Elbridge, 48, 51

Gershwin, George, 208

Gettysburg, Battle of, 149

Ghent, Treaty of (1815), 74, 78, 89

Gibbons v. Ogden, 75

G.I. Bill of Rights (1944), 243, 247–48

Gilded Age, 166–72, 175, 177–78

Gilded Age, The (Twain and Warner), 166

Gingrich, Newt, 297, 309–11, 319–20

Glass-Steagall Act (1932), 217

Glenn, John, 265

Glorious Revolution (1688), 23

Godkin, E. L., 177

gold: mining, 128–29, 189; New Deal and, 221; reserves, 184–85, 217; rush, 128–29; standard, 171–72, 185–86, 193, 215, 221–22

Gold Standard Repeal Act (1933), 222

Goldwater, Barry, 271

Gompers, Samuel, 229

Gooch, Daniel W., 144

Goodyear, Charles, 118

Gorbachev, Mikhail, 300–301, 303

Gore, Albert, Jr., 302, 306, 321–22

Gorgas, Col. William C., 195

Gorges, Sir Ferdinando, 16

Graham, Rev. Billy, 323

Grain embargo (1979), 291

Grangers, 177–78, 183

Grant, Ulysses S., 149–50, 152–53, 160–67, 169–70, 173, 176

Grasse, Adm. François de, 45

Great Awakening: First, 25–26; Second, 115–16, 134

Great Britain: American colonies and, 23–30, 29; American Revolution and, 32–34, 35–39, 41–45; Canada and French and

Indian Wars and, 27–28; Civil War and, 144, 147–48; exploration and settlement of North America by, 9–23; Glorious Revolution, 23; impressment and, 60–61, 70–72; Iraq War and, 329; Jay Treaty and, 61; New Netherlands taken by, 18–19; Orders-in-Council, 60, 70, 72; Oregon Territory and, 123; Parliament, 22–24, 26–27, 30, 32–36, 43, 298; post–WW II, 246–47, 249; Privy Council, 22; Quadruple Alliance and Monroe Doctrine, 84–85; Spanish Armada defeated by, 9–10; war of 1763 and, 31–32; war of 1793 vs. France, 59–61; War of 1812 and, 72–74; WW I and, 203; WW II and, 231–36, 240–41, 243–44

Great Society, 271, 276

Greece, 233, 240, 247, 249

Greek and Turkish Aid Act (1947), 249

Greeley, Horace, 169

Greenback Party, 176–77, 183

Greene, Nathaniel, 97

Green Party, 321

Greensboro sit-in, 263

Grenada, 304

Grenville, George, 32

Griffiths, Martha, 315

Grimes, James W., 160, 163

Groves, Gen. Leslie R., 240

Grow, Galusha A., 309

Guadalcanal, Battle of, 242

Guadalupe Hidalgo, Treaty of, 125–26, 128

Guam, 192, 236, 241–42

Guantanamo, 327

Guiteau, Charles J., 177

Gulf of Tonkin Resolution (1964), 274; repeal of (1971), 280

Gulf War (1991), 304, 306, 326

gun control, 278, 308

habeas corpus, 108, 143, 148, 165

Habeas Corpus Act (1863), 148

Haiti, 68

Haldeman, H. R., 283, 285–86
Half Breed faction, 176
Hall, Dominick, 108
Halleck, Gen. Henry W., 146
Halliburton, 324
Halsey, Admiral, 242
Hamas, 331
Hamilton, Alexander, 47–48, 54–60,
    65–66, 106, 116
Hamilton, Lee H., 335
Hamlin, Hannibal, 141
Hancock, John, 40
Hancock, Winfield Scott, 176
Hanna, Marcus A., 185–86, 193
Harding, Warren G., 205, 209–10
Harlem Renaissance, 209
Harpers Ferry raid, 140–41
Harriman, Job, 193
Harrison, Benjamin, 180–82, 184
Harrison, William Henry
    "Tippecanoe," 98, 111–12, 116, 122, 180
Hart, Gary, 302
Hartford, 16; Convention (1814–1815),
    74
Hastert, J. Dennis, 320
Hawaii, 189, 191, 236, 265
Hawkins, John, 9
Hawthorne, Nathaniel, 112, 117
Hay-Bunau-Varilla Treaty (1903), 195,
    290
Hayes, Rutherford B., 173–76
Haymarket Massacre (1886), 183
Hayne, Robert Y., 103
health insurance, 253, 296, 308–9
Hearst, William Randolph, 190
Helper, Hinton R., 139–40
Hemingway, Ernest, 209
hemp, 91–92, 132, 134, 199
Hendricks, Thomas A., 173, 179
Henry VII, king of England, 9
Henry the Navigator, prince of
    Portugal, 5
Henry, Patrick, 33, 37
Hepburn Act (1906), 194
Hersh, Seymour, 280
Hicks, John D., 205

Higher Education Act (1965), 271
Highway Act (1956), 259
Hill, Anita, 305
Hill, Isaac, 97
Hillman, Sidney, 229
Hinckley, John W., Jr., 295
Hiroshima and Nagasaki bombing,
    244
Hispanic-Americans (Latinos), 307,
    317–18
Hispaniola, 5
Hiss, Alger, 246, 254, 257
History of New York (Irving), 75
Hitler, Adolf, 220, 230–32, 235, 244–45
Holding Company Act (1935), 225
Hollywood Ten, 245–46
Homeland Security Department, 327
home mortgages, 217
Home Owners Loan Corporation
    (HOLC), 223
Home Owners Refinancing Act
    (1933), 222
Homestead Act (1862), 146, 194
Homestead strike, 183
Hong Kong, 236, 241
Hooker, Gen. Joseph, 148
Hooker, Thomas, 15–16
Hoover, Herbert, 202, 213, 215–20
Hopkins, Harry, 224
Horseshoe Bend, Battle of, 73
House of Seven Gables, The
    (Hawthorne), 117
housing, 228, 253, 258, 272, 296
Housing and Urban Development Act
    (1965), 272
Housing and Urban Development
    Department, 272, 301
Howe, Elias, 119
Howe, Gen. Sir William, 38, 42–44
Hudson, Henry, 9
Hughes, Charles Evans, 200
Hughes, Langston, 209
Hull, Cordell, 236, 237
Hull, Gen. William, 72
Humphrey, Hubert H., 279, 288
Hundred Days, 221–23

Hungary, 240, 260, 303, 312
Huron tribe, 8–9
Hussein, Saddam, 303–4, 306, 326–30
Hutchinson, Anne, 15–16
Hutchinson, Thomas, 34–37
Hyde, Henry, 319, 320, 321
hydroelectrical projects, 218, 253
hydrogen bomb, 247

Iceland, 247
Ickes, Harold, 231
Illinois, 82, 178
immigration, 76, 86–87, 131–32, 136–37,
    172, 179, 210–11
Immigration Act (1924), 210
Immigration Act (1965), 272
Immigration Agency, 327
Immigration Reform and Control Act
    (1986), 317
impeachment, 61; Andrew Johnson
    and, 163; Clinton and, 319–21;
    Nixon and, 285–86
Impending Crisis of the South, The
    (Helper), 139–40
impressment, 60–61, 70–71
Inca tribe, 2, 7
indentured servants, 22
Independence Party, 197, 200
Independent Treasury Plan, 111
India, 4–5, 8, 336
Indiana, 82
Indian Citizenship Act (1924), 210–11
Indian Removal Act (1830), 100–102,
    101
Indians (Native Americans), 1–2, 3,
    5, 8–12, 14–15, 18, 20, 26–28, 31–32,
    61, 72, 99–102, 118, 136, 158, 238;
    in Congress, 307. *See also* specific
    tribes
Indian Wars, 111
indigo, 18, 22, 24
Indochina, 236, 260
industrialization and manufacturing,
    76–79, 91–93, 116, 131–32, 167,
    172–73, 180, 182, 206, 240
inflation, 276, 289, 294

influenza epidemic, 208
INF Treaty (1987), 300–301
initiative, referendum and recall
    reforms, 184, 196–97
Insurgent Republicans, 197–98, 211
interest rates, 225, 289, 294
Interior Department, 170, 210, 228
Internal Revenue Act (1862), 146
Internal Revenue Service (IRS), 284
International Business Machines
    (IBM), 315
international power, 188, 194–95, 244
Internet, 316
interstate commerce, 47, 49, 75, 176
Interstate Commerce Act (1887), 180,
    194
Interstate Commerce Commission
    (ICC), 180, 197
Intolerable Acts (Coercive Laws,
    British, 1774), 36–37
Iowa, Granger laws, 178
Iran, 326, 336; -Contra scandal,
    298–301; hostage crisis, 291–93; and
    nuclear program, 336
Iraq: Gulf War and, 303–4; War and
    occupation, 326, 328–36
Iraq Study Group, 335
Irish immigrants, 131, 136, 179, 181
Iron Curtain, 246
iron industry, 132, 199
Iroquois tribe, 8–9, 18, 27–29, 79, 92
Irving, Washington, 75–76
Islam: fundamentalists, 291; Shiite vs.
    Sunni, 329, 333; terrorists, 325–26,
    330–31
isolationism, 188, 204–5, 209–11, 244
Israel, 290, 298, 312, 326, 330–31
Italy, 203, 230, 247, 249, 329; WW II
    and, 231, 235, 237, 240–41, 243
Iwo Jima, Battle of, 242

Jackson, Andrew "Old Hickory," 67,
    72–73, 80–82, 87–91, 94–110, 116–17,
    122, 132, 142, 165, 238
Jackson, Gen. Thomas J. "Stonewall,"
    144, 149

Jackson, Jesse, 302
Jackson, Rachel D. Robards, 94
Jackson, William, 48
Jackson State College killings, 280
Jamaica, 44
James I, king of England, 10–12, 14
James II, king of England, 18–20, 23
Jamestown colony, 10–12
Japan, 231, 235–38, 241–44, 255
Japanese-American Commercial
    Treaty (1911), 236
Japanese-American Reparations Act
    (1988), 302
Japanese-Americans, removal of, 238,
    302
Jaworski, Leon, 285
Jay, John, 45, 54, 61, 65
Jay Treaty (1796), 61–62
Jeffers, Robinson, 209
Jefferson, Thomas, 34, 36–37, 40,
    46–47, 54, 56–62, 64–71, 79, 199, 103,
    116, 119
Jewish Americans, 212, 241, 321
Jim Crow laws, 178, 261
Johnson, Andrew, 144, 151, 154–63, 167,
    169, 189
Johnson, Herschel V., 140–41
Johnson, James W., 209
Johnson, Lyndon B., 259, 262–63,
    269–79, 281, 284, 305
Johnston, Gen. Joseph E., 144, 147,
    152
Joint Commission on Atomic Energy,
    247
Jones, John Paul, 44
Jones, Paula, 318
Jones Act (1916), 192–93
Juarez, Benito, 148
Judd, Walter H., 254
judicial branch, 50, 66, 70, 227
Judicial Procedure Reform Act (1937),
    228
judicial review, 70, 226
Judiciary Act: (1789), 54, 70; (1800),
    66; (1802), 69–70
Julian, George W., 144, 161

Jungle, The (Sinclair), 195–96
Justice Department, 262

Kansas, 135–39
Kansas-Nebraska Act (1854), 136–37
Karzai, Hamid, 326
Katrina, Hurricane, 327, 334
Kearny, Col. Stephen W., 125
Keating-Owen Child Labor Act
    (1916), 199
Kefauver, Estes, 257
Kelley, William D. "Pig Iron," 169
Kendall, Amos, 97
Kennedy, Edward M. "Ted," 279, 292
Kennedy, John F., 263–69, 279, 284,
    292, 306; assassination of, 269–70
Kennedy, Robert F., 277–79, 292;
    assassination of, 278
Kent State killings, 280
Kentucky, 134, 143
Kentucky and Virginia Resolutions
    (1798), 64
Kern, Jerome, 208
Kerry, John, 331–32
Key, David M., 174
Khalilzad, Zalmay, 333
Khmer Rouge, 281
Khomeini, Ayatollah, 291
Khrushchev, Nikita, 266–67
King, Adm. Ernest J., 237
King, Dr. Martin Luther, Jr.,
    117, 261–62, 268–69, 272–73;
    assassination of, 278
King George's War, 27
King Philip's War, 27
King William's War, 27
Kitty Hawk flight, 207
Kleindienst, Richard, 284
Knowland, William, 254
Know-Nothing Party, 136–38, 141
Knox, Henry, 46, 54
Knudson, William S., 240
Korean War, 255–60
Kosovo, 304, 312
K Street Project, 323
Ku Klux Klan (KKK), 165, 209, 212

Ku Klux Klan Act (1871), 165
Kuwait, 303–4, 306, 329
Kyle, James, 183, 7

Labor and Commerce Department, 194
labor movement, 86–87, 183–84,
    193, 223, 225, 229–30, 248–49, 253;
    unions, 217, 225, 229–31, 248, 313
Ladd, William, 115
La Follette, Robert M., 196–97, 211–12
La Guardia, Fiorello, 211, 217
Landon, Alfred M., 226
Lane, Joseph, 141
Laos, 280
Last of the Mohicans, The (Cooper), 76
Latin America, 84–85, 93–94;
    immigrants from, 317–18
Laurens, Henry, 45
League of Nations, 202–5
Lease, Mary Elizabeth, 183
Leaves of Grass (Whitman), 118
Lebanon, 300, 304; hostages, 298
Lee, Mother Ann, 114
Lee, Richard Henry, 37, 39–40
Lee, Gen. Robert E., 147, 149–50,
    152–53
legislative branch, executive power vs.,
    48–50, 67, 159–63, 223, 228, 282
Lend-Lease Act (1941) 234–35
L'Enfant, Pierre Charles, 64
Leningrad, siege of, 241, 243
Letters from an American Farmer
    (Dickinson), 34
Lewinsky, Monica, 318
Lewis, John L., 229, 248
Lewis, Meriwether, 39, 69
Lexington, Battle of, 37, 41
Leyte Gulf, Battle of, 242
Libby, I. Lewis "Scooter," 334–35
Liberal Republican Party, 169
Liberator, The, 135
Liberia, 134
Liberty Party, 112, 128
Libya, 304
Lieberman, Joseph, 321
Liliuokalani, queen of Hawaii, 189

Lincoln, Abraham, 67, 84, 131, 135, 137,
    141–47, 149–54, 162, 165, 189, 269;
    assassination of, 153–54; -Douglas
    debates (1858), 140
Lincoln, Gen. Benjamin, 44, 46
Lincoln, Mary Todd, 145
Lindbergh, Charles A., 207
Lippmann, Walter, 268
literature, 75–76, 117–18, 209
Lithuania, 231, 303
Little Rock integration, 262–63
Livingston, Bob, 319–20
Livingston, Robert R., 40, 53, 68, 75
Lloyd, Henry Demarest, 196
Lloyd George, David, 203
lobbyists, 97, 110, 178, 180, 323
Locke, Alain, 209
Locke, John, 17
Lodge, Henry Cabot (elder), 204
Lodge, Henry Cabot (younger), 257,
    263
Logan, John A., 179
London Company, 10–13
Long, Hucy P., 224
Long, Jefferson F., 164
Longfellow, Henry Wadsworth, 118
Longstreet, Augustus B., 118
Longworth, Alice Roosevelt, 208
Longworth, Nicholas, 208
Lookout Mountain, Battle of, 150
Louisiana, 28, 82, 134, 141, 155, 162, 178,
    271, 273; Purchase, 39, 68–69, 77,
    82–84, 188
Lowell, James Russell, 118
Lumpkin, Wilson, 102
Lusitania (RMS), 200
Luther, Martin, 5
Luxembourg, 232, 247
Luzon, Battle of, 242
lynching, 165, 251

MacArthur, Gen. Douglas, 216–17,
    237, 241–42, 244, 256
MacFarlane, Robert, 298, 299
Macon, Nathaniel, 88
Macon's Bill No. 2, 71

Madison, James, 48, 53–54, 56–57, 59, 64, 70–72, 78–79, 107, 116, 307–8
Mafia, 208, 252
Magellan, Ferdinand, 8
Maine, 16, 83, 84
Maine (USS), 190
Malay Peninsula, 236, 241
Maliki, Nuri al–, 333
Mallory, Rollin C., 91
Manassas. *See* Bull Run, Battle of
Manchuria, 235, 244
Manhattan Project, 240
Manifest Destiny, 122–26, 189–90, 195
Manila, capture of, 242
Mann, Horace, 115
Mann-Elkins Act (1909), 197
Mansfield, Mike, 269
manufacturing. *See* industrialization
Mao Tse-tung, 254
Marbury v. Madison, 70
Marcy, William L., 97
Marne, Battle of, 202
marriage, 114, 317; same–sex, 332
Marshall, George C., 237, 249, 254, 257–58
Marshall, John, 66, 70, 75, 102, 106
Marshall, Thurgood, 305
Marshall Plan, 249–50
Martin, Joseph W., 256
Martin v. Hunter's Lessee, 75
Maryland, 16–17, 28, 41, 47, 51, 134, 143
Mason, George, 48, 51
Mason, James M., 144
Massachusetts, 23–25, 28–29, 34–37, 46, 51, 87, 198, 332; Bay Colony, 14–16
Maurer, James H., 219
Maximilian, emperor of Mexico, 148
Mayflower Compact, 13–14
McAdoo, William G., 212
McCarran Internal Security Act (1950), 255
McCarran-Walter Immigration and Nationality Act (1950), 255
McCarthy, Eugene, 277–78
McCarthy, Joseph R., 254–55, 257

McClellan, Gen. George B., 144–47, 151
McClure's, 196
McCormack, John, 269
McCormick reaper, 118, 187
McCulloch v. Maryland, 75, 106
McDowell, Gen. Irwin, 144
McGovern, George, 281–82
McGuffey, William H., 116
McKay, Claude, 209
McKinley, William, 181, 183, 185–86, 189, 191–93
McKinley Tariff Act (1890), 181–85
McNary, Charles L., 233
Meade, Maj. Gen. George G., 149
Meat Inspection Act (1906), 195–96
Medicaid, 271
Medicare, 271, 294, 325, 333, 335
Medina, Capt. Ernest, 280
Mellon, Andrew, 216
Melville, Herman, 117
Menéndez de Avilés, Pedro, 7
Menneville, Marquis Duquesne de, 27
Meredith, James, 268
Mergentheber, Ottmar, 187
Merrimac and *Monitor*, Battle of, 147
Metacom, Chief, 27
Mexican-Americans, 211, 317, 238
Mexican War, 118, 123–28, 124, 189
Mexico, 84, 148, 201, 313; Texas independence from, 122–23
Mexics, 6–7
Microsoft Company, 316
Middle East, 260, 303–4, 326, 330–31, 336
"midnight appointments," 66, 70
Midway, 236, 242
military-industrial complex, 260
Military Reconstruction Act (1867), 161
Milosevic, Slobodan, 312
Mims, Fort, massacre, 72
minimum wage, 227–28, 253, 335
Minimum Wage and Hours Act (1938), 229
Missionary Ridge, Battle of, 150

Mississippi, 8, 82, 134, 141, 162, 164, 251, 263, 267, 271, 273; University of, desegregated, 268
Missouri, 84, 134, 143; Territory, 82–84
Missouri Compromise (1820), 82–84, 119, 135–36, 139
Missouri Enabling Act (1820), 82–83
Moby-Dick (Melville), 117
Mohawk tribe, 9
Mohican tribe, 100
molasses tariff, 91–92
Moley, Raymond, 219
Mondale, Walter F., 288, 292
Monmouth, Battle of, 44
monopolies and trusts, 177–80, 182–83, 188, 194, 196, 199
Monroe, James, 68, 79–80, 84–87
Monroe Doctrine, 79, 84–86, 204
Montana, 200
Montcalm, Gen. Marquis de, 28
Montezuma, emperor of Aztecs, 6
Montgomery, Gen. Sir Bernard, 241
Montgomery bus boycott, 261
Montgomery Convention (1861), 141–42
moon mission, 265
Moore, Sara Jane, 287
Moral Majority, 314
Morgan, J. Pierpont, 185
Morgenthau, Henry, 239
Mormons, 114–15
Morrill Land Grant College Act (1862), 146
Morris, Gouverneur, 48, 51
Morse, Samuel F., 119
Morton, Levi P., 180
Morton, William T.G., 119
motion picture industry, 207, 246–46
Mott, Lucretia, 115
muckrackers, 196
Mugwumps, 177, 179
Mühlenberg, Frederick, 61
Munich Agreement (1938), 231–32
Munn v. Illinois, 178
Murders in the Rue Morgue (Poe), 118
Murtha, John, 295

music, 260–61; jazz, 208, 212; rock and roll, 261
Muskie, Edmund S., 279
Mussolini, Benito, 230–31, 241, 245
Myers, Michael, 290
My Lai massacre, 280

Nader, Ralph, 321, 322
Naples, Battle of, 241
Napoleon Bonaparte, 68, 70–72
Napoleonic Wars, 70–71, 73, 99
Napoleon III, emperor of France, 148
National Aeronautic and Space Administration (NASA), 265
National Association for the Advancement of Colored People (NAACP), 198
National Budget and Accounting Act (1921), 211
national debt, 54–55, 59, 239, 295–96, 325
National Defense Act (1916), 200
National Defense Program, 243
National Employment System Act (1933), 222
National Endowment for the Arts and Humanities, 296
National Farmers' Alliance of the Northwest, 179
National Guard, 200, 262–63, 268–69, 280, 332
National Housing Act (1937), 228
National Industrial Recovery Act (NIRA, 1933), 222–23, 226
National Intelligencer, 107, 121
nationalism, 74–76; new, 197–98
National Labor Relations Act (Wagner Act, 1935), 225, 228
national parks, 310
National Progressive Republican League, 197
National Republicans, 91, 108
National Security Council, 298
National Union ticket, 151
National Woman Suffrage Association, 159

National Youth Administration, 225
Naturalization Acts (1795, 1798, 1802), 64
Navigation Acts (British), 24
Navy Department, 63, 170, 210
Nazi-Soviet Pact, 231, 232
Nebraska, 135–36
Nelson, Donald M., 240
Nelson, John M., 211
Netherlands, 56, 59, 232, 247
neutrality, 60, 188, 200, 204
Neutrality Acts (1937, 1939), 232
Nevada, 126
New Amsterdam, 9, 18–19
New Deal, 218, 221–31, 253, 257–58
New Echota, Treaty of, 102
New England, 4, 13–16, 20, 21, 24–26, 43, 56, 70, 72, 74, 76, 91–93
Newfoundland, 4, 9, 27
New France, 8–9
New Freedom program, 198
New Frontier, 267
New Hampshire, 16, 23, 28, 51
New Harmony, 113–14
New Jersey, 19, 23, 51
New Jersey Plan, 49–50
Newlands Act (1902), 194
New Lights, 25–26
New Mexico, 125–26, 129–30, 189, 317
New Netherland, 18–19
New Orleans, 68, 69, 108, 147, 160; Battle of, 73–74, 116; Katrina and, 334
New Spain, 7–8
New World: exploration and settlement of, 2–11; first inhabitants, 1–2; named America, 6
New York Central Railroad, 132
New York City, 52–53, 56, 76, 131, 149, 175, 212, 218, 314; Custom House, 176
New York: colonial, 9, 19, 21–23, 28, 34, 36, 42, 46; State, 51, 198
New York Daily News, 311
New York Herald, 158–59
New York Journal, 190
New York Sun, 167
New York Times, 280

New York Tribune, 98, 169
New York World, 190
Nicaragua, 298–99; Contras, 298–99; Sandinistas, 298–99
Niger, 328
Niles Weekly Register, 74
Nimitz, Adm. Chester, 242
Nineteenth Amendment (1920), 200
Nixon, Richard, 246, 257, 263–65, 279, 281–87, 306; resignation of, 286–88, 299
NLFB v. Jones and Loughlin Steel Corp., 228
Noah, Mordecai, 97
No Child Left Behind Act (2001), 324
Non-Importation Act (1809), 71
Noriega, Manuel, 303
Normandy invasion, 243
Norris, George W., 197, 211, 217
Norris–La Guardia Act, 217
North, 82–84, 120, 129–31, 158
North, Lord, 34, 37, 43, 45
North, Oliver, 298–99
North Africa, 241
North American Free Trade Agreement (NAFTA), 312–13
North Atlantic Treaty Organization (NATO), 247, 304, 312
North Carolina, 10, 17–18, 39, 51, 134, 143, 162, 263, 273
Northern Securities company, 194
North Korea, 255–56, 260, 326
North Vietnam, 274, 276, 278, 281
Northwest Ordinance (1787), 46–47
Northwest Passage, 8
Northwest Territory, 47
Norway, 232, 247
nuclear weapons, 266, 336. *See also* atomic bomb; weapons of mass destruction
nullification doctrine, 93, 102–5
Nussle, James, 307

Obey, David, 297
Odell, Moses, 144–45
Office of Censorship, 240

Office of Economic Stabilization, 240
Office of Production Management, 240
Office of Scientific Research and
    Development, 240
Office of Strategic Services, 240
Office of War Information, 240
Oglethorpe, James, 20
Ohio, 76, 198
oil, 178, 182, 187, 189, 209–10, 236, 289,
    303–4
O'Keeffe, Georgia, 209
Okinawa, Battle of, 242
Oklahoma City bombing, 309
Olmert, Ehud, 331
Olympics (Moscow, 1980), 291
Oneida tribe, 9
O'Neill, Eugene, 209
O'Neill, Thomas P. "Tip," 272,
    288–89, 293–94, 296, 299
Onondaga tribe, 9
Opechancanough, Chief, 10–12
Oregon, 238, 332; Territory, 69, 123
Orlando, Vittorio, 203
O'Sullivan, John L., 122, 189–90
Otis, James, 32, 35
Ottawa Indians, 31
Our American Cousin (play), 153
Overlord, Operation, 243
Owen, Robert, 113–14

Pacific Railroad Act (1862), 146
pacifism, 200–201
Packwood, Robert, 309
Paine, Thomas, 38–39, 42
Pakistan, 326
Palestinians, 312, 331
Palmer, A. Mitchell, 209
Panama, 195; invasion of 1989, 303
Panama Canal, 194–95; Treaty (1977),
    195, 290
Panama Congress, 93–94
Pan-American Exposition (Buffalo,
    1901), 193
Panetta, Leon, 310
Panic: of 1837, 111, 132; of 1873, 171, 173,
    176; of 1893, 184–85

Paris, Treaty of: (1763), 28, 29; (1783),
    45, 52; (1898), 192
Paris Peace talks (Vietnam War), 278,
    280–81
Parker, Alton B., 195
Parks, Rosa, 261
Partisan, The (Simms), 118
Paterson, William, 49
Patriot Act (2001, 2003), 327
patronage system, 175–77
Patton, Gen. George S., 241
Pawtuxet tribe, 14
Payne-Aldrich Tariff Act (1909), 197
Peace Corps, 267
Pearl Harbor attack, 192, 236–39
Pelosi, Nancy, 315, 335
Pemaquid tribe, 14
Pendleton, George H., 151
peninsulares, 7
Penn, William, 19–20
Pennsylvania, 19–20, 22, 25, 28–29, 36,
    47, 51
Pennsylvania Railroad, 132
Pentagon Papers, 280
Pequot War, 27
Perot, H. Ross, 306, 312
Pershing, Gen. John J., 202
Peru, 7, 84
Pétain, Marshal Henri-Philippe, 233
Petersburg, siege of (1864–65), 150,
    152
phalanxes, 113
Philadelphia, 47, 56, 131
Philip II, king of Spain, 9–10
Philippines, 8, 191–93, 211, 236–37,
    241–42
Phillips, David Graham, 196
Phips, Sir William, 27
Pilgrims, 13–14
Pilgrim's Progress (Bunyan), 196
Pinckney, Gen. Charles C., 65
Pioneers, The (Cooper), 76
Pitt, William, 28
Pizarro, Francisco, 7
plantations, 22, 77, 132–34
Plessy v. Ferguson, 178, 261

Plumer, William, 83
Plymouth, 13, 27
Pocahontas, 11
Poe, Edgar Allan, 118
Poindexter, John M., 298, 299
Poland, 202–3, 231–32, 241, 303, 312, 329
political campaign contributions, 180
political machines, 179
political parties: evolution of two-party system and, 59–62; Jacksonian age and, 91, 96–97; labor and, 248; nominating conventions begun, 65; refashioned, with Kansas-Nebraska dispute, 136–37; reform movement and, 197. *See also* elections; *and specific parties and factions*
Polk, James Knox "Young Hickory," 98, 111, 116, 123–24, 128
Pollock v. Farmers Loan and Trust Company, 185
poll taxes, 251, 267
Polo, Marco, 4
Ponce de Leon, Juan, 8
Pontiac, Chief of Ottawa, 31
popular sovereignty doctrine, 128, 130, 140
population, of 2000, 318
Populist Party (People's Party), 183–86, 193, 195, 197
pork barrel, 97, 180, 218
Porter, Cole, 208
Portugal, 5–6, 247
Potter, John F. "Bowie-Knife," 139
Pound, Ezra, 209
poverty, 115, 317
Powell, Colin, 304, 328, 329
Powhatan, Chief, 10–12
Powhatan War, 12
Preliminary Emancipation Proclamation (1863), 147
Presbyterians, 18
Prescott, Col. William, 38
president (executive branch): nominating system, 65; nominating system, changed in 1824, 87–88;

power of, 49–50, 67–68, 107–10, 182, 223, 228, 239, 282, 327, 336; power of, vs. legislative branch, post–Civil War, 158–63; salary of, 171; separate ballot for vice president and, 66; veto by, 50, 106–8, 110, 180; veto by, first major congressional override, 159, 161–62
Presley, Elvis, 261
Preston, Capt. Thomas, 35
Prevost, Gen. Sir George, 73
Priest, Oscar S., 213
Princeton, Battle of, 42
Proclamation of 1763 (British), 31
Proclamation of Amnesty and Reconstruction (1863), 150
Proclamation of December 10 (1832), 104–5
Proclamation of Neutrality (1793), 60
progressive movement, 109, 184, 193–99, 211
Progressive Party, 197–98, 200; of 1924, 211–12, 217; of 1948, 251–52
Prohibition, 207–8, 212, 219, 221–22
Prohibition Party, 169, 176–77, 184, 193, 195, 197, 219, 220
protectionism, 91. *See also* tariffs
Protestant Reformation, 13
Prussia, 84
public works, 215, 217–18, 259
Public Works Administration, 223
Puerto Rico, 192, 317
Pulitzer, Joseph, 190
Pullman strike of 1894, 183
Pure Food and Drug Act (1906), 195, 229
Puritans, 13–17, 19–21, 24–25, 27, 112
Purloined Letter, The (Poe), 118

Quadruple or Holy Alliance, 84–85
Quakers, 19–20, 24, 25, 119
Quartering Act (British, 1765), 32, 36
Quasi-War with France, 63
Quayle, J. Danforth, 302, 306
Quebec, 8; siege of, 28
Quebec Act (1774), 36

Queen Anne's War, 1702, 27
Quincy, Josiah, 35, 67

Rabin, Yitzhak, 311
race riots, 121, 267
racial discrimination, 166, 206, 251,
    262, 270
Radical Republicans, 144–45, 150–51,
    155–57, 159, 162–64, 175–76
radio, 206–7, 212, 219, 222, 234
railroads, 76, 132, 135–36, 166–67,
    168, 171, 177–80, 187–88, 193–94,
    196, 202, 211, 217, 223; segregation
    and, 178; seizure of, 248;
    transcontinental, 146, 172
Rainey, Henry T., 221
Rainey, Joseph H., 164
Raleigh, Sir Walter, 10
Randolph, Edmund, 48, 51, 54, 60
Randolph, John, 67, 71, 83, 90–91
Rangel, Charles, 319
Rankin, Jeannette, 200, 201, 237
Ray, James Earl, 278
Rayburn, Sam, 259
Reader (Webster), 116
Reagan, Ronald, 288, 292–301, 304,
    308, 324, 325
recession: of 1780s, 46; of 1833–34, 108.
    See also Depression; Panic
Reciprocal Trade Agreement Act, 223
Reconstruction, 152, 155–66, 169, 172,
    174–75, 178, 262, 270, 271
Reconstruction Acts (1867), 162,
    164–65
Reconstruction Finance Corporation
    (RFC), 217, 218
Red Scare, 209, 253–55. *See also* anti-
    communism
Reed, Thomas Brackett, 181–82
reform movement: antebellum, 109,
    112, 115–17, 119; post–Civil War,
    179–80, 193, 195–96
Reform Party, 312
Regan, Frank S., 219
Rehnquist, William, 285, 321
Reid, Whitelaw, 184

religious freedom, 13–17, 46–47
religious fundamentalists, 212, 308–9
religious Right, 314, 323
Reno, Janet, 318
Republican National Committee to
    Reelect the President (CREEP), 281
Republican Party: anti-labor
    legislation, 248–49; antitrust
    legislation and, 182; Bush II
    administration and, 323, 328, 332,
    334–35; civil service reform and,
    179; Clinton administration and,
    308–12; Clinton impeachment
    and, 318–21; conservative coalition
    with southern Democrats and, 227;
    created by Whigs, Free-Soilers,
    and antislavery Democrats, 121,
    136; development of, and Civil
    War, 140–42, 144–45; early-20th-
    century reforms and, 197; elections
    of 1856 and Frémont candidacy,
    138; elections of 1864, 151; elections
    of 1870, 163–64; elections of 1876,
    173; elections of 1876 and deal with
    South, 174–76; elections of 1880,
    176–77; elections of 1890, 183;
    elections of 1892, 184; elections of
    1896, and control of Congress and
    presidency, 185–86; elections of
    1900, 193; elections of 1912, 197–198;
    elections of 1916, 200; elections of
    1918, 203; elections of 1920, 205;
    elections of 1924, 212; elections of
    1928, 213; elections of 1932, 219, 220;
    elections of 1934, 224; elections of
    1936, 226; elections of 1948, 250–53;
    elections of 1952, 257, 258; elections
    of 1956, 261–62; elections of 1960,
    263–65; elections of 1964, 270–71;
    elections of 1968, 279; elections of
    1972, 281–82; elections of 1974 and
    1976, 288; elections of 1980, 292–93;
    elections of 1988, 301–2; elections
    of 1992, 306–7; elections of 2000,
    321–22; elections of 2006, 335;
    majority, and Sun Belt, 313;

Republican Party (*continued*)
New Deal and, 222–23; Nixon
impeachment and, 286;
Reconstruction and dispute with
Johnson, 155–61; reform movement
among, 177; religious right and, 314;
South and, post–Civil Rights Act
of 1964, 271; split between Stalwart
and Half Breed factions, 176; split
in, with Liberal Republicans,
169; tariffs and silver issue and,
180–82; television and, 297; Truman
administration and, 253–54; WW II
and, 233. *See also* Half Breed faction;
Insurgent Republicans; Radical
Republicans; Stalwart Republicans
Republican Party (Jeffersonian). *See*
Democratic-Republican Party)
Reserve Officers' Training Corps
(ROTC), 200
Residency Act (1790), 64
Revels, Hiram R., 164
Revenue Act: (1940), 233; (1941), 239;
(1942), 239
revival meetings, 115
Revolutionary War, 38–39, 41–45
Rhode Island, 15, 23, 28, 48, 51
Rice, Condoleezza, 328
rice plantations, 18, 22, 24, 132, 134
Richardson, Elliot, 284
Richmond, 143, 146, 152
rights: assembly and petition, 54,
121–22; ; to bear arms, 54; free
speech, press, and religion, 54; not
delegated, reserved to states or
people, 54, 57; privacy, 283
Ripley, George, 112, 113
Roanoke colony, 10
Roaring Twenties, 205–13
Robards, Lewis, 94
Robber Barons, 178, 188
Robinson, Joseph T., 213
Rockefeller, John D., 188
Rockefeller, Nelson, 286, 288
Rockingham, Lord, 45
Rodino, Peter, 285

Roe v. Wade, 283, 314–15
Rogers, Edith Nourse, 239
Rolfe, John, 11
Roman Catholics, 4–5, 8, 13, 16–17, 137,
179, 212; sexual abuse scandal, 313
Romania, 233, 240, 303
Romanticism, 112, 117–18
Rommel, Field Marshal Erwin, 241
Roosevelt, Franklin D. (FDR), 205,
211–12; New Deal and, 218–31; WW
II and, 230–45
Roosevelt, James, 237
Roosevelt, Theodore, 191, 193–98, 200,
208, 306
Rosenberg, Julius and Ethel, 254
Ross, Edmund G., 163
Ross, Gen. Robert, 73
Rough Riders, 191
Rove, Karl, 322–23, 323, 332
rubber, 118, 229
Ruff, Charles, 321
Rumsfeld, Donald, 326, 328–30, 333
Rural Electrification Administration,
225
Rush, Richard, 85
Russell, John, 169
Russia, 84, 85, 189; post–Soviet, 303,
329; Revolution, 202–4. *See also*
Soviet Union
Rust Belt, 313

Sackville-West, Sir Lionel, 180–81
Sadat, Anwar el-, 290–91
St. Augustine, Spanish settle (1565), 7
St. Lawrence River, 4, 8, 9; Seaway, 259
St. Louis Democrat, 170
Saipan, Battle of, 242
Salary Grab Act (1873), 171
Salerno, Battle of, 241
Samoset, 14
Sandburg, Carl, 209
San Ildefonso, Treaty of (1800), 68
San Salvador, 5
Santee tribe, 18
Saratoga, Battle of, 43, 44
Sargent, Nathan, 129

Saturday-night massacre, 284–85
Saudi Arabia, 304
Savannah, 20, 44, 152
savings and loans crisis, 301
Sawyer, William, 98
scalawags, 162, 175
Scarlet Letter, The (Hawthorne), 117
Schechter Poultry Corp. v. United States, 226
Schenck v. United States, 202
Schurz, Carl, 169, 177
Schwarzkopf, Gen. Norman, 304
Scofield, Glenn W., 169
Scott, Dred, 139
Scott, Gen. Winfield, 124–25, 143–44
Scowcroft, Brent, 328
secession: New England and, 74; Mexican War and, 126; South and, 82–84, 104–5, 119, 127–31, 136–37, 139, 141–43
Second Amendment, 278
Secret Service, 327
Securities and Exchange Commission (SEC), 222, 224, 225
Sedgwick, Theodore, 56
Sedition Act: (1798–1801), 64; (1918), 201–2
segregation, 178, 213; abolished in civil service and armed forces, 253; ruled unconstitutional, 261–63
Selective Service Act: (1917), 201; (1940), 233
Selective Service boards, 239
Selma–Montgomery Freedom March of 1965, 272–73
Seminole tribe, 79–80, 100, 101
Seneca tribe, 9
separation of church and state, 15
September 11, 2001, attacks, 325–26
Serbia, 304
Seven Cities of Cibola, 8
Seven Days Battle, 146
Seven Pines, Battle of, 147
Seventeenth Amendment (1913), 198
Seven Years' War (French and Indian, 1755–1763), 28–29

Sewall, Arthur, 186
Seward, William H., 141, 144, 148, 189
sex discrimination, 270, 315
sexual harassment, 305, 309
sexual revolution, 313–14
Seymour, Horatio, 164
Shakers, 114–15
Sharon, Ariel, 331
Shaw, Lemuel, 87
Shays' Rebellion, 46, 59
Shepard, Alan, Jr., 265
Shepperd, Augustine H., 92
Sherman, John, 163
Sherman, Roger, 40, 48, 50, 54
Sherman, Gen. William T., 150–52
Sherman Antitrust Act (1890), 182–83, 198–99
Sherman Silver Purchase Act (1890), 181–82, 185
Shriver, R. Sargent, 281, 282
Sicily, Battle for, 241
Siegfried Line, 243
Silicon Valley, 316
silver (free silver), 171–72, 176, 181–82, 185–86, 193
Simms, William Gilmore, 118
Simple, Oliver, 287
Simpson, "Sockless Jerry," 183
Sinclair, Upton, 195–96
Singapore, 241
Single Taxers, 211
Sirhan, Sirhan, 278
Sirica, John J., 283–85
sit-ins, 263, 273
Sixteenth Amendment (1913), 198, 199
Sketch Book (Irving), 75–76
slaves and slavery, 17–18, 22, 47, 50, 82–84, 103, 105, 118–23, 127–42; abolished, 145–48, 152; revolts and, 119–20; trade in, 24, 50, 130. *See also* abolitionists
Slidell, John, 144
Smith, Alfred E., 212–13, 218
Smith, John, 10, 11, 14
Smith, Joseph, 114
Smith, Margaret Bayard, 66

Smith, Mrs. Samuel H., 95–96
Smoot-Hawley Tariff (1930), 213–14
Social Destiny of Man (Brisbane), 113
socialism, 218
Socialist Labor Party, 197
Socialist Party, 184, 193, 195, 197, 211, 219, 220
Social Security, 228–29, 253, 257–58, 271, 310, 325, 331
Social Security Act: (1935), 225, 228; (1954), 259
Soil Conservation Act (1935), 225
Solidarity Movement, 303
Somalia, 304, 312
Sons of Liberty, 33, 36
Soto, Hernando de, 8
South: civil rights movement and, 262, 267–71; colonial, 20, 21, 22; Civil War and, 142–44, 147–56, 161–62; dispute over treatment of, post–Civil War, 155–58; elections of 1924 and, 212; federal troops removed from, with Hayes election, 174–77; literature and, 118; plantation and slavery system in, 76–77, 132–33; readmitted to union, 159, 164; Reconstruction and, 155–66; rural life in, during 1920s, 206; secession threats of, over slavery in territories, 82–84, 104–5, 119–20, 127–31, 136–37, 139–43; slave revolts and, 119–20; state debt assumption and, 56; tariffs and, 92–93, 99; white rule restored in, 165–66, 178, 209. *See also* Civil War; Confederate States of America; slavery; *and specific acts, colonies, individuals, and states*
South America, 7
South Carolina, 17–18, 51, 93, 102–5, 134, 141–42, 162, 271, 273
Southern Alliance, 179
Southern Christian Leadership Conference, 268
Southern Democrats, 227, 250–53, 271, 294
South Korea, 255–56, 260

South Vietnam, 274, 280–81
Soviet Union: Cold War and, 246–47, 249–52, 254–56, 260, 265–67, 291, 297–98, 300–301, 325; disintegration of, 303; WW I and, 202; WW II and, 230–32, 235–36, 241, 243–44. *See also* Russia
space program, 265
Spain, 5–11, 18, 28, 44, 59, 80–82, 81, 84–85, 247, 329; civil war of 1936–39, 230; Spanish-American War (1898), 190–92
Sparkman, John, 257
Special Orders, 297
Specie Circular (1836), 110
Specie Resumption Act (1875), 172
Spelling Book (Webster), 116
Spirit of St. Louis, The (monoplane), 207
spoils system, 99
Spotsylvania, Battle of, 150
Sprague, Adm. Clifton, 242
Sputnik, 265
Spy, The (Cooper), 76
Squanto, 14
Stalin, Joseph, 230–32, 243–44, 246
Stalingrad, Battle of, 241, 243
Stalwart Republicans, 175–77, 197
Stamp Act (British, 1765), 32–33, 35
Stamp Act Congress, 32–33
Standard Oil Company, 178, 196
Stanton, Edwin, 154, 162–63
Stanton, Elizabeth Cady, 115, 159
Starr, Kenneth, 318–19
Star Wars, 296
State Department, 53–54, 246, 254
state(s): Constitutional Convention and, 47–48, 51–53; debts, assumption of, 56, 58; disputes under Articles of Confederation and, 45–47; election reform and, 196; militias, 59, 143; legislatures, 196; new, admitted between 1810 and 1819, 82; new, admitted by War of 1812, 77; provisions for adding future, and Northwest Ordinance, 46–47;

slave vs. free, 82–84, 119–21, 130–31, 135–39. *See also* specific states

states' rights, 49, 52, 54, 57, 64, 91, 93, 103, 159

States' Rights Democratic Party, 251

Steagall, Henry, 228

steamboats, 77, 132

steel industry, 167, 187, 229; embargo, 236

stem cell research, 116, 323

Stennis, John C., 284

Stephens, Alexander H., 129, 136, 142, 166

Stephens, Lincoln, 196

Stevens, Thaddeus, 142–44, 156–57, 161, 163, 296

Stevenson, Adlai (elder), 184, 193

Stevenson, Adlai E. (younger), 257–58

Steward Machine Co. v. Davis, 228

Stimson, Henry L., 237

stock market: crash of 1893, 184; crash of 1929, 213–15; crash of 1987, 301; decline of 1938, 229

Stowe, Harriet Beecher, 135

Strasser, Adolph, 229

strikes, 87, 183, 205, 211, 229, 248–49

Stuyvesant, Peter, 18, 19

suffrage: adult male, 86, 88, 97–98, 173; black male, 159; women's, 159. *See also* voting rights; women; *and specific constitutional amendments*

sugar, 24, 44, 132, 134, 182, 187, 199, 214

Sugar Act (1764), 32

Summary View of the Rights of British America, A (Jefferson), 36

Summers, Hatton, 227

Sumner, Charles, 137–38, 157

Sumter, Fort, attack on, 142

Sun Belt, 313, 314

Sundquist, Donald, 294

Supplementary Reconstruction Acts (1867), 161

supply-side economics, 292, 294

Sutter, John, 128–29

Swallow, Silas C., 195

Swift Boat Veterans for Truth, 332

Taft, Robert A., 233, 252–53, 257

Taft, William Howard, 192–93, 197–98

Taft–Hartley Act (1947), 248–49, 252–53

Taiwan, 254, 290

Taliban, 325, 326

Talleyrand, Charles–Maurice de, 68

Tallmadge, James, 82–83

Taney, Roger B., 139

Tarawa, Battle of, 242

Tarbell, Ida, 196

tariff(s), 76, 79, 91–93, 99, 122, 167, 179–82, 184–85, 197–99, 213–14, 219, 223; of 1828 (Abominations), 93, 99, 102–3; of 1832, 103–5; of 1833 (Compromise), 104

taxes, 276; American colonies vs. British, 22–23, 26–27, 32–34; Articles of Confederation and, 41, 49; Bush I and, 305–6; capital gains and, 302; Civil War and, 146; Constitution, and federal power of, 49; cuts in, 247, 292, 295–96, 302, 310, 324–25, 331; earned income credit, 324; estate, 324; excess profits, 211, 239; excise, on liquor, 58–59; gasoline, 259; income, 176, 184–86, 188, 196, 198–99, 202, 239, 295–96, 302, 324; payroll, 225, 228–29; poll, 251, 267; resistance, 117; states, of federal institutions, 75; victory, 239

Taylor, Glenn, 251

Taylor, Zachary "Old Rough and Ready," 98, 116, 123–24, 128–130

Tea Act (1773), 34–37

Teapot Dome scandal, 209–10

technological advances, 76–77, 118–19, 172, 197, 206–7, 277, 315–17

Tehran conference, 243

telegraph and telephone, 118–19, 172, 197

television, 212, 277, 296–97; presidential debates, 306

Teller Amendment, 191

Temperance movement, 115
Tennessee, 8, 134, 143, 155, 159, 178
Tennessee Valley Authority (TVA), 222, 253
ten-percent plan, 150–51
Tenure of Office Act (1867), 161–63, 175
terrorism: domestic, 308–9; Islamic, 325–26, 330–31; war on, 327, 332
Tet Offensive (1968), 277
Texas, 122–24, 127, 130, 134, 141, 156, 164, 178, 189, 267, 317, 323, 334
Texas v. White, 165
Thailand, 241
Thirteenth Amendment (1865), 151–52, 155, 166
Thomas, Clarence, 305
Thomas, Jesse, 83
Thomas, Lorenzo, 162
Thomas, Norman, 219, 220
Thomas, Parnell, 245
Thompson, A. M., 176
Thoreau, Henry David, 112, 117
Three-fifths Compromise, 50, 121, 159
Thurmond, J. Strom, 251, 252, 271
Tiananmen Square protests, 303
Tilden, Samuel J., 173–75
Time, 246
Tincher, J. N., 210
Tippecanoe Creek, Battle of, 111
tobacco, 11, 18, 22, 24, 50, 92, 132, 134
Tocqueville, Alexis de, 90–91, 97–98, 113
Tojo, Gen. Hideki, 236
Toleration Act (Maryland, 1649), 17
Toombs, Robert, 129
Tordesillas, Treaty of (1494), 6
Toussaint-Louverture, 68
Tower, John, 298
Tower Commission, 298
Townsend, Dr. Francis E., 224
Townshend, Charles, 33–34
trade, 49–50, 313, 70–71, 301. *See also* tariffs; *and specific treaties*
Trade Acts (British), 24
Trail of Tears, 102

Transcendentalists, 112–13, 117–18
transportation and communications, 76, 79, 90, 116, 184, 259, 316
Treasury Department, 53–59, 65, 107, 170, 181, 211
treaties of alliance and amity and commerce (1778), 43, 60
Treaty of 1783, 45
Treaty of 1846, 123
trial by jury, 47, 54
Triple Alliance, 235–37
Tripoli, undeclared war with, 67–68
Trist, Nicholas, 125–26
Truman, Harry S., 243–57, 261
Truman Doctrine, 249
Trumbull, Lyman, 158–59
Tubman, Harriet, 135
Tugwell, Rexford G., 219
Turkey, 247, 249
Turner, Benjamin S., 164
Turner, Nat, Rebellion, 120–21
Tuscarora tribe, 9
Twain, Mark, 166
Tweed Ring, 173, 175
Twelfth Amendment (1804), 66, 88–89
Twentieth Amendment (1933), 52, 220
Twenty-Fifth Amendment (1967), 283
Twenty-First Amendment (1933), 221
Twenty-Fourth Amendment (1964), 267
Twenty-Seventh Amendment (1992), 54, 307–8
Twice-Told Tales (Hawthorne), 117
Tyler, John, 111, 122–23, 142

Ukraine, 303
Uncle Tom's Cabin (Stowe), 135
Underground Railroad, 120, 135
Underwood-Simmons Tariff (1913), 199
unemployment, 184–85, 215–16, 219, 221, 223, 229, 305; compensation, 225, 294
Union Army, 143–53
Union Navy, 147
Union Pacific Railroad, 167, 169, 171

United Arab Emirates, 334

United Christian Party, 197

United Mine Workers Union, 229, 248

United Nations, 255–56, 291, 304, 328–29, 331; Charter, 244; General Assembly, 256; Security Council, 249, 266

United States: border with Canada, 123; border with Mexico, 126; boundaries of, and Treaty of 1783, 45; maps of, 55, 58, 264; as Union of people vs. confederation of states and nullification issue, 102–5. *See also* federal government

U.S. Air Force, 236

U.S. armed forces, 50, 79, 202: civil rights in, 253; gay and lesbian personnel in, 308. *See also* specific branches and wars

U.S. Army, 79, 200, 239, 241; engineers, 195; -McCarthy hearings, 254–55

U.S. Coast Guard, 239, 327

U.S. Congress: African-Americans in, 164; airplanes and, 207; Alien and Sedition Acts and, 63–64; Andrew Johnson impeachment and, 155–63; anti-communism and, 230–31, 245–46, 249, 253–55; antitrust suits and, 194; atomic energy and, 247; Bank of U.S. and, 57, 79; Bush I and, 305–6; Bush II and, 323, 325–26, 334–35; Carter and, 288, 289; civil rights and, 251, 261–62, 268–71; Civil War and, 142–46, 148–52; Clay vs. Madison and, 71–72; Clinton and, government shutdown, 308–12; Clinton and, impeachment, 319–20; Coolidge and, 210–11, 213; corruption and, 167–71, 178, 290; created, and Connecticut Compromise, 49–50; C–Span and, 296; Democrats take control of, with election of 1892, 184–85; Eisenhower and, 258–60, 262; elections of 1890, and shift to Democrats, 183; elections of 1948, 250–53; elections of 1964 and Republican South, 271; elections of 1980, 292–93; elections of 1988, 302; elections of 1992, 307; elections of 1994 and Republican control of, 309–10; elections of 2006 and Democratic control of, 335–36; environment and, 269–70; FDR and, 220, 224, 226; FDR and New Deal and, 221–28; first convened in New York, 1789, 53–54; first convened in Philadelphia, 56, 64; first convened in Washington D.C., 64–65; Gulf War and, 304; Hawaii and, 189; Hoover and, 213–14, 217–18; immigration and, 317–18; Iraq War and, 328; Jackson and, changes in practices and character of, 97–98; Jacksonian reforms and, 98–99; Jacksonian veto of bank bill and power of, 106–9; Jackson's seizure of Florida and, 80–82; Jefferson's use of, as spokesmen, 67; John Quincy Adams and tariffs and, 90–93; Korean War and, 256; labor and, post–WW II, 248–49; LBJ and, 271–73; Louisiana Purchase and, 69; Mexican War and, 124, 126; Monroe Doctrine and, 85–86; navy and army and, 63; new parties in, and Kansas controversy, 137–39; new states and, and Northwest Ordinance, 47; Nixon impeachment and Watergate investigation and, 284–88; Nixon impoundments and, 282–83; Panama Congress and, 93; Panic of 1893 and, 185; patronage system and reform and, 175–77; presidential elections of 1824 and caucus system, 87–88; railroad regulation and, 180; Reagan and, 293–96, 298, 299; Reconstruction and, 155–57, 164–66; Republican revolution and partisanship in, 297; salaries of, 54, 171; silver coinage and, 171–72;

U.S. Congress (*continued*)
  slavery abolition adopted by, 151–52;
  slavery disputes and, 82–84, 119,
  121, 127–31, 140–41; space race and,
  265; state militias authorized by, 59;
  Supreme Court and, 212; tariffs,
  silver and antitrust of 1889–1890,
  181–82; tariffs and nullification issue
  and, 103–4; trade and embargos
  during Napoleonic Wars and, 70;
  Vietnam War and, 274, 280; War of
  1812, 72, 74; war powers and, 304;
  war with Tripoli and, 68; Wilson
  and progressives in, 198–99; WW
  I and, 201–2, 205, 216; WW II and,
  230, 235, 237, 238, 239, 243. *See also*
  U.S. House of Representatives; U.S.
  Senate: *and specific acts, individuals,
  laws, and political parties*
U.S. Congress Joint Committees: of
  Fifteen on Reconstruction, 156–57,
  159, 162; on the Conduct of the
  War, 144–45, 151, 243
U.S. Constitution, 59–60, 135, 142,
  222; Bank of U.S. and, 57, 106–7;
  bill of rights added to, 51–52, 53;
  drafted and ratified, 50–52; "implied
  powers" clause, 57, 106; Louisiana
  Purchase and, 69. *See also specific
  amendments and Supreme Court cases*
U.S. House of Representatives:
  African-Americans in, 164,
  213; anti-communism and, 254;
  assumption of state debt and, 56;
  Bank of U.S. and, 79; Bank scandal
  and, 307; Bank War and, 109; Bill
  of Rights and, 54; Bush II and,
  322–23, 334; civil rights legislation
  and, 268; Clay as first great Speaker
  in, 71–72, 79; creation of, 49, 50;
  "Czar Reed" and, tarifffs, 181;
  Democrats control, with elections
  of 1912, 198; elections of 1916, 200;
  elections of 1992, and diversity
  of, 307; elections of 2006, 335–36;
  ERA and, 315; first female Speaker

in, 315; Gingrich revolution and,
  309–12; impeachment of Clinton
  and, 319; impeachment of Johnson
  and, 162–63; impeachment of
  Nixon and, 284; Jacksonian era
  and change in, 96–98; Jay Treaty
  and, 61; New Deal and Democratic
  control of, 224, 226, 251; presidential
  election of 1800–1801 decided in,
  65–66; presidential election of 1824
  decided in, 88–89; presidential
  election of 1876 decided in, 173–75;
  Reconstruction and, 157; reform
  movement and, 197–98; seats added
  in, with Fourteenth Amendment,
  159; slavery debates in, 82–84,
  127–31, 139; slavery debates in,
  and gag resolution, 121; Spanish-
  American War and, 190–91;
  television and, 296–97. *See also*
  U.S. Congress; *and specific acts,
  individuals, and political parties*
U.S. House of Representatives
  committees: Budget, 310;
  Dies, 230–31, 245; Ethics, 307;
  Housing, 228; Judiciary, 227,
  268, 285–86, 319, 320; Judiciary
  Subcommittee on Criminal Justice,
  287; Manufactures, 91; National
  Currency, 79; Un-American
  Activities (HUAC), 231, 245, 246;
  Ways and Means, 67, 143, 181
U.S. Housing Authority, 228
U.S. Marines, 239, 300
U.S. Navy, 79, 233, 236, 239, 242
U.S. Post Office, 170
U.S. Senate: African-Americans in,
  164; anti-communism and, 254–55;
  Bill of Rights and, 54; Bush I and,
  305; Bush II and, 323; civil rights
  filibuster and, 270; Clinton and,
  309; Clinton impeachment and,
  320–21; Compromise of 1850 and,
  130–31; corruption in, 196; creation
  of, 49–50; elections of 1916, 200;
  elections of 2006, 335–36; Jackson

censured by, 108; Jay Treaty and, 61; Johnson impeachment and, 163; Missouri Compromise and, 83; New Deal and, 224, 226; Panama Canal and, 290; Reagan and, 301; Reconstruction and, 157; United Nations and, 244; Versailles Treaty and, 204; Watergate investigation and, 284; Wilmot Proviso and, 127–28; women in, 307. *See also* U.S. Congress; *and specific acts, individuals, political parties, and treaties*

U.S. Senate committees: Foreign Relations, 204; Judiciary, 158; Watergate, 284

U.S. Steel Company, 194

U.S. Supreme Court, 60, 69; abortion and, 283, 314–15; Bank of U.S. and, 106; Bush I and, 305; civil rights and, 261, 262; congressional right to override, proposed, 212, 226; creation and powers of, 49; election of 2000 decided by, 322; FDR's New Deal and effort to pack, 225–28; federal government favored by, vs. states, 75; first appointed, 52; Granger laws and, 178; income tax and, 185–86; Indian removal and, 100–102; segregation and, 178; Marshall, and opposition to Jefferson, 70; Marshall appointed to, 66; Nixon impeachment and, 285; reorganization of, under Judiciary Act of 1789, 54; railroads and big business and, 180; Reagan and, 301; Reconstruction and, 164–65; salaries, 171; sedition and, 202; slavery and, 138–39; WW II and, 238. *See also* specific cases and justices

United States v. Butler, 226

Upshaw, William D., 219, 220

urban areas, 205–6; aid and renewal, 272, 296; riots of 1960s, 268, 276, 278

Urban II, Pope, 4

Utah, 126, 130

Uzbekistan, 303

Vallandigham, Clement, 148

Valley Forge, 43–44

Van Buren, Martin "Little Magician," 87–88, 91, 97–98, 110–11, 116, 128, 302

Vandenberg, Arthur H., 233, 249

Van Rensselaer tract, 22

Van Tuong Peninsula, Battle of, 274

Vatican Council, Second (1965), 313

Versailles, Treaty of, 203–4, 231

Vesey, Denmark, 119

Vespucci, Amerigo, 6

Veterans Administration, 243

vice president, separate balloting for, 66

Vichy France, 233, 236

Vicksburg, capture of, 149

Viet Minh, 260

Vietnam War, 260, 274–81, 275, 281, 331, 332

Vikings, 2–4

Virginia, 10–12, 13, 28, 36, 41, 46, 47, 51, 56, 134, 143, 155, 164, 267, 273; House of Burgesses, 11–13, 33; University of, 46

Virginia Company, 16

Virginia Dynasty, 79

Virginia Plan, 48–50

Voldstead Act (1920), 207

voting rights, 196–97; blacks and, 164–65, 177, 181, 262–63, 267–68, 272–73; secret ballot, 184. *See also* elections; suffrage; women

Voting Rights Act (1965), 273–74

WAACs, 239

Waco, Texas, Branch Davidians, 308

Wade, Benjamin, 144–45

Wade-Davis Bill, 150–51

wages, 87, 184, 193

Wagner, Robert, 225, 228

Wagner-Steagall Housing Act (1937), 228

Waite, Morrison R., 174
Walden (Thoreau), 117
Waldseemuller, Martin, 6
Wallace, George C., 268–69, 279
Wallace, Henry A., 234, 251–52
Walls, Josiah T., 164
Walsh, Lawrence E., 299, 300
Wampanoag tribe, 27
war, power to declare, 67–68
War Department, 53, 54, 145, 170, 247
War Hawks, 72
War Industries Board, 202
Warner, Charles Dudley, 166
War of 1812, 72–75, 86, 89, 97, 116, 119,
    122, 134
War of the Austrian Succession, 27
War of the League of Augsburg, 27
War of the Spanish Succession, 27
War on Poverty, 269
War Powers Act: First (1941), 239;
    Second (1942), 239; (1973), 282, 304
War Production Board, 240
Warren, Earl, 252, 257, 261, 269
Washington, D.C., 56, 64–65, 121;
    burning of, 73; Civil War and, 143;
    March of 1893, of unemployed, 185;
    March of 1963 for Civil Rights,
    269; peace convention of 1861, 142;
    segregation in, 213; slavery in, 130, 145
Washington, George, 28, 38–39, 41–45,
    48, 52–54, 57, 59–62, 71, 87, 116, 188,
    197–98, 234
Washington Globe, 104
Washington Post, 268
Washington State, 238
Water and Air Quality Acts (1965),
    272
Wateree tribe, 18
Watergate scandal, 281, 283–88
Watson, Albert W., 271
Watson, Thomas E., 186, 195
WAVEs, 239
Waxhaw tribe, 18
wealth, concentration of, 109–10,
    187–88, 324–25, 331. *See also* Robber
    Barons

weapons of mass destruction (WMD),
    326–30
Weaver, James B., 176, 183–84
Webster, Daniel, 77, 92, 95, 102–3,
    107–8, 111, 126, 130, 296
Webster, Noah, 116
Weinberger, Caspar, 300
welfare reform, 302, 310
Welles, Gideon, 97, 160
West Bank, 312, 331
West Coast Hotel v. Parris, 227–28
West Indies, 24, 44
West Point Military Academy, 90
West Virginia, 143
westward expansion, 39, 41, 46–47, 56,
    76–77, 82, 122–26, 125, 146, 188–90.
    See also Manifest Destiny; *and
    specific states and territories*
Wheeler, Burton K., 211
Wheeler, William A., 173
Wheelwright, John, 16
Whig Party, 108–9, 111, 121–22, 124,
    128, 136, 141
Whiskey Rebellion, 58–59
Whiskey Ring, 170
White, Hugh L., 111
Whitefield, George, 25
white rule, in South, 165–66
Whitewater investigation, 318
Whitman, Walt, 118
Whitney, Eli, 77
Whittier, John Greenleaf, 118
Wilderness Campaign (1864), 150
Wiley-Dondero Act (1954), 259
William and Mary, king and queen of
    England, 23
William II, kaiser of Germany, 203
Williams, John Bell, 271
Williams, Roger, 15
Willkie, Wendell L., 233–34
Wilmot Proviso, 127–28
Wilson, Henry, 167, 169
Wilson, James, 48
Wilson, Woodrow, 110, 198–205, 207,
    218, 257
Wilson-Gorman Tariff (1894), 185

Winthrop, John, 14
wiretapping, 327, 335
Wisconsin, 178, 196
Wolfe, Gen. James, 28
Wolfowitz, Paul, 328
woman and child labor laws, 184, 193, 198
women: citizenship rights, 315; education movement, 115; elected to Congress, 307; excluded from Fourteenth Amendment, 159; flappers and new freedom of, 208; rights movement, 115, 159, 315; suffrage movement, 176, 200–201, 208, 315; voting rights extended to, 200
Women's Army Auxiliary Corps Act (1942), 239
Wood, Col. Leonard, 191
wool industry, 79, 91–93, 167, 199
Worcester, Samuel, 102
Worcester v. Georgia, 102
working class, 86–87
working conditions, 115, 184, 193
Workingmen's Party, 87
workmen's compensation, 198
Works Progress Administration (WPA), 224, 229
World Trade Center: bombing of 1993, 308; September 11, 2001, and, 325

World War I, 199–203, 205, 207, 216
World War II, 231–44, 245, 255, 258
Wright, Fielding, 251
Wright, Frances, 115
Wright, Frank Lloyd, 209
Wright, Jim, 299, 300
Wright, Silas, Jr., 91
Wright, Wilbur and Orville, 207
writs of assistance, 35
Wynkoop, Henry, 53
Wyoming, 126

xenophobia, 210–11
X,Y,Z Affair, 63

Yalta Conference, 244
Yamamoto, Adm. Isoroku, 236, 242
Yamassee tribe, 100
Yancey, William, 91
"yellow dog" contracts, 217
yellow journalism, 190
Yeltsin, Boris, 303
Yemassee, The (Simms), 118
Yorktown, Battle of, 44–45
Young, Brigham, 114
youth culture, 260–61
Yucatán, 6
Yugoslavia, 233, 304, 312–13

Zimmerman, Arthur, telegram, 201
Zoot-suit war, 238